AN OUTSTANDING
LUXEMBOURG DIPLOMAT:

Hugues Le Gallais in the Turmoil
of the Second World War

Paul Schmit

D1734458

AN OUTSTANDING LUXEMBOURG DIPLOMAT

Hugues Le Gallais in the Turmoil
of the Second World War

Paul Schmit

EDITIONS
SCHORTGEN

To all who made this biography possible.

© 2021 Editions Schortgen
B.P. 367
L-4004 Esch-sur-Alzette
Luxembourg

editions@schortgen.lu
www.editions-schortgen.lu

French Original Version: © Editions Saint-Paul (2019)
French E-Book Version: © Editions Schortgen (2020)

Published with the support of the Fonds culturel national, Luxembourg
Editorial consulting: Jean-Jacques Granas
Front cover photo: Thomas D. Mc Avoy/Getty Images
Back cover photo: Hugues Le Gallais en 1952 with the Statue of Saint Antoine from
his collection. (Photo: Victor Salvatore/Washington Post)

ISBN: 978-2-919792-14-6

MADE IN
LUXEMBOURG

TABLE OF CONTENTS

IV. DIPLOMATIC ACTIVITIES AFTER THE WAR AND RETIREMENT IN VENICE ... **251**

APPENDICES **423**

PREFACE

"The diplomatic body is never a beautiful body; it is often a body that's aged; at times it is a wise body, but it is always a body at the feet of the minister of foreign affairs… Good embassies are those that make no noise and whose activities are conducted without fanfare. Like happy peoples, they will have no history… Like children, diplomats should be seen, not heard. The less they say, the more they will be heeded."

Quote of Charles Maurice de Talleyrand
found in the papers of Hugues Le Gallais

Over the last twenty years or so I have become increasingly familiar with the life and work of Hugues Le Gallais. Through ups and downs, more or less intense research, depending on my availability and my hobbies, I have learnt more and more about this multi-faceted character, whose trajectory I crossed several times. At the end of 2001, I was appointed Deputy Chief of Mission at the Embassy of the Grand Duchy of Luxembourg in the United States and came across many traces left by the first resident Head of Mission in Washington. Le Gallais lived and worked for almost eighteen years at 2200 Massachusetts Avenue, in what is, still today, the Luxembourg Embassy. Most of the documents related to Ambassador Le Gallais, especially his correspondence with Luxembourg's political actors, have been in the National Archives of Luxembourg since the summer of 2002, having first been inventoried after my arrival at the embassy as a young diplomat. The exchange of letters between the ambassador and a wide variety of persons covers everyday aspects of the life of Luxembourg exiles during the Second World War and political and economic issues alike.

The possibility of analyzing these documents at the National Archives in Luxembourg was of great help, as was the additional insight provided toward the end of my research by a few highly personal handwritten letters from Le Gallais to the Grand Duchess of Luxembourg and which the Archives of the Grand Ducal House permitted me to consult. This allowed me to discover another side of the diplomat, who was also Chamberlain to the sovereign. During the years of exile, he had to work tirelessly and find his way between the head of state and the government's two most important figures, Minister of State Pierre Dupong and Minister of Foreign Affairs Joseph Bech, regardless of whether they were in the United States, Canada or the United Kingdom.

Numerous meetings in the United States, but also in Luxembourg, Germany, France and Italy have provided me with an even fuller picture of an outstanding diplomat, who was at times criticized or even mocked, and who led a very different life from that of today's diplomats. There are ever fewer family members, friends and contemporaries who knew Le Gallais and can speak of him firsthand. The ambassador's son and grandson, with whom I met several times in Venice in 2018, answered a number of questions and allowed me to examine photo albums from the Japanese and American stage of Le Gallais' career. Other members of the family helped to flesh out and even corroborate certain aspects of the busy life of Le Gallais and his entourage. Another invaluable source was the *Scrapbook* compiled over many years in Washington by Le Gallais' Secretary, Eleanor Maloney. In it, she gathered press clippings about the Luxembourg Embassy and added photos and other documents, such as the seating plans and menus at major Washington dinners. Some of Ambassador Le

Gallais' correspondence with Mrs. Maloney was handed to me by her daughter in 2004.

The authors of many books and publications made an essential contribution to my understanding of Le Gallais' actions during the Second World War. Among them I would like to mention the former ambassador of Luxembourg to the United States, Georges Heisbourg, author of the four-volume *Le gouvernement luxembourgeois en exil* (The Luxembourg Government in Exile). At the National Archives, I was able to view the documentation produced by his detailed research in the 1980s. It is undoubtedly demanding for Le Gallais' successor as ambassador to draw an objective and accurate portrait of him. I have also drawn inspiration from several studies and publications on this difficult period. Research at the National Archives at College Park has greatly supplemented these sources.

I do not want to take sides, to question, let alone judge, but simply try to better frame and describe Hugues Le Gallais' character. In essence, I agree with the theme of an exhibition held at the Musée de la Ville de Luxembourg in 2002: *Et war alles net esou einfach* (It wasn't all that simple). This formula also applied to a diplomat like Le Gallais, who was, by definition, far from the heat of military action or active resistance in his native country. As the writer and journalist Alfred Fabre-Luce put it: "It is always difficult for the historian to recreate the atmospheres of an era for a subsequent generation. A man who looks back tends to consider as known at that given moment something that will only be known later."

Consultation of other sources was, of course, essential to retrace the thread of a diplomatic life rich in often fascinating adventures. The Library of Congress was not only a great resource in this respect, but also allowed me to locate or verify at a distance information that had appeared in American press articles.

The views, thoughts, comments and interpretations contained in this study of the life of Hugues Le Gallais are mine and in no way reflect those of the Ministry of Foreign and European Affairs or those of the Luxembourg Government. Any erroneous interpretation or transcription in this account is my sole responsibility. I wanted to express myself in a personal capacity and give an account of the life of a Luxembourg diplomat, a subjective undertaking by definition. This account is not intended as an apology, a scholarly study, or a detailed biography. Rather, it is an attempt to better understand and bring to life the broad outlines of Le Gallais and his work and to follow the many written and photographic records left by him. Not being a historian, I do not wish to enter into any polemics in connection with the activities of the Luxembourg head of state and government in exile in the context of the lot of those who remained in the country under occupation.

What I found fascinating in trying to piece together the puzzle of Le Gallais' career is to come across many actions and reflections, even reflexes, which have survived in some form and to a certain degree in diplomatic life today. Without wishing in the least to idealize or systematically justify Le Gallais' actions, I have often wondered whether, at another period in our history and having other means at our disposal, we are not, in the end, motivated by the same aims for our country, our career, our professional and private life. Above all, I wanted to place Le Gallais' complex itinerary in its historical context and try to make his public and personal actions, as well as his intimate aspirations, more understandable. Le Gallais' participation in numerous international conferences that have given rise to multilateral institutions still relevant today, as well as his interaction with very high-ranking representatives of various countries, no longer necessarily reflect the daily reality of all those who work in the diplomatic sphere today. In short, I have sought to immerse myself in Le Gallais' family and social background and this made me realize that he had very little contact with people from a less affluent background than his own.

To my knowledge, this biography is the only one that tells the story of a Luxembourg diplomat. Few politicians of this country (Emmanuel Servais, Nik Welter or, more recently, Pierre Werner) or ambassadors (Auguste Collart and Adrien Meisch) have published their memoirs. I hope that this gap will one day be filled by other studies of this kind or that other research on a pivotal period of our history will be published.

Finally, I wish to let the reader know, as a matter of honesty, but also family loyalty, that my wife's paternal grandfather was one of Le Gallais' privileged interlocutors, at least during the Second World War. While this connection with a man whom I did not know personally was not of a nature to facilitate my research, I state this fact at the outset to help to avoid the reproach of having written an apology, if only indirectly.

What follows, therefore, whether the result of chance encounters or assiduous research, is only a modest contribution helping to preserve the memory of an outstanding diplomat and singular character interested in the good of his country and its people.

Luxembourg/Warsaw,
September 2019 (1st Edition)
2020 (e-book) and
2021 (English Edition)

I.

An adeventurous childhood and youth

THE BIRTH OF HUGUES LE GALLAIS

Diplomacy is an art. Hugues Le Gallais was not an artist. Yet, from the very beginning, his life was a spectacle. He turned his life into an art form, enjoying at every moment all the advantages of being well-born into a world that no longer exists and doing everything to be well seen in it.

Hugues Le Gallais, the eldest of the four children, was born to Norbert Le Gallais and his second cousin, Juliette Metz, on May 15, 1896 in Dommeldange, on the outskirts of the capital of the Grand Duchy of Luxembourg. At his baptism four days later, he was given the first names Gustavus Emilius Augustinus Hugo. As godfather, his parents had chosen Auguste Collart, his maternal aunt's husband, and as godmother Léonie de Mathelin, the wife of industrialist Gustave Metz and the maternal grandmother of the newborn child. The fact that no one was chosen from the paternal side can hardly lead to conclusions about misunderstandings or preferences of the mother's family over that of the father. At most, it makes it possible to wonder about the nature of the relationship between Hugues' parents and the two closely linked families. Perhaps choosing the godfather in the Metz family and not in the Le Gallais family simply reflected the dominant position of this alliance between the most prominent family of Luxembourg industrialists, the Metz, and the affluent and noble family which owned several castles, the Collarts.

Hugues' birth certificate, with the first two names reversed, is kept at the civil registry of Dommeldange. According to this certificate, the birth took place at 5:30 PM. The witnesses were the doctor Auguste Faber and Paul Mayrisch,[1] mayor of Eich from 1911 to 1915, son of the doctor Jean Mathias Édouard Mayrisch and

Mathilde Metz (daughter of Adolphe Metz and niece of Norbert Metz, one of Hugues' great-grandfathers). This Paul Mayrisch was the brother of the great potentate of the Luxembourg iron and steel industry, Émile Mayrisch, whom we will meet again, along with his wife Aline de Saint-Hubert,[2] in the course of this account. Hugues' family had very close ties to Luxembourg's iron and steel industry. Hugues remained faithful to this milieu throughout his life, but was guided, above all else, by his very own brand of patriotism and a loyalty, if not unconditional veneration, for the Grand Duchess and her family.

Less than five months earlier, the second daughter of the Hereditary Grand-Ducal couple, the one who would become Grand Duchess Charlotte 23 years later, was born in Luxembourg. Hugues Le Gallais was to be very attached and loyal to this sovereign who reigned for 45 years. She plays a major role in this biography, especially during the exile years (1940-1944/5).

Before going over the somewhat original life of Hugues' father and his three sisters, let us examine his ancestry. His grandparents were aristocratic bourgeois and, at the same time, first cousins. The life of these families of Luxembourg notables at the turn of the 19th century was marked by a prestigious genealogy and an attachment to conservative values leaving little room for originality, even if some members of Hugues Le Gallais' close family had some experiences that were out of the ordinary. In the second half of the 19th century, Hugues' maternal grandfather and paternal uncle preceded him to the lands of America and India, which he would soon come to know in the course of his professional career.

A QUASI ARISTOCRATIC ANCESTRY

The paternal line of Hugues Le Gallais can be traced back ten generations, to Francis Le Galles. The name was also spelled Galles or Gallez, before definitively becoming Le Gallais at the beginning of the 18th century. The pronunciation suggests the family's origins lie in Brittany.

Le Gallais' ancestors were lords of Chasteau Crocq in Brittany. From 1607 onwards, the presence of a member of the family is recorded on the Isle of Jersey, in the English Channel between the United Kingdom and France, as lord of Rouge Bouillon. Later, this branch of the Le Gallais family settled at La Moye. Given that the Le Gallais family's titles of nobility were confirmed in 1669 and 1702, and taking into account the coat of arms of the Amy, Hugues' great-grandmother being of this lineage, the family is authorized to bear the arms described in detail in the *Biographie nationale du pays de Luxembourg*. The Le Gallais had their own coat of arms and their own motto: *jamais chancelant* [never wavering].[3] As we will see, Hugues Le Gallais would live up to this family motto and always remain true to himself and his ambitions.

The paternal and maternal families, even if they were quite closely related, will be examined separately. The paternal grandparents Le Gallais-Metz and the maternal grandparents Metz-de Mathelin knew each other very well since they were first cousins and belonged to the same bourgeois society linked to industry and construction. The residences of these families were among the most imposing in the capital. The last residences of these families also reflected their social affluence, even if they no longer belong to the family today or have disappeared. The tomb of the Metz family in the Notre-Dame cemetery near *Le Glacis* is imposing, reflecting the grandeur of one of the most illustrious families in the Luxembourg steel industry. Hugues' mother was buried there with her family. The paternal grandparents are buried in a separate grave next to that of the Metz family. Hugues' father, Norbert Le Gallais, and his second wife found their final resting place in a separate grave, but still in the same cemetery.

THE PATERNAL GRANDPARENTS

Hugues' paternal grandfather, Edmond, was born on September 9, 1814 in La Moye St-Brelades/Jersey, and died on July 20, 1873 in Wildbad, a spa in what is now Baden-Württemberg in Germany. He was the son of Philippe Le Gallais and Marie Margaret Amy from Jersey who never came to Luxembourg. This great-grandfather of Hugues was a judge and had nine children.

The paternal grandfather arrived in the Grand Duchy around 1856 from Jersey, the largest of the Channel Islands. Edmond Le Gallais was to integrate quickly in Luxembourg. The country was embarking on an economic boom which would last for about a century. An engineer and entrepreneur, he came to the Grand Duchy about ten years before the major changes in the economic and political centre of the country began with the dismantling of the fortress following the Treaty of London of 1867. The first Le Gallais to settle in the Grand Duchy came there with the Waring brothers and the Irish engineer Thomas Byrne to build the Guillaume-Luxembourg railway lines and the viaducts of the Northern Railway. He was admitted to the Masonic Lodge around

1866, along with his cousin by marriage Gustave Metz. Once the construction of the viaducts was completed, he remained in the country and invested in various businesses.

About three years after settling in the country where he did not have any immediate relatives, Edmond managed to ally himself with one of the leading families in the capital. He married Léonie Metz, born on February 2, 1836, in Luxembourg on May 2, 1859. She was the daughter of Charles Metz (1799-1853) and Justine Vannérus (1808-1849), daughter of a notary from Diekirch. This Charles Metz, one of Hugues' great-grandfathers, was the brother of Norbert, the latter being one of the three other great-grandfathers. Norbert was in fact the grandfather of Hugues' mother, Juliette Metz. Hugues' paternal grandmother, called 'Granny' by her descendants, died on October 27, 1909 in the family home on Boulevard Royal in Luxembourg. From this union were born five children, all of whom married and had children, except for the second son.

The eldest child was Hugues' father, Norbert Le Gallais, born on April 17, 1860 in Septfontaines and deceased on March 6, 1934 in Luxembourg. Then came Walter Le Gallais, who was born on August 17, 1861 in Luxembourg and fell in battle on November 6, 1900 near Bothaville during the Boer War. He first served in the Indian Army and had risen to the rank of Lieutenant-Colonel in the 8th Hussars Regiment by the time he died. A lifelong bachelor and a very good polo player, he was a cavalry leader who, after his studies in England and Germany, joined the Jersey militia, then served in India under Lord Kitchener, the British military commander during the Nile campaign, and finally took part in the South African campaign. That general, who distinguished himself during the Second Boer War, described Hugues' paternal uncle in his book *Three Years of War* as 'without doubt one of the bravest English officers I have ever met'. This uncle, who fell in battle when Hugues was six and a half, had an adventurous spirit and lived a life off the beaten track—not unlike his nephew and, as we shall see later, Hugues' maternal grandfather. From 1891 to 1895, he was aide-de-camp to the Commander-in-Chief of Bombay, the city where Hugues Le Gallais was going to travel in 1926 for Columeta, and be in charge of Arbed's exports. Walter Le Gallais' epic was widely commented on, particularly in the American media of the day.

The Le Gallais-Metz couple had a third son, Marc Le Gallais, who was born on September 30, 1863 in Eich, and died on August 30, 1906 in Broadsland, Jersey, where he had returned, to his roots as it were, to settle on a property purchased by his family. In 1901 he became Adjutant General of the militia in Jersey. He followed the same career path as did his brother Walter. In 1891 he married Joséphine, known as Finky Schaefer (1863-1933), daughter of the banker Ferdinand Schaefer-Nothomb. The Schaefers were one of the wealthiest families in the country, the banker's daughters were called 'the three graces' and all made great matches. Marc and Joséphine had four children:

Léonie, known as Lily (1892-1959), in 1914 married her cousin Paul Simons (1877-1936), who was President of the Administration des Biens de la Grande-Duchesse, and the son of the Minister of State Mathias Simons. Léonie had been lady-in-waiting to the Grand Duchess. Then came Edmond, born in 1893, on whose behalf Colonel Charles Schaefer approached his friend Kitchener to get him into the Cadet School. Edmond Le Gallais became a major in the 1st Royal Sussex Battalion, and died a retired colonel. Edmond was followed in 1898 by Réginald, who became a captain in the Royal Air Force and died in a plane crash in 1917. And the last was Simone, born in 1905, who married Claude-Frederick-Forestier Walker, who was born in 1892 and became a captain in the 3rd Hussars of the Guard in London in 1933.

The fourth child of the Le Gallais-Metz couple was Edmée, who was known as Missy Le Gallais (1864-1917) and who in 1896 married her first cousin Jules Schaefer in Kanzem in Rhineland-Palatinate, where the Metz and then the Le Gallais families had a winery. This engineer (1862-1904) was the son of C.-J.-A. Schaefer and Irma Metz. This couple lived in Paris, but also in the Villa Simons in the Montée de Gasperich. Schaefer was also the first cousin of Marc Le Gallais' wife. They had several children.

Finally, there was Marguerite Le Gallais (1868-1950), known as Daisy, who, in Kanzem in 1890 married Ernest H. Burney (1860-1905), a colonel of the Royal Berkshire Regiment, Commander of the Bath. They lived in England and had two children.

Hugues' paternal grandparents lived alongside the enterprising and well-to-do Tesch, Mayrisch and Barbanson families. Hugues' paternal and maternal families had known each other very well since always, as it was customary to say, long before their children Norbert and Juliet were married in 1895. From this union Hugues was born, on whose baptismal font his paternal grandmother Léonie Le Gallais-Metz and her first cousin, the maternal grandfather Gustave Metz, were reunited. It was a Catholic family then, at least in appearance. The affiliation of Hugues' two grandfathers with the Freemasons, however, carries a certain mystery. As in all families, then as now, some must have been more practicing than others.

THE MATERNAL GRANDPARENTS

Hugues' mother was the daughter of Gustave Metz (1838-1895, the son of Norbert Metz and Eugénie Tesch) and Léontine de Mathelin (1845-1925), daughter of Léopold de Mathelin (1815-1880) and Baroness Marie de Steenhault (1815-1894). Mrs. Gustave Metz-de Mathelin came from a Spanish family ennobled by the King of Spain in 1672. Hugues' maternal grandmother, called *Bonne-Maman*, who lived in the capital, supported the four children of her daughter who died early and did not have the best of relations with her son-in-law's second wife. The Metz family represented the Iron Dynasty, but had allied themselves with noble families of the region, such as the de Mathelin family, owners of a castle in Messancy, a French-speaking commune of Belgium situated in the Walloon region. They were men of action, even if not all of them were always willing to make a career in industry. Hugues' maternal grandfather was one of these rebels. He was, at least in his youth, a sort of ugly duckling and stayed clear of his family's ready-made path. As would be the case for Hugues a generation later, he had lost his mother at a very young age. Gustave's father remarried his mother's cousin. Due to difficulties at school, Gustave spent several years in boarding schools. After working for a while, he emigrated at the age of twenty to the United States where he stayed for six years in Louisiana, Wisconsin, Iowa and California. This 'lost' son, not to say the black sheep, of the Metz family returned briefly in 1860 to settle an inheritance and set off again on the other side of the Atlantic. There he carried on at various jobs (farmer, horse breeder) in order to create a somewhat dignified existence for himself, but which, in the end, was to lead to bankruptcy and to his return to Luxembourg, failed, disillusioned and destitute. A letter from 1864 to his sister testifies to this: 'This country of America... is only a lottery country, where men are millionaires today and poor tomorrow, doesn't do me much good, and although I have gone to great lengths to achieve something, luck does not smile on me'.[4] Gustave was sent to his cousin Léonie Metz who had married Edmond Le Gallais (they were, as we have seen, Hugues' paternal grandparents). From 1860 onwards he worked for Waring Brothers, the firm for which Edmond Le Gallais had come to Luxembourg. A year later, he worked for his father's factory, even becoming director of the Dommeldange Ironworks before marrying, a year later, the daughter of the banker and Baron de Mathelin. Everything was back to normal and, having become factory manager, Gustave ended his life as he began it: in comfort and respected. He died on March 3, 1895 at the age of 57 and was therefore unable to pass on his American stories in person to his grandson who was to be born the following year.

From the Metz-de Mathelin union, concluded in 1868, five children were born, one of whom died in infancy. The eldest was Alice Metz (1870-1948), who first married L. Auguste Collart (1859-1906) and then François Mathieu (1876-1930), in 1915. They were the parents of a daughter who died young and of the owner of the castle of Bettemburg castle, Eugène-Auguste Collart (1890-1978), a politician and diplomat. In 1914 he married Daisy Weber (1889-1969), daughter of Auguste Weber and Berthe Gansen, who had been the Grand Duchess' lady-in-waiting since 1937.[5]

The Luxembourg chargé d'affaires in the Netherlands, Eugène-Auguste Collart, and his first cousin, the chargé d'affaires in the United States, Hugues Le Gallais, were indirectly linked to the industrialists Emile Mayrisch (1862-1928) and Gaston Barbanson (1976-1946) who had taken over the reins of the Arbed in 1911. The two diplomats shared a great-aunt in Mrs. Edmée Tesch (1843-1919), the daughter of J. B. Victor Tesch and Caroline Nothomb, widow of the master of the forge in Dommeldange and founder of the Institute bearing his name, Emile Metz (1835-1904), who was the son of Norbert Metz and Eugénie Tesch. After the death of Mrs. Emile Metz-Tesch in 1919 at the Château de Beggen (which her husband built), the fortune passed partly to Emile Mayrisch, whose mother had been Emile Metz's first cousin, and partly to Gaston Barbanson, the latter nephew of Edmée Metz-Tesch.

However, the marriages between the different offspring of these families and their efforts to keep the common patrimony undivided and the family prosperous were not going to keep these bourgeois at the top of Luxembourg society forever. As early as the First World War and especially with the crisis of 1929 and the period of virtual stagnation that marked the inter-war period, the Metz and Le Gallais families began to loose their hold on many residences and properties, including their most prestigious villas.

Let us continue our examination of Hugues' maternal family. His mother Marie-Juliette, known as Juliette Metz (1872-1909), was the second child of the Metz family, followed by Léopoldine called 'Poldie' (1873-1904), wife of Jean-François Mersch called 'Fritz' (1862-1937), a lawyer and member of parliament. Finally, the Metz-Mathelin couple had a son, Jean Metz called 'Chany' (1879-1922), who was attached to Arbed's central administration and who, in 1906 in Bettembourg, married Elisabeth Jacquinot called 'Maisy' (1884-1975), daughter of Baron Charles Jacquinot and Joséphine Collart.

Hugues had five cousins on his mother's side, one of whom died in infancy, and seven on his father's side, one of whom died during the First World War. The death in a plane crash of this young 19 year-old cousin left an indelible mark in the family, according to the recollections of Hugues' sister Rozel, and cast a shadow over the reunions in the house in Kanzem where all the Le Gallais cousins liked to gather in the summer. For Hugues, this period in his life was marked by various bereavements. At a very young age, before he was thirteen, he had already lost his 36 year-old mother, and his 73 year-old paternal grandmother, both in the same year. The family's happiness had been short-lived, the more so as three years later his father would remarry, with a 46-year-old woman. This new union was supposed to help ensure a dignified standard of living for the bereaved family made up of a widower with four children, but did not bring any stability to the family.

A COLOURFUL FATHER

Hugues' father, Norbert Le Gallais, had first married his mother's first cousin's daughter, Juliette Metz, on June 19, 1895 in Luxembourg, before marrying Anne-Marie de Gargan, from Preisch Castle in Basse-Rentgen, on October 5, 1912, in Luxembourg. Norbert Le Gallais was 35 years old at the time of his first marriage to his 23-year-old second cousin, and 52 years old at the time of his second marriage, while his second wife was 46 years old.

Norbert's first wife and Hugues' mother, whom her children called 'Mummy', had died after an illness that greatly diminished her, possibly tuberculosis, on February 3, 1909, in the villa on Boulevard Royal. For the four children, Hugues, Aimée, Alice and Rozel, aged 12, 10, 7 and 5, this was the beginning of a difficult period which Rozel described very well in her memoirs, speaking of the terrible silence and absolute emptiness surrounding the half-orphans. The adults apparently did not know how to deal with it and spoke, according to Rozel's recollection, of the mother's ascent to the sky, which would allow her now to remain above the clouds. Dark clouds appeared when Norbert remarried, with Anne-Marie, de Gargan, called 'Marie'. She was an old friend of the family, of noble descent and very pious, not to say extremely religious.

Anne-Marie was born on August 28, 1866 in the castle of Preisch, on the other side of the border in France. Also known as Marie de Gargan, she was the daughter of Baron Charles-Joseph de Gargan (1831-1920), whose mother was a de Wendel, and Emilie Pescatore (1840-1913), the only daughter of Pierre-Antoine Pescatore and Emilie Daelen. Pierre Pescatore was the nephew of the businessman and patron Jean-Pierre Pescatore. Anne-Marie de Gargan's parents had ten children and lived in the castle located between Frisange and Rodemack. The estate still belongs to the family. The de Gargan family, probably one of the richest in the region along with the Pescatore family, was therefore linked to the French industrial family of the de Wendel. The family moved to Luxembourg, to the Villa Vauban, they had bought in 1874. At that time, the surroundings of the residence were laid out and the garden landscaped thanks to the genius of the French landscape gardener Edouard André. Winter was spent here for the most part, whereas in summer the family preferred Preisch Castle. As Anne-Marie's father had wanted to retain French nationality, he had to leave Preisch in 1872 after the annexation of Lorraine by the German Empire, only acquiring Luxembourg nationality five years later. The Baron had acquired a collection of objects with which he furnished the castle. He acquired them during his travels to Italy, Austria, Portugal, Flanders and the Palatinate.

The Gargan family had prestigious relatives and alliances. One of Anne-Marie de Gargan's sisters, Marguerite de Gargan (1862-1948), was married to François Gérard d'Hannoncelles (1861-

1940) and lived in the villa now known as Villa Foch, next door to the Villa Vauban. Marshal Foch lived there during his 1918/1919 stays in the area. A niece of Anne-Marie de Gargan, Thérèse de Gargan (1903-1996), in 1925 married Philippe de Hauteclocque, known as Leclerc de Hauteclocque, who was one of the main military leaders of the Free French during the Second World War.

The Le Gallais-de Gargan couple was not going to have any children. The marriage gave rise to a scandal described as 'catastrophic' by members of the bride's family. The union had been contested by the de Gargan family to the point that the parents, who opposed it at all costs, wanted to have their daughter interned. They did not accept this marriage to a widower who was, moreover, the father of four teenage children, and a commoner with a slightly tarnished reputation since changes that had taken place the year prior to the marriage, namely the takeover by Mayrisch and Barbanson of what had been managed in the Luxembourg steel industry in part by Norbert Le Gallais. Even if the bride's mother, born Pescatore, was not noble either, the fact that Le Gallais led the life of a spendthrift bourgeois may also have influenced the attitude of the Gargan family. The differences between the old and the new nobility, as well as between the nobility and the bourgeoisie, were considerable at the time. Hugues' father had written several letters and brought in a lawyer, brandishing the threat of a lawsuit, in his bid to prevent having his future wife declared not of sound mind. His new wife was no longer going to see her mother and father and was not going to attend their funeral, although contact was maintained with her sisters and brothers. Hugues' father's second marriage was apparently a happy one. Photographs showing Anne-Marie Le Gallais-de Gargan with two of her husband's children suggest that a certain understanding existed for some time. However, this was not the case in reality, to say the least. In fact, the mother-in-law's relationship with the four young Le Gallais children was abysmal. Anne-Marie de Gargan had announced in one of her fits of rage that the Le Gallais children wouldn't inherit anything. During her lifetime, she had given part of her jewelery to decorate the statue of the Blessed Virgin in the Cathedral, which, according to Rozel, had earned her the protection of the bishop himself in the face of accusations about her relationship with her husband's children. Indeed, Hugues and his sisters hardly seem to have recovered their mother-in-law's inheritance, her personal belongings having been returned to the de Gargan in Preisch, as were the proceeds from the sale by auction of the Villa Vauban and its furniture in 1948 and 1949.[6]

At the civil marriage on October 4, 1912, which took place in front of mayor Alphonse Munchen, Norbert was described as an industrialist, his late father as an engineer. The marriage certificate does not really reveal the difficulties that preceded the marriage. As it mentions an *Ehrerbietigkeitsakt* drawn up and issued by the notary Camille Weckbecker in Luxembourg on August 24, the bride respectfully asked her parents' opinion on the said marriage. A marriage contract was drawn up the day before by the same Luxembourg notary. As on other occasions, the witnesses for this marriage were chosen from among family members, this time even from the close family of the first wife who had died three years earlier. They were Henri Vannérus (1833-1921), President of the Diekirch court, who belonged to the Governments of Tornaco and Servais as Minister of Justice and was a member of the Council of State. He was the brother-in-law of Charles Metz, and therefore the uncle of Norbert's mother; of Léon Metz (1842-1928), an engineer, member of the Arbed council after 1911, member of parliament and vice-President of the Chamber of Commerce, mayor of Esch-sur-Alzette and first cousin of Norbert Le Gallais' father and of the father of Norbert's first wife; Auguste Weber (1852-1936), a doctor who had performed the first operation at the hospital in Eich, son of Jacques Weber and Justine Metz, husband of Berthe Gansen, and father of Daisy Weber, wife of Auguste Collart, whom we met earlier in describing Hugues' maternal family. He was therefore Norbert's second cousin; and finally someone not directly allied or related but from the Arbed sphere, namely Émile Bian, an industrialist and politician, member of parliament from 1916 until his death, son of the notary in Redange and politician Léopold Bian.[7] On the day of the wedding, Rozel, who was the only child present, began to cry, so that she had to leave the church. When Norbert and Marie came back from their honeymoon in Italy, the stepmother struck the ten year old child because she had dared to welcome her in the parents' bedroom. It should be noted that the year the war broke out,[8] the eldest daughter, Amy, had been sent to a convent in Spa in Belgium, and the third child, Alice, to another boarding school, so that only the youngest child, Rozel, remained in Luxembourg. She was the only one to endure the wrath of her stepmother as soon as their father remarried. We shall see that the son of the family, Hugues, had also been sent away. Although relations with Anne-Marie de Gargan had been excellent until the marriage, the children always refused to call their father's second wife 'mother' and, with support from the servants, gave her a hard time.

Having seen her take up more and more space with their father and having given her the name Aunt Marie, they began calling her *die Alte* (the old woman) or *la Stief* (short for *Stiefmutter* or stepmother). The new Mrs. Le Gallais was described by Rozel as having suffered from a split personality. Her upbringing was said to have been spartan, which the stepmother, who was most prudish and jealous, considered suitable to her stepchildren a generation later. She is described by Rozel as very generous towards the poor and religiously fanatic at the same time. She suffered nervous breakdowns and was interned in her youth when she wished to marry Norbert Le Gallais, before the latter decided to marry Juliette Metz. Hence the transposition of pathological feelings of jealousy according to Rozel's autobiography, and the wish to cast aside or even eliminate everything that was reminiscent of this episode, in particular the existence of the four children.

Hugues' father, whom his children called 'Daddy', had much character, but little willpower. His daughter Rozel portrayed him as jovial, funny, always joking, even insolent. His lively and amusing temperament in society did not, however, reflect his lack of decisiveness with regard to the behavior of his second wife, against whom he was hardly ever overly opposed. He had strange ways of educating his children and was rarely present, if we are to believe his daughter's account. According to her, he was very successful with the ladies and his second wife was very jealous, probably with good reason. Known for his strong, rather authoritarian and imposing personality, Norbert Le Gallais had studied law and was a lawyer by profession. In 1890, the year in which the Nassau-Weilburg dynasty arrived in Luxembourg, Norbert Le Gallais became general secretary at the Forges d'Eich and then, a few years later, its director.

Norbert Le Gallais was in fact an industrial magnate who had horses at Bonnevoie, rue de l'Hippodrome, including a racehorse named 'Camperdown'. The facility was even named at the time the *petit Auteuil du Luxembourg*. He was President of the Jockey Club in Paris where he sometimes travelled by special train. Races were organized there in the presence of the Grand Ducal couple and the heirs to the throne as well as 10,000 spectators, which included allied and related bourgeois families (the Blochhausen, the Schaefer, etc.), in 1897. Hugues was only four and a half years old, but the different occasions of this impressive event must have reached him, among others the fact that his father's racehorse had won the Prix de Bonnevoie, and was awarded 300 francs plus 50% of ticket sales.

Hugues' father also hunted, particularly in the Troisvierges region, on the Moselle and in the vicinity of the capital. He had a pheasant farm in the *Baumbusch* and went fishing, likely with more commitment than he gave to family affairs. He had a dog, Lexy, which accompanied him everywhere.

In 1904, after the company's name, "Les Forges d'Eich", was changed to "Le Gallais, Metz & Cie", Norbert Le Gallais took over from his mother's cousin and his wife's uncle, Emile Metz, as general managing partner. Norbert Le Gallais had already invested in electric steel works (*Elektrostahlwerke*), a choice of process that proved misguided and was replaced in 1928. In fact, he had little to say when the merger with Dudelange and Burbach took place in 1911. Hugues father had gobbled up part of the family fortune. In reality, the business of the Metz family was in very bad shape, close to ruin. Mayrisch and Barbanson were somehow going to restore the coat of arms, by turning Arbed into a profitable enterprise and, in a few decades, into a state within the state. Norbert Le Gallais had succeeded in joining the board of directors of the new company. The family used to say that "what the Metz family accumulated in two generations, the Le Gallais spent just as quickly." "Maître des Forges", Norbert Le Gallais was director of the Aciéries Réunies Burbach-Eich-Dudelange, but also, from 1919, director of the Société métallurgique des Terres Rouges. Rozel described the financial situation as precarious, due also to the bankruptcy of the stable in Paris, which had been inherited from a great-aunt who proved to be less generous as expected, so that around 1920 the children, especially the girls, were sent on trips, especially to England, but also to Romania. Rozel even speaks of journeys on the Orient Express. Stock market speculation seems to have dealt the final blow to the carefree lifestyle led until the 1920s by Norbert Le Gallais, who became increasingly dependent on his second wife financially. A family friend, the notary Félix Bian,[9] looked after the material affairs of the Le Gallais children and tried, as best he could, to act as an intermediary when their relationship with their stepmother reached the point of no return or even to a momentary lack of communication with their father.

Norbert Le Gallais was also President of the Luxembourg Automobile Club, which he had founded in 1906. The prodigious Norbert Le Gallais went in style and rode in a Panhard with chains. This rolling fortress, a French automobile construction,[10] was also used by Hugues' father's second cousin, the 'imperial bourgeois' Emile Mayrisch.[11] This car brought a definite change in the life of the Le Gallais family. It emancipated them from constraints that are difficult to imagine in our days, when everything is instantaneous and when we imagine ourselves as being able to know and attain everything, to be everywhere and nowhere. This means of locomotion put everything within the reach of a well-to-do family, eliminating distances and bringing distant people and places closer.

Le Gallais was a member of the board of directors of the Institut Emile Metz, a British Consul and a member of the town council from 1892 to 1895. He was also a member of the first National Committee of the Fédération Nationale des Eclaireurs et Eclaireuses du Luxembourg (FNEL), whose English origin was close to his heart and which reminded him of his father's country of origin.

Hugues Le Gallais' father had been a liberal member of parliament since 1908 when, according to the biography of his daughter Rozel, he acquired Luxembourg nationality. Political life at that time was extremely turbulent, and the First World War would change the balance of political forces. Norbert Le Gallais belonged to the party that would barely escape disaster after the war, although he himself retained his mandate. Before the war, he, Maurice Pescatore and Joseph Funck had been convicted of electoral corruption after offering their constituents drinks, which was prohibited by the electoral law. Remaining in Luxembourg when the war began, he gave up his seat on April 4, 1916. He joined the Luxembourg Relief Committee for the Disabled and Discharged Veterans of the Allied Armies, which had been founded on the initiative of Gaston Barbanson. This committee was in fact an organization that propagated the Belgian option, i.e., it favored the incorporation of Luxembourg into Belgium, in contrast to the attachment of Le Gallais père to the Grand Ducal family and also in opposition to those who advocated a rapprochement with France. He had subsequently gone into exile, so to speak, in Paris, but also, in part, in Switzerland, according to corroborating sources.[12] In Switzerland, according to a report by the French diplomat Berthelot,[13] he had been 'either in Ouchy-Lausanne or in Evian-les-Bains for eight months'. Berthelot had been informed at the end of October and in a 'completely confidential' manner by the director of the Syndicat des Fontes that the latter had been mandated by the Luxembourg Minister of State Eyschen to sound out Le Gallais if he, as British Consul, could check in London whether a Luxembourg chargé d'affaires would be accepted there. Eyschen supposedly thought of Le Gallais for this position. The Luxembourg socialist minister Michel Welter,[14] for his part, stated in his memoirs that, at the beginning of November 1915, Le Gallais was 'at present without known domicile or residence (it seems that he lives sometimes in Switzerland and sometimes in Paris; he left the country because, in his capacity as British Consul, he no longer felt safe enough in the country)'. According to the memoirs of his daughter Rozel, Hugues' father had lived lavishly, first in the Grand Hotel, Place de l'Opéra, and later in two increasingly less prestigious hotels, his financial means having apparently suffered a few setbacks, thus mandating that savings be made. Nonetheless, in Paris the Le Gallais spouses each had a room to which were added those of the three daughters plus those of two ladies who accompanied them throughout the Parisian episode.

Norbert Le Gallais returned to the Grand Duchy after the First World War. In October 1919, he presented his candidacy in the electoral district of the Centre and was elected along with Brasseur, Diderich and Ludovicy, and regained his seat in the Chamber of Deputies. His re-election was even more brilliant in 1922, including this time as well the election of Brasseur, Cahen, Diderich, Ludovicy and Gallé. In 1925, as the Liberal Party split into two groups, he joined the Brasseur list. Only Brasseur was elected from the list, and following his resignation, Le Gallais took his place. After the war, he remained loyal to the conservative group of Liberals, supporting the Government of Pierre Prüm until the latter submitted a bill granting workers paid leave. Norbert Le Gallais' vote against the bill contributed to the fall of the Government, which resigned on July 16, 1926. Prüm had left the Party of the Right (*Rechtspartei*) and founded the Independent National Party in 1918. Now came the time of Joseph Bech, who had been propelled to the post of Head of Government. When, on November 16, 1926, the Government presented the bill to parliament, Norbert Le Gallais did not attend the vote in the House. In 1931, he was elected for the last time from the list of the future mayor of the capital, Gaston Diderich, against Cahen's list. He belonged to the moderate wing of the Liberal-Radical Party and it was therefore understandable that he finally 'did not hesitate' to join a coalition with the right-wing party. He was elected twice as Deputy Speaker of the House—on November 4, 1919, when he did not take office for political reasons, and again in 1931.

Norbert Le Gallais was not prone to long speeches but a man of action, always very courteous and polite. He was described as a perfect gentleman who had his own opinions but never put them forward in a harsh or offensive manner. Although he had clear interests in industry, one can't accuse him of promoting them in a partial manner. The common good was his aim and guiding principle.

An amusing description of the Le Gallais milieu has been made in *La Foire* by Pierre Viallet,[15] who admirably set down on paper the carefree, even unconscious life of the 19th and early 20th century Luxembourgish bourgeoisie. In this account of the rise and fall of the author's maternal family, the Brasseurs, a clan also linked to the steel industry, are minutely dissected, a little like in Thomas Mann's *Buddenbrooks*. The reader learns about the deeds of a well-to-do social class that shows little reluctance when it comes to flaunting its ascending glory, but keeps silent about any dirty laundry, preferring to dissimilate its intellectual or financial mediocrity. The insolence, eccentricity and prodigality of Viallet's novel bear witness to life in a bourgeois family similar to that of Hugues Le Gallais' own, at least in his youth.

Hugues' father had a weakness for card games. It was in particular at the Place d'Armes, the meeting place in the middle of the capital, that he lost considerable sums of money, as well as some of the family's furniture. His second wife kept him on a leash and gave him a few francs on Sundays, on condition that he also went to church. Norbert Le Gallais played cards with friends at the Bridge Club de Luxembourg (the premises of the Automobile Club du Luxembourg at the Porte Neuve) when he suffered an attack to which he succumbed shortly afterwards. He was struck down as he responded with an energetic 'redouble' to an opponent's 'double'.[16] He died barely 14 days after the death of his friend and comrade-in-arms Robert Brasseur.[17] His successor in parliament was the former deputy Jacques Gallé. In the country's second largest city and centre of its steel industry, Esch-sur-Alzette, a street was named in honor of Hugues Le Gallais' father. In the obituary, the right-wing Catholic daily *Luxemburger Wort* recalled that from a religious point of view, the deceased regularly fulfilled his duties and that his personal friend abbot Gemen de la Chapelle du Glacis was able to administer the last rites to him, as far as 'it was possible'. On March 8, 1934, the leftist *Tageblatt* described the funeral of Norbert Le Gallais held on the previous day. A large number of participants from all walks of life accompanied the deceased on his final journey. A dignified funeral for a father who was often absent or even wavering, contrary, one would almost say, to the family motto. This disappearance left Hugues an orphan with a stepmother who was going to settle in the South of France and with whom he no longer had much contact. Of the two surviving sisters, one was married in Germany and the other lived in England. We do not know if Hugues came home from Japan given this unexpected change in his family in Luxembourg.

THREE SISTERS WITH SINGULAR DESTINIES

Hugues was four years older than the eldest of his sisters. Aimée Maria Edmée, also known as Amy Le Gallais, was born on July 9, 1898 and baptized on July 16. Her paternal uncle Walter Le Gallais was her godfather and her maternal grandmother was her godmother. The Civil Registry shows the names in a different order: Léontine Marie-Amy. According to family legend, while she was expecting a child by the painter Pierre Thévenin, born in

1905 and younger than her, Aimée did not get off the train that was taking her to the village in the south of France where she was to be married. The artist came from a family of musicians and became first prize winner in cello in 1923. At the same time he studied painting and attended the School of Fine Arts in Lyon. From 1932, and for 4 years, he travelled extensively as a professional musician on cruise ships. He also travelled to Morocco, as had Delacroix and Matisse. On his return to Lyon in 1936, he lived through an important creative period and produced vast mural compositions for clients. At the same time, he was active as a portraitist, painting friends and acquaintances, notables from Lyon and children. The father of Hugues' nephew died on October 12, 1950 in an accident that occurred while he was working in his studio in St-Just. Aimée had become a schoolteacher, teaching English, and lived at Watermans Cottage Ewhurst in Sussex, 40 kilometers from London. She singlehandedly brought up her son David, born on September 5, 1934. She was the talk of the family with this child, who also perpetuated the name Le Gallais. Hugues' sister had led her son to believe that she had been married to a Le Gallais, only revealing the truth to him much later.[18] Hugues Le Gallais regularly sent money to his sister, with whom he maintained close ties.[19]

Alice Barbara Le Gallais, Hugues' second sister, was born on March 28, 1901. At her baptism on April 2 she was given the name Caecilia Alicia Brigitta. The other paternal uncle, Marc Le Gallais, was her godfather and her maternal aunt, Alice Collart-Metz, her godmother. Of the four children, this sister of Hugues was the most sensitive, and apparently suffered most from the conflicts with her father's second wife. One day, she reportedly confessed to her father that she wanted to poison her stepmother. The young woman, who suffered from depression, experienced an episode of speechlessness and was treated with electric shocks before being sent to Switzerland, far away from her step-mother, which helped to improve her condition. Alice Le Gallais drowned in Algiers on February 7, 1928,[20] in a suicide resulting from an unhappy love affair. She had followed a French doctor who was married and living in Algeria.[21] The family's announce-ment in the newspaper *Indépendance luxembourgeoise* spoke of an accident and stated that 'it had pleased Almighty God to call for a better life' for the 'piously deceased', while the newspaper, in an announcement of the funeral a few days later, stated that a car accident had been the cause of the young woman's death. She was buried in Kanzem, Rhineland-Palatinate, with her aunt Daisy Burney-Le Gallais joining her 22 years later in the family grave. This suicide was to be another motive leading the survivors to depart from Luxembourg. The two surviving sisters were soon to leave, one for the United Kingdom, the other for Germany. This made it the easier for Hugues to pursue his international career and avoid having to confront the tragedy, which was stigmatizing at the time.

Rozel Le Gallais, who was born on May 16, 1903 in Luxembourg City, seven years to the day after her brother, was christened Ma-ria Edmunda Simona Rozella on 26 May. The birth certificate lists the following first names: Cunégonde Marie Edmunda Rozelle Simone. Her godfather was Anatole de Mathelin, the brother of the maternal grandmother.[22] Her godmother, her paternal aunt, who was prevented from coming due to a more or less prolonged sojourn in Paris, was replaced by the paternal grandmother who lived in the family home surrounded by vineyards in Kanzem.

This sister of Hugues always used the name Rozel, after a small port town in Jersey, and was still called 'Pignose' or 'Monkey' by some relatives. In 1920, she went to London to study English. There she discovered tennis. Her father, in order to save money and to keep the children away from their stepmother, had allowed his eldest daughter and his youngest daughter, aged 17, to leave Luxembourg. Rozel joined the Botanic Garden Club in the British capital where her coach Worthington was a pioneer in this rather exclusive sport. A talented player, she took lessons up to four times a week and also participated regularly in tournaments in Britain. In 1924, Rozel returned to Luxembourg, where she trained in preparation for the Paris Olympic Games, which she entered on her own initiative. Rozel Le Gallais had little luck, as in mixed singles and doubles with Camille Wolff,[23] she had to withdraw. After her tennis career, the youngest of the Le Gallais children took up motor racing.

While Hugues was in Asia, on June 6, 1932 his younger sister married in London.[24] Her husband, Edmond Reverchon,[25] ten years her senior, was a vineyard owner and wine merchant in Filzen near Konz and Kanzem, the stronghold of Le Gallais. The son of Alice von Boch and Adrian Reverchon, a banker in Trier, Hugues' brother-in-law was a descendant of the couple who founded the Villeroy et Boch factory, Eugen von Boch and Sophie Octavie Villeroy. The Reverchon family was allied to the von Papen family, the later German Chancellor Franz von Papen having married a Boch-Galhau cousin in 1932. Hugues' brother-in-law was also allied with Sayn-Wittgenstein, and in Luxembourg with the Pescatore, Schorlemer and Barbanson families. In a way repeating the family history, the husband had been married for the first time to Maria Brügmann, from whom he had two children, Heinz and Günther, who were less than ten years old. Rozel's civil marriage to a divorced man does not seem to have met with as much opposition as his father's had twenty years earlier. This union produced one son, Eddie Reverchon, born in 1934, the same year as his first cousins Norbert and David were born.

To a greater degree than her husband, Rozel was partial to Nazi ideology and was supposedly considered *persona non grata* by part of her family in Luxembourg. Hugues seems not to have wished to maintain this connection. He no longer went to Germany after the Second World War and did everything he could to divest himself of his share in the Weingut of Kanzem despite the fact that it had come from his mother's family. After Hugues' death, his sister and her husband came to Venice and were among the first to sign the 'guest book', in 1965, expressing their gratitude to Hugues' widow, who had always been very welcoming. A reconciliation of sorts seems to have taken place after Hugues' passing. Rozel was touched by an artistic streak and, ten years after her brother's disappearance, she would exhibit her paintings in the villa, which had belonged to her mother-in-law and had become the Marie-Thérèse gallery before being known as the Villa Vauban. Rozel Reverchon-Le Gallais died on June 27, 1988 in Konz.

HOMES OF THE NORBERT LE GALLAIS FAMILY

Hugues' father was born in the Château de Septfontaines, one of the most beautiful mansions in Luxembourg. In the 1880s, he lived at 7, rue Marie-Thérèse, and now rue Notre-Dame. He was the neighbor of the Maurice and Bertha Gernsbacher-Durlacher, whose son Hugo, the future 'father of modern science fiction', was born on August 16, 1883 at number 9 of the same street. After the merger of the various entities that produced Arbed, he was content to receive dividends and lived from various incomes. At the beginning of his first marriage, he had a property as director of the Dommeldange factory, before moving to the former Hotel

Pescatore on the corner of Boulevard Royal and Avenue Amélie. Hugues' mother died there. Today it is headquarters of the Banque de Luxembourg.[26] Finally, Norbert Le Gallais lived with his second wife in the Gargan family home, the Villa Vauban, on Avenue de l'Arsenal, which has since been renamed Avenue Emile Reuter. The Le Gallais also had a holiday home on the other side of the border with Germany.

❋ THE KANZEM WINE ESTATE ❋

The Kanzem estate comes from the Metz family and passed into the hands of the Le Gallais family in the mid-19th century. The buildings of the Le Gallais vineyard are located in Kanzem on the Saar, with vineyards in the neighboring districts of Wiltingen and Wawern. Since the early Middle Ages, Kanzem and Wiltingen were a Luxembourg seigniory as an exclave in the *Kurstaat* of Trier. Today, the property is much smaller than before. Lesser vineyards have been sold and only Riesling vines are cultivated. Since 1954, the administration of the estate has been in the hands of Egon Müller, in whose cellars, not far away in Scharzhof, the wines are produced. Norbert Le Gallais is the one who established the reputation that the estate enjoys today. Even in his day, his wines were highly appreciated.

Rozel Le Gallais describes happy summers spent in Kanzem, where the young Le Gallais were surrounded by many cousins, with whom they had fun, often at the expense of the adults and their guests. The house had no less than sixteen bedrooms, plus mansard rooms, allowing their aunt Daisy Burney-Le Gallais from England and their aunt Missy Schaefer-Le Gallais from Paris to come with their families. Numerous guests from Luxembourg, France and England also came to Kanzem. At a very early age, the Le Gallais children could thus meet people of influence, notably some Prussian officers, such as those of the troops garrisoned in Trier.

During the First World War, the German authorities placed the vineyard under sequestration, and even housed Russian prisoners there, so that when family returned to Kanzem at Easter 1919 they found it in a rather desolate state. Considerable damage had first to be repaired before the young Le Gallais could resume the carefree life they had known there. After the Second World War, the house in Kanzem belonged in 2/8 parts to Hugues Le Gallais and his sisters, and in 3/8 parts to his two cousins Yvonne Rochon, born Schaeffer, who was of French nationality, and Violet Douglas Brown, born Burney, who was of British nationality. The domain was experiencing difficulties in connection with the future of the wine estate, which had been damaged during the war. Hugues Le Gallais undertook to repair the destruction sustained in what was an estate and not a château. He did not wish to maintain ties with a property located in a country which he had done everything to oppose, even though he did so from the other side of the Atlantic. This sale therefore brought some funds to the head of the mission in Washington.

❀ THE CASTLE OF SEPTFONTAINES ❀

The property where Hugues' father had been born was no longer for sale, as the family had sold it before the First World War. Hugues' paternal grandparents, Edmond Le Gallais and Léonie

Metz, had lived in the superb château of the Boch family in the Rollingergrund. The fabulous seigniorial residence known as Septfontaines, one of the glories of the Rollingergrund district, is indissolubly linked to the nearby earthenware factory. The castle, as it is now called, was built between 1780 and 1785 on the foundations of a house erected in 1684 by a retired member of the Spanish army. It was built by the three Boch brothers, Pierre-Joseph, Jean-François and Dominique, after they had built the earthenware factory and the houses of the first workers. They were the sons of François Boch, a foundryman in Hayange, Lorraine, in the employ of the De Wendel master forgers' family. This exceptional place is surrounded by a large park. At the time it overlooked the Rollingergrund forest. It was sold in 1913 to the Maurice Pescatore-Barbanson couple.[27] Since then, the Château de Septfontaines has become a site for exceptional receptions.

❧ THE DIRECTOR'S HOUSE IN DOMMELDANGE ❧

The house in Dommeldange where Hugues was born was located near the station and resembled a residential pavilion with a balcony above the door and several windows on either side of the main entrance, giving the house a grand, even noble appearance. The building was originally inhabited by the Collart family and had been rented to the family of the famous botanist Tinant. Acquired in 1873 by Metz & Co., it became the home of the director of the Arbed Dommeldange factory. The Norbert Le Gallais-Metz family lived here from 1895 to an unspecified date at the beginning of the 20th century, succeeding Norbert's father-in-law Gustave Metz and preceding Emile Bian, who lived here until the end of the First World War, both as directors with residence in Dommeldange. The house was demolished in 1955.

The Norbert Le Gallais-Metz family lived in the former Hotel Pescatore on the corner of Boulevard Royal and Avenue Amélie. According to the account of Norbert's daughter Rozel, this residence remained the family home after the mother's death in 1909 and after the father's second marriage in 1912, until he left, alone and without a word, to join his second wife at the Villa Vauban, more or less abandoning his children. The villa had a veranda with palm trees and other exotic plants. The family had at its disposal seven people, two servants, a cook and her kitchen helper, two maids and an assistant, plus two drivers. These persons were the children's allies and even, according to Rozel, their best friends, especially after their father's second marriage. In addition, there was a governess who changed often as the situation became more and more complicated for the Le Gallais. For a time the villa served as the home of the Belgian ambassador, only to be destroyed later and replaced by the present Banque de Luxembourg.

In 1912, Norbert Le Gallais, husband of Anne-Marie de Gargan, was named as the owner of the Villa Vauban from the dowry of his second wife. The residence is located in the middle of the municipal park at 18, avenue de l'Arsenal, which has since become avenue Emile Reuter. The site benefits from its proximity to the lively centre of the upper town, but also to the outlying residential areas, which are highly prized for their quality of life. Norbert Le Gallais' father-in-law, Baron Charles Joseph de Gargan came from an illustrious steel family from Lorraine. They fled the Franco-Prussian War of 1870-71, and his wife Emilie Pescatore settled there in the middle of Luxembourg city. In 1874 they acquired the property of the glove-maker Mayer.

Anne-Marie de Gargan moved to the South of France in 1934, following the death of her husband. The Nazi occupation authorities confiscated the villa to house the Ministry of Agriculture and, from July 1 940, the *Office des Prix*.[28] While Hugues dealt with the reconstruction and war damages of Kanzem, it does not seem to have been the case for this property of his mother-in-law. After the war, Pierre and Henriette Werner-Pescatore lived in the villa from the summer of 1945 until February 1948. The wife of the future politician and Minister of State was a distant cousin of Anne-Marie de Gargan. The latter died there on January 16, 1946. In 1948 and 1949, the heirs of the Le Gallais-de Gargan couple auctioned off, respectively, the furniture and real estate. The City of Luxembourg bought back the Villa Vauban for 5 million francs and transformed it into the Pescatore Museum.[29]

These beautiful and prestigious villas and residences were the setting for a youth which, despite all the surrounding luxury, proved rather unhappy. Hugues Le Gallais must have been delighted to leave the Grand Duchy to pursue his studies in Brussels.

YOUTH AND STUDIES

Various photos of Hugues' youth have come down through time. A photo of the couple Le Gallais-Metz with their first two children shows a mature man with a moustache, with a very high and straight forehead, reflecting a measure of self-confidence. His wife, twelve years his junior, seems dreamier and gives a more composed impression, something which at first glance cannot be seen in this photograph. It shows her sitting on a sofa with the

Hugues Le Gallais with his parents and his sister Aimée.

(Photo: Fonds Jules Mersch).

Hugues Le Gallais as a child.

first daughter, Aimée, on her lap, dressed all in white and Hugues
in tartan with a hoop and a ball at his feet, standing next to his
father. Another photograph shows Hugues with a beret in the
driver's seat, with his three sisters seated comfortably in the back
of one of the first cars to be driven in Luxembourg. A rather colorful but nevertheless romantic picture of Hugues in a Scottish
kilt and a photo of a sad pre-teen boy, sitting nonchalantly on a
chair and pouting his full lips that one might think swollen, give
a not overly joyous picture of the young Le Gallais, but nevertheless reflect a privileged life without too many material woes.
In this portrayal free of sentiment, personality and individuality,
the young Hugues seems closed, dreamy and introverted, with
empty, if not extinguished, eyes. Rozel describes his brother as
having their mother's large eyes. He was apparently surprisingly
calm and serious, aware of his masculine dignity. He couldn't bear
to be made fun of, and in such tense moments he would grow pale

Hugues Le Gallais and his sisters in their father's car.

and chatter his teeth. Hugues was then called 'the white rage'. He was not, however, brave and drove his father to despair, especially after he became a widower, and even more as he began seeing Anne-Marie de Gargan.

Always unwavering, Hugues seems to have been a disturbed child, hardly loved by his father's second wife. He was, therefore, placed in a boarding school in Brussels and left to the care of the Petrucci couple. Professor Raphaël Petrucci[30] would try to help and socialize

Hugues, passing on to him his love for oriental art. Raphaël Petrucci was born in Naples in 1872 of an Italian father and a French mother. He spent his childhood and his teenage years in Paris. Petrucci's interest in Far East art was apparent from his formative years, around 1890. He moved to Belgium in 1896, where he held the chair of positivist aesthetics at the *Université nouvelle de Bruxelles* and, in 1902, scientific adviser to the Solvay Institute of Sociology. His authority in the field of Chinese painting and, more generally, Far Eastern art, recognized throughout Europe. He influenced the young Hugues for the rest of his life, fulfilling his educational mandate. Le Gallais had apparently presented himself to him in Brussels from atop his horse, in continued defiance of all authority. Schooling far away from his family environment ultimately benefited him. Hugues was a bit insolent, but that was about to change. Petrucci's book *The Philosophy of Nature in the Art of the Far East* accompanied Le Gallais throughout his life.

Over the years, our young Hugues became methodical. Even if he remained somewhat dissipated and did not become very orderly, he developed a collector's soul that he was to put to good use in Japan a few years later. Nevertheless, he remained a silent and conventional being with a scrutinizing gaze. He was not very personable, he lost his hair early on and did not have a very slender stature. Hugues had received a complete education making him an accomplished man. While his father had been a colorful and eminent figure, the same could not be said of Hugues who, in his early days, maintained in all circumstances a ceremonious affability. He loved sports and the outdoor life so much appreciated by the English. On May 22, 1922, Andrée Mayrisch wrote to her mother that Hugues is well behaved and increasingly British—at least he believes so. He has 'Hugh Le Gallais' business cards, discusses rugby using technical terms, but it's not a game for me, it's much too rough".[31]

Hugues studied at the University of Liège and continued his studies at the Swiss Federal Institute of Technology in Zurich from 1914 to 1918, thus largely escaping the torments of the First World War. Luxembourg was occupied by the German Imperial Army and was subject to Governmental instability after the death of Minister of State Paul Eyschen in October 1915, with six successive Governments in two years. In addition, after the armistice of 1918, there was institutional instability, with the reign of Grand Duchess Marie-Adélaïde being questioned, leading to her abdication and the referendum of September 28, 1919 on maintaining the monarchy and economic association with Belgium or France. 1919 was also the year in which universal suffrage was introduced in the Grand Duchy. From wartime, Rozel recalled a story about her brother, who was already very gallant as he approached his nineteenth birthday. Hugues was to join his father in Paris, but had encountered problems at the border because of love letters he wished to take to France. Norbert apparently intervened to have his son released. Since then Hugues enjoyed a certain fame among women following his gesture, which he apparently considered one of bravery. Minister Michel Welter describes in his memoirs dated April 25, 1915 how Hugues had been the victim of a border examination, the Swiss authorities wanting to see whether travelers were smuggling letters: "Recently, the young Le Gallais traveling to Switzerland was sentenced to five days in prison for having (had) letters on him. The letters he had been given were quite harmless, but despite this, the young man was sentenced to five days in prison and was only released on bail of 10,000 francs after spending several days in pre-trial detention. It seems that this was counted as part of his sentence".[32]

The young Le Gallais always spoke slowly and thoughtfully, expressing himself in Luxembourgish with a pronounced accent. French was his mother tongue, as it was that of Luxembourg bourgeoisie. He was also fluent in English. From his nannies he had learned the language of his paternal ancestors, which he was later able to perfect in the American style. Later, once married, Hugues learned Italian without ever being able to express himself in a way enabling him to really integrate with high Venetian society, which was very picky in this respect.

Since his childhood, Hugues had been called 'Doody' by some close friends. His sister Rozel mentions this nickname in her memoirs. Its origin is unknown. Le Gallais mainly signed his correspondence with his wife's Italian family with this familiar nickname.

Hugues Le Gallais on horseback.

LINKS WITH THE MAYRISCH-DE SAINT-HUBERT FAMILY

The mothers of Norbert Le Gallais and Emile Mayrisch were first cousins. The Mayrisch-de Saint-Hubert family initially lived in Dudelange. In 1920 they moved to the Château de Colpach, where they worked to bridge the gap between France and Germany, he in the field of steel industries, she in the field of ideas. Around this time, the Mayrisch acquired a *bastide* in the South of France for Elisabeth van Rysselberghe.[33] This acquisition of a country house in Provence for the daughter of Mrs. Mayrisch's great friend was the subject of a letter[34] from Hugues Le Gallais to the French writer André Gide.[35] There was another link between the two men. In 1921, Gide presented Hugues Le Gallais with the first volume of the complete works of the German Minister of Foreign Affairs, Walther von Rathenau,[36] for him to take it from Paris to Emile Mayrisch in Luxembourg. On January 21, 1921 Aline Mayrisch wrote to André Gide: 'I have given Hugues the first volume of the complete works of Rathenau in 5 vols. which arrived for you in Colpach, so that you can send him a note of thanks (perhaps through me)'.[37]

A year earlier, Hugues Le Gallais had travelled to Geneva where the daughter of the Mayrisch-de Saint-Hubert, Andrée, known as 'Schnucki', was studying.[38] From September 1919 to January 1920, he acted as a sort of chaperone for what could have been an ideal party, although the outline of no idyll can be sensed in the correspondence between the young girl and her mother. The only daughter of the Mayrisch couple was five years younger than Hugues and studied natural sciences in Geneva before continuing her studies in London. She lived in a boarding school in Geneva. During her stay, Hugues was also accommodated in this mixed boarding school. To her mother, with whom she had a complex relationship, Andrée Mayrisch described the only son of the Le

Gallais and her distant cousin as a spendthrift, but one who taught her how to deal with certain financial questions, such as the tips that it was customary to give.

A few years later, Aline Mayrisch asked the German-French journalist and writer Jean Schlumberger[39] to invite Hugues Le Gallais to the 2nd Decades of Pontigny. These intellectual meetings had been held since 1910 and were led by Paul Desjardins,[40] who consented to the presence of the young Le Gallais.[41] However, on July 18, 1925, Aline Mayrisch wrote that she gave up on the presence of her young protégé, who was nevertheless able to mingle with the other guests, either famous or less well-known, talking and discussing with them on literary, philosophical or religious subjects.[42] In contrast to what Aline Mayrisch said, Hugues Le Gallais attended the 2nd Decades which had as its theme: 'We Europeans. Europe and Asia'.[43] He apparently also gave a talk on Japanese tea ceremonies.[44] Quite a program and a premonitory subject for Hugues' future career![45] It was a fine introduction to an elite literary and intellectual world where, every day, a writer, academic or scientist dealt with a chosen subject of quality.

The relationship—which can be described as close—between the great intellectual and patron of the Grand Duchy and the young Le Gallais had its ups and downs. In 1930, Aline Mayrisch wrote in any case to her friend Schlumberger that Hugues was in Luxembourg, 'more of a nincompoop than ever'.[46] In other words, she considered him to be, at least at the time, imbecile, idiotic, stupid even. The reason for this unflattering qualifier has not been revealed.

In spite of some occasional annoyance, Aline Mayrisch apparently had a certain esteem for Hugues Le Gallais. She called her travelling companion Hugues Le Gallais, 'Hugo San'. She went to visit him in Japan in 1930 and 1934. With Hugues Le Gallais, Aline

Mayrisch-de Saint-Hubert travelled to Asia for three months (October 7 to January 8), first to New York, then Shanghai and Hong Kong in January 1931, and finally to Tokyo.[47] From Nara, a city with important works of art and temples a few kilometers from Kyoto and Osaka, Aline Mayrisch described to Schlumberger the living conditions of Le Gallais, who was still single at almost 35 years of age. We pick them up again later, describing the 1930s, spent in the Japanese Empire of the Rising Sun. Aline Mayrisch-de Saint-Hubert attended in October 1934, as Vice-President of the Luxembourg Red Cross, the 15th International Conference of the Red Cross and the baptism of Hugues' son. Photos show her holding her godson Norbert in the company of an unidentified couple. After the death of her husband in a car accident in France on March 5, 1928, Aline undertook daring journeys, to Persia and Japan, for example. From Tokyo, Aline Mayrisch first reported 'rather violent assaults on [her] disarmed heart', facing a capital 'where the old Japan exists only in small islands (...) and where the rest reflects our present rout, grafted onto theirs'.[48]

Aline Mayrisch wrote on May 10, 1930 to Isabelle Rivière, the widow of Jacques Rivière, a French man of letters, director of *La Nouvelle Revue française* from 1919 until his death in 1925: 'Only the month of August will remain for me to prepare my great departure for the Far East in September. I am leaving with a young friend who is almost an adopted son of my husband and me, and who lives in Tokyo on behalf of the Aciéries Réunies. I intend to spend the winter there'.[49] Mayrisch's trips to Japan were intellectually and personally mediated by orientalists who were interested in old traditions and objects even though she perceived Japan as disastrously Americanized.[50]

Aline Mayrisch had also, in 1933, welcomed Hugues and his young fiancée to Colpach, just before their wedding.[51] On June 17,

1933, she wrote to Jean Schlumberger: 'Back here for the whole month of July, with quite numerous and varied guests: Goret, Haas, Gertrude Eysoldt, Hugues Le Gallais'.[52] And in another letter, also of 15 July, to Schlumberger: 'Here, people come and go. Hugues surrounded by golden screens, and Haas, a melancholy Jew, whose sarcasms do not always manage to hide his deep distress'.[53] A hitherto unsuspected environment opened up to the young thirty-year-old man who was also going to bind himself for life to the woman who seemed to him to be his soul mate.

It should also be mentioned that Mrs. Mayrisch bequeathed a painting by Signac to her friend Hugues when she died in 1947. The painting had been bought by Emile Mayrisch in 1909 and is called 'Venice'.[54]

In the meantime, Hugues had met in the lagoon city the woman who would become his wife. Some time before the wedding, Hugues went with his fiancée for a fortnight to the home of Aline Mayrisch-de Saint-Hubert at the Château de Colpach. According to the guest book, they stayed there from September 15 to 30. ❀

II.

Marriage in Venice and happy years in Asia

A HAPPY UNION WITH AN ITALIAN
OF ILLUSTRIOUS ANCESTRY

It was through Battista Nani Mocenigo, an Italian diplomat post-ed in Tokyo, that Hugues Le Gallais met his future wife, Pisana Velluti. She lived in the Ca' del Duca on the Grand Canal in Venice, with her sister and brother-in-law, whose cousin was a friend of Hugues. Pisana was in fact just waiting for an opportunity to escape from the uncomfortable situation of a young single woman in her early thirties. She saw Venice as a small village, and worse, a nest of vipers. She was quoted as saying loud and forcefully: "I will marry the first one who passes." Le Gallais, who was at the time the Tokyo representative of Columeta, a subsidiary of the Luxembourg metal conglomerate Arbed, with which his family had very close ties, seems to have chosen the right moment to return and go on an excursion to Venice. Things rapidly became more concrete from then on. Pisana's aim seemed accurate, as Hugues offered her a life of dreams and stability in a faraway country. While love is earned, theirs seems to have been somewhat driven by the desire to leave their respective countries and to put all their ambition to good use in new lands and new circles to conquer. Pisana with her Latin sensuality conquered Hugues, the Nordic man with his discreet and reserved charm. The young couple sought a life for themselves far from their families or what was left of them. Both were trying to find their way in a period that was just catching its breath after the Great Depression that followed the stock market crash of 1929 and at a time when intolerance was rising dangerously in Europe with the rise of Fascism, since 1922, of Nazism and, above all, the German menace that was soon to hang over Luxembourg. Together, Pisana and Hugues appropriated Oscar Wilde's maxim: "Be yourself; everyone else is already taken." As displaced and, at times, even uprooted people, theirs was a life of hard work but also one that was exceptional in many ways for a few years in Japan and, after a spell in Luxembourg, in the United States.

On November 6, 1933, Hugues Le Gallais and Pisana Velluti were married in the church of Santa Maria dei Carmini in Venice. The church is in Renaissance style and is located in the Venice borough of Dorsodouro. It is grandiose with a counter-façade and a convent next door. A photo shows the young couple in an almost majestic scene, disembarking from a gondola onto the steps of the house where the young bride lived with her sister and brother-in-law, and another photo with the father of the bride and probably his second wife and two train bearers. The latter photograph was taken in the courtyard of the house, which was very old and which had long belonged to the family of the bride's brother-in-law. This residence of the Count and Countess Marino and Katy Nani Mocenigo was located at 3051 San Samuele and was called Ca' del Duca. Marino owned another palace in Dolo, in the Veneto region.[55] The Ca' del Duca, a palace situated on the Canal Grande, a few steps from the Palazzo Grassi, owes its name to the Duke Sforza of Milan who commissioned the architect Filarete to build it in 1453. The project lived up to the Duke's ambitions, as the palace was supposed to become the largest in Venice. However, the *Serenissima* Republic of Venice, always concerned not to allow anyone to overshadow its authority, expropriated the palace and the work, which had barely begun, was suspended. The building was later completed by the Republic in a more modest size. Only the foundations and the corner of the palace, with its column and the beginning of the façade in *bugnato* style, bear witness to that past which should have made it the first example of Renaissance architecture in the lagoon. Ca' del Duca was used as a workshop by Titian for the production of paintings for the Doge's Palace, before coming into the possession of the Nani Mocenigo family, and in particular of Marino Nani Mocenigo. The palace was open to the public for a long time and used to house Count Marino Nani Mocenigo's collections of porcelain and the Asian art objects collection of Hugues Le Gallais until the 1960s, when he retired as the Grand Duchy's ambassador to the United States. It was he who turned it into a museum in 1963.[56]

The bride was born in Venice in a house on the Campo de San Stefano located between the church of the same name and the church of Vidal, on January 28, 1900 (according to a passport application). The young woman actually altered her date of birth and, out of expediency or vanity, modified the year of her birth with a small line and made herself 6 years younger. The fact that the year 1906 appears on many official documents has given rise to administrative complications and complex rectifications in later years. Only four years separated her from Hugues, not ten, as sometimes claimed by the interested party herself. She may have played somewhat on both the day and the year of her birth to hide the fact that she had remained unmarried for longer than was usual.

The very beautiful 33-year-old woman, claiming to be only 27, had curly blond hair that would one day lead to comparisons to a painting by Titian. In addition to her dazzling physiognomy, Pisana had great presence, knew how to dress and had a self-confident and incredibly classy air. She was 1.65m tall, while Hugues, who was 37 years old, was ten centimeters taller, which did not make him a giant, far from it. The young woman was judged to be of princely rank by some of the ambassador's colleagues. She was very elegant and had an undeniable presence, while her husband was somewhat withdrawn, but also intellectually grounded. Both shone in society thanks to their demeanor and their readily forgiven ambition.

Hugues Le Gallais' marriage with Pisana Velluti in 1933 in Venice.

Pisana was the daughter of Francesco Velluti and his first wife Elisabetta Carrara, who died in 1918 in Naples from the Spanish flu, in the prime of life. Pisana's father died in 1957 at the age of over 80.[57] Two daughters were born of this union: Caterina, known as Katy, born in 1898, and Pisana, born in 1900.

Pisana's father's family came from Italy's southern Adriatic coast. Pisana's grandfather had opened an earthenware factory in Venice. The father, an agricultural engineer, had made his fortune by draining and irrigating marshland to make agricultural estates behind the Lido de Jesolo. The credits for this had been provided by the Italian Fascist Government. Francesco Velluti had, moreover, been somewhat attracted to fascism and, despite letters from his daughter warning him that Mussolini would not survive the war, believed in an Italian victory. Pisana's father had remarried, with a younger woman. The two daughters didn't appreciate her too much. This marriage with Zemira de Lorenzi, a woman of vaguely Armenian origins, produced three children, with whom the contact was better than with their mother: Francesca married Alberto Baldissera from a large Venetian family and had two children: Giuseppe and Jacomo. Then came the son long hoped for by his father, Gianni-Luigi, who married Anna-Luisa Cazorzi, with whom he had four children. And finally Alberto, who died young, married Maria Padovan, with whom he had two children.

Hugues' wife was named after her maternal grandmother, Pisana Carrara-Nani Mocenigo, who belonged to the prestigious and wealthy family into which her elder sister Catherine would also enter by marrying Count Marino Nani Mocenigo. It is one of the most illustrious and powerful Venetian families, which produced seven doges. Following in the footsteps of the Venetian Marco Polo, who revealed to Europeans the existence of Cipango, later to be known as Japan, Pisana and Hugues would try, with perseverance and tenacity, to find their own way with at least the satisfaction of conquering everything through their own energy and enthusiasm. Like the Luxembourg steel magnates of the Metz and the Le Gallais, the Velluti and even more so the Nani Mocenigo had great houses at their disposal. In 1947, Mrs. Le Gallais and her sister, Countess Marino Nani Mocenigo, co-owned a building in Campo San Maurizio called the "Palazzo Bellaviti". The building had been occupied since the end of the war by an organization attached to the Italian Government, known as the *Ente Nazionale post-Bellica*, which had not paid rent for three years. In December 1947, the Le Gallais couple wished to occupy one of the two flats in the palazzo and, with this aim, undertook assiduous steps which involved even the Luxembourg Minister of Foreign Affairs, Joseph Bech, and his Italian counterpart, Carlo Sforza. The Italian Chief of Protocol Taliani, the Italian ambassador in Washington Tarchiani, the Prefect of Venice Gargiulo, the Governor of the Province of Venice and the Luxembourg Consul in Venice Bartolomé Bellati also intervened in this matter. The Le Gallais were now planning to make extended stays there in the years to come. The palace in Venice was finally returned to the family on December 1, 1950. In fact, the two Velluti sisters wished to recover Palazzo San Maurizio so that the Le Gallais could sell it and buy with their share the palace opposite the Ca' del Duca, a matter to which we will return. The two couples, and especially the two sisters, lived in harmony and unity reigned in this family.

In the meantime, the youngest of the Velluti sisters began her married life far from her home town with a man she hardly knew. The Le Gallais, who were rather sociable and liked to be in company, were a couple living in osmosis and united by a strong affection. They led a peaceful but never monotonous family life. Numerous photographs bear witness to past memories, almost forgotten today, and still carefully preserved in numerous photo

Another photo of Hugues Le Gallais' marriage with Pisana en 1933 in Venice.

albums in Venice. Hugues was apparently formal and a little demanding, even harsh towards his wife, who supported him as she could. It was Pisana who wrote the invitations and menus for the big dinners. A mutual sense of division of labor prevailed. She had a Latin character that could be described as "fiery", while he often remained silent, seeming to find it difficult to express his feelings.

Highly demanding in terms of etiquette and protocol, Hugues seems to have been touchy in the face of criticism that was even slightly unfair. With tact and distinction, without getting lost in unnecessary verbiage, he knew how to impose his vision of things. He always expressed himself in a thoughtful manner and described himself as tolerant and valiant.

Hugues seems to have kept few friends from his youth who accompanied him throughout his journey. Family ties almost always dominated and, most of the time, conditioned Hugues Le Gallais' acquaintances and friendships. One friendship seems to have lasted, that with Georges Brasseur, who worked for a while in Marrakech. Various things linked Hugues to Brasseur, who was born in 1894 and who died two years later than Hugues, in 1966. He was the son of the Member of Parliament Xavier Brasseur and of his wife Jeanne de Saint-Hubert. This couple had divorced in 1910, Georges' mother subsequently marrying his father's first cousin. Georges Brasseur's mother was the daughter of industrialist Xavier de Saint-Hubert-Mongenast and the sister of Aline Mayrisch-de Saint-Hubert. Georges Brasseur married Annette Mayrisch in 1922, granddaughter of a Metz and, therefore, a relative of Hugues. An engineer, Brasseur was director and administrator of the Compagnie des Mines et Métaux and attached to the general management of Arbed.[58] This friend of Hugues Le Gallais was the subject of a letter written by the Minister of Justice Victor Bodson on May 28, 1941.[59] Georges Brasseur had come to the United States in May 1941 "with papers issued by the German authorities who forbade him from seeing the Grand Duchess or any member of the Luxembourg Government in exile, but at Brasseur's special request he was authorized to see you [Hugues Le Gallais] as a former friend from his studies... the visit is of interest as regards the questions raised by the Government ...". Rather confidential contacts in the middle of the war. Brasseur was back in Washington in January 1942 where he met Dupong and traveled on business to Ohio in March. During this visit, he was arrested and Le Gallais had to intervene with the Federal Bureau of Investigation (FBI). A large bail was paid to put an end to suspicions against Brasseur who had been considered a military and was carrying letters written in German, making him suspect according to Heisbourg.[60] Brasseur was still in Washington in January 1944 and handed over a note on the Luxembourg steel industry explaining the difficulties of sabotage in a small country, which would later become important in explaining the wartime attitude of Arbed and Aloyse Meyer. During the war, Brasseur joined the Allied war effort as an American soldier, not at the frontlines but as a G2 (security and intelligence) operative in the War Department.[61] In Luxembourg, the acquaintances of the Le Gallais included the Alexandre couple, whose daughter, Madeleine, was to marry Robert Flesch,[62] who had married a Leclère, who was a niece of Emile Mayrisch and a cousin of the Le Gallais on the Metz side, and who died young in 1915. It was only in Washington that the Le Gallais would make real friends, such as the Maurice Frère couple or certain fellow ambassadors with whom they would remain in contact even in retirement. Pisana no longer had many ties in Venice outside her family, and after their return from Washington in 1958, real friendships there became increasingly rare for Hugues, who did not know the Italian language well enough. Prominent Venetian residents, such as Élie Ludovic Henri Christian Decazes,[63] 5th Duke Decazes, owner of the Contarini Polignac Palace, and the heiress and modern art collector Peggy Guggenheim,[64] were almost neighbors, but it is difficult to know whether they had also become real friends. There was also the Curtis couple, from an old Boston family, who had bought the beautiful Barbaro Palace, on the Grand Canal opposite the Polignac Palace, which had an interesting cultural and artistic life. Such is the life of diplomats who, more often than not, lose many ties and friendships during their career. As far as possible, one remained among one's kind, caring for numerous and diverse but always carefully chosen ties.

The two offspring of bourgeois and even aristocratic families were linked not only by all the talents of youth combined with ambition, but also and above all by the fact that they wanted to escape complicated family situations, especially the ones caused by the remarriage of their respective fathers. Their relations with their respective stepmothers were hardly satisfactory and neither Luxembourg nor Venice sufficed to hold back the adventurous couple which, without much hesitation, set off far away. Hugues knew high society and the great game of life, and Pisana was going to fill his unspoken enthusiasm for exotic lands and his ambition to pursue a career that was, after all, promising. Pisana has been described by some as a very nice girl but not knowing how to look after a household

And so they left for Japan. The airplane, that symbol of man's conquest of the air, does not seem to have been within reach for the young Le Gallais. Pisana had used this means of transport only once in her life, to go to Cuba, and Hugues may have done so to go to Mexico, but not as often as it would have been possible for them at a time when aviation was no longer in its infancy but still considered dangerous. Cars were non-existent and impossible to use in Venice, so they travelled almost exclusively by train and boat. In any case, on the threshold of their new life, an adventurous page would open for Pisana and Hugues. The couple would lead a dream life, skillfully making their talents to good use, whether in Tokyo, Luxembourg, later in Washington, or finally in Venice.

PRE-WAR PROFESSIONAL ACTIVITIES AND DIPLOMATIC POSTING IN WASHINGTON

Hugues' family had been at the origin of the Arbed, whose head office was the symbol of Luxembourg's flourishing economy. This edifice from the 1920s reflects the glorious history of an era when the iron and steel industry was dominant. The building has been and continues to be the emblem of the Avenue de la Liberté. The architecture and town planning of the capital remain imprinted by this jewel of the country's architectural and industrial heritage.

According to a member of the family, Hugues had in fact no real position after the First World War. Not very inclined to be expansive, at least in public, he also lacked the soul mate that would really enable him to play his role with more ardor and passion. At the end of his studies, he was happy to be able to represent Columeta, where someone had to put in a good word for him and recommend him. He was apparently not known for being overly assiduous at office work, with some people saying at the time that his number two was always doing a significant part of the job. This is also what transpires from a letter from Andrée Mayrisch to her mother dated November 19, 1921 when she and Hugues were both in London: "Hugues is becoming more and more comical in spats[65] and *gibus*.[66] He utters so many memorable words that they are not remembered. Here are some of the best: 'I find it amoral for someone as rich as Gaston to work',[67] 'I am handsome, I am intelligent, I have broad ideas.' About business and about the money he'll make later: 'When I want to, I'll always succeed, at anything.' In addition to his other faults, he has become a snob and full of worldly prejudices—but he is a dear boy all the same, even though Poussy[68] and I believe him capable of the worst rogueries, in full innocence".[69] Hugues was not too inclined to work, but was nevertheless interested in playing in the big league. Hugues had ideas and, in keeping with his family's motto, was determined to see them materialize one day. A few years later, perhaps out of necessity, he proved that he knew how to work and earn a living, whether in the commercial or diplomatic fields.

Successively, Hugues Le Gallais was attached to the Comptoir Métallique Luxembourgeois (Columeta), the sales counter created in 1919/1920 by the Arbed with the aim of distributing the products manufactured by the metallurgical group throughout the world. As the German market had collapsed after the First World War, the Luxembourg steel industry had to look for new ones. The cartellization or alliances between the German, French, Belgian, Luxembourg and Saarland steel producers reached its peak between the two world wars. Two cartels were headquartered in Luxembourg and were successively presided over by Emile Mayrisch, Hugue's main promoter, and then by Aloyse Meyer.[70]

Occupying a number of posts in succession, Hugues was first sent to Paris from 1919 to 1920. At the end of the Paris Peace Conference on June 28, 1919, the Treaty of Versailles, having rejected Belgium's annexationist visions, devoted a few articles in response to questions about the status of Luxembourg. These must have been observed with interest. Subsequently, he was appointed to London from 1921 to 1922, where two international conferences were held to seek solutions to the difficulties of implementing peace treaties. Subsequently, he left for Saarbrucken for the Aciéries Réunies de Burbach-Eich-Dudelange in 1923. At the time, the Saarland was subject to the international administration of the League of Nations administration under French control. Hugues Le Gallais was in Tokyo in 1924, in Luxembourg in 1925, in Bombay in 1926, as director in Tokyo from 1927 to 1936 and again in Luxembourg from 1937 to 1939 as "Chief of the Rail Export Division". Columeta's network was based on representatives who often came from families linked to Arbed. It formed something of a diplomatic network *avant la lettre*. The Grand Duchy had only a few diplomats, most of them itinerant, who were supplemented in their work by Honorary Consuls.

IN THE SERVICE OF COLUMETA IN BOMBAY (1926)

We have seen that Hugues' uncle on his father's side, Lieutenant-Colonel Walter Le Gallais, had served in India from 1891 to 1895 as aide-de-camp to the Commander-in-Chief of Bombay. Hugues had heard about him and was all the more curious to retrace the footsteps of this relative, who had been dead for over a quarter of a century, and whose adventures and bravery had left a trace in the form of many photos and, no doubt, anecdotes. In the 1920s, Bombay was the economic hub of India and the world's largest cotton market. Under British rule, the country's second largest city after Calcutta had a population of one million. It was also one of the major centers of the Indian nationalist movement. During these years, Gandhi and Nehru, the leaders of the Congress Party, called for democratic reforms and then for autonomy for the metropolis. These demands were accompanied by non-violent action, a boycott of British products and a civil disobedience. Delhi was the capital of several Indian empires, but the administration of the British Indian Empire was based in Calcutta. It was not until 1911 that King George V announced the transfer of the capital of the Empire from this city, considered too out-of-center, to Delhi, whose more central position would make the administration of the empire easier.

In October 1927, Columeta conducted sweeping reassignments in several of the cities where it had representatives: Hugues Le Gallais was moved to Tokyo, from where his predecessor Guy Noesen was transferred to Brazil, while Victor Buffin, until then in Milan, was sent to New York, and finally the representative in Brazil, Jacques Neef, was to represent Columeta in Dublin. All these changes were published in the Luxemburger Wort on October 15, 1927.

In May 1929, two years after Le Gallais had left India, the Luxembourg Government requested that Alphonse Als, director of the Belgian Manufacturing Industry Corporation, be recognized as Honorary Vice-Consul in Bombay. This brother of Robert Als, the future minister and diplomat, was to become minister Bech's chief of staff in London at the end of the war.

IN JAPAN (1927-1936)

Columeta Tokyo, founded in 1925 in order to conquer new markets, offers an insight into the cultural mechanics of a European company in Japan during the inter-war period. While Luxembourg had since 1923 a Honorary Consul in Japan, Mr. Imaizumi Kaichiro, head of Japan's largest private steel mill, Nippon Kôkan Kabushiki Kaisha, Columeta's and therefore le Gallais' role by far exceeded the sale of steel products.[71] While business went well in the 1920s, the situation became more difficult in the 1930s due to the global economic crisis, the boom in Japanese steel production and the country's increasing protectionist economic policies. In the Land of the Rising Sun, Hirohito, grandson of Emperor Meiji, ascended to the throne on December 25, 1926 under the name of Shôwa ("Shining Peace") reign. He had already assumed the regency in previous years due to his father's illness and he survived the Second World War. Minister Plenipotentiary Hugues Le Gallais was one of the signatories of the peace treaty in San Francisco in 1951 that formally ended the state of hostility with Japan.

By the 1930s, when Le Gallais came to Japan, first alone and then with his wife and son, the country's population had almost doubled since 1868, from 34 million to nearly 60. The country had a dynamic economy and a powerful, globally competitive industry. In urban areas, mentalities became closer to the Western world and modern districts were developing in large cities such as Tokyo and Yokohama. However, the majority of the country had remained agricultural and artisanal. Westernization was seen as a challenge to traditional Japanese ideals, with the result that a conservative, even reactionary, opposition favored a strong military regime with ultra-nationalist tendencies. Universal suffrage, introduced in 1925, was but a façade of liberal democracy. In 1931 the military placed the Emperor and the Government before a fait accompli by invading Manchuria. Then the assassination of Prime Minister Inukai in 1932 and the attempted coup d'état of February 26, 1936 led the Emperor and the Government to give power to the General Staff in order to escape from its most extremist officers. The regime put in place by the military soon took the form of Japanese totalitarianism.

There are not many traces of Le Gallais' private life from the early years of his life in Japan, apart from those left by Aline Mayrisch-de Saint-Hubert who visited him in 1930. On December 7, 1930, she wrote on Le Gallais' house in Tokyo, from Nara to Schlumberger:

Hugues Le Gallais in the 1930s in Japan, in front of a *torii*.

"I am continuing from one of the most beautiful and oldest places. I hope to stay here for eight days in relative solitude, which I need very much. Hugues' house, tiny and uncomfortable, hardly allows one to isolate oneself for long, and he himself, affectionate, generous, attentive as much as possible, does not bring you a very nourishing atmosphere [with, on the margin: many elements of comic unconsciousness], with which he is relatively absorbing with his tinkering mania. Every day one has to accompany him to another sale, or to some other antique dealer. Moreover, thanks to him, I have become acquainted with several interesting circles and have also been able to make several acquisitions, with which I am happy, including a very beautiful Chinese painting. But that was not the purpose of this trip and the stay in Tokyo [...] was certainly, by the force of circumstances, a little long for the interest it entails".[72]

Hugues and Pisana Le Gallais-Velluti.

A more harmonious depiction from Mrs. Mayrisch this time, than that of Hugues as a "pickle", from about the same time.

From the photo albums of the Japanese episode, carefully kept by Pisana and Hugues, one can feel a great tranquility and admiration for a country with a culture several thousand years old. Pictures of temples and splendid nature alternate with photos, sometimes in extremely small format, of country scenes or views of the modern, spacious, Bauhaus or even Art Deco style house that the Le Gallais must have lived in. It was a welcoming house of cubic construction with a roof terrace, situated on a hill that made it possible to receive friends and acquaintances. The visiting cards and menus from those years bear witness to a busy social life. A few pictures of various hotels suggest that they were used to extended stays or trips outside the capital. Hugues Le Gallais also visited the Wall of China and the Temple of Heaven in Beijing. The program also seems to have included climbing Mount Nantai, almost 2,500 meters high, on the Japanese island of Honshu, North of the Tokyo metropolitan area. This whole life, quite unique for a Luxembourger in the 1930s, alternating illusions and setbacks, allowed Hugues to shine and break out of old habits and conventions. These years were often punctuated by sophisticated encounters with locals or expatriates, dinners in jackets and long evenings alone and with his young wife. Pisana was in a way Hugues' double. She had a strong personality, which was much needed with regard to someone who had the advantage of having already lived alone in Asia for six years, or even seven if one is to count the 1926 stay, before she joined him. A very chic Venetian, Pisana must have been perceived as glamorous, even emblematic, in a Japan that was formal and hierarchical to the extreme. A photo of her in a long dress and one of him in a dinner jacket, ready to entertain or to go out, lascivious and philosophical at the same time, testifies to an art of living, even a mastery of this high-society mundane life which had everything to please a dynamic couple.

Married on Monday November 6, 1933, the young couple left Italy from Genoa on November 15 on board the "Super Expresso Conte di Savoia" for faraway Asia, of which Pisana knew nothing. Soon after arriving in the Japanese capital, which had its very particular atmosphere, Pisana was expecting her first child. Far from her family, she gave birth to a son named Norbert Ludovico Marino Maria in Tokyo on August 26, 1934. The child's godmother was Aline Mayrisch-de Saint-Hubert.

By the time of the birth of their son, the Le Gallais had been well introduced in Japan, as shown by the countless messages of congratulations received from locals (Nantaisan, Junko Hagiwara) and expatriates like them (Tony Rollman,[73] who also worked in Japan for Columeta from 1926 to 1935, Wilfried Fleischer, Mrs. Georges Stoïesco, Mr. and Mrs. Luigi Mariani). There was also Katharini Sansom, professor emeritus of Japanese at Columbia University, British representative in Tokyo, Singapore, Washington and New York, probably the wife of Sir George Bailey Samsom who left valuable works on Japan, and of whom there is a trace several years later in the *Scrapbook* organized at the embassy in Washington. Other messages came from people long forgotten and impossible to place in the context of their relationship with the young Le Gallais couple. Telegrams or simple business cards with a word or two were sent at the time. Pisana stuck them in an album with photos of their stay and photos of their baby which filled and changed their lives profoundly. One nanny or another was available so that Pisana would not be too absorbed by the child. There are photos of the very young Norbert with sometimes a Japanese nanny and sometimes one of European origin.

Aline Mayrisch-de Saint-Hubert with her godson Norbert Le Gallais
and two unknown guests.

During these years in Japan, the Le Gallais were rather close with
the Baron and Baroness Albert de Bassompierre.[74] In December
1920 the Belgian Baron had been named envoy extraordinary
and minister plenipotentiary in Tokyo, where he arrived in May
1921. He remained in Japan until February 1939. Thanks to the
development of relations between Belgium and Japan, de Bassompierre became the first Belgian diplomat in Japan with the
rank of Ambassador Plenipotentiary Extraordinary in June 1922.

Le Gallais was to follow this path of a change of status in 1955 in Washington. The Baron and Baroness had, for example, organized a dinner with the Le Gallais and the Portuguese, German and French diplomatic representatives. A Luxembourg couple, Joseph Hackin and his wife Marie Ria Parmentier, called Ria,[75] were in close contact with Hugues Le Gallais. Hackin, a native of Boevange-sur-Attert, was director of the *Maison franco-japonaise* in Tokyo from 1930 until 1933, after having been curator of the Guimet Museum in Paris. He befriended Le Gallais, ten years his junior, as he would befriend minister Bech in wartime London where he joined de Gaulle and before he died at sea, a hero of France, on February 24, 1941, when his ship was torpedoed near the Faroe Islands. Hackin wrote to Mrs. Mayrisch that he had "steered Hugues towards studying art. He gave me a study on his screens which, thanks to my friend Espezel,[76] will be honored by the *Gazette des Beaux-Arts*. It's good work. I hope that Le Gallais will not stop there".[77] He describes Hugues as "stoic and phlegmatic" in the face of Tokyo's unbearable summer temperatures.[78] Luxembourger Tony Rollman, whom Jean Monnet later described in his memoirs as "a precise Luxembourg steelmaker whose reputation extended beyond the borders of his country",[79] worked in Japan at the same time as Le Gallais. We do not know the exact private links between them. This compatriot had three children during those years. He worked under the direction of Le Gallais, who remained in Tokyo. Rollman moved twelve times in nine years, mainly to Osaka, the industrial centre where Columeta opened offices in 1928, and to Kobe. In the Japanese capital, Le Gallais had his offices in the Marunouchi commercial district,[80] located in Chiyoda between Tokyo station and the Imperial Palace. While daily life was described as exotic, Rollman asked, as early as January 1935, not to return to Japan for another three years after his planned leave in Europe, for family and health reasons. Le Gallais was supposed to settle the last affairs before returning himself. In fact, Columeta's business seems to have run into difficulties due to the fall of the Yen and the Japanese employees, at one point more than a dozen people, who left the Luxembourg representation to join Japanese cartels. Hugues Le Gallais apparently pleaded for the recruitment of Europeans, as the Japanese preferred to negotiate with foreign representatives. He also sought to obtain the payment of an annual bonus, which was an indispensable custom in Japan. He wrote on October 19, 1931 to Columeta in Luxembourg: "We have always insisted on the importance of personal contacts in business affairs between Europeans and Asians. The latter consider themselves inferior to Europeans and like it and are flattered when they can interact with them from equal to equal."

More or less regular trips to Luxembourg allowed Le Gallais to keep in touch with his native country, but also to travel via the Suez Canal and India or the Trans-Siberian Railway or even across the Pacific and North America. Columeta closed its Osaka office in November 1938 and its Tokyo office in June 1939.[81]

In 1936, Pierre Ruppert took over from Le Gallais in Japan. The latter took no less than 39 crates to the Grand Duchy, an undertaking described as considerable and time-consuming. He took with him many antiques and works of art acquired over the years. The suicide of Lieutenant Aoshima Kenkichi on February 28, 1936, in the midst of a rebellion, attracted the attention of Le Gallais, who kept among his souvenirs and photos an article of March 2 from the newspaper *Hochi Shimbun* on: "Lieutenant Aoshima commits hara-kiri to show rebels how to die. Wife follows." The suicide of the member of the "Imperial guards' division transport corps" would have been due to "nervous prostration from studying too hard", a posthumous letter testifying to the fact that the unfortunate man worked day and night. It is telling to see this tragic episode, which must have reminded Hugues Le Gallais of his sister Alice's suicide eight years earlier, appear so vividly in the memories of this stay in Japan. In fact, the incident of February 26 or "incident 2-2-6" was an attempted coup d'état that was organized by the ultra-nationalist faction of the Japanese Imperial Army and took place from February 26 to 29, 1936. This violent episode may have been the final straw for the Le Gallais. Pisana wanted to leave this country, with its customs and morals so different in many respects, as soon as possible. So the couple returned to Europe with their three-year-old son.

Hugues Le Gallais would long remember their time in the land of the Rising Sun. In his speech delivered in English at the signing of the peace treaty with Japan in September 1951, Le Gallais pointed out that he had spent some ten years in Japan, where he arrived briefly after the great earthquake of 1923, which had caused enormous damage, and was able to see with his own eyes what hard work can accomplish in the face of a national disaster. He also said that he saw a real avalanche of American aid and that he realized for the first time the generous spirit of the American people. He also paid tribute to this approach which has benefited many peoples, including his own. He mentioned that during these years he had been in contact with the different classes of the Japanese people and that in general the Japanese people are good and peaceful by nature. He recalled that, unfortunately, after the Mukden Incident,[82] a 1931 provocation which served as the pretext for Japan's invasion of Southern Manchuria, Japan was led by military fanatics, and that the conciliatory nature of the peace agreement was intended to prevent a return to such circumstances. He stressed that during his ten years in Japan he had not seen a single Japanese not keeping his word. His position had been patiently thought out and worked out in concert with his capital and its authorities.

In the meantime, Le Gallais was back to square one, to Luxembourg, a country unknown to Pisana. With complacency and casualness, the couple returned to the Old Continent, which was also threatened by totalitarianism, especially National Socialism. Before reaching Washington, the place of power projection par excellence, the couple had to face their own destiny in this provincial capital before the new explosion that was to set Europe ablaze. Le Gallais was the amiable gentleman par excellence, while becoming more and more "imperial bourgeois" in the image of his ancestors and relatives. He was to make a name for himself at the Grand Ducal Court and seek refuge in the examination, preservation, study and contemplation of his collection of oriental art that he had built up over the preceding decade.

HONORARY POSITION WITH THE GRAND DUCHESS AND LINKS WITH THE GRAND DUCAL FAMILY

A monarchist, conventional at times, Le Gallais was a mixture of elite aristocrat and great lord who knew where to go and who to attach himself to in order to continue on his path, especially at the Luxembourg court.

Hugues' father, Norbert Le Gallais, had already been close to the Grand Ducal Court. Hugues' sisters had been invited to play at the Grand Ducal Palace with Luxembourg Princesses and the children of diplomats. Rozel remembered that Princess Charlotte had been locked up and forgotten in a cupboard containing coats that had been treated with mothballs. This special relationship explains in part the rather close link between Le Gallais and the sovereign, to whom he could sometimes address himself differently, more intimately than was usual and traditional, as we shall soon see.

Hugues was Chamberlain to Her Royal Highness the Grand Duchess from February 1939 until the end of his life. 1939 was the centenary of the Treaty of London and therefore of Luxembourg's independence. Commemorations and celebrations were held throughout the country and bore witness to the independent spirit and sovereign pride of Luxembourgers. Hugues Le Gallais must not have been insensitive to this national fervor, which was also intended to show the menacing Germans that Luxembourgers wanted to remain independent according to the motto *Mir wölle bleiwe wat mir sin* (We want to remain what we are). Hugues certainly wanted to progress in his professional life. The fact that he had become a Chamberlain at Court was undoubtedly a welcome and appreciated boost. He was also willing to leave his native country again. Many of these events must have led him to believe that man is responsible for his own destiny in more than one respect, and it was in this sense that he would approach the Washington-related opportunity that was about to present itself. The quality of Chamberlain was for Hugues a welcome step on his diplomatic journey. As a person close to the Court, he was somewhat envious, distinguishing himself from the lot of civil servants and courtiers among whom he would soon evolve as a diplomat.

The function of chamberlain (camerarius in Latin) and therefore of a gentleman in charge of the chamber service of a Monarch or Prince, at whose court he lived, had changed somewhat over time. Hugues Le Gallais mainly took part in certain ceremonies, but could also advise the Court. During the war, he would make use of it. A photo taken during the last Te Deum on National

Day,[83] on January 23, 1940, before the German occupation shows Auguste Collart, Hugues Le Gallais, the aide-de-camp of Prince Félix, Guillaume Konsbruck called Guill,[84] the Grand Marshal of the Court, François de Colnet d'Huart, and the President of the Administration des Biens, Alfred Loesch.[85] The men of the Grand Ducal Court are lined up in keeping with precedence in front of the cathedral while waiting for the Grand Ducal family. A whole range of acquaintances, even familiars, thus regularly met for festive and solemn occasions.

It is probably thanks to his first cousin Auguste Collart that Hugues entered this restricted and coveted circle of Luxembourg dignitaries, and it was also that cousin's example that he would follow in becoming a diplomat. The owner of the castle of Bettembourg, where he was also mayor, Auguste Collart was six years older than Hugues. He had been Director General, i.e. Minister of Agriculture, Trade, Industry and Labour from 1918 to 1920 as an independent supported by the People's Party (*Freie Volkspartei*). He had also been chargé d'affaires in The Hague. During the Second World War he was interned in the Hinzert concentration camp and later deported with his family to Leubus. He wrote his memoirs and a book about the turmoil surrounding the dynasty after the First World War. He was a member of the Historical Section of the Grand Ducal Institute. He lived in The Hague in a mansion located in the middle of a vast park, first rented and then bought by the Luxembourg state. A good host, demanding and qualified by some as difficult, Collart often lived there alone, his wife and two daughters remaining, at least at the beginning of his mandate, in Luxembourg. Although there is no known correspondence or particular link between the two cousins, whose destiny was in many respects similar, the younger one seems to have often drawn inspiration from the older one.

Beyond this honorary position at Court, Le Gallais also had a special, not to say privileged, link with the Grand Ducal family. While most of his letters to the Grand Duchess ended with the words, "I am, Madam, with the deepest respect, Your Royal Highness' most humble, most obedient and most faithful servant and subject", Le Gallais also took the liberty of addressing the Grand Duchess in a rather personal, even intimate manner. During the war, Le Gallais gave his opinion on personal matters affecting the sovereign. Thus, on October 8, 1942, he went so far as to philosophize, as it were, recalling his education, setting himself up as an example to invoke and take the opportunity to

"ask Madam if She does not think it would be appropriate, each time She writes to Her son, to speak to Him about His future responsibilities. Anything Your Royal Highness writes from here (the American continent), for Him there (the United Kingdom), will be of much greater importance than words exchanged on the spot. The great failing of men of this century has been the indecisive and floating side of their character. The men of the occupied countries who will remain after this ordeal will be different and will show firmness of character. They will demand that the sovereign set a good example. To see Prince Jean's character strengthened is my only concern and only Madame can have an influence in this direction. My teacher never missed an opportunity to point out the soft side of my character and to strengthen my will. For Your Royal Highness, there is no shortage of examples to cite. That of H.R.H. Grand Duchess Marie-Anne in the positive sense. In the negative sense one can always come back to the danger of getting caught up in words, instead of reflecting oneself on the ideas behind the words. Perhaps Madame could get Prince Jean to summarize certain conversations for Her; this is an excellent exercise for the mind and for memory. Out of pride He will wish to do well and Madame will be able to encourage Him, which is very important."

Here is Hugues Le Gallais trying his hand as an adviser on the training of the future sovereign, two days after the Crown Prince's departure from the American continent. Perhaps this sermon by Le Gallais simply reflects the bitterness of its author to see a member of this family for whom he was willing to do anything, leave the American continent. Other subjects, far more politically sensitive, will also be the subject of a similar letter, which we quote here as testimony to the liberties Le Gallais took towards the Grand Duchess. Also in relation to political and economic topics such as the Ensch Plan[86] and his discussions on this subject with the American Under-Secretary of State Sumner Welles, Le Gallais duly informed the sovereign to whom he sent not only his report of his talks with Welles (notably the ones of November 30, 1942 and December 21, 1942), but also a note from Dupong on the latter's conversation with Welles on February 9, 1943.[87] Although Le Gallais was loyal to his direct authorities, he considered it his duty to inform his sovereign first and foremost. The Grand Duchess was going to express her appreciation to him after an incident with Minister Bodson in Chicago.[88] He was also going to telephone and write without intermediary during the period of exile.[89] Before recounting the epic of this period, here are some excerpts from various letters from Le Gallais to the Grand Duchess written as legibly as possible in his own hand and expressing his very personal and pronounced emotional attachment and bond of admiration:

"Let us be realistic in foreign policy: Let us give in order to receive and let us not rely on the law. Mr. Dupong told me that Madame had the impression that she was faced with a fait accompli. I don't quite understand... I apologize if I misunderstood. In fact, when I telephoned Madame last night, with what I thought to be good news (the invitation to go to Louisiana), it seemed to me that Your Royal Highness was not very pleased. I am still very saddened by it, because when I don't think about foreign policy and become a naughty realist, I always wish to please Madame. It is not easy to find the right balance between acting according to one's conscience and reason on the one hand and one's heart and feelings on the other. What I know is that I love Madam deeply. I hope with all my heart that when Your Royal Highness, who is so receptive to new things, sees Louisiana, She will be pleased again and that She will forgive Her servant his latest sin" (Letter of December 12, 1942).

Two weeks earlier, Le Gallais, in the context of his aborted idea to have Aide-de-Camp Konsbruck appointed as military attaché, gave a definition of the role he considers to be his: "I would still very humbly like to ask Madame's forgiveness for having caused Her trouble. My only excuse is that I wanted to play Madame's game for the best and that I wanted to use the Konsbruck card to the fullest. May Your Royal Highness not worry; She will win anyway" (Letter of November 28, 1942).[90] Quite a bit of familiarity from a faithful and devoted servant!

Let us mention at this stage that the Le Gallais attended the wedding of the last of the six children of the Grand Duchess and Prince Félix. Indeed, Chamberlain Le Gallais and his wife adapted their summer holiday arrangements to be able to attend the wedding of Princess Alix of Luxembourg with Prince Antoine de Ligne at Luxembourg Cathedral on August 17, 1950. Hugues Le Gallais liked to meet royal and even imperial highnesses and frequented several of them, not only the Luxembourgers, but also the Bourbon-Parmas and the Habsburgs during the war. Afterwards, he kept in touch with some of them and closely followed their careers in the media. In the *Scrapbook* kept by Mrs. Maloney there are reports on the marriages of Otto of Habsburg, of the Luxembourg Crown Prince Jean and of his sister Marie-Adélaïde to Count Henckel von Donnersmarck, a ceremony which Le Gallais does not seem to have attended.

In his retirement, he regularly returned to Luxembourg for the Grand Duchess' birthday on January 23. A reception was held at the Grand Ducal Palace on such occasions.

Hugues Le Gallais was Grand Officer of the Order of Civil and Military Merit of Adolphe de Nassau, Grand Officer of the Order of the Oak Crown, Grand Cross of the Order of Leopold II of Belgium and Grand Cross of the Order of Orange-Nassau. He was appointed Grand Officer of the Order of the Crown of Thailand, probably as Chamberlain, during the visit of the Thai sovereigns to Luxembourg in 1960.

By Grand Ducal decree of January 21, 1950, he was awarded the title of Commander of the Order of the Crown of Oak, along with some others that he had frequented during his career, such as Robert Als and Albert Wehrer.[91]

On the occasion of her birthday, in January 1960, the Grand Duchess conferred the rank of Grand Officer on "Hugues Le Gallais, Plenipotentiary Minister Honorary, Venice", in the decree dated March 11, 1960. Recognition for services rendered, but also for seniority, with the Grand Ducal decoration of the Order of Adolphe de Nassau being awarded in a more personal way for services rendered to the Grand Ducal House. Hugues Le Gallais must have known the reason for this and had indeed always been a loyal servant. For him, devoid of modesty and hardly discreet about his own actions, the decorations certainly constituted a source of gratitude and satisfaction. In any case, as soon as he was "upgraded" from Commander of the Order of Adolphe de Nassau to Grand Officer, Le Gallais asked the publisher of the *Interna-*

tional Year Book, published in London, to make a note of this in his curriculum vitae.

As everyone has to be a judge in certain circumstances, the ambassador must have felt a sense of fulfillment as he reviewed, at the end of his life, all the historical moments he had attended or has had to take part in. Feeling at ease in the company of the great and mighty of this world, Hugues Le Gallais, knowing how to receive with perfect grace, had everything one needed to become a diplomat. A man with the beautiful manners of times gone by and a ceremonial appearance, Hugues Le Gallais always tried to understand, interpret and transmit. From February 1937 to early 1940, he waited patiently in Luxembourg for the right time to leave for other countries with his wife, his son and the extensive art collection he had acquired in Japan.

A COLLECTOR OF ORIENTAL ART

During his assignment in Japan in the service of Columeta, Hugues Le Gallais had acquired numerous pieces of oriental art which he had been able to recognize as objects of value on the basis of his initiation to the subject by the expert Petrucci. In 1929, for example, Le Gallais bought a painting of the 18th century painter Toshusai Sharaku. He even sent the information to Columeta headquarters that he continued to be interested in Japanese art and bought a work of this ukiyo-e [a genre of Japanese art which flourished from the 17th through 19th centuries] print designer, known for his portraits of kabuki actors. He himself spoke of himself as of a collector of Far Eastern art objects. His personal collection exhibited at the embassy in Washington included swords, screens and Japanese kimonos. The atmosphere in that dark house of sumptuous splendor became more personal, but also more exotic with the overabundance of works reminiscent of the Orient. Despite his status as a diplomat, Hugues Le Gallais had become a master in the art of entertaining, and his open-mindedness allowed him to frequent collectors and sophisticated people interested in art as he was. Always on the lookout for the most beautiful that does not saturate, unearthing marvels and highlighting them where they were not expected, Hugues Le Gallais was dazzled by Japanese works all his life. He also authored several articles on Far Eastern art that appeared in the *Gazette des Beaux-Arts* in 1933, 1947, 1948 and 1949.

The year of his departure from Washington was also the year of his separation from part of his collection. Perhaps the Le Gallais saw things coming or simply wanted to downsize. In any case, on November 20, 1958, Hugues Le Gallais wrote to his faithful ex-secretary Ms Maloney that the sale of objects had not had the desired effect and that he intended to visit the British capital shortly. Selling 178 pieces at Sotheby's in London obliged him to demonstrate that a Ming Dynasty saucer showing fish with a wavy rim had been part of his collection before 1951, so that the Chinese Communists would not show an undue interest in this object and demand its return. As a loyal soldier, Ms Maloney certified in a letter to the purchaser that the object and the collection were at the embassy from 1940 to 1958 and had been acquired by the ambassador before his departure from the Orient in 1935. In another document, Hugues Le Gallais asked that it should be mentioned that the objects in his collection were more than 100 years old and that those dating from the 19th century were from the "early 19th century". On August 17, 1958, while in Venice, Le Gallais asked Ms Maloney to write to Sotheby's that he maintained his appreciation of the quality and value of certain pieces about which the auction house had expressed disappointment. These were the painting *The Philosopher* and a Tibetan scroll qualified as "one of the strongest seen by (expert) Laurence Bingon". The sale of part of Hugues' collection and of the Palazzo San Maurizio, which Pisana owned with her sister, enabled the acquisition of a palace next to Ca' Rezzonico, the Palazzo Contarini Michiel, where the Le Gallais would remain until the end of their days. In fact, the ambassador had not only disposed of part of his collection at Sotheby's, but had also sold to the Freer Gallery of Art, a museum of Asian and Near Eastern art founded in 1923 in Washington and located on the National Mall, two lions that had initially sat on either side of the fireplace in the entrance hall of the embassy. What a passion for a collection we will come back to! All of this was also intended to make it some day possible to receive his many friends in Venice in a more than dignified and distinguished manner.

Let us now return to the tense and complex pre-war period. The Grand Duchy felt threatened by its German neighbor, but continued to observe its "perpetual and unarmed" neutrality, imposed on it by the Treaty of London of May 11, 1867 and violated for the first time in 1914 by Imperial Germany's invasion. 1937, the year in which Pisana and Hugues settled in Luxembourg, was the year in which the so-called *muselière* or muzzle law was rejected in June. This bill threatening public liberties and in fact intending to ban the Communist Party was rejected in a referendum by the majority of the electorate. It was a scathing disavowal for the Christian-social Minister of State of the time, Joseph Bech,[92] who had to give up this post to Pierre Dupont,[93] the figurehead of the left wing of his party. Bech, who was close to the Grand Duchess and for whom Le Gallais would develop a certain admiration, would nevertheless keep the Foreign Affairs portfolio until 1959.

Some people saw him as a Luxembourgish Talleyrand. Le Gallais developed a certain admiration for both. We do not know to what extent Le Gallais frequented these important actors in his life over the next few decades during his three-year stay in Luxembourg. A letter written by Bech to the minister in Washington at the end of August 1944, just before the liberation of the country, seems to indicate that Le Gallais had already been seeing the Bech couple before the war: "My wife recently reminded me of the tour of the Siegfried Line that you gave her before the war and from which she came back very impressed".[94] Luxembourg was a country of just under 300,000 inhabitants, and almost everyone knew each other. The Le Gallais lived in the Belair district, a few hundred meters from the Bech house. Le Gallais was soon to enter the service of this experienced minister.

DIPLOMATIC REPRESENTATION OF THE GRAND DUCHY BEFORE THE SECOND WORLD WAR

As outlined above, at the time, Luxembourg's diplomatic representation was limited and often linked to the interests of Arbed. This conglomerate and its commercial arm, Columeta, gave an international dimension to the small Grand Duchy. In 1940, the Grand Duchy was represented in Washington by Hugues Le Gallais, in London by André Clasen[95] and, during the war, in London by Georges Schommer[96] to the Czechoslovak, Polish and Belgian Governments. Antoine Funck,[97] who had been stationed in Paris since 1934, remained in Vichy until the autumn of 1942. Hugues Le Gallais' first cousin, Auguste Collart, was at The Hague.[98] In Berlin, Albert Wehrer and the secretary of legation Jean Sturm represented Luxembourg until the occupation. Count Gaston de Marchant et d'Ansembourg[99] was chargé d'affaires of Luxembourg in Brussels with Nicolas Cito as Consul. During this dark and uncertain period, the perception of the war varied from person to person : Hugues Le Gallais, who was in the United States, did not experience that cataclysm in the same way as André Clasen, who experienced the Nazi bombing of London, Auguste Collart, who experienced the occupation in The Hague before being incarcerated in the Hinzert concentration camp, and, later deported with his family, or Antoine Funck, who was in forced residence in Vichy and fled to Switzerland after the occupation of the so-called Free Zone by the Nazis.[100] As far as possible, these diplomats maintained contacts with the Government in exile, a demanding function presupposing a certain humility, which Le Gallais learned on the job. At the beginning of the war, the Minister of Foreign Affairs, Joseph Bech, displayed an innate panache similar to the one of Hugues Le Gallais. Bech for his part, travelled to Spain and Portugal before settling in London, where he was confronted with the *Blitz* of the British capital. Most of the time, Bech maintained friendly relations with Pierre Dupong and made sure that the two other ministers, the Minister of Labour, Pierre Krier,[101] and the Minister of Justice, Victor Bodson, did not cause any commotion. This was only natural, just as it was inevitable that the initial agreement between ministers from competing political families would be undermined as the period of exile went on and the problems became more numerous and thorny.[102] At times, friction arose between Bech and Le Gallais. Bech resented the separation of the ministers, half of whom were in Montreal and half in London, and he suffered from the ambiguity that this split caused about the official seat of Government. Luxembourg's minister plenipotentiary in Washington skillfully maneuvered to keep the Grand Duchess in the Western Hemisphere. For Le Gallais, the United States was destined to become the force that would determine the outcome of the war and organize the new international order. Prime Minister Dupong was not insensitive to Le Gallais' arguments, which included the existence of a major Luxembourg community in the United States and the role that the Grand Duchess could play in mobilizing American public opinion for the cause of oppressed countries. It was at Bech's insistence that the President of the Government agreed, in May 1941, to declare London the official seat of Government, and he went there several times to underline the seriousness of the decision. Ambassador Heisbourg, the author of four volumes on the war years, concluded in his books on exile that Le Gallais and Bech were each right in their own way. Bech expressed his opinion to Le Gallais in a letter dated September 10, 1941. One of his political opponents, René Blum, who had been Minister of Justice before the war and who was appointed Minister of Luxembourg to the Soviet Union in 1944, wrote to Dupong on September 9, 1945, when the election campaign in Luxembourg was in full swing: "It burns my tongue to have to proclaim aloud in the face of the ignorant the truth that you and Joseph Bech have, thanks to your efforts, saved the existence of our country *quorum testis fui* [of which I was a witness]!" In so far as Le Gallais had a strong opinion on this subject, we shall return to it in detail.

Therefore, it was a diplomatic corps limited in number, to the point that the Minister of Foreign Affairs Joseph Bech had wondered, in a note of 1937, "if we can speak of a foreign policy when it comes to a small, mostly neutral country?"[103] As so often in a diplomatic corps, points of view diverged, although the general interest overcame particular desires most of the time. In fact, Hugues Le Gallais had no predecessor in Washington, at least no one who had resided there. He may, therefore, not have thought, as some of his colleagues so often did, that the predecessor was incompetent and the successor prone to intrigue. He will, as we shall see, support Heisbourg as his successor in Washington. Without disturbing either customs or etiquette, our representative of industry, converted into a diplomat, was different and far removed from the other actors in the capital or those in post. He was moving his chess pieces and looking for markers in a country he didn't really know, apart perhaps from the memories passed on from the journey of his maternal grandfather and one passage or other while returning from Japan in the 20s and 30s.

LUXEMBOURG BEFORE MAY 10, 1940

The German invasion of 1940 did not really come as a surprise in the Grand Duchy, whose neutrality had already been flouted by the German Empire in 1914. Luxembourg had been preparing for it. This was evidenced by the intention of some, kept secret in January 1940 by the Grand Duchess and the Government, not to remain in the country in the event of a new German invasion. Was Le Gallais aware of those discussions and preparations before his arrival in the United States in March 1940? It is doubtful. The trip by Princes Félix and Jean to the United States eight months before the outbreak of hostilities in Luxembourg and at the very moment of the invasion of Poland on September 1, 1939, took place against the background of a potential German invasion and, therefore, of a more or less long exile. This princely visit had determined, if not prepared, part of the course of the exile which was to take the Grand Ducal family and the Government across the Atlantic for an exile of about four years.

Prince Félix and the Hereditary Grand Duke, accompanied by the prince's nephew, Archduke Félix of Austria-Hungary, travelled to the United States and Canada at the end of August 1939, notably to visit the World Fair in New York. On August 24, 1939, the Grand Duchess' husband and their eldest son first travelled to Canada for a brief stay in Montreal and Quebec City. From August 27 to September 5, 1939, the Luxembourg Princes were received with full honors in the United States. On August 28, 1939, a luncheon was held in Washington with President Franklin Delano Roosevelt (FDR). From this summit meeting with the President who originated the New Deal was born a bond that would prove most useful in the years to come. On August 30, the Princes opened an exhibition of Luxembourg painters (Beckius, Stoffel, Kutter, Lamboray, etc.) and sculptors (Trémont and Wercollier in particular) at the Arthur U. Newton Gallery in New York. William H. Hamilton, the Honorary Consul General of Luxembourg,[104] was also present as he had been appointed Luxembourg curator for the New York Exhibition. On September 1, the Princes attended a lunch at the New York Stock Exchange. On September 4, 1939, Luxembourg Day was held at the International Exhibition in New York. The princes returned earlier than had originally been planned, on September 5, 1939, on board the Dutch ship *Nieuw Amsterdam*, along with Herbert Claiborne Pell,[105] American minister in Lisbon in 1940, and Captain John Gade, naval attaché at the American embassy in Brussels. These two men would prove to be important contacts during the exile of the Grand Ducal family and the Luxembourg Government. It was somewhat by chance that these Americans were on board the ship bringing the princes back to Europe eight months before the invasion of Luxembourg and the government's departure into exile. Hugues Le Gallais was not present during this visit, which marked out the trail for the future actions of the Luxembourg exiles. The letter of thanks from Prince Félix to the American President,[106] which Le Gallais could have considered as a mandate for his future activities as a diplomatic representative, mentions the terms: "recognition, admiration, deep respect, paternal kindness", concluding with the "conviction that Luxembourg will emerge unscathed from the turmoil that threatens it", with FDR's views "fully covering" those of the Luxembourg Prince. Thereafter, and once accredited in the United States, Le Gallais was not going to do or say anything contrary to these premonitory words.

In 1939, with the threat of war looming, Le Gallais, who had lost his father five years earlier, had little to draw him to the country where only his stepmother and two aunts remained. Nothing beyond what was necessary attracted him to Luxembourg. He had returned there in February 1937 to live with his small family in a house in Belair. At the time, it was a new part of the city where a certain bourgeoisie was beginning to settle in newly built houses. The three-sided house at 29 Arthur Herchen Street was a three-storey building and it was built according to the plans of the architect Schmit-Noesen.

Just before the war, as the old world was slowly but inexorably coming to an end, the climate was marked by a renewal of Luxembourgers' identity, culminating in the celebrations of the Centenary of Independence, but also in anxiety about an increasingly threatening Germany. The country remained marked by its rural origins, with forty percent of the population still working in the agricultural sector. Four out of ten people were employed in industry, mainly in Arbed, for which Hugues Le Gallais was working. For three years, Le Gallais was Chief of the Rail Export Division. His superior by the name of Molitor would make life difficult for Le Gallais, as he apparently hated the members of the founding families of Arbed,[107] who remained involved in the firm, often out of sheer complacency. Nothing exciting, therefore, from

1937 to 1939, unless it was to serve as a springboard for a post abroad, a mission that was to be made possible in early 1940 in Washington. ❀

III.

In the United States during the Second World War

WASHINGTON IN 1940

Washington, D.C. was a provincial city until the 1930s, due in part to its insularity and its remoteness from the great metropolis of New York. The U.S. capital changed during World War II, when it became the headquarters of the world's largest war machine.[108] The city also became more cosmopolitan. As one journalist described it, "Washington never did explode. Instead, it began to adjust to a new form of existence: more harried, more crowded, more contentious, faster, lonelier, bigger. And while some of the strains of wartime would subside when the fighting was over, the city would never again live by its old rules".[109] From 1940 to 1943, the number of federal employees increased from 134,000 to 281,000. The region around Washington D.C. now had about 1.4 million citizens.[110] The American capital didn't have Luxembourg's thousand-year history or the cultural abundance of Venice, but it was well laid out thanks to the plans of the Franco-American engineer Pierre Charles l'Enfant. It was a clean city to live in, especially if you could escape from it during the hot and unpleasant summer months. Hugues Le Gallais didn't have to be asked twice and took extended holidays during these difficult months marked by high humidity and a subtropical climate that could last from the end of June to the beginning of September. The town, with its almost exclusively administrative functions, had everything to please Le Gallais: prestigious buildings and a concentration of power, all coupled with an intense social life. The capital was the seat of federal institutions and its economy was largely dependent on activities related to the federal Government. For Le Gallais, this city had become the centre of the world. It should be noted that the construction of the State Department's headquarters at Foggy Bottom had begun in 1939 and was only completed in 1941.

The first diplomatic representative of the Grand Duchy of Luxembourg in the United States was Baron Raymond de Waha, who travelled to the United States in September 1920.[111] He was Minister of Agriculture and Industry at the time, but with his appointment on September 6 of that year, had held the title of chargé d'affaires. De Waha's name had, however, disappeared from the directory of diplomats published in Washington in 1940.

When Prince Félix and Hereditary Grand Duke Jean travelled to New York and Washington in September 1939 for the World Fair, and more precisely during their meeting at the White House with President Roosevelt, the question of appointing a chargé d'affaires in the United States was "discussed and arranged". De Waha had only been informed in writing by Minister Bech on February 19, 1940. He had therefore accepted his own honorable resignation, which he had already submitted a first time on November 6, 1926 to prevent his removal from the diplomatic list of the United States. He had been unable to actually reside in Washington until the early months of 1926 at the latest, as the Government had not obtained the necessary funds from Parliament to send a chargé d'affaires. Already in de Waha's time, in 1928 to be exact, the question of a residence had been addressed. De Waha had reported in February of that year that he had visited the widow of Senator John B. Henderson of Missouri who wanted to help Luxembourg get a foothold in Washington. However, ten months later, in December, via de Waha, an instruction was sent to Consul Cornelius Jacoby in Washington to express Luxembourg's gratitude, while informing Mrs. Henderson that her eagerly considered project had made it necessary to enact a law. Nowhere did the Grand Duchy own a legation at the time. The building would have cost some US$100,000, including land and furnishings.

Hugues Le Gallais' application for approval was submitted in February 1940. The American chargé d'affaires in Luxembourg, Platt Waller, had explained, while recalling the de Waha episode, that Luxembourg only had diplomats of this rank charged with carrying out the duties of head of diplomatic mission. The American diplomat explained to his authorities that instead of a fixed salary of $1,000, Le Gallais and the Government had agreed that:

"he is conscientiously to ascertain through actual experience the minimum costs of living with dignity as chargé d'affaires, and reasonably reciprocating hospitalities and other courtesies, and after a few months reporting his findings, probably during leave of absence here, at which time the Grand Ducal Government will provide him with a fixed salary and allowance, I imagine about $6.000,00 per annum, plus $2.000,00 or $3.000,00 for allowances, will be found sufficient, inasmuch as Monsieur [sic] Le Gallais does not think for a moment of saving anything from his salary and allowances. On the other hand, he is not desirous except under circumstances when the fate of his sovereign and country might be in greater danger than at present, to spend anything from his private purse, inasmuch as his own fortune has suffered severely from the world crisis and grave errors of judgment on the part of his late father, and he is already making a real sacrifice in separating himself from the Steel Trust. ... Monsieur Le Gallais is the only person available who unites gentle birth, educational background, fluent knowledge of English, and experience gained through many years of foreign service in the interest of the Steel Trust, to a personality which can depend upon in every way. For the Department further information, the President and Vice President of the Steel trust might have been willing in a greater emergency to represent Luxembourg in Washington, but such an appointment could have been at best but temporary, and would have lacked some of the advantages attending the present nomination".[112]

In a form also found in the Heisbourg papers, he is described thus:

"Personality: very quiet, slow spoken, rather phlegmatic, not impulsive; [...] Influence: no political influence but considerable family & financial influence; [...] Service in the United States: He has never had an assignment in the U.S. but has visited the U.S. from time to time, en route to Japan, etc. [...] Attitude toward other nations: Very friendly toward England and France, and while lacking fascist sympathies has excellent relations with friends in Italy, due to his wife, who is Italian."

To this one should add, and Platt Waller may not have known this, that Hugues' father is described in the autobiography of the future ambassador's sister as having had a pronounced antipathy towards the Americans. This could have harmed him or even prevented him from being granted approval. The description goes on: "Remarks: Mr. Le Gallais is very discreet, but his predilections are emphatically for England, the United States, and France. The Department will find him worthy of every consideration and confidence. His English is perfect, as are his French & German".

For Haag and Krier, "the choice of the first diplomatic envoy to Washington was a most welcome one".[113]

It should be noted that on February 29, the Le Gallais were granted diplomatic visas by the State Department. The form states that the Le Gallais couple was domiciled at the Grand Ducal Palace,[114] as they no longer maintained a residence in Luxembourg. Le Gallais embarked with his family on March 20 on the cruise ship *Conte di Savoia* in Genoa.[115] The Luxembourg chargé d'affaires *in spe* is said to have met during this trip with Under-Secretary of State Sumner Welles and the Director of European Affairs of the State

Department, Jay Pierrepont Moffat. This meeting with American officials, like that of Princes Félix and Jean in 1939, would form the basis of the relations that would unfold in the months and years to come. The Le Gallais arrived in Washington at the end of March 1940.[116] The Luxembourg legation was established at the Shoreham Hotel at the intersection of Connecticut Avenue and Calvert Street, two blocks from the Wardman, where the Le Gallais family would stay some time later. Built in 1930, the hotel had become "the place to be", with several American politicians staying there and President Roosevelt holding his first inaugural ball, a custom that has since become a tradition. Following his interview with Le Gallais, Georges Schommer reported in a long letter to Minister Bech on September 7, 1940, that "Our legation is very comfortably installed at the Shoreham Hotel in Washington and one can say that our country has *pignon sur rue*"..[117]

Family life revolved around Pisana and Hugues' only son, who went to school in Washington, D.C., where he arrived while not yet six. Norbert Le Gallais would also remember an extended stay in a New York hotel with a swimming pool that made life much more enjoyable. Le Gallais' son first attended the Convent School of Sacred Heart at 1719 Massachusetts Avenue, where he won the prize for French and for his penmanship. He then attended the public Laundon School in Bethesda, Maryland, before leaving for the prestigious Harvard University, where he studied from 1952 to 1956, and then for the Institut d'Etudes Politiques in the rue Saint-Guillaume in Paris. A fine career path, therefore—one that probably didn't cause his parents too many worries, as they were so often busy elsewhere. Finally, he graduated after four years at the Institute of International Studies in Geneva in 1956.[118]

April 3, 1940 was the date on which the legation moved into the Shoreham Hotel and took up its duties. Hugues Le Gallais was received that day by Secretary of State Cordell Hull.[119] The latter was Secretary of State from 1933 to November 30, 1944, leaving the administration for health reasons shortly after President Roosevelt's re-election to a fourth term. On January 2, 1945, Le Gallais wrote him a personal message thanking him for their long-standing relationship and his continued support for the Luxembourg cause, stating: "in you I always recognize a champion of the principles of decency, fairness and mutual respect which should govern relations between countries." The Luxembourg minister did not fail to ask for a photo signed by the Secretary of State. Another important relation at the State Department was with Under-Secretary of State Sumner Welles.[120] Between November 1940 and April 1943, Le Gallais left no less than twelve reports on his meetings with the number two in the State Department.[121] Originally from New York and educated at Harvard, he entered the State Department to become ambassador to Cuba in 1933, then Assistant Secretary of State for Latin America and number two in the State Department as Under-Secretary of State. He resigned at the end of September 1943 because of tensions with Secretary of State Cordell Hull and revelations about an alleged homosexual affair. Welles was close to the Luxembourg community, as was confirmed by the Grand Duchess' aide-de-camp, Guill Konsbruck, who wrote to Hugues Le Gallais on September 2, 1943 on this subject: "I read with emotion the very charming and touching letter which Mr. Sumner Welles addressed to you. It is unfortunate that he is leaving his post, for we all lose in him a faithful and sure friend of our country and our cause, and you lose a devoted personal friend on whom you could count at all times." Welles was married three times. In 1925, he married his second wife, Mathilde Townsend, one of the wealthiest divorcees in Washington. The couple lived at 2121 Massachusetts Avenue. The beautiful turn-of-the-century mansion opposite the building that was to house the Luxembourg legation was sold in September

1950 to become the headquarters of the Cosmos Club.[122] Like Le Gallais, Welles was a collector of Japanese art.[123] At the beginning of his diplomatic career, he was briefly posted to Tokyo where his son was born in 1916. So he and Le Gallais had much in common. Sumner Welles was also behind the famous "no comment" made famous by Winston Churchill in 1946.[124] After a meeting at the White House with President Truman and an American diplomat, the British prime minister is said to have reported: "I think 'no comment' is a splendid expression. I got it from Sumner Welles."

Other key dates in Le Gallais' career before his retirement on September 30, 1958 were his promotion to Minister Plenipotentiary on October 2, 1940, with the presentation of his credentials on November 8, 1940. Hugues Le Gallais' accreditation in Washington was to prove a major asset. The absence of a diplomatic representative in Washington would not have allowed the Government in exile to be represented and advised, or even to open the doors adequately.

The Luxembourg legation was set up at 2200 Massachusetts Avenue in March 1941. On September 10, 1955, it was granted embassy status. So many reports sent, instructions received, causes and ideas defended, information gleaned and contacts and bonds of friendship woven over the years by the head of mission Le Gallais! Hugues and Pisana Le Gallais were charming and had a taste for society. Over the years, they had become outstanding socialites and gathered the top names of American political, economic and social world around their splendid table and in a choice location in the embassy quarter. Despite the fact that the minister plenipotentiary had not held the rank of ambassador for 15 years and was only going to take full advantage of it during the last three years of his presence in Washington, the Luxembourg legation became a place frequented with happiness and pleasure by those in the

American capital who counted or thought they did. Especially after the war, the Le Gallais knew how to receive and make their guests feel at ease. In their presence, conversation flowed and time passed happily. In a special universe that would soon be of no interest to many, they opened the doors of their home to the whole of Washington. They were going to make their own way without ever fearing or verging on the ridiculous. To Le Gallais worked continuously and relentlessly to put himself in the limelight. He surrounded himself with dedicated staff and top chefs, serving the finest wines, and became a member of closed clubs, such as the Metropolitan Club in Washington. The club's proximity to the White House and other key addresses in the nation's capital made it a destination for many local, national and international leaders, including nearly every American President since Abraham Lincoln. Minister Le Gallais was also a member of the Council of the American Geographical Society. The aim of the Professional Geographers' Association was to encourage activities that spread geographical knowledge.

When presenting his credentials, Le Gallais limited himself to stating that "he had no special problems in mind to take up with the United States Government, but pointed out that increasing trade between this country and Luxembourg—a steel-producing state whose greatest imports from the United States are motor cars—made it advisable to maintain full diplomatic contacts."[125] At the time, to promote their country and present it in its true dimension Luxembourgers already had to fight clichés and stereotypes that were circulating. This description in the Evening Star at the beginning of April was to be followed a few days later by an article describing the couple and their only son:

"Signorina Pisana Velluti, is a native of Venice and her family is one of the old and distinguished families of that ancient city. Both the Charge [sic] d'Affaires and Mme Le Gallais are young and both are ardent fishermen. The chatelaine of this newest legation has a sparkle in her eye, which gives a hint of her keen sense of humor. Although her English is not fluent she understands it easily and in addition to her mother tongue she speaks French. The young son of the family, Norbert, now five years and a half, will attend a Kindergarten in Washington and learn the ways of his American contemporaries. He has a bright face with expectant and interested expression and is eager to learn about this country, though he speaks no word of English. Mme. Le Gallais, although not a musician, has the love for the art, which is native with Italians, just as she has an appreciation and knowledge of painting and sculpture. She will make many friends here with her gracious and friendly manner."

Le Gallais' predecessor was also described at length; as was the fact that now some 54 diplomatic missions were present in Washington.[126] As reported in the *Evening Star* of April 18 in its "Notes From the Social Calendar of Washington and Its Environs", the special assistant to the Secretary of State and former ambassador to Belgium, Mrs. Joseph E. Davies, received the couple quickly, as she had received the Belgian ambassador and Countess van der Straten-Ponthoz and their daughter Betty the previous day:[127] "Mr. and Mrs. Davies will be hosts again at dinner tomorrow, when they will entertain in honor of the newly appointed Charge [sic] d'Affaires of Luxembourg and Mme. Le Gallais."[128] In April 1940, Le Gallais handed over books to the Library of Women's Group. The *Evening Star* reports that:

"An Interesting gift of pamphlets and books was made to the library of the Newspaper Women's Club of Washington by the Charge [sic] d'Affaires of Luxembourg, Hughes [sic] Le Gallais, at the tea given by the club yesterday at the Raleigh Hotel, when

M. and Mme. Le Gallais were guests of honor. M. Le Gallais gave an informal talk about his country which has a population of only 300,000 and has a half dozen newspapers, some printed in French, some in German and one in the native dialect. There are no women in newspaper work in Luxembourg, he said, although women are numbered in other professions, such as law and medicine. Mme. Le Gallais also spoke a few words expressing her enjoyment of American motion pictures".[129]

What a great initiative to make their country better known across the Atlantic!

Le Gallais was not the only Luxembourger in the United States. Many others had come there at the end of the 19th and the beginning of the 20th centuries to find a better future. In the summer of 1940, Bernard Zimmer,[130] who had arrived in the United States in 1905 and who had been President of the organizing committee of the Luxembourg pavilion, was appointed Honorary Consul on July 2, 1940. In December 1946, he was to become Honorary Consul General, as President of a newly created section of the American Red Cross Relief Fund for assistance to Luxembourg refugees. Heisbourg traces the initiative back to the newly arrived chargé d'affaires in Washington: "When Le Gallais envisaged the creation of a Luxembourg Relief fund,[131] the American Red Cross agreed to cooperate and the attitude of the Luxembourgish colonies in the United States was also positive."[132]

According to the Official Yearbook of 1940, the newly accredited Luxembourg diplomat could count on certain consuls who had been appointed to look after Luxembourg's interests. The list of the Grand Duchy's consuls abroad included Honorary Consul General in Chicago John Marsch, who had two Vice-Consuls, a vacant Honorary Consul post in Minneapolis with, however, a Vice-Consul in St. Paul, Minnesota. William Hamilton was Honorary Consul General in New York with Corneille Staudt as Honorary Vice-Consul. The relationship between the two men was deplorable, and in September 1943 Le Gallais recommended that Mr. Hamilton, who had already offered to resign in November 1941,[133] be replaced by Ben Zimmer.[134] In Washington Cornelius Jacoby was Honorary Consul and had his offices at 5423 13th Street. The Honorary Consulate in San Francisco was vacant, as was the position of Honorary Vice-Consul. Captain Peary Daubenfeld was Honorary Consul in Redfield, South Dakota. The Yearbook of 1958/59, around the time of Le Gallais' departure, mentions in Chicago: John N. Treveiler, Honorary Consul General, with William Capesius as Honorary Vice-Consul and Fred Gilson as chancellor; in North Hollywood, Eugène Huss was Honorary Consul; in New York, Bernard Zimmer was Honorary Consul General and the diplomat and future Ambassador Adrien Meisch, Consul. In Washington, the post of Honorary Consul was vacant, Le Gallais no doubt believing that this largely honorary function was not meant to assist him or could even overshadow him.

The news of the German invasion and the departure of the Grand Ducal family and the Government had of course been noted with concern on the other side of the Atlantic. The Luxembourg representative in Washington, Hugues Le Gallais, seems at first to have been rather distraught, at least according to memories of Jacques Lennon, future Honorary Consul of Luxembourg in New York.[135] Having gone to the United States before the war, he had met Le Gallais on May 10, 1940 and was asked by the latter: "*A wat maache mer dann elo?*" (What are we going to do now?). Seeing the desolation that had gripped Luxembourg's official representative in Washington, Lennon sought to make himself useful elsewhere.[136]

In a letter dated March 31, 1941, Le Gallais announced to Prime Minister Dupong that the legation was now installed in Massachusetts 2200. It was Prince Félix who bought the house in the presence of two witnesses, Le Gallais and Konsbruck. From March/April 1941, the Le Gallais family, the Dowager Grand Duchess and Countess of Lynar, the chambermaid Lucie Hansen and the valet Edouard Georges lived there. For a while, the third daughter of Grand Duchess Marie-Anne, Princess Hilda de Schwarzenberg, also lived here. Logically, the legation should have been established at Massachusetts Avenue 2200 from the same date. At the end of September 1941, Le Gallais left the legation to stay at the Wardman Park Hotel to make way for the Grand Duchess and her mother and Konsbruck. The children of the Grand Ducal couple living in Canada met in Washington for Christmas (1941 and 1942 surely, 1943 perhaps). Le Gallais returned to stay at the legation after the death of Grand Duchess Marie-Anne in the summer of 1942.[137] From then on, the legation continued to function at Massachusetts 2200 without interruption.[138]

The Louis XV-style seigniorial house was built at the beginning of the century on the basis of a plan by New York architects Jules Henri de Sibour and Bruce Price. In 1909, the timber merchant and Wisconsin Congressman Alexander Stewart lived there.[139] Attached to another, less imposing house, it is free on three sides with an alley where roses have been a reminder for decades that the property is Luxembourgish. It is one of the most beautiful houses on one of the main avenues of the American capital. The interior has always been rather dark, with cherry wood panels on the first and second floors and windows that only timidly let in natural light. Stucco work enhances all these rooms, with the living and dining room on the first floor and a library of sorts on the second floor. The Le Gallais couple had decorated the house with Hugues' valuable acquisitions, and the house, populated with works of oriental art, resembled, according to photographs of that period, a huge museum, with panels hanging on the walls and silks and cushions covering the sofas and armchairs. The house remained austere, however, despite the couple's efforts to give it a personal, elegant and even exotic touch. The third floor was reserved for the family, with the servants living on the fourth floor, under the roof, which covers the building like a copper lid.

While waiting to enjoy the exclusive use of the legation, Hugues Le Gallais, his wife and their son lived for less than a year in the Wardman Tower, originally called the Wardman Park Annex. The family must have been comfortable there. As always, Le Gallais had selected one of the best places to stay. Hotel accommodation was also chosen as a makeshift solution in London by Minister Bech, as the country did not have a permanent embassy in the British capital. So Le Gallais could not complain too much, since a member of the Government and at the same time his superior, alone and without a secretary, was in addition subjected to regular bombardments.

Let's now talk about two ladies, Mrs. Eleanor Maloney and Countess Marguerite of Lynar, who played a significant role in the diplomatic career and private life of Hugues Le Gallais.

MRS. ELEANOR MALONEY,
AN UNFAILING ASSISTANT

Hugues Le Gallais' always faithful, conscientious and enterprising social secretary was Mary Eleanor Maloney. Born Mary Eleanor Comes on November 4, 1903 in Pittsburgh, Pennsylvania, she was a brilliant officer in the chancellery as principal assistant to the head of mission.[140] Of Luxembourgish descent, she served the country of her ancestors with dignity and devotion. She was one of the three daughters of John Theodore Comes, born in 1873 in Larochette, Luxembourg, who died in 1922, and of an American, Honora, known as "Mother". Eleanor's paternal grandmother had been the niece of the Luxembourg poet Michel Rodange, author of the famous satirical poem *Rénert*. Like about a third of the Luxembourgers who had sought a better life, the family left for the United States in 1881 with two of their four surviving children. The couple settled in Minnesota, in St. Paul. Eleanor Comes had married James Menton Maloney, a Navy officer who died in the service during World War II. The couple, who were in separation, had two children: Sara and John Maloney.[141]

We don't know how Eleanor Maloney was recruited, but her descent certainly contributed to get her this job with the Luxembourg envoy. Her additional skills and knowledge certainly helped in obtaining this position. She was fluent in Italian as she had spent time in Italy with her family after her father had died. She held a Master's degree in French, the subject of her thesis having been Molière. She was going to fill a role as an unfailing adviser, with an often accurate and insightful perception of both Washington and Luxembourg political realities, but also a first-rate faculty of observation. She had graduated from Trinity College in Washington. It was especially during Le Gallais' prolonged absences that the two exchanged news on an almost daily basis. Whether during the long summer holidays in Europe or his travels to Maine and New York, especially after the United Nations had established its headquarters there, news continued to be transmitted with great regularity and detail. Correspondence with the head of mission was an inexhaustible source for documenting the activities of the embassy and the daily life of the ambassador and his family. Hugues Le Gallais' writing was often very chaotic and difficult to decipher. He wrote on loose paper, sometimes with the details of the embassy or hotel where he was staying on his letterhead, most of the time in English, but sometimes also in French. Mrs. Maloney always used a typewriter and wrote only in English. Occasionally, telegrams or even sporadic telephone calls made interpretation and the handling of a case or file even more complex. Hugues Le Gallais also wrote instructions or draft typescripts on small pieces of paper without numbering or even dating them. The exchange between the two was always professional, rarely intimate or going beyond the public domain and embassy business. Correspondence sometimes took several days to reach its destination, whether it was Luxembourg, Venice,[142] Paris, Le Havre, New York or the Seal Harbor resort in Maine. Always very courteous and conventional, these letters nevertheless reflect an enormous amount of trust between the main actors in Luxembourg's diplomatic representation during 18 years. A great deal of respect on both sides, each trying to do their best and in their own way to act on behalf of the Luxembourg state and to defend its legitimate interests with a great power. Many of the private affairs of the Le Gallais family passed through the hands of Mrs. Maloney, who was aware of everything and showed determination in taking care of the smallest details while running the embassy, such as social affairs, maintenance, housekeeping, or personnel matters. The ambassador, with or without his family, was often away for long holidays and the embassy did not have a second diplomat.

For at least one-third of the year, including various trips and a three-month summer holiday of Le Gallais, Mrs. Maloney was the sole master on board. Political issues were addressed more sporadically in their correspondence, and Mrs. Maloney intervened only occasionally to represent the ambassador. On the other hand, she had her own social activities and occasionally attended receptions or events organized at her level. She willingly mingled with the socialites and social secretaries of the American capital. Thus, there are many photos showing her with other ladies or with ambassadors who are received in an official building or embassy. Eleanor Maloney was indeed the alter ego of Hugues Le Gallais. She remains inseparable from his activity, and it is difficult to determine which one of them could have acted for a long time without the advice and guidance of the other.

She maintained an unfailing relationship of trust with Hugues Le Gallais, confiding many details about her private life and her relationship to her mother, her two sisters and her two children. Her relationship with Mrs. Le Gallais seems to have been more distant, never mentioning more personal considerations and always calling her *Madame*. She addressed her as "Dear Eleanor" after her husband's death, when they continued to exchange a few letters sporadically. As can be seen in the countless letters from Mrs. Maloney to her chief on which much of this story is based, Mrs. Maloney was very attached to her "Dear Ambassador" and his family. She looked good in all circumstances and presented herself well, had a charming smile and knew how to convince. Hugues Le Gallais even asked her, two years before his departure, what gift would make her happy, to which she replied: "from Italy a simple pair of gold hoop earrings, about the size of an American five hundred piece and not larger than a quarter (25 cent coin) since my ears are not clipped on or put on with screws."

In 1958, the year of the ambassador's departure, a single letter found among others leaves one perplexed as to the relationship between the two as Le Gallais promises that he will no longer leave any documents in his office. Was this a joke before the storm? This paper is of a completely different and, above all an unusual nature, with Mrs. Maloney for once appearing to have laid down the law and most likely no longer felt like having to absolutely obey a messy if not chaotic ambassador. The real issue at stake in the dispute within the embassy itself could not be detected.

Mrs. Maloney had her office at the entrance to 2200 Massachusetts Avenue and thus had control over the comings and goings in the whole mansion. She represented the soul of the house and ensured a certain continuity even after the departure of Le Gallais in 1958. Eleanor Maloney had to remain loyal to the ambassador, who had retired in a hurry. She had a more detached bond with Le Gallais' successor, accusing Mr. Heisbourg of being "responsible for several nails in her coffin".

She was the author of the embassy's famous *Scrapbook*, which is preciously preserved in Venice. An anecdote reveals the nature of her relationship with her boss, to whom she regularly asked: "how was lunch Mr. Ambassador?", to which he would have replied one day: "the Old one came", when the lunch had been organized with the son instead of the Secretary of State Dean Acheson himself.[143] Nothing is more painful for a diplomat than such a mistake or to be confronted with last-minute cancellations.

Eleanor Maloney first lived in Georgetown, 3406 O Street, then, from October 1955, at 3812 Fulton Street NW in a house owned until then by Senator and Mrs. Paul Douglas of Illinois.[144] The house, located two blocks from Massachusetts Avenue, had been bought for $22,500. Mrs. Maloney's salary, which in 1952 she considered too low in view of the rising cost of living in Washington and her expenses which increased with the age of her two children, was $375 in June 1957, when it was increased by 4.1%, so that she received $4,680 a year. To this amount was added an annual gratification in the sum of a month's salary. In this respect, all correspondence from the 1950s with the authorities in Luxembourg is preserved.

Another word on the evolution of the role of the "social secretary" which remains an institution, even if she is nowadays called a "personal assistant" or a "coach". Over time, the means available to these people have become increasingly efficient and rapid, to the point where they have become demigods of instantaneity and control of almost everything, including their superior. In Mrs. Maloney's time, a certain amount of computerization was introduced on Massachusetts Avenue. Apart from letters, telegrams and telephone calls, modern means of communication and work have become indispensable. Thus, in March 1952, an "electric typewriter ordered at IBM" appeared at the Luxembourg Embassy. As early as August 1955, the replacement of this typewriter prompted Mrs. Maloney to request three quotations from IBM, Smith Corona and Royal, this time with a price comparison showing that competition, but also accords, were already possible at the time. At the beginning of August 1958, Mrs. Maloney, knowing that the ambassador was no longer going to return to Washington, proposed to buy a Thermo-Fax for $218 to make copies at the embassy, thus saving time and making life easier.

Eleanor Maloney must have told herself that "there is never a dull moment" with Hugues Le Gallais. Even if in the life of a diplomatic representation, as in most professional experiences, there was a certain routine, the English sketch "The same procedure as every year" was hardly applicable with such a leader. Some improvisation and innovation were always on the agenda for someone like him. This relationship was definitely marked by mutual attachment and dedication.

Mrs. Maloney was to see Hugues Le Gallais again after his retirement during a trip to Venice from July 10 to 14, 1961, about a month after the visit of the Hereditary Grand Ducal couple, to whom Le Gallais had also shown the most exquisite and exclusive places in his adopted city. Le Gallais and Mrs. Maloney had many memories to share from almost 18 years of intense collaboration in the interest of the country that they always cherished in a special way. Everything had seemed to work well for them in Washington, D.C., and over the years the two had become an unbeatable and well-honed tandem.

During the war, Eleanor Maloney was the Washington counterpart of Mary Estelle McKenna, who had been working in Montreal since the summer of 1941 for the Government in exile, and, in October 1945, had married Pierre Elvinger called Pieps,[145] a senior Government advisor at Bech's Department of Foreign Affairs and at the Department of Justice. In her post-war life in Luxembourg, the latter published the story *Adventures in Foreign Land*, consisting of a collection of letters sent regularly to Mrs. Maloney about her life in Luxembourg. Thus, an undated letter to Eleanor Maloney informed of her unfavorable assessment of the new US minister in Luxembourg, Perle Mesta:

"I have been wondering if you met Mrs. Mesta and if so what you think of her... I privately refer to her as Vera Vague,[146] because unless you are an absolutely big wheel, she can never remember you. It is so embarrassing and hardly a quality advantageous to a diplomat. When she first came here I was introduced to her at a reception given by the British minister during the course of which

Mrs. Mesta asked the wife of the British minister 'to introduce her the charming young lady speaking English (me)'... however we smoothly got through the third introduction when she asked me what my husband did. That was the end of everything... Pieps had been officially presented by Mr. Bech and she had already done business with him."

Or again, on December 11, 1952, following the presidential elections giving victory to the Republicans after Democratic President Truman's two terms: "everyone here was thrilled with the outcome of the elections. It must be interesting to watch the heads falling in Washington. Shall we be losing the valuable services of Madame... I hope. I saw her at a dinner last night and she was telling me how pally she is with Ike [Eisenhower, the Republican] and how much she dislikes Acheson [the Democrat]..."

Similarly, Mrs. McKenna wrote in early August 1952 that she had met Le Gallais in Luxembourg: "As I told you in my note, your boss gave a lovely speech at the 4th of July dinner; I must tell you something just between us. I said to Mr. Dupong: 'Imagine Mr. Le Gallais making a speech without Mme Maloney' and he replied with a big smile: 'He is making progress; I suspect the speech was written and typed at the ARBED'."[147]

Another peculiar character at 2200 Massachusetts Avenue, at least for a dozen years, was the Countess Marguerite of Lynar.

COUNTESS MARGUERITE OF LYNAR

The Grand Ducal family was accompanied by the families of four of the members of the Government, the Dupong, Bech, Bodson and Krier, as well as those of its retinue and staff. Among the latter was Countess Marguerite de (in German: Margarethe zu) Lynar,[148] of German origin. Countess of Lynar was born on January 25, 1871 in Berlin, and was the daughter of a Prussian lieutenant-general. She had been in the service of the Grand Ducal family for a long time. In a letter dated July 25, 1952, she stated that she had known it for 40 years. The Grand Duchess' niece, Princess Irmingard of Bavaria, describes her in her memoirs thus:[149] "She was tall, stiff with a very fine mouth [Strichmund] and a double chin. She was called 'the turkey' [Truthahn] because she often blushed and kept going in circles [loskullern]."

In May 1940, probably by chance, she was in the company of Grand Duchess Charlotte and her family. At the age of 69, she was, as it were, part of the Court's "baggage". She was later to accompany the Grand Duchess throughout her exile in the United States. She remained there with the benevolence of the Le Gallais couple beyond the end of the conflict and before returning at the end of her life to her native Germany.

After the war, she remained in contact with the Grand Ducal family through regular letters sent to the Grand Ducal Palace. Despite her German, not to say Prussian, origins, Countess of Lynar gave unfailing support to the Grand Ducal family throughout the war and beyond. She had links with a lady-in-waiting who, like her, followed in the footsteps of an august family, the Habsburgs, the Grand Duchess' in-laws. Countess Theresa S. Kerssenbrock remained in the service of former Empress Zita of Austria-Hungary, born Princess of Bourbon-Parma, while the latter's mother, the Duchess of Parma, had returned to Europe in the 1950s to die at Colmar-Berg Castle in 1959, the residence of her son and daughter-in-law. The correspondence between these two ladies-in-waiting, that of the Grand Duchess and that of the Duchess of Parma (mother-in-law and maternal aunt of the Grand Duchess who spent part of the war in Canada) and the former Empress Zita (sister-in-law and first cousin of the Grand Duchess, who remained in Canada at the Villa St-Joseph until 1949 and in the United States in New York from then on to 1953) is quite bucolic. It reveals the deep attachment of such ladies, who remained unmarried, to the august families in whose service they were to spend their entire lives.

The Countess of Lynar maintained, when she was away from Washington, a regular exchange with Eleanor Maloney and her mother, and even her sister. She once described herself there as a "lonely refugee". Much later, Mrs. Maloney, in an August 21, 1950 letter to Countess Kerssenbrock,[150] recalled that she called Countess of Lynar "a good soldier". Countess of Lynar also reflected in her correspondence certain news received from Luxembourg, such as the liberation from the concentration camps of the Grand Duchess' sister, Princess Antonia,[151] wife of the Bavarian Crown Prince, who, with her daughters, had suffered a real ordeal during the Second World War. In a letter written from Quebec on September 5, 1945, Countess of Lynar summed up the political and economic news in the Grand Duchy in a brief but insightful way: "The enclosed letter will also give you pleasure, please keep it till I come back, I am naturally not quite happy about Mr. Konsbruck, especially as it will be nearly impossible for him to have a time of rest. It seems that Luxembourg and Belgium are the two countries, which recover the quickest and best. In France it is still to be very hard with food, clothing and fuel."

The Countess of Lynar continued to reside at 2200 Massachusetts Avenue after the war for a rent of $150 per month paid by the Administration des Biens of the Grand Ducal Court. She helped raise Norbert Le Gallais and oversaw his piano and violin lessons given by a professional piano teacher. She had no means of her own. According to a letter from Mrs. Maloney addressed on January 7, 1947 to Mrs. Putz, who was to visit her son in the United States, Mrs. Maloney stated that the Countess would be willing to accompany her on her travels in Washington, but that "The only thing that I think I must tell you is that she has no money for herself to spend on taxis, luncheons in restaurants etc. She is an interesting person and of course knows Washington very well."

The Countess of Lynar celebrated her 80th birthday in Washington on January 25, 1951. Having become ill, and following an asthma attack, she had already been hospitalized in May and July 1950. This revealed her precarious and fragile situation. Hugues Le Gallais and even more so his secretary Eleanor Maloney immediately began corresponding with the Marshal of the Court and Countess Kerssenbrock to bring the former lady-in-waiting back to Europe as soon as possible.

At the end of December and in April, plans for the return of the Countess of Lynar to Europe became more concrete, and following a reservation which was postponed, the final arrangements for the transfer were made and implemented. Finally, the Countess returned to Europe on July 10, 1952 on the SS *Veendam* (Holland America Line) which arrived in Rotterdam on July 21. Former Empress Zita together with Mr. Corneille Staudt, Honorary Vice-Consul of Luxembourg, and Mrs. Staudt,[152] were at the pier in New York to bid her farewell. Then the Countess went briefly to Luxembourg to visit the Grand Ducal family. The Grand Duchess had just returned from the castle of Beloeil in Belgium where her daughter, Princess Alix de Ligne, had just given birth to a second son. Here is the description of this reunion at Colmar-Berg Castle in a letter dated July 5, 1952: "I supposed the Grand Duchess still with Princess Alix but an hour after my arrival the door opens and in come in their old liveliness (just as before 40 years) the Grand Duchess and Princess Hilda Schwarzenberg! Grand Duchess very well looking and just the same in her 'unique' personality. Pr. H.[153] looking 20 years older than her sister, but every one finds her greatly improved in health and enjoying life—but one sees immediately that she misses deeply her husband."[154]

The Countess was due to return to Germany on August 4, to spend her old age in her native country. She stayed for a while at her niece's house in Karlsruhe before moving to Bad Tölz near Lenggriess South of Munich.[155] She was waiting for a place in Lenggries and then joined the Heiss Pension Home.[156]

A few letters remain from this period, addressed to Eleanor Maloney, 33 years younger than Marguerite of Lynar. The Countess thanks her for everything, especially for sending her Reader's Digest and National Geographic. One can sense in them a certain loneliness, even weariness. Secretary Maloney and the Le Gallais family seem to have been her only lasting links with Washington. Not many traces of the Countess of Lynar's family remain, except on an Internet site devoted to the genealogy of this German family. The eldest of five children, she devoted her entire life to the Grand Ducal family and the Le Gallais family. She had epistolary contact with her only surviving brother after the war and with her niece to whom she had assigned the pension that was paid in discharge of the Grand Ducal Court.[157] She died alone on August 26, 1959 in Bad Tölz.

Let us now go back a little further, to 1940, a most dramatic year for Luxembourg. Le Gallais was far from the European continent which had been heavily tested and had known an influx of countless refugees, only some of whom made it across the Atlantic. In the first stage, about 50,000 Luxembourgers fleeing the German invader had been evacuated to France.

THE DEPARTURE FROM LUXEMBOURG OF THOSE WHO WERE SOON TO JOIN HUGUES LE GALLAIS ON THE OTHER SIDE OF THE ATLANTIC

Hugues Le Gallais had escaped the effervescence of the hasty departure of Friday, May 10, 1940, but had to follow very closely what some would interpret as an escape from the Nazi invader. The details of this Grand Ducal escape are recounted in numerous publications, notably the works of Georges Heisbourg, Emile Haag and Emile Krier on the year 1940. The departure from Luxembourg on the morning of May 10 was also commented on by supporters and opponents of this decision, which, as we have seen, was taken as early as January. First lieutenant and aide-de-camp of Prince Félix, Guill Konsbruck, put this fateful day down on paper in a letter written a few days after the events, and the details of the journey must certainly have reached the ears of Hugues Le Gallais fairly quickly. The Grand Duchess, the Prince and the Dowager Grand Duchess left for France by way of Rodange and Longwy. Guill Konsbruck was entrusted with the Hereditary Grand Duke and the Princesses Marie-Gabrielle and Alix. They left with a second car in the direction of Esch and Audun-le-Tiche around 6 o'clock in the morning. Together, the Habsburgs and three of the Grand Ducal children who were with them (17 people in all) left

Steenockerzeel castle with three cars between Brussels and Leuven, where the former Empress of Austria-Hungary lived in exile with her family. During their exile in the United States, the heir to the Austro-Hungarian throne and his brothers maintained close contacts with President Roosevelt and the American administration. The Habsburgs and Le Gallais crossed paths several times during these years.

Back in Luxembourg, the prevalent atmosphere back in the community, which Le Gallais had not experienced directly, probably corresponds to that described by Guill Konsbruck, who summed it up in simple and touching words: "It is above all as an officer that one has a certain depressing feeling and one despises oneself a little for having left one's country in these sad and painful hours." This is indeed the dilemma that all exiles, be they politicians, diplomats, civil servants or soldiers, faced on May 10. The situation was definitely not easy for anyone.

In France, the first stage of exile brought the "official" Luxembourgers to Sainte-Ménehould, a town on the road to Paris, from May 10 to 11. In the French capital, on May 17, 1940, the Grand Duchess and Prince Félix were received at the Elysée Palace by President Lebrun. Three days earlier, Le Gallais had been mandated by the Grand Ducal couple to warmly thank President Roosevelt for his offer to send the Grand Ducal children safely to the United States. A few weeks later, this was going to materialize with the departure from Lisbon of the Prince and his six children.

In May 1940, the Grand Ducal exiles stayed for a week near Paris, at the Château de La Celle Saint-Cloud, owned by Auguste Dutreux, Chairman of the Board of Directors of the Société du Chemin de Fer Guillaume-Luxembourg, and his wife Elisabeth Pescatore. He was a relative of Le Gallais' stepmother. As a result of the German advance, the Luxembourgers had to travel to the South of France. For ten days, from May 17 to 28, 1940, the Grand Ducal family lived at the Château de Bostz in Besson near the city of Moulins. The chateau belonged to Prince Xavier of Bourbon-Parma, the elder brother of Prince Félix of Luxembourg. Then, from May 27, the Château de Lamonzie-Montastruc in the Dordogne, 124 km East of Bordeaux, was made available by the French Government. Forty kilometers away, the Domaine de la Poujade housed the members of the Luxembourg Government, about fifty people in all.

The passage through Spain lasted three days and led from Saint-Jean-de-Luz to San Sebastián and via Burgos and Salamanca to Lisbon in Portugal, where the 72 people, in 17 cars, arrived on June 25. While the head of the Portuguese Government, António de Oliveira Salazar, had given his approval for the arrival of the Luxembourg sovereign and her family "in an individual capacity", the Portuguese Consul General in Bordeaux and former Consul General in Antwerp, Aristides de Sousa Mendes, had granted visas to them and other Luxembourgers. He had done the same for thousands of Jewish refugees, contrary to Salazar's instructions. For several weeks, the Grand Ducal family stayed in Cascais in Portugal in the property of the Honorary Consul General of Luxembourg, Manuel Ribeiro Espírito Santo Silva. Then, from July 30, 1940, the Grand Duchess, Dupong and Bech were at the *Casa Posser de Andrade* and in other lodgings near Lisbon.

These were provisional solutions dictated by the progress made by German troops and the uncertainties of the moment against which Le Gallais was trying to highlight the advantages of exile in the United States. In these exceptional circumstances, he felt that an American stay, preferably in Washington, was more necessary than ever. Throughout that summer, Le Gallais took note, after the invasion that began on May 10, of the surrender of the Dutch forces on May 14, that of Belgium two weeks later, followed by France, which laid down its arms on June 22, 1940. Hope now lay with the United Kingdom and on the other shore of the Atlantic.

THE ARRIVAL OF PRINCE FÉLIX AND THE GRAND DUCAL CHILDREN IN THE UNITED STATES

In a letter from Hugues Le Gallais to Prince Félix at the beginning of July 1940, the chargé d'affaires, still alone in Washington, tried to convince the Luxembourg exiles in Portugal to come and join him in the United States. He put forward the argument that

"the President told me verbatim: 'Europe is not a place for children'... I would like to draw the attention of Your Royal Highnesses to the excellent propaganda that the arrival of the Princesses and Prince Charles in New York would constitute for our country, so that the Children of Your Royal Highnesses would be in the custody of the President. In a certain sense, by assimilation, it would be the Grand Duchy itself which would come under the protection of the United States of America, which could one day be important. Here it is necessary to be constantly 'in the spotlight', which is what the Grand Duchy of Luxembourg could become if Your Royal Highnesses could decide to adopt the President's proposal. Americans would be individually proud to have to protect the Children of Your Royal Highnesses, and in this country it is individuals who create public opinion".[158]

This is one of the most important reports written by Le Gallais. It says it all, or almost everything, in an admirable and premonitory manner, at least from the point of view of a diplomat on the other side of the Atlantic. It seems that in the end his arguments prevailed, at least for a time. Always obliged to testify, not necessarily able to convince, this time Hugues had managed to rally more or less everyone to his vision of things. He would soon have the Grand Ducal family and the Government in exile close to him, and would feel from time to time that he had become the pillar around which this Luxembourg microcosm revolved.

On July 15, 1940, Prince Félix and his six children, as well as valuables from the Grand Ducal House, embarked in Lisbon on the American cruiser USS Trenton sent by President Roosevelt. During the journey, the Prince could communicate with the Grand Duchess, Le Gallais and the former American ambassador to Belgium and Luxembourg, Joseph E. Davies, and send and receive telegrams. A few days earlier, Le Gallais had received a mandate to request permission from President Roosevelt for members of the Grand Ducal family to board. They were accompanied by the driver Eugène Niclou and his wife, born Joséphine Wagner, as well as chambermaid Justine Reinard. On the day of departure from the Portuguese capital, Le Gallais sent to Lisbon the advice of the Belgian ambassador (on special mission) Theunis,[159] and the Brazilian ambassador Martins,[160] advising the Grand Duchess not to return home.[161] On July 25, 1940, the first Grand Ducal exiles arrived in Annapolis, the capital of Maryland, where the headquarters of the American Naval Academy was located. Roosevelt had requested that the American warship stop there, an hour's drive from Washington, instead of going directly to its port of destination Norfolk.[162] Let us just mention that beforehand Le Gallais had been invited by Prince Félix to take along $1,000, probably to pay for expenses on the Trenton, and that privileges and exemptions had been granted.[163] Welcomed by Hugues Le Gallais and his wife[164] as well as by the acting Chief of Protocol and the Under-Secretary of State, Prince Félix, the Hereditary Grand Duke, Prince Charles and the Princesses were invited to have lunch with President Roosevelt from 13 to 14.42 hours. The lunch was attended by 18 people. Among them were Acting Secretary of State Sumner Welles and his wife, the Le Gallais and Joseph Davies couples. The Luxembourgers then travelled by train to Roslyn near New York. A few days later, Le Gallais meticulously reported to his minister who remained in Lisbon on this event.[165] He described the welcome as "quite dignified, marked by simplicity due to the circumstances, very hospitable and well organized down to the smallest details." He also mentioned that the Prince Consort would return to Washington soon and meet there on July 31 and August 1 with the Under-Secretary of State, with whom he had not been able to speak on arrival. This time, the recommendations were clearer than ever: that the Grand Duchess not return home, but come to the United States without delay.

From the beginning of the American stage, the Grand Ducal exiles resided in New York at the house of the Davies-Merriweather Post couple. In Washington, Le Gallais protested in mid-August and early September against the measures imposed in her country in violation of the law of nations, treaties and promises made by the Germans, hoping that the Grand Duchess would draw the world's attention to the situation in Luxembourg as soon as possible. He subsequently reported the reaction of many colleagues and sent valuable information to Lisbon.[166] In New York, Davies, and especially his wife, Marjorie Merriweather Post, welcomed the Luxembourg Princes to their property in Roslyn on Long Island near New York. The third husband of the wealthy heiress of C.W. Post estate and owner of the General Foods Company had been American ambassador to Moscow from 1936 to 1938 and ambassador to Brussels from 1938 to 1939. In this capacity, he was accredited as a minister in Luxembourg. In Nancy Rubin's book *American Empress* on the life of Marjorie Merriweather Post, we learn that: "By the time Marjorie was attracting press attention of her own through her charities and kindness to others. With the threat of a Nazi invasion of Luxembourg, Marjorie helped the Grand Duchess spirit her six children out of the country and send them to the United States. By the spring of 1940 they had arrived in New York and were taken to Hillwood and Long Island. Mother took one look at the boys in their heavy wool serge jackets and the girls in their middy blouses and heavy wool serge shirts and said: 'By God, this won't do. Come on, we'll go to Garden City'. Then she piled them into the car and took them to Best and Company to buy them new clothes... For months the children lived at Hillwood and that summer visited Marjorie and her family at Topridge".[167] A certain simplicity therefore characterized the Luxembourg refugees who were discovering the world of American politics, finance and industry. The aristocracy of American finance was not stingy when it came to supporting recently exiled royalty. At least at the beginning and up to the financial arrangement with the Belgians, the Luxembourgers, and especially the members of the Government, were rather destitute. The only one who was somewhat settled and had taken his furniture and works of art with him was Le Gallais. He helped as much as he could, but did not have the means to install, equip or dress all these people. He only had Mrs. Maloney at his disposal to help him with administrative matters. The relative initial destitution of some of the exiles was also reflected in the fact that Le Gallais was responsible for providing for the needs of the Government in exile and the embassy a copy of the Luxembourg official gazette, the *Mémorial*. The legal texts had to be taken into consideration, but the exiles had left without a copy of the essential foundations of the Constitution, the Nassau Family Pact or the *Official Journal of the Grand Duchy*. The Library of Congress has apparently helped to remedy these shortcomings. During these years, questions relating to matters of portfolios of shares in Portuguese-speaking countries, insurance contracts, car registration, exemptions, etc. were the subject of correspondence between Le Gallais, Mrs. Maloney and Guill Konsbruck. The detail would be too tedious to report in this context and is largely a matter for the Court's private life. Part of the Grand Ducal collections had left the Grand Duchy in 1939, and Le Gallais was involved in their preservation once they were sent to the United States. Thus, valuable items of Nassau silverware were preciously kept in the United States until their return in 1952/1953.[168]

In addition to the remoteness of the Luxembourgers who lived in New York and not in Washington, preparations for the move to Canada were started in the summer by the embassy in Washington. The transfer was envisaged with certain displeasure by Le Gallais who saw the small Luxembourg community that had just joined him in the United States escaping further. It was President Roosevelt and Undersecretary of State Sumner Welles who encouraged the Grand Duchess to settle in Canada where Le Gallais would not be accredited and was not accredited until much later. This solution made it possible to act from a Commonwealth member state while respecting American neutrality imposed by the Neutrality Act, at least until the Americans entered the war after the Japanese attack on Pearl Harbor on December 7, 1941. It also made it possible for young exiles to study in French if, as would be the case, the choice fell on Montréal rather than Ottawa.

In a telegram of August 28, 1940, the Canadian minister accredited in Belgium described from London to the Secretary of State for Foreign Affairs the composition of the delegation accompanying the Grand Duchess:

"Following persons all being Luxembourg citizens born in the Grand Duchy, except Lynar Lady-in-Waiting born in Berlin, January 25th, 1871, but holds Luxembourg travelling permit;

- HRH Grand Duchess Marie-Anne of Luxembourg;
- Countess Marguerite de Lynar;
- Lieutenant Guill. Konsbruck, ADC; Madame Konsbruck and her two sons, Guy, 3 years old and Carlos [sic], 7 months;
- Alice Sinner, maid to HRH;
- Lucie Hansen, nurse;
- George Edouard, valet;
- HE M. Pierre Dupong, President of Government; Madame Dupong and family: Marie 24 years, Lambert 23 years, Jean 18 years, Henrietta 16 years;
- Suetnne [Suzanne] Busch, maid to Madame Dupong;
- HE M. Joseph Bech, Minister for Foreign Affairs, his wife and family: Charles 21 years, and Elizabeth 18 years;
- Victor Bodson, Minister of Justice and his wife;
- Pierre Krier; Minister of Labour;
- Leon Schaus; Government Counsellor;
- Pierre Elvinger, Judge attached to the Ministry of Justice."

Le Gallais was not enthusiastic about the correspondence between the Canadian minister in Belgium and the Secretary of State for Foreign Affairs or his deputy[169] concerning the arrival of the exiles in the United States. For the purposes of transferring the Luxembourgers to Canada, their financial situation was examined thoroughly. Their admission or not to Canada and their status and privileges in Canada depended upon this examination. Thus, several steps and correspondence preceded the actual transfer. One example is the correspondence of August 28: "The Grand Duchess is reported having 1,000,000 gold francs in the US, providing for herself and suite. Out of Belgium reserve now in England, 12,000,000 gold francs property of Luxembourg Government. Convention entered whereby £3,000 payable quarterly in Canada for Governmental expenses and remuneration for ministers and officials awaiting Bank of England's ratification. Government about 1,000,000 francs in Portugal." And that of September 25: "The Prime Minister stated last night that he doubted the advisability of permitting the establishment in Canada of a number of Governments of European countries. In the case of Luxembourg, the matter was not particularly important but the precedent established in such a case would be made the basis for other demands." October 15: "Laissez-passers valid for three months have been granted to Grand Duchess and immediate family. Application for laissez-passers for Grand Duchess' mother and personal suite now pending; understand from Washington that financial arrangements which M. Gutt[170] attempted to negotiate were intended for maintenance of ministers and their families, and that Grand Duchess' own means of support are already assured." And finally, May 3, 1941: "…express regrets for delay which has occurred in dealing with this matter… Canadian Government is prepared to recognize the Grand Duchess as a reigning sovereign provisionally abroad and as such enjoying, as of right under international law, the generally accepted immunities from civil and criminal jurisdiction and from taxation." Everything was therefore concentrated on the material conditions under which Luxembourgers settled in Canada. Whereas in the United States wealthy relations had prepared for the most urgent needs, the Canadians were more demanding than the Americans. They wanted to ensure that the Luxembourg exiles had sufficient means of subsistence. This attitude was made up of prevarication, which Bech described as "inexplicable difficulties" and which he urged Le Gallais to put an end to. The whole situation was complicated by the fact that the Americans, notably Sumner Welles in an interview with Le Gallais on September 20, made the visas of exiled Luxembourgers wishing to come to the United States dependent on obtaining those from Canada. The Grand Duchess having sent a personal telegram to FDR, Le Gallais was finally able, on September 23 and 30, 1940, to announce that there was no longer anything to prevent the last Luxembourg officials remaining in Portugal from coming to the United States. Le Gallais was grateful to the American Under-Secretary of State, as he notified the President of the Government a few days later. Despite the prospect of the exiles moving away, Le Gallais had succeeded in his mission.

In August, there was a moment of uncertainty to which we referred earlier, as the Grand Duchess had received letters from the Speaker of Parliament and former Minister of State Emile Reuter and the Chairman of the Administrative Commission, Albert Wehrer, inviting her to return to the country. Opinions described as unfortunate,[171] addressed to the Grand Duchess by American diplomats, were along the same lines. After some hesitation, this invitation was not followed up, as it would have, at the very least, subjected the Grand Duchess to the goodwill of the Nazi occupiers. Hugues Le Gallais, after having initially suggested (as mentioned above) to the Grand Duchess the possibility of an arrangement with the occupier, even under unfavorable conditions for a while, is said to have made it known that Under-Secretary of State Sumner Welles had made it clear that such a return to the country would serve no purpose.[172] Nor would this alternative have been in keeping with his plan for the future of the exiles, which he saw mainly in Washington. On several occasions, Prince Félix intervened in a determined manner in order to have the Grand Duchess follow. He even sent a telegram to the Under-Secretary of State asking him to receive Le Gallais and saying "Feeling rather concerned about Grand Duchess".[173]

On August 29, 1940, the Grand Duchess, preceded two days earlier by her Minister of Foreign Affairs Bech, travelled from Lisbon to London to meet King George VI and Prime Minister Winston Churchill. On September 5, 1940, the sovereign was also to record the first of her messages broadcast by the BBC and listened to clandestinely in the Grand Duchy. In all, fourteen of the Grand Duchess' speeches were broadcast from the autumn of 1940 to the end of 1944.[174] It should be noted that in March 1941 Le Gallais told her that during an interview with Welles, the latter had told him that Roosevelt approved of the actions of the Luxembourg sovereign in the United States and regretted that the Crown Princes of Norway and the Netherlands were not allowed to do the same.[175]

This move to the British capital took place while Prince Félix did not favor it.[176] Aide-de-camp Guill Konsbruck remained in Portugal with his family. Minister Bech returned from London on September 6, 1940. Apparently the idea of acquiring an aircraft circulated around this period, as Schommer wrote in his report to Minister Bech on September 7, 1940: "A letter from Mr. Clasen of London to Mr. Le Gallais suggests an action among the Luxembourg colony in order to raise the necessary funds for the acquisition of an aircraft, named 'LUXEMBOURG'. Because of the unclear situation I mentioned above, I advised Mr. Le Gallais to wait for the arrival of the Government and not to expose himself to a possible failure. He was of the same opinion."[177] For once Le Gallais was not thinking as big as usual and was not following the suggestion of his colleague in the British capital, an idea already mentioned two days earlier in a letter from Dupong to Bech: "I have received from Monsieur Legallais [sic] the attached report concerning a possible subscription for the acquisition by free Luxembourgers of an aircraft for the English army. What do you think? I think that the gesture should be encouraged, without however the Government as such appearing in the affair. Let me know how you see it."[178]

Meanwhile, on August 31, 1940, Prince Félix and the Grand Ducal children were in New York for "Luxembourg Day" at the International Exhibition. Hugues Le Gallais also participated at the beginning of September, with Prince Félix giving a speech in the presence of King Haakon of Norway and Queen Wilhelmine of the Netherlands.[179]

For those Luxemburgish who remained in Portugal, the departure to the United States took place in late-September/early October. Thus, on September 25, 1940, Minister of State Pierre Dupong and his wife, Mrs. Bech-Delahaye and his daughter Elisabeth, known as Betty Bech, left Portugal for the United States on board the SS *Excalibur* of American Export Lines. On October 2, 1940, Prince René of Bourbon-Parma and his children, Minister Bodson and his family (his wife Gilberte Bodson-de Muyser, his daughter from a first marriage, Andrée, and the children of the couple Mimy, Sonia, Léon and Robert),[180] attaché then Government adviser Léon Schaus,[181] Pierre Elvinger, the children of the President of the Government Dupong (Lambert, Marie-Thérèse, Jean and Henriette dite Jetty) and the son of the Minister of Foreign Affairs, Charly Bech, left on the SS *Excambian*, also of American Export Lines, which arrived in New York on October 11.[182] Le Gallais insisted that the Luxembourg ministers reside at the Waldorf Astoria, for "reasons of standing in front of American opinion". Schommer had suggested in early September the renting of furnished flats in the suburbs of New York.[183] A few days later, Dupong had all these people moved to a less luxurious hotel. One sometimes wonders to what extent Le Gallais was aware of the very difficult situation of the exiles, even if, with regard to the host country, one had to remain dignified and credible. In their book on 1940, Haag and Krier describe this attitude as follows:

"After the Court's civilian list, the Washington legation, whose costs amounted to $1000 per month, was the largest ordinary expense. Dupong complained to Bech that these fees were too high: 'He's living a little too expensively, in the best hotel in Washington.' He also had a 'frank' exchange of letters with Le Gallais himself in order to reason with him and persuade him to reduce his lifestyle. Le Gallais countered by insisting that a certain standing was indispensable for a diplomatic representative in the American capital. Dupong, always discreet and not very ostentatious, was not convinced and went so far as to suspect Mrs. Le Gallais of being behind her husband's spending habits."[184]

On October 3, 1940, the Grand Duchess left Lisbon with her mother, Countess of Lynar, Alice Sinner, the couple Konsbruck-Hartmann and their two sons on board the Pan American Airways Yankee Clipper.

The day before, on October 2, 1940, Hugues Le Gallais had just been promoted to Minister Plenipotentiary. It was a consecration that should facilitate access to him and to exiled Luxembourg officials, all of which were soon to be on American territory, to act otherwise than through a simple envoy. Equipped with the title of chargé d'affaires, while not yet granted the rank of ambassador, the Luxembourg diplomat could hope to act more effectively and in accordance with the interests of his country.

THE ARRIVAL OF THE GRAND DUCHESS
IN THE UNITED STATES, OCTOBER 4, 1940

The arrival at New York's La Guardia Airport was described in the New York Times on October 5:

"Royalty of Luxembourg and Austria were at the marine terminal of La Guardia Field yesterday afternoon to welcome Grand Duchess Charlotte of Luxembourg, hereditary ruler of the tiny country annexed by Germany, who arrived from Lisbon aboard the Yankee Clipper of Pan American Airways. Prince Félix of Bourbon-Parma [sic], her consort, and five of their six children, all of whom came to this country on July 25 aboard the United States cruiser Trenton; her nephew, Archduke Otto of Austria, Hugh [sic] Le Gallais, Chargé d'affaires of the Luxembourg legation in this country; representatives of the US Department of State and the City of New York as well as several hundred private citizens bowed, cheered and waved tiny Luxembourg flags to the Grand Duchess and her entourage of seven persons when they debarked. ... The six other members of the party left later in two other cars. They were Guillaume Konsbruck, aide-de-camp; his wife Nelly; their children Guy, 3 years old and Carlo, 7 months, Countess Marguerite of Lynar, and Alice Sinner, a maid."

A photo of all Luxembourgers smiling reflects the dismay at the uncertain future, but also the great dignity of the main exiles. The sovereign was greeted by Le Gallais and the American ambassador to Belgium in the 1930s, Dave Hennen Morris.[185] One wonders who the hundreds of people who joined the reception committee might have been, even if the descendants of Luxembourg immigrants were already numerous at the time.

Welcoming of the Grand Duchess to the United States, 4 October 1940.
To the right of the Grand Duchess, her mother Grand Duchess Marie-Anne,
and the American ambassador D. H. Morris. Behind the Grand Duchess,
her chambermaid Alice Sinner, Mrs. Konsbruck and her son Carlo Konsbruck,
Countess de Lynar, Grand Duchess Marie-Anne's lady-in-waiting, aide-de-camp
Guillaume "Guill" Konsbruck, and the chargé d'affaires Hugues Le Gallais.

A new existence had to begin for all those who were in no way
prepared for a life marked by uncertainty and the unknown in
a country of which they knew almost nothing, even and above
all the language. While the former President of the Government
and now President of the Chamber, Emile Reuter, and the Minister for Agriculture and Education, Nicolas Margue, remained
in Luxembourg, Ministers Bech and Krier were to spend most

of their period of exile in London. Their families, like those of Dupong and Bodson, were settled in Montreal. All of them were divided between the different places of exile. For the children, as had been the case a few months earlier for Norbert Le Gallais, adaptation to the turbulent life of exile was certainly easier. From an early age they had been in contact with French (spoken by the Grand Ducal family), German (spoken as a mother tongue by the Dowager Grand Duchess, *Infanta* of Portugal, whose mother was of German origin, and by the Countess Marguerite of Lynar, also of German origin) or English (the language spoken by most members of the Grand Ducal family). While the move to South-Western Europe had been eventful, the settlement on the American continent was to be just as uncertain, with successive stages in different places. Whether it was Washington or New York, Montreal or Quebec City, they were big cities very different from the capital of Luxembourg. For this very disparate community, the future was also, at times, to be marked by doubts and constraints that were difficult to overcome. Le Gallais was focused on the American capital, even if he travelled across the United States from time to time.

We have described above how the Davies-Merriweather Post couple, as well as later Franklin Delano Roosevelt and his wife Eleanor, committed themselves to make the move across the Atlantic as easy and enjoyable as possible for those who had left everything behind. Prince Félix and the princely children had already been residing on Long Island with the Davieses since their arrival on American soil. The Grand Duchess and her mother joined them near New York. The ties between the Grand Ducal family and the presidential couple seem to have been particularly close, since the President had developed a weakness for monarchies and a real attachment to the sovereign of the little Grand Duchy. Several meetings were organized during the American stay of the

Hugues Le Gallais with his secretary Mrs. Eleanor Maloney, née Comes and of Luxembourgish extraction, in the ground-floor office of the embassy at 2200 Massachusetts Avenue in 1953.
(Photo: Stewart Photographers Washington, D.C./Revue).

Luxembourg exiled. During research for the documentary *Leif Letzebuerger*, it was noted that the Grand Duchess and/or members of her Government and thus Le Gallais were received a dozen times by Roosevelt. By way of comparison, Belgian Minister Paul-Henri Spaak was received only once by the President, who had a certain disdain for the attitude adopted at the beginning of the war by the Belgian authorities at the highest level. A photo of the Grand Duchess with the President does not seem to exist. On the other hand, at least two pictures exist of the sovereign with Eleanor Roosevelt who, as her husband, was born into the Roosevelt family, which had already had an American President in the beginning of the century.

Hugues Le Gallais was a privileged witness to this growing attachment over the years of exile. Reports by Le Gallais have been found recounting the extraordinary ties of the time between the Grand Ducal and Presidential families.

Following the arrival of the sovereign, regular correspondence between the chargé d'affaires Le Gallais and the aide-de-camp Konsbruck started. Le Gallais' first letter to Konsbruck was dated October 24, 1940, while on November 12, 1940 he wrote to Le Gallais for the first time. Most of the quotations and interpretations on the daily life of the Luxembourg exiles which will be used to support the following pages come from this correspondence. It should be noted that the first letter found from Hugues Le Gallais to Guill Konsbruck contains an annexed letter from Maître Alex Bonn,[186] addressed to the Grand Duchess and concerns immigration issues and a contact between Minister of Justice Bodson and a delegate of the Jewish Committee of New York. The letter is formally addressed to "Mr. Lieutenant" and ends with the polite phrase "Please accept the expression of my highest consideration". The reply to the Minister Plenipotentiary is addressed to "Dear Mr. Le Gallais" and ends with the following: "Please accept, with my most respectful regards, the assurances of my best and most devoted sentiments that you will convey to Mrs. Le Gallais." A week later, the reply is addressed to "Dear Mr. Konsbruck". A certain formality therefore, reflecting a certain professionalism on both sides, which should not prevent cordiality, even familiarity and the exchange of news, sometimes personal. It should be noted that the two men's correspondence changed from July onwards, as Le Gallais wrote "My dear Captain" instead of "Dear Mr. Konsbruck". It seems that the differences in social background and age, for example, but also the style of the ambassador did not allow an intimacy similar to that of Konsbruck with the other correspondents in Montreal, such as Schommer, Schaus or Elvinger.

Hugues Le Gallais and Guill Konsbruck did not address their letters in their personal names ("Cher Guill", "Cher Hugues") until 1957. It should also be noted that correspondence, especially during the war, often took a very long time to reach its destination and that even if the legation used, for transatlantic letters, the diplomatic mail of American, Belgian and Dutch colleagues from Washington to London, it was only after Le Gallais' intervention that the American embassy in London was authorized to forward mail intended for Luxembourgers in Washington.[187] Mail between Washington and Montreal was faster, so that depending on whether Dupong or Bech were in London, the exchange of correspondence with the minister plenipotentiary was more or less regular. The telephone between Washington and Canada was easier and cheaper, and therefore supplemented or replaced the mail service from time to time.

We have just seen that on October 2, 1940 Hugues Le Gallais was promoted to Minister Plenipotentiary, giving a new status to Luxembourg's representation in the United States. Less than three weeks later, the White House seemed not to have taken note of Le Gallais' change of rank, still designating him as chargé d'affaires. On Sunday October 20, 1940, the Grand Duchess, Prince Félix and the Le Gallais couple were invited to lunch in Hyde Park with Earl Athlone and Princess Alice.[188] Stanley Woodward,[189] of the State Department's Protocol Division, was at the side of the President who, for the occasion, was accompanied by his mother, Sara Ann Delano. According to the New York Times, "The conversations between Mr. Roosevelt and his guests were clothed in strict privacy, but it is obvious that they concern recent reports of the progress of the war in Europe. None of the guests, however, was in a position to discuss these affairs." It is probably on this occasion that the story developed around the link between FDR and a certain de La Noye, who in the 17th century had come from

Clervaux in the North of the country. This distant relative of the President, whose parents had converted to Protestantism and had, for this reason, settled in the Netherlands, emigrated to North America, where his name became Delano. The President's mother descended from this de la Noye. Roosevelt, whose name means "field of roses", adored royal families. It was therefore astute of the Luxembourg exiles to refresh the history of his not only Dutch, but probably also Luxembourgish origins. The Luxembourg legation was undoubtedly involved in this little subterfuge to bring itself to the President's mind. In mid-September 1944, the link was to appear again in an article in the weekly *The New Yorker*: "The Delano branch of the President's family stems from Luxembourg." To which FDR replied that he simply did not know. The idea may have originated with Le Gallais, who had to deal with many details concerning the Grand Ducal family and members of the Government. On the Grand Duchess' first meeting with FDR, Le Gallais reported to Bech: "The President was particularly kind to Their Royal Highnesses and twice extended an invitation to Her Highness the Grand Duchess to come to Washington. I will take up this matter again when I deliver my Letters to the President." This "question" was indeed to the liking of the Luxembourg Minister Plenipotentiary, who wanted to bring the main Luxembourg players as close as possible to him. However, from the outset, this wish was going to prove more complex to put into practice than expected.

THE DEPARTURE OF THE GRAND DUCHESS FOR CANADA

Until December 1941, the United States was not a party to the conflict unleashed by the Germans. It was above all "old Europe" that was concerned during this year filled with war news that was unfavorable to the US allies. The Luxembourg exiles nevertheless enjoyed the benevolence of the American administration and of the President in particular, but also of former Ambassador Joseph Davies and Representative Herbert Claiborne Pell. In spite of this support, it was therefore logical that as long as the United States wished to see its neutrality respected and did not allow political action, the Luxembourgers would fall back on Canada. In Quebec, moreover, the population is predominantly Catholic and French-speaking.

Three weeks after her arrival on the American continent, on October 24, 1940, the Grand Duchess and her retinue arrived in Montreal. This change was intended to allow for more committed political action, whereas in the United States this was not yet possible. Less than three weeks later, on November 8, 1940, Hugues Le Gallais was received, this time alone, in audience by President Roosevelt to present his credentials. On this event, Le Gallais sent a direct letter to the Grand Duchess.[190] Guill Konsbruck, in his letter of November 12, congratulated Le Gallais on this audience: "H.R.H. read with the greatest interest the report on your audience of November 8, with President Roosevelt. You can imagine how pleased and happy Their Royal Highnesses were with it." This was soothing for the heart of Le Gallais, who was left alone in Washington with perhaps one or two members of the Government who had not yet left for Canada. The presentation of his credentials to the President was for Le Gallais the crowning achievement of his new diplomatic career. It is customary to write a report with the details of the accreditation ceremony, which varies from country to country and consists, in Washington, of an exchange of "remarks" from the accredited ambassador and a presidential response that was not very engaging for a small country the size of Rhode Island. In his report of November 12, 1940,[191] Le Gallais described the ceremony as simpler than in Luxembourg, even though the President had been very kind. Le Gallais addressed the American President as follows:[192]

"Mr. President, I have the honor to place in the hands of Your Excellency the Letters which accredit me to you as Envoy Extraordinary and Minister Plenipotentiary of Her Royal Highness the Grand Duchess of Luxembourg. It is a great honor for me to have been appointed by my Sovereign Grace to fulfill this high mission, the importance of which I fully appreciate. Mr. President, the fact that the Luxembourg people have always shown the most friendly feelings towards the people of the United States is no doubt not unknown to you. To these feelings was added, after the 1914-1918 war, that of deep gratitude when the United States and its allies gave back to the Grand Duchy its independence and liberty. At this tragic hour in the history of my country our eyes turn once again to the United States which, under your enlightened leadership, has become the foremost guardian of the traditions of Justice and Law. You have made it known, Mr. President, that the United States would never recognize the acquisition of territory by violence. This statement supports the courage of my fellow citizens as they wait for a better future. Mr. President, all my efforts will be aimed at strengthening the spiritual and economic ties between our two countries, and I am convinced that I can always count on your kind support in carrying out my task."

Heisbourg mentions two versions of the Presidential reply, the second one having a warmer and more reciprocal character, related to feelings of friendship. The first version was allegedly sent by mistake... Le Gallais also reported that FDR had described the *Gauleiter* as "German pig", which would have given him some pleasure. Le Gallais informed the President "of the incident at the Brasseur Hotel mentioned in your report of October 8. President Roosevelt replied: 'That's not such bad news, the action of this German pig can only strengthen the Grand Duchess in Her Own Country'." In addition, Le Gallais has sent notification of his accreditation to all diplomatic missions, with the exception of the German embassy. From his Italian colleague he did not receive the traditional reply welcoming him and congratulating him on his accreditation. From all this, the now duly accredited Minister was writing long reports to Bech.[193] For once, Le Gallais showed moderation in this report in relation to a travel project of the Grand Duchess, stating: "I did not present any objections since we cannot always be on the front page and we have to space out our effects [efforts]." However, he sent a *New York Times* clipping at the same time, stating that he had "reported the article to the British chargé d'affaires, the *London Times* Correspondent and the Reuters Service Correspondent", while asking Schommer "to take action at his information desk to get the article spread." Le Gallais definitely wanted to get Luxembourg and its accreditation talked about, but also to help make himself known.

On November 12, 1940, Guill Konsbruck wrote a letter, also concerning the postponed broadcast of the Grand Duchess' speech recorded in Montreal on November 6. Henceforth, the Grand Duchess family was installed at the Manoir St-Henri de Mascouche, a suburb Northeast of Montréal in the province of Quebec.[194] The *New York Times* of November 17, 1940 reported that the "Grand Duchess Charlotte of Luxembourg, with her consort, Prince Félix of Bourbon-Parma, and six of their children have left the Hillwood estate here of Joseph E. Davies, former US ambassador to Belgium, and have gone to Canada to remain indefinitely, it was learned today. They left last week for St. Henri de Mascouche, thirty-three miles from Montreal, where the exiled ruler has set up a provisional Government." Hugues Le Gallais had to accept with great regret that the seat of the Luxembourg Government in exile was at 809 Sun Life Building, one of the best addresses in Montreal. We do not know if the Luxembourg "tenants" of the Sun Life Building were aware that this prestigious 24-storey, 122-metre high building, completed in 1931, contained in its cellars the jewels of the British crown and the gold bars of the Bank of England. The renown of the building made it the choice par excellence for the conservation and protection of the British Government's important assets during the Second World War. To this end, the third basement was reinforced with steel beams. All this did not really concern Le Gallais, who was not accredited to Canada and therefore did not go there on official business. From that moment on, the question of the headquarters arose, as Le Gallais had, on the 15th of that month, raised the question of the diplomatic representation of the United States to the Grand Duchess. From Montréal, Dupong replied:

"It is advisable, even necessary, that all the countries with which we are still in contact should be represented to us. As for the United States, it does not seem to me that for the time being the representative can reside in London. It is true that our plan to go with the sovereign to London to establish the seat of Government there still stands. However, we do not yet know when and how we can carry out this project. Even leaving aside these considerations, it is a fact that as long as the Grand Duchess resides in Canada, the seat of the Government can only be in Canada. If the sovereign later travels to England, it will be at that time that the seat of the Government will be transferred to London. Therefore, for the time being, it could only be envisaged that the diplomatic representative of the United States in Ottawa would also be accredited to the Grand Duchess. You could examine the question from this point of view. I have brought the matter to the attention of Mr. Bech, to ask his opinion. As soon as he has written to me, I will inform you and give you precise instructions. In the meantime, you can always deal with the matter informally."

Dupong was right. Le Gallais was going to do as he pleased and above all to do everything possible to attract the Grand Duchess back to Washington.

From mid-November until the first week of December, the Grand Duchess was back in New York, then she left for Montreal. Without the Grand Duchess and the Ministers, Le Gallais must already have felt a little lonely in trying to keep American interest focused on the small, occupied and repressed Grand Duchy. Thus, he had to note that in November/December 1940, for example, the case of Luxembourg was not mentioned in several official statements by the English and American authorities. President Roosevelt had indeed forgotten to mention the Grand Duchy among the victims of Germany in a speech in November 1940.[195] This was a great disappointment for all Luxembourgers, especially for the minister plenipotentiary whose primary mandate was to keep the American administration informed of the sad developments in his country. Other omissions of this kind were to cause Le Gallais to intervene over the next two years, also with regard to the Soviet ambassador, whose bulletin did not mention Luxembourg as an occupied country either.[196] However, a *Memorandum* from FDR to Sumner Welles of December 30, 1940 suggests that Roosevelt had, from the beginning of their stay in the United States, paid particular attention to the Grand Ducal exiles: "To prepare a personal reply. They are the Luxemburgs".[197]

The Le Gallais family spent their first Christmas across the Atlantic at the Shoreham Hotel. In Montreal, an imminent change of residence for the Grand Ducal family became necessary, as "the state of the roads no longer allows us to drive around; it is as if we were buried", as Guill Konsbruck mentioned in a letter of December 28. He described the holidays spent in Canada far from Luxembourg: "We celebrated Christmas with our families. It was very nice and moving: midnight mass was also celebrated at the manor house. All our Princes and Princesses came back and are enjoying the snow and the charming places where they engage in winter sports." As of January 2, 1941, "we will live" at 1305 Pine Avenue in Montreal, which was, in fact, the residence, in turn, of Bech and Dupong. The bourgeois house in downtown Montreal was a few blocks from the Sun Life Building.[198] The Dowager Grand Duchess and the Countess of Lynar resided at the Ritz Carlton Hotel in Montreal. From Jean-Claude Coutu's book "La millionnaire de Mascouche: le manoir seigneurial de 1930 à 1954", we learn that "The Grand Ducal Family stayed in Mascouche until January 8, 1941 and then temporarily lodged on Avenue des Pins in Montreal, not far from the former residence of Mrs. Hazel-Béatrice Kemp-Colville.[199] However, in May, the Prince and the Grand Duchess returned to the manor house to plant a tree each, as a souvenir of their stay in Mascouche."

On January 6, 1941, Le Gallais informed Dupong that he took part in the *Town Hall of Washington Broadcast Radio Station* WINX at the Shoreham Hotel on Sunday January 5, from 8:00 to 8:15 AM, welcoming the opportunity to address the American population directly and to explain the difficult situation in which his country found itself. On this occasion, he presented the heir to the Austro-Hungarian throne, in exile in the United States, as well as his Luxembourg cousins. According to the story, Archduke Otto of Austria spoke about "Christianity and War" and "was very successful in answering the questions put to him after the conference with great intelligence and tact". Le Gallais also spoke of an actress and author, Mrs. Isabel Leighton, who wrote a letter to him about a forthcoming play entitled *Marie-Adélaïde*, about which he asked for information from the Honorary Vice-Consul Corneille Staudt and the Theater Guild. There is also mention of a visit the next day by William H. Hamilton, Honorary Consul General in New York, and Mrs. Leighton and the intention to submit the play about Grand Duchess Marie-Adélaïde (who had abdicated in 1919 and died in 1924), to her younger sister, the Grand Duchess, and to Prince Félix.[200]

Certain circumstances therefore lent themselves to bringing the serious situation in the Grand Duchy to the minds of the authorities on the other side of the Atlantic, some with a more mixed reception, others with undeniably tragic connotations. Thus, on January 16, 1941, Le Gallais wrote to the Secretary of State to transmit a report received from Luxembourg from a source described as "most reliable" about the dramatic events taking place there under the Nazi occupation. He further expressed in this letter of protest "my contempt for the methods described above which are designed to impose submission on an entire population". The minister plenipotentiary concluded: "Luxembourg does not want to go *Heim ins Reich*, its people wish to remain a free nation at home in their own independent Country under the wise rule of their beloved Grand Duchess. I believe, Mr. Secretary, I am not going too far in stating that I can find no words to express my contempt for the above-mentioned methods to enforce submission upon a whole population."[201] The next day, Cordell Hull stated that he read the report with interest and sympathy for the victims of this situation. However, Le Gallais had taken this initiative without waiting for instructions. On February 5, the note was formally delivered, this time by Bech in London to his Allied counterparts and in Washington by Le Gallais.

The first birthday of the Grand Duchess in exile, on January 23, 1941, was celebrated without festivities, as had been the case a year earlier in Luxembourg. On the day of her sovereign's 45th birthday, however, Le Gallais hosted a reception attended by a large number of high-ranking American officials as well as most ambassadors and minister plenipotentiaries. Democratic Senator Walter George,[202] chairman of the Foreign Affairs Committee of the Senate, and Republican Congressman Lewis Thill,[203] of Luxembourg origin, were also present.[204]

DISCUSSIONS ABOUT THE SEAT OF GOVERNMENT

Despite the difficult situation, a real battle began between the exiles to keep the Grand Duchess in the United States and to establish a real legation there, or to see her settle in London. On January 22, 1941, Le Gallais wrote a long letter to Konsbruck in which he outlined all the "dangers" for the Grand Duchess of going permanently to Great Britain. He drew up a number of "advantages" favoring her settlement in Washington. It was important for the Luxembourg representative in the United States to see his sovereign and a large part of his Government move as close as possible to his personal sphere of influence.

"... What is in my opinion most important at the present time is that neither H.R.H. nor Her Government as a whole should run any risk, and that the isolated members of the Government should run as little risk as possible; for as the situation now stands, if Great Britain, with the help of the United States, is victorious, it may be said, by reason of our position vis-à-vis these two countries, that the Grand Duchy is already saved. I remind you that the cardinal point of the foreign policy of the United States is the recognition of the maintenance of the independence of small countries."

Subsequently, and still in the context of this letter, Le Gallais' arguments and conclusions were as follows:

"1. It is in the interest of the Country that H.R.H. does not go to England.

2. It would be unwise for all members of the Government to move to Great Britain at the same time.

From a practical point of view this amounts to saying:

1. that H.R.H. may continue to live in Canada or come to live in the United States as She wishes... It seems that we can find a legation large enough for H.R.H. to reside there; the most favorable solution would be for H.R.H. to come there from time to time for a few weeks. The climate in Washington is not pleasant during the summer, and the problem of the studies of the younger Princesses and Prince Charles would arise again if a prolonged stay here were envisaged. H.R.H. could possibly ask President Roosevelt for his opinion on this matter.

2. that Mr. Dupong would do well to travel to London to replace Mr. Bech for a while."

This last point was considered essential by Le Gallais, as it would make Mr. Bech's task easier and it might be possible to get the United States Government to appoint a chargé d'affaires to the Grand Ducal Government in London. All this seems to augur well for what was to follow, but is nevertheless rather daring for a head of post, even if he addresses the aide-de-camp of his sovereign, whose Chamberlain he is, as we should not forget. In his reply of January 25, Guill Konsbruck states that the Grand Duchess has taken note of the recommendations she submitted to Prime Minister Dupong. The latter was to write directly to Le Gallais to instruct him on how to proceed. And Guill Konsbruck added: "The only thing that Madame told me was that your way of thinking about the 'London' decision was right. Mr. Dupong was aware of everything. As soon as I have any news, I will not fail to let you know." In the days that followed, Le Gallais wasted no time in his correspondence with Konsbruck, and wasted no time in presenting the merits of the United States over England in the defense of the interests of small countries. On January 31, Le Gallais described a house for rent in Washington "which might very well be suitable as a legation and for the stays that Their Royal Highnesses would like to make in Washington". On February 3, Konsbruck informed Le Gallais that Dupong, who had just seen the Grand Duchess at the time the letter was written, did not accept the offer; and commented:

"There you have it. And to say that as soon as I received your letter, I telephoned him because Madame wanted to talk to him about this very matter. But of course it is much simpler to decide without asking anyone, see the famous telegram to Mr. Bech, etc. I shall report to you orally some more observations by Mr. Dupong. Unfortunately, Monseigneur (the Prince) had been away all morning; I made a point of informing Him as soon as He returned home. He told me that He would call you again this evening on this subject."

In the same letter, Konsbruck wrote that the decision on a possible trip to London was postponed till after the forthcoming meeting with Roosevelt scheduled before mid-February and on the advice of the British ambassador Lord Halifax:[205] "In any event She [the Grand Duchess] sees perfectly well the merits of your judicious remarks on the same question [the decision to travel to London]." This was now the obsession of Le Gallais, himself admitting only a year later to Dupong that he had, prior to the visit, and when FDR had just been freshly sworn in for a new term, insisted that the visit take place quickly in order to prevent a premature departure of his sovereign for London.[206] On February 7, Le Gallais returned to the matter: "I refer to our conversation on the telephone last night and confirm that in certain circumstances one must have convictions. Mine is that H.R.H. the Grand Duchess and the Luxembourg Government should not travel to England. I do not think there is any argument that will make me change my mind unless, and then entirely, if the British Cabinet's reply to Lord Halifax's cable is negative. This is not a matter of considering arguments, or a matter of sentiments, but of considering facts. The facts are that the war must be won and helped to be won. Belgium, Norway, the Netherlands and Poland have armies and two of these countries have colonies. Luxembourg has no weapons other than propaganda, and this weapon resides almost entirely in the personality of H.R.H. This weapon cannot be used in England, where H.M. the Queen of the Netherlands and H.M. the King of Norway are already present. On the contrary, in the United States, where there is no foreign sovereign other than H.R.H., there is a way of exercising effective propaganda that is absolutely unique. In short, in England we will be the fifth wheel of the cart, while here we will be able to occupy a leading position which will increase as the United States takes a more active part in the war. I cannot understand why we would want to abandon this unique fighting position in the United States for a secondary position in England, unless Her Britannic Majesty's Government directly informs Lord Halifax that Her Majesty's Government is anxious that Her Royal Highness the Grand Duchess and Her Government should move to Great Britain."[207] Not only did Le Gallais courageously and persistently oppose the visions of some ministers, but he often saw further and more accurately than others, at the risk of making himself unpopular. On the physical presence in the United States and on their location, he was going to be right in so far as the Grand Ducal family was going to buy property in Washington and Pennsylvania. However, in the end, he could not win this battle. A future relocation to London would become inevitable, and Le Gallais had to deal with it. And there goes the word "propaganda"! On February 11, Le Gallais repeated his convictions in a letter to Bech: "We must help win the war; we don't have an army, nor a colony, and we only have one weapon, that of propaganda, which lies in the personality of H.R.H. Grand Duchess." While waiting for the propaganda tour through the United States, the Grand Ducal couple and the Crown Prince were back in Washington.

From February 12 to 14, 1941, President Roosevelt officially welcomed them. On that occasion, the President advised the Luxembourgers not to settle in London for the time being.[208] Le Gallais, comforted in his position, must have been overjoyed, and the details of the visit that was important to him are recounted *in extenso* in the book by Heisbourg on the year 1941. The delegation from Montreal made a stop in New York/Pennsylvania Station before going to Washington. The Luxembourgers were received at the station by Secretary of State Hull and

Army and Navy officials. Also on the program was a lunch at the Executive Mansion, a visit with the President's wife to Mount Vernon, the home of the first American President. This was followed by Prince Félix's meeting with Congressional leaders (with the Chairman of the Senate, the Foreign Relations Committee and the House Foreign Affairs Committee), the state dinner at the White House on February 12, with among others the Vice President and Mrs. Wallace, the Speaker of the House of Representatives Rayburn, the Secretary of State and Mrs. Hull, the Treasury Secretary Morgenthau, the Attorney General and Mrs. Jackson, the Secretary of the Navy, the Secretary of Agriculture, the Secretary of Commerce, the Secretary of Labor and the Mayor of New York and Mrs. La Guardia. On February 13, the Grand Duchess participated in one of Mrs. Roosevelt's press conferences, before visiting the American Red Cross headquarters and having lunch with Mr. and Mrs. Davies. This was followed by a "musical afternoon" followed by a dinner at the White House and a visit to the Luxembourg legation. On February 14, the Grand Duchess, her husband, their eldest son and Lieutenant Konsbruck attended the President's press conference in the Executive Office of the White House.[209] Guill Konsbruck, in a letter dated February 21,[210] informed Minister Bech, still in London, about this official visit, which was described as very successful: "The visit was a great success, the welcome cordial everywhere, President R. [Roosevelt] of unparalleled kindness and thoughtfulness. He addressed the Grand Duchess, saying: 'My child'; Mgr. [Monseigneur] the Prince and Prince Jean were for him: 'Félix' and 'Jean'. Their Royal Highnesses approached on the first evening at dinner at the White House all the senior officials of the State Department and some representatives of the Diplomatic Corps; 87 guests in all. On the second evening there were a good number of Senators and Congressmen at dinner." Le Gallais had already communicated to his Minister three days earlier the outcome which seemed to him to be the most important: "The main point of the conversations was Roosevelt's statement that the place of H.R.H. the Grand Duchess was here and not in England..."[211] About the official place of exile and the presence of the Grand Duchess on the American continent, Le Gallais seemed to have been right on all counts, even if the dossier would soon bounce back.

On February 16, 1941, the Grand Duchess and the Government travelled to Chicago, a cosmopolitan city and a center of modernity. It was the nerve centre of the Midwest where many Luxembourg migrants had settled and prospered at the end of the 19th century. As mentioned above, the "National Relief Fund" was established there to raise funds for the Luxembourgers' struggle against the Nazi occupation. The idea for this fund goes back to the previous year when Le Gallais asked for money to pay the debts of the Luxembourg pavilion at the 1939 exhibition and Bech suggested that he seek the help of the Luxembourg community in the United States. Also in his February 21 letter to Bech, Konsbruck describes the visit as follows: "In Chicago the Luxembourgers were touchingly simple in their love and veneration for the Grand Ducal Family. Everything was wonderfully arranged." And then he described the happiness and thoughtfulness of Consul General Marsch[212] towards Their Royal Highnesses, and revealed to Minister Bech some of his personal feelings as a soldier far from the field: "...we so often think of you who are in reality the only one at the real battle station", i.e. London under the bombardments of the German Luftwaffe. Le Gallais must have had this feeling only in a mitigated way as a recent diplomat. In fact, the meeting in Chicago had been a painful moment for the diplomat who found himself in opposition with Minister Bodson in relation to the treatment of interventions in favor of the Jews, but especially on the question of the seat of the Government:[213] "I asked him

Mrs. Eleanor Roosevelt, the Grand Duchess, Mrs. Le Gallais and Guill Konsbruck at Mount Vernon near Washington, D.C.

for certain steps and interventions to place our compatriots in South America. As he was doing this from his head and a little carelessly, I did not fail to tell him so politely. He wrote a letter to Mr. Dupong saying that he, Le Gallais, has only Mr. Bech as his boss, but even though it would be a bit complicated, all his letters would in the future go through Mr. Dupong." Also in Chicago, in mid-February, the atmosphere was not the best, Bodson not appreciating Le Gallais' presence at a meeting of the Grand Duchess with her ministers. While Bodson protested against Le Gallais' presence at the meeting, as Prince Félix had said he would not attend either, it was the Grand Duchess who intervened to ensure that everyone stayed in the room and calmly discussed the issues at stake. Le Gallais reported to Bech, concluding: "I regret, Mr. Minister, that I have been obliged to note the indecisive side, in my opinion, of your report, but there are circumstances in which one must have the courage to express one's convictions. I dare to hope that you will not hold it against me."[214] Heisbourg's assessment, more than 45 years later, is worth quoting: "...it would be a mistake in my opinion to believe that Le Gallais acted only out of ambition or to improve his own situation. He may not always have had a very accurate conception of his function, but in his letters to Dupong and Bech he made no secret of his opinions. The postscript reproduced above shows that he was aware that he had gone a bit over the top with regard to his boss. He would not have written everything he wrote if he had wanted to deceive Bech. It can therefore be said that his conduct was inspired above all by the interest of the country as he understood it. The Minister of State and the Minister of Foreign Affairs did not hesitate to call him to order when they considered it necessary. But in doing so they remained within the limits of courtesy and decorum, even if Bech sometimes had a touch of malice. Thus, after reading Le Gallais' document on the Chicago meeting, he congratulated him on 'surviving Bodson's savage attack'. Can it be said, moreover, in the light of the role that American forces would play in the liberation of the country and the part that the United States would take in its reconstruction after the war, that Le Gallais was not right? Bech was right, but perhaps his Minister in Washington was not entirely wrong."

The fact remains that Le Gallais' situation had not been the most comfortable during this stormy meeting even though he was enjoying support from the top. A draft letter from the Grand Duchess to Bech following Bodson's "derogatory" protest against Le Gallais refers to an eight-page letter written by Bech to Dupong on January 5, 1941: "You can imagine how painful and unfair this whole affair is, and you will understand with what delight they all threw themselves, Ministers and Secretaries, at the passage in your report of January 5, saying: 'Moreover, I have a little impression that he [Le Gallais] is being tempted by high diplomacy. It is an excessively slippery ground for the representative of a small country.' Now they were satisfied, as the 'master' himself [Bech] condemned Mr. Le Gallais." The unsent text takes sides and is most complimentary to Le Gallais. Thus, and it should be pointed out that even though the letter was not sent, it describes him as follows: "In Washington itself, all we have heard about Mr. Le Gallais has been nothing but praise. He has an excellent press. Mr. Sumner Welles told us about him: 'Your Minister is really excellent, I think very highly of him. Mr. Cordell Hull, Dunn, the President himself have the same feelings for him. We have seen him in action, he does it very well. Everybody loves and esteems him. I agree that he may be overzealous at times, but he is surely honest, sincere and has the courage of his opinion.'" This draft of the letter grants Le Gallais, with regard to Bech, "feelings of the highest esteem and veneration". The draft letter expresses doubts to the extent that Le Gallais would have confided, bordering on resignation following this unfortunate meeting in Chicago: "I am so sad and sorry; I thought I was doing the right thing by always acting as my conscience dictates. I am convinced that Mr. Bech, thinking me too young and inexperienced, will no longer listen to me at all. It's hard to work under these conditions".[215] In the end, the draft text is indicative of the difficult and unique position of Le Gallais, who was valiantly trying to do his best and to be appreciated and well regarded not only by the American authorities but also by his own. Following Le Gallais' altercation with Bodson, Dupong had apparently told Le Gallais not to worry.

With regard to the prevarication and travels of the various parties, already proposed by Le Gallais in his letter of January 22, Le Gallais expressed pleasure in a letter to Konsbruck on March 6 that they had finally been accepted: after receiving Lord Halifax's reply, the sovereign was going to ask Dupong to go to England to replace Bech for a certain period of time in Canada and the United States. Bodson would remain in Canada until Dupong returned from London and Bech returned to London. It was furthermore understood that during the absence of the President of the Government, the Grand Duchess would not sign any document.[216] And after having alluded to the necessity of ministerial countersignature for the constitutional monarch, to be even clearer in his letter of March 8 to Konsbruck:

"I would be grateful if you would explain to H.R.H. that it is only my deep conviction, in the wisdom of the path I suggest to adopt, that allows me to speak so frankly. As much as I am wary of what might be undertaken by the four Ministers in London now, I have not the slightest doubt that the decisions that might be taken by H.R.H. and Mr. Bech in Montreal would be good ones. Therefore the sooner Mr. Dupong could go to London, carrying a special message from H.R.H. for Mr. Bech, expressing the sovereign's settled desire to make personal contact with her Minister of Foreign Affairs, the better, it seems to me; I do not understand why Mr. Dupong wishes to wait until after Easter."

For once, the thoughtful and cautious Le Gallais, almost always so reserved and stoic, had gone beyond his competence, transmitting to Guill Konsbruck his deepest convictions. Sometimes described as unoriginal and not very enterprising, Le Gallais has, in this matter that affects him, shown all his character and determination. He was not, however, at the end of his troubles.

Heisbourg concluded in his book on the year 1940 that when in February 1941 the American diplomat Pierrepont Moffat was appointed Minister to the Luxembourg Government in Montreal, Bech was annoyed and Dupong was displeased because, in spite of himself, he [Dupong] had been put in an embarrassing situation vis-à-vis Bech, to whom he had said a little earlier that he felt that chargés d'affaires should be accredited to the Minister of Foreign Affairs, unlike ministers plenipotentiaries and ambassadors. Le Gallais remained consistent, wishing that all countries be accredited to his sovereign and that the seat could only be in Canada[217] and the Grand Duchess, if possible, in the United States. Heisbourg was right, however, when he stated[218] that Le Gallais "had overstepped his powers. He was probably unaware of this, perhaps unconsciously deriving from his title of chamberlain the rights that this honorary office hardly entails", this after the Minister had submitted this request for approval to the Grand Duchess. Dupong was going to speak, in a protest on February 3, 1941, of "very unpleasant annoyance ... dangerous initiatives",[219] Bech being now more convinced than ever that he was right to have stayed in London and that: "one thing is certain: we have made a mistake in establishing the seat of Government in Canada. No advantage there and multiple disadvantages here."[220] Le Gallais' determination to keep everyone as close as possible to him had earned him a protest that could have cost him dearly. In addition, in preparation for his meeting with Dupong in Chicago (mid-February 1941), as recounted above, he had submitted to the Grand Duchess an "Analysis of Mr. Bech's report of 5 January 1941", where he concluded: "I would go so far as to say that it seems to me essential that Mr. Bech should leave the atmosphere of London and get to know the influential men in the United States Government through direct contact; my reports have no bearing on him."[221] He decidedly never gave up and clearly exceeded his powers here, despite several prior clarifications and even warnings on the subject. Since November 1940, Le Gallais had not ceased to plead and to do his utmost to please the Americans or even to avoid offending their sensibilities and try to bring Bech to the United States. Heisbourg evaluated that "one would think one hears a Minister of Foreign Affairs giving instructions to one of his diplomats!" Heisbourg quoted Bodson who estimated on February 4, 1941[222] that Prince Félix and Le Gallais prevented the Grand Duchess from going to London and for whom

"The case of Le Gallais is quite different (from that of the Prince described as brave and fearful for his wife's safety). Le Gallais is here playing his fifth Minister and with great success... Le Gallais is working hard with the American authorities to get an American representative next to the Grand Duchess... Le Gallais ignores this and gives the approval (to Moffat)... The reasons for his attitude are clear. The title of Minister we gave him, not because of him, but because of the Americans, makes him too self-confident. He believes that his situation is brighter if the Grand Duchess stays in America, and that is why he asked for an increase of $400 per month, or a total of $1,400, to rent a large house in Washington so that the Grand Duchess could come and stay from time to time."

Opinions therefore differed seriously in relation to the seat of the government.

PROPAGANDA EFFORTS AND HOSTILITY
TOWARDS GERMANY

In addition to his efforts and even his determination to keep the sovereign in the United States, if not Canada, Le Gallais began around this time his numerous interventions and speeches situating the Grand Duchy in Europe and describing Luxembourg almost every time as a small country that is nevertheless a serious and respected contributor to the common war effort against Nazi tyranny.

Thus, Le Gallais described himself during his speech to the Overseas Press Club entitled *In tribute to the Unity of the Democracies*, at the Waldorf Astoria in New York, on February 27, 1941,[223] as a representative of the smallest of the nations present that evening, recalling that "the strength of a State does not depend solely upon the number of its nationals, but upon the will of the people to uphold certain spiritual values, such as patriotism, loyalty to the sovereign and courage. I am happy and proud to be in a position to tell you that the people of Luxembourg are living up to these values and showing their determination not to let themselves be nazified." He recalled the thousand-year-old history and even the recent destruction of the monument in memory of the Luxembourg soldiers who died in the First World War (*Gëlle Fra*) described as "the latest anti-French act in Luxembourg", to remind that "the most popular verse in a Luxembourg song was: 'We don't want to be Prussians'... a thousand-fold stronger 'we don't want to become Nazis'" and, lastly, to express his hope that "Luxembourgers are again living in the hope that right and justice will triumph in the long run and they will see their country free and independent under the wise Constitutional rule of their beloved sovereign". This incantation of a tiny country was to recur regularly throughout his career and was also taken up in the speeches of Dupont and Bech. The latter were made to complement each other and remain friends despite the vicissitudes of their political careers. Efforts were made in this direction not only in the United States but also in London. On March 9, 1941, the BBC began to broadcast a program in Luxembourgish.[224] The Grand Duchess' speeches were regularly broadcast on the airwaves and listened to clandestinely by the population remaining in the country. At the beginning, they were more focused on the idea of resistance, making the sovereign increasingly appear as an active force that nourished and strengthened the identity aspiration of the Luxembourg people.[225] Le Gallais' opposition to Germany and the Germans became more and more pronounced, to the point that, in a letter to the Minister of State of June 15, 1942, he considered that there was no reason to "want to make Hitler and his people solely responsible, like the Kaiser [German Emperor] in the other war".[226] A poll had shown "that the American public considers the German Government the great enemy and not the German people", which Le Gallais described as dangerous. Le Gallais' bitterness against the Nazi Germans was not going to diminish even after the war.

EFFORTS IN FAVOUR OF REFUGEES, ESPECIALLY JEWS

Before the outbreak of hostilities, Hugues Le Gallais had been confronted for three years in Luxembourg with the rise of Nazism in Germany. The Jewish community of some 2,000 people before the 1930s had seen the arrival of about 1,500 Jews, mainly from Eastern Europe. After May 10, 1940, this community of almost 4,000 people was to be severely depleted during the war. 1,300 of those Jews lost their lives during the war. The head of diplomatic post in Washington had to intervene in accordance with the instructions of his authorities in favor of those Jews, especially the ones of Luxembourg nationality. The Chief Rabbi from 1929 to 1946, Robert Serebrenik,[227] was among those who had taken refuge in the United States. In New York, he founded the Luxembourg-Jewish Information Office. He was also the Rabbi of the Ramath Orah Congregation, founded in 1941 by refugees from Luxembourg. While still in Europe, Serebrenik went to Berlin in 1941 to negotiate with Adolf Eichmann the liberation of the surviving Luxembourg Jews.

Le Gallais was going to concentrate on the exiles he considered "prominent". He also had to consider his direct superiors, the Grand Ducal family and four of the five members of the Government, who had managed to leave the country. This did not prevent him from intervening, even on a regular and assiduous basis, with the State Department to grant visas to Jews who wished to leave the European continent, especially those of Luxembourg nationality and who had resided in Luxembourg.

In addition to Luxembourg officials, the Minister in Washington, but also the Honorary Consul in New York would very quickly be taken with the fate of the many Jewish refugees who had left Luxembourg and tried to come to the United States, particularly via Portugal. The correspondence, especially that between Le Gallais and Bodson, concerned emergency visas, Luxembourg passports obtained under false pretences, the necessary moral guarantees (affidavits) for obtaining visas and recovering the costs incurred, and the addresses of various Luxembourgers. Those were situations and procedures which the former representative of Columeta had not been confronted with in his previous professional and personal career and which the necessity of the moment had made crucial for a great number of people.[228]

In December 1940, while Bech was in Brazil, Le Gallais presented to the chargé d'affaires of the Brazilian embassy in the United States a request from the Grand Duchess for visas for Jews detained in a camp at Mousserolles near Bayonne, a town in South-Western France. These people had been turned back at the Portuguese border of Vilar Formoso in November 1940. They were the 293 occupants of the third convoy which had been organized by the president of the Consistory Albert Nussbaum.[229] He was, from the end of November 1940 until December 1941, assistant to the Minister of Justice Bodson as Commissioner for the emigration of Jews from Luxembourg.[230] At the beginning of 1941, the Government in exile tried to get things moving in favor of its interned citizens. In January 1941, Le Gallais intervened again at the request of Bodson, writing to the State Department to protest against the conditions of detention of Jews in the internment camp.[231] In a report of January 24, 1941, Georges Schommer had advised the Government to intervene officially, despite the breakdown of diplomatic relations between France and Luxembourg: "[I]t might be appropriate to ask the State Department to intervene through the [United States] embassy in Vichy and to bring the case of the internees to the attention of the French authorities. As soon as the material means of subsistence are or appear to be assured, as in the present case, there is, it seems to me, no reason to justify the prolonged detention of these unfortunate compatriots, who are, in this case, of French descent." At Bodson's request, on February 26, 1941,[232] Le Gallais sent a letter of protest to the State Department against the conditions of internment of Luxembourgers at Gurs near Pau in the South of unoccupied France. This letter was delivered to Admiral Darlan, head of the French Government, by the American ambassador in Vichy. Bodson also intervened with Le Gallais so that the latter would try to obtain visas for South American countries.[233]

The difficulties were not over yet. Following the opinion of the State Department, the Luxembourg Government decided that "no Luxembourg title will be extended in countries other than France and Portugal, which are, for the needs of the cause, considered as waiting countries." The titles could be extended in these two countries on condition that the holder had resided for at least ten years in the Grand Duchy or that his/her spouse or mother had Luxembourg nationality.[234]

Other specific cases were being dealt with through Le Gallais. Thus, in June 1941, the Minister of Justice Bodson informed Le Gallais that "Troeller,[235] Luxembourgish but of German descent [sic]", general representative of the *Metallgesellschaft* in Frankfurt, who was with his wife in Lisbon, was known in Luxembourg as a pro-Nazi, could possibly apply for a visa and that it would be appropriate to inform his authorities ("please consider whether it would not be appropriate at this stage to enquire about a possible visa application by this Troeller and informally communicate what we know about this individual"). Charles, known as Gordian Troeller, who had taken part in the civil war in Spain and who, after fleeing to Portugal, set up there, with the support of the Allies, a secret service allowing the escape of those pursued by the Nazis.[236]

Le Gallais was not the only Luxembourg official who intervened on the administrative level. Dupong, Bech, Bodson and Krier, but also Elvinger, Schommer, Schaus and Staudt in New York, where the American Jewish Joint Distribution Committee was located, were active in this context. Thus, on May 5, 1941, Georges Schommer informed Minister Bodson that he had certified to Minister Le Gallais a few days earlier that "the visa for René Blum[237] would have been refused by the Washington Committee; no specific reason for this, but it seems that the state of danger in which Mr. Blum would find himself would not be sufficiently characterized." While Minister of State Dupong left New York for Lisbon on May 4/5, 1941 and then travelled to London, those who remained on the American continent continued to intervene on behalf of Luxembourgers in difficulty on the European continent. Le Gallais was invited to take further steps immediately, taking into account that this was not an official request and that the situation was due to the former Minister of Justice himself. He had not kept his former Government colleagues sufficiently informed beforehand, which did not help the situation. It is to be noted that once he had arrived in New York, Blum wrote a warm letter of thanks to Le Gallais on February 20, 1942:

"It is with immense pleasure that I fulfill, in acknowledging receipt of your kind telegram of today, a duty of deep gratitude for all the trouble you have taken to solve my desperate case. I am, at the same time, the interpreter of all my compatriots residing in non-occupied France, who entrust me with the task of expressing to you their deepest gratitude for the very appreciable services you have rendered them in the accomplishment of your so delicate and arduous mission. Better than anyone else, they know how precious your solicitude has been to them."[238]

A moral affidavit for Blum and his wife was sent by Elvinger to Serebrenik on April 29, 1942. In connection with Blum and his wife's stay an intermezzo followed between Le Gallais and Dupong, who was asking for an intervention in order to secure the support of the State Department in securing the extension of their residence permit. According to Heisbourg, Le Gallais interjected the "spectre of the establishment of a hotbed of Socialist propaganda", to which the Minister of State, assuming his role as head of the entire Government, replied: "Let this be my concern." Le Gallais, not giving up, replied:

"I am solely responsible to H.R.H. the Grand Duchess and the Grand Ducal Government in its entirety of the Luxembourg activities in the United States and I have to foresee and act under any circumstance when I believe that an act could impair my Country… I know that Your Excellency shares the same concern and to the same degree as the undersigned and I can only note that in general terms we have always been in agreement. I express the firm hope that this good understanding will continue."

Heisbourg described this as "a challenge to the authority" of the Minister of State. Dupong pointed out that "it was not that I disagree with you… but I wanted to say that I have a little more experience in this matter [ensuring that New York does not become a hotbed of Socialist unrest] than you do, and knowing better the character and personality of Mr. Blum, I know how to deal with him." In the meantime, Le Gallais had met Blum in New York, the former minister assuring that it was not his intention to create such a Socialist agitation movement. Mr. and Mrs. Blum left shortly afterwards for Canada on visas provided by the minister in Washington.

In addition to Blum's thanks, let us mention the equally warm thanks of Nussbaum on May 28, 1942:

"Having so quickly and unexpectedly obtained my visa for the United States, I learned on my arrival here that my emigration so quickly was only possible thanks to your high intervention. I cannot express to you what the value and the continuation of this happy result obtained by you means, but be convinced that you have saved me from a very sad situation. I can never forget the effort you have been willing to make for me and also for my mother, and I ask you, Mr. Chargé d'Affaires, to accept the expression of my deepest gratitude".[239]

Let us conclude with the praise cited by Heisbourg[240] from the jurist and former Secretary of the Consistoire Israélite de Luxembourg, Alex Bonn, for "the generosity and energy that he [Le Gallais] never ceased to show his compatriots in their misfortune."

Le Gallais was not alone in his efforts. Others urged him to act and intervene as quickly as possible. Thus, Victor Bodson[241] was particularly active in the United States in order to move the dossiers of Jews in difficulty. Minister Bodson had, for example, asked in a letter addressed on May 9, 1941 to a Belgian, Alfred L. Vanden Broeck, for news of several Jews, to which he replied on June 7: "I understand your desire to know which Luxembourgers had arrived and their addresses. I believe that they all go to the Consulate of Mr. Staudt." Washington and New York were therefore to cooperate very closely on a number of issues.

The Chief Rabbi of Luxembourg Serebrenik arrived in New York at the end of June 1941 where he founded a new congregation at 550 West 110 Street at Broadway in New York, the Ramath Orah Congregation, "City of Light" in Hebrew, a reference to the etymology of the name Luxembourg, as well as the Luxembourg Jewish Information Office (LJIO). In passing, dealing with a specific case of a Jew, Le Gallais congratulated Serebrenik on the creation of this office when, on July 27, 1941, he had written on LJIO letterhead: "Our work will be based principally on the precious help that Her Royal Highness the Grand Duchess will give us through Her Government in Montreal and you, Minister, in Washington" in order to "organise the emigration of our compatriots or co-religionists who are in the Grand Duchy, in non-occupied France or in Portugal, to overseas countries and notably to the United States." He concluded: "I firmly hope that in the future you will also place at our disposal for the success of our rescue action your high credit and authority which you enjoy with the State Department and with the various branches of the United States Government." Le Gallais could have considered himself flattered and be more grateful.[242] However, he was not able to work miracles either. As early as June, Serebrenik addressed urgent requests to the Grand Duchess and to the Government in exile for support in obtaining entry visas for the United States. Maître Alex Bonn also sent a letter to this effect to Le Gallais, asking, on June 6, 1941: "... to intervene in the case of the unfortunate people concerned (co-religionists from Luxembourg who are still in the Grand Duchy and who would also like to obtain a visa enabling them to enter this magnificent and hospitable country) with the generosity and energy that you never cease to show to our compatriots in misfortune. We thank you from the bottom of our hearts!"[243] The State Department was reluctant to accept people who could not prove they had a place on a boat. As described in Vincent Artuso's February 2015 report on 'La Question Juive' au Luxembourg (1933-1941), on the Luxembourg State in the face of Nazi anti-Semitic persecution:

"the State Department was particularly reluctant to receive non-Luxembourgish Jews who were resident in Luxembourg. On July 2, Serebrenik was received at the State Department, together with Hugues Le Gallais. The latter had opened the doors, as was his duty, asking, among other things, that despite the new regulations that had come into force the day before, Platt Waller was still allowed to issue visas to Jews residing in Luxembourg,[244] but obtained nothing. In any case, the American Consulate in Luxembourg was closed on July 7. Following this, Victor Bodson made one last attempt to approach the State Department. With the agreement of the Swiss Government, he suggested that the American Consulates in Switzerland could grant visas to Luxembourgers in countries occupied by Germany. This proposal failed due to German hostility."[245]

After examining a few specific cases, let us return to Le Gallais' relationship with Chief Rabbi Serebrenik. On August 26, 1941, Le Gallais wrote to Dr. Robert Serebrenik, Luxembourg Jewish Information Office in New York, with a copy to Dupong and Bodson, about the Germans who did not allow Luxembourg Jews wishing to emigrate to go to Switzerland, but demanded that they go to the Consulate of the United States in Barcelona to obtain a visa. Le Gallais approached Mr. Avra Warren, head of the visa division, showing him the Consistory cable and saying that the American Consulate in Barcelona had to be able to guarantee that the visa was granted before the people concerned could leave Luxembourg, which was considered absolutely impossible. It was agreed that as long as the Luxembourgers were aware of this and the tickets for the group had been secured for them by a boat leaving on a certain date, Mr. Warren should be informed. He was aware of 38 Luxembourg Israelites and that "reasonable assurances can be given that their visas will be passed", without however giving any guarantee. For Le Gallais, it was impossible to intervene in this affair with the Spanish embassy in Washington. On September 26, Le Gallais informed Serebrenik that Warren had refused the visas because it was a matter of principle for the State Department and there was no way of getting him to reverse that decision. The State Department had given this matter careful consideration before taking a decision. The next day, Bodson said that Le Gallais had done well and that

"we have to be a little wary, because in their desperation, both the Rabbi and the Jewish Information Office are trying in one way or another to get more than we can actually give them. Under these conditions... tell them to refer each new request to Mr. Dupong... and to remember that the Germans had escorted two full trains of Israelites to the Portuguese border through Spain. So they will be completely free to give a visa to Barcelona, when in fact they are ordering in Spain."

Then, in a letter dated October 21, Serebrenik informed Le Gallais of the existence of 134 people who had arrived (on the last convoy leaving Luxembourg) in Barcelona on October 20, and for whom it was necessary to act quickly. Le Gallais reminded Minister Bodson's Secretary General, Pierre Elvinger, on September 8, 1941, that he could only intervene with the State Department if American citizens filed affidavits in favor of those seeking immigration visas. The aim was to prevent these individuals from becoming a public liability. Serebrenik informed Dupong on October 16, 1941 that the situation of the Jews in Luxembourg, about 700 souls, had tragically worsened in recent weeks and that the *Gauleiter* had decided the day before to deport all Jews from the Grand Duchy to the ghetto in Litzmanstadt (Łódź), with the exception of the sick and elderly and those who were able to prove the prospect of emigration overseas. He asked for a solution for these people, among whom there were 60 Luxembourgers. This request was made after Serebrenik had collected 5,000 dollars and exhausted the resources of his fellow countrymen and women to guarantee the maintenance of the forced transport of 132 people to Spain and to prevent their imprisonment. The intention was to make these funds available to Albert Nussbaum, Commissioner for emigration attached to the Grand Ducal Government in Lisbon. Everything would depend on Le Gallais and the State Department obtaining American visas, which should not arrive too late to save these Jews. The next day, October 17, 1941, Serebrenik spoke to Dupong about his intention to rebuild a Congregation whose material foundation was assured.[246]

In December 1941, Le Gallais asked the State Department why the American Consulate in Barcelona had not yet been informed following the prior request for urgent examination of the situation of the passengers of the convoy held at the Spanish border and in Barcelona. In the context of this convoy, a letter sent by Chief Rabbi Serebrenik to the Grand Duchess was badly received, and Le Gallais wrote to his Minister on January 19, 1942 that he was displeased with this way of approaching the Grand Duchess, while he and Dupong were in the process of making representations to the State Department on behalf of the group in Barcelona.[247] While Hugues Le Gallais had asked Dupong to be able to reply to Serebrenik that this was not appropriate, the Minister of State dissuaded him from doing so. Dupong had a better character than his minister plenipotentiary in the United States. On December 12, 1941, Serebrenik had sounded the alarm to Dupong about 121 people in Barcelona ("the American Consul in Barcelona is in trouble while for about 50 people the State Department has cabled advisory approvals...") and 45 refugees in Portugal ("exposed to the greatest danger"). Heisbourg and Koch-Kent discuss this episode and the manner of the Chief Rabbi who displeased Le Gallais, Koch-Kent adding at the bottom of the page,[248] as for Minister Bodson a little further on, that they were "trying to use the prestige of the Head of State". Henri Koch-Kent added on behalf of the diplomat in Washington: "Puffed up with pride, Le Gallais tried to mobilize, for his own benefit, the interventions of the sovereign."

Nevertheless, the Luxembourgers on the other side of the Atlantic, like all the other Governments–in-exile faced with a similar situation, sought to save first and foremost their nationals, the "real Luxembourgers". As Le Gallais wrote, this attitude was motivated by fear, reinforced by the American conviction that among the stateless there were infiltrated German agents. A distinction was therefore made between Jews of Luxembourg nationality, also referred to as "the cases of genuine Luxembourgers", for whom the Government intervened, and stateless persons who had been or were in Luxembourg.[249]

In summary, Le Gallais' diligent and legalistic approach, hardly driven by initiative, was that of an intermediary who was called upon and carried out the instructions received mainly from his Prime minister and his Minister of Justice. The latter had a hotter temperament and became impatient at times, harassing the diplomat, who sometimes considered Bodson's instructions to be untimely and inconsistent with diplomatic practice.

"The Minister of Justice believed that the question of Jewish refugees did not find the interest it deserved in Le Gallais, who was taking great pains (Elvinger in a letter from Montreal to Bodson dated September 18, 1941)... If the question of the Jews had contributed to this mini-crisis (see above for details on the Government Council in Chicago where the Grand Duchess had had to arbitrate) between the Minister and the diplomat, it would have been a very serious matter, Their relations soon normalized, and on March 5, 1941, Bodson told Le Gallais that he appreciated his work very much."[250]

According to Heisbourg,[251] Dupong, Bodson, Bech, Le Gallais, Schommer, Krier and others undertook numerous efforts over many months in the direction of Brazil, Belgian Congo, Cuba (Le Gallais had also to intervene in relation to the abhorrent conditions in the Tiscornia camp in Cuba, this detail being reported by Heisbourg),[252] Santo Domingo and other countries. Le Gallais worked with varying degrees of success and commitment and in accordance with the maxims applied by other bureaucracies. The legalistic manner in which the Government came to the aid of its nationals, trying as best it could to advance the various individual cases, but also the collective cases of the various convoys, was to keep the legation in Washington busy, especially during the first two years of its operation. In the archives left by Le Gallais there are, now classified under "Fate of the Jews during and after the Second World War", dozens if not hundreds of cases on which Le Gallais intervened with the most diverse American institutions and authorities. Working conditions were extremely complex due to the scattering of Luxembourg officials and the unprecedented situation, to say the least. Thus, much later, in a letter to Dupong, then in London, concerning the recent arrival of Luxembourgers in Spain, Le Gallais still regretted that Luxembourg did not have consular representation in Portugal and that, in addition to strengthening national sovereignty, the precarious conditions of compatriots who were in Portugal without transit visas could have been alleviated if such a presence had been ensured. Of course, in Washington this was not the case, as he himself was accredited in due form and was working on all fronts.

THE PURCHASE OF 2200 MASSACHUSETTS AVENUE

As mentioned above, the purchase of the property at 2200 Massachusetts Avenue in Washington occurred on February 25, 1941.[253] The property had been owned by the family of a Canadian lumber merchant from Wisconsin who had become a Senator. The mansion was acquired by the Grand Ducal Court for $40,000. On March 10, Le Gallais informed Konsbruck: "Finally I have the honor to inform you that I have taken possession of the keys of our legation at 2200 Massachusetts Avenue and that we will begin to put it in order in the next few days. ...I have taken out a five-year fire insurance policy for $75,000 (the house only, i.e. without the furniture)." Subsequently, the two correspondents discussed the layout of the legation's rooms, particularly in the basement, in order to store boxes containing valuable belongings of the Grand Ducal family previously held by the Manhattan Storage Company in New York. This was followed by discussions on the insurance of the contents of these crates. According to Heisbourg, Le Gallais moved to Massachusetts Avenue on March 31, with the Grand Duchess and Prince Félix offering dinners there during their first visit, from April 30 to May 1, 1941. The Dowager Grand Duchess and her lady-in-waiting only lived there from early October until June 1942. During this time, Le Gallais stayed with his family at the Wardman Hotel.

At the Shoreham Hotel, Le Gallais had been paid $1,000 a month, which the Minister of State had reduced by $350 in consideration of the fact that hotel costs had amounted to about $360 a month.[254] This was followed by a fairly frank exchange between the two, Dupong writing: "It is rather unpleasant for me to have to be the boring lecturer. But circumstances oblige me to carry out this thankless task." And a week later, following Le Gallais' complaints: "You say that you do not live as a private individual, but as a representative of our country. As I am identically in the same case as you, I have full understanding for that. Knowing the rather narrow limits of a small country like ours... we all have to make certain sacrifices." Finally, Le Gallais' personal remuneration was separated from the management fees, part of which was paid by the Court as owner of the building. At the outbreak of the war, Le Gallais had, apparently at the request of his authorities, to apply for advances from his acquaintances in Washington. Dupong, in a letter of November 18, 1940 to Bech in London, recalled that Le Gallais had borrowed $1,500 from Davies and

2200 Massachusetts Avenue in Washington, D.C., first the legation, then the embassy of the Grand Duchy of Luxembourg.

$500 from Prince Félix.[255] On July 17, 1941, Minister Bech made it quite clear to Le Gallais:

"In agreement with the Minister of State, I had informed you by cable on May 29 last that as from June 1 the Government would pay you the sum of $650 per month for your personal budget, adding that the other expenses would be liquidated on production of the supporting documents required by our law on State accounts. In giving you these instructions, Mr. Dupong and I were basing ourselves on the indications contained in your previous correspondence with the Minister of State. According to this correspondence, your disbursements were estimated by you to average between $1,000 and $1,100. However, your last monthly statement is over 1700 dollars. ... in the meantime you will therefore want to take steps to limit your monthly expenses to a maximum of 1100 dollars."

In November 1942, the question of the "monthly lump sum as indemnity and legation expenses generally of any kind" was again raised between Le Gallais and Dupong,[256] with the clarification that "the Belgian ambassador receives 2,300 dollars, the expenses for the Chancellery being separate." Le Gallais asked that the lump sum be allocated to him retroactively from September 1, "to allow me to take over the deficit that you are aware of", Dupong having invoked that "our limited availability has already obliged me to refuse certain other requests [and] impose a great reserve on me".[257] Hugues Le Gallais' unreal expectations about the lifestyle and standing of diplomatic envoys were all the more painful as they occurred in times of war. It should also be mentioned that on behalf of the Court, Hugues Le Gallais, both as a civil servant and Chamberlain, also had to deal with various practical and financial matters.

TRAVEL AND POLITICAL CORRESPONDENCE

The Luxembourgers travelled a lot between the American and Canadian capitals and New York during this time. From March 31 to April 2, 1941, the Grand Duchess and Guill Konsbruck travelled to New York, then to Philadelphia, where they were joined by the Le Gallais.[258] The Grand Duchess made one of her first public appearances there, on April 3, and gave a speech. She also visited the Liberty Bell at Independence Hall. The sovereign uttered phrases that Le Gallais would use many times in the years to come:

"I would like to say how deeply grateful I am to President Roosevelt for the address he made after the passing of the Lend-Lease Bill, and I am thinking not only of the words. .. 'immediate all-out aid for Britain, Greece, China, and for all the Governments in exile whose homes are temporarily occupied by the aggressors...' but more particularly of the phrase, '...we believe that any nationality no matter how small, has the inherent right to its own nationhood...'. God bless America."

In thanking the United States, the Grand Duchess, and later the authorities in exile, would never fail to link their recognition of the American commitment to the fact that Luxembourg considered itself a full-fledged partner.

From April 26 to May 1, 1941, the Grand Duchess, Prince Félix and Guill Konsbruck stayed in Washington, where dinners were held at the Belgian legation and embassy by the Count and Countess van der Straten-Ponthoz,[259] and at the British embassy by Lord and Lady Halifax. The Apostolic Delegate Monsignor Cicognani offered lunch after Mass on Sunday morning, April 27.

Le Gallais had proposed a whole list of persons (senators George and Green, representatives Bloom, Atherton, Dunn, Acheson, Summerlin and Woodward from the State Department, Red Cross representatives Mrs. William Corcoran Eustis and Mrs. Truxtun Beale) to Konsbruck for the event at the legation while specifying in his letter of April 15 that "as we can only place 18 people at the legation table, we can only invite 13 people at a time, but there are 26 on our list, so we would have to plan two dinners..." All these precautions seem a little exaggerated in the middle of the war, especially as Le Gallais insisted on receiving a telephone call so that he could get the invitations out. But Le Gallais wanted not only to do well, but also to shine.

Subsequently, Minister of State Dupong, who had met Belgian Finance Minister Camille Gutt in New York a few days earlier and reached an agreement on the terms of the cash advances, left the United States to travel via Bermuda to Lisbon with some delay and then on to London.

Fortunately, there is no shortage of political subjects in the correspondence found by the minister plenipotentiary in Washington. In Le Gallais' papers, dated May 26, 1941,[260] there is a report of an interview with Leo Pasvolsky, Special Assistant for Economic Affairs to the American Secretary of State, on the possibility of a customs union in Europe once the war is over. This was the time when the needs of post-war Europe and the collection of data on raw materials undertaken by the British were also discussed. On June 5, 1941, the minister plenipotentiary reported his meeting with Soviet ambassador Umansky, who reportedly stated that each country should first think of its own interests, basing this assertion on a recent statement made by President Roosevelt. Le Gallais wrote the same day to Minister Bodson that the Soviet ambassador had reported from his conversation with the Under-Secretary of State that it had had "an obituary character and can be considered a rupture in economic relations for political reasons." Documents from Luxembourg gave an idea of the suffering of the population. Thus, on June 3, 1941, Le Gallais sent Konsbruck, as an appendix to his letter, a petition addressed to the Grand Duchess transmitted by the State Department. It came from Platt Waller, who had received it personally from someone whose name he did not reveal. In reply, Konsbruck wrote as early as June 4 that the Grand Duchess had been very moved by it and wondered how she could help... This does not prevent personal motivations sometimes taking precedence, especially when it was, again and again, a question of the seat of the government. This time it was more a question of assessing the consequences of the actual transfer of the Grand Duchess' residence. Thus, for example, in his letter of June 4, 1941, Guill Konsbruck recounted a dispute with Justice Minister Bodson over "our establishment in the States", which gave rise to three telegrams exchanged with London. Bodson reproached Konsbruck this time "that he, as the only adviser to H.R.H., he had not been informed and consulted in advance... And it is my fault that only London received a telegraph and he was summoned by the Grand Duchess! Never mind, it's all right..." The telegrams (five in all, which will be communicated to Le Gallais in two stages) in fact specify that, although the Grand Duchess intends to settle shortly in the vicinity of Washington and buy a house and farm there, the seat of the Government will remain, following talks and prior information with the State Department, in London. This arrangement will remain provisional and intermediate and will not give rise to inappropriate publications and comments in the press. The stay in Canada and the one in the United States are to be considered provisional only. Bech, who gave his indications to the Grand Duchess, following the information he had received from her and Bodson, concluded in his telegram of May 31: "We ask you to prevent above all Hugues from giving the opposite impression Stop Higher interest country at stake." This time, Bech's confidence in his diplomat in Washington had reached its lowest level.

The Grand Duchess replied by stressing:

"State Department fully agrees... Buying property will allow us to 1. Good investment 2. save on rent 3. be close to Washington 4. and New York in view of business and radio. Our residence will continue to be in Montreal at the Ritz Carlton Hotel. This will be all the more practical because our children will continue to attend Canadian schools and will also resolve the issue of the future residence of the Ministers and the situation of accredited foreign Ministers".[261]

The Grand Duchess concluded that the seat of the Government should remain London and that "Hugues was warned". Le Gallais had therefore partially won his case insofar as the Grand Ducal family was getting closer to Washington, but at what price! However, he seemed alarmed by the prospect of the Grand Duchess' rapprochement with New York, and not Washington, as can be seen from his letter to Konsbruck of June 10, 1941, here quoted in full:

"I believe it is my duty to express my opinion very clearly on the question of the advisability of the purchase of a property in the vicinity of New York by H.R.H. This opinion is negative because, from a political point of view all the benefit that could be derived from the proposed transfer of domicile from Canada to the United States is lost if H.R.H. takes up residence in the vicinity of New York,[262] and not in the vicinity of Washington. Indeed, on the New York side, the contact that TT.RR.HH. will have will be composed of businessmen, retired people and wealthy refugees, a whole world that has no political influence in the first place and whose neighborhood must harm TT.RR. HH.'s cause with the American public at large. And even if this contact is kept to a minimum, it will be considered to be the same thing. If we were happy to learn that H.R.H. wanted to leave Canada to come to the United States, it was always with the idea that TT.RR.HH. would come to the outskirts of Washington to see the official American world and the political world and to live a life withdrawn and necessarily withdrawn by the very situation of the chosen place. In our minds this is the only thing to do if we want to see the growth of influences in the United States favorable to the cause of the Grand Duchy. I even believe that it would be preferable from a political point of view for H.R.H. to stay in Canada rather than to come and reside in the vicinity of New York. As Minister on the one hand and as Chamberlain on the other, I have always tried to reconcile the interests of the Country and those of the Grand Ducal House, but in this case and after careful consideration I find that this is not possible and that I must put forward what I believe to be the interest of the Country. I would be grateful if you could explain the above to H.R.H. and apologize to Her."

This is another proof of Le Gallais' courage and frankness, but also of his stubbornness. This time, however, Dupong, who had just joined Bech in London, clarified to the Grand Duchess that: "Mr. Bech has already expressed to You political concerns about Your decision to transfer the actual headquarters of Your residence from Montreal to the outskirts of Washington ... the announcement came as a bit of a surprise to me, whereas in our last meeting in New York on May 2, it had not yet been mentioned... The new situation will make personal contact between the Government and Your Royal Highness more difficult and necessarily rarer." And, while questioning whether this decision "implies the renun ciation of the project to make, at a time yet to be determined, a stay in England", to appeal to the sovereign on the need for "solidity of our position within the group of democratic countries" and to mention "the apprehension that the increasingly wide geographical dispersion of these same leaders might give the uninitiated the impression of a less close collaboration".[263] For little, Le Gallais' determination could have alienated everyone.

On June 4, 1941, the Luxembourg community in New York had invited the Grand Duchess and the Prince of Luxembourg to attend a solemn mass celebrated by Cardinal Spellman in St Patrick's Cathedral.[264] On June 12, 1941, the Grand Duchess and Hugues Le Gallais went to Philadelphia.

In June and July 1941, a campaign against European royalty was launched by various American newspapers. Thus, on June 21, the Chicago Tribune Service listed the contacts between the Roosevelt administration and members of the European royal families, including: the lunch offered on August 28, 1939, to Princes Félix and Jean of Luxembourg and the lunch offered on July 25, 1940, to the Prince and princely children. On February 12, 1941 contact was made with the Grand Duchess and Princes Félix and Jean. Other royal guests were the Crown Princes of Norway (July 17, 1941 in Hyde Park) and Denmark (two days later) [this is most probably inaccurate. P.S.], Princess Juliana of the Netherlands (December 19, 1940 and June 17, 1941) and the British royal couple (June 8 and 9, 1939). With a similarly critical attitude, on July 5, 1941 the Chicago Tribune explained that the Dutch could not have their headquarters in the United States, as it was a royal, not a republican, Government. Following a request from Boston residents, one Congressman even asked why seven royal refugees had been welcomed to the United States with all the honors reserved for reigning families. The State Department replied that: "the transportation (on the Trenton) ...was a curtesy [sic] extended to the immediate family of the head of a foreign State with which the Government maintains friendly relations. Upon arrival they were, of course, treated as official visitors to the United States".[265] This might have dissuaded Le Gallais from bringing the Grand Duchess to the United States, but he was stubborn and wanted Luxembourg to play a major role at the side of the American administration.

On July 17, Bech sent Le Gallais, along with instructions on the legation's expenses discussed above, a political directive which he found difficult to comply with, as it was hardly in keeping with his personality and way of doing things: "Your interesting reports come to me regularly. I sincerely thank you for this and ask you to continue to keep me informed of any conversations you may have with foreign diplomats. Just be careful not to get involved in high politics, which has never worked for the representatives of small and especially very small countries".[266]

The Eldorado Farm was bought by Mrs. Charlotte and Mr. Félix de Clervaux on August 4, 1941. The 247 acre property, with an additional 50 acres of land purchased two years later, was ultimately sold.[267] Konsbruck had informed Le Gallais of the purchase in July 1941 of this property/farm,[268] which, ironically, was called Eldorado Farm and was located on Core Creek, three miles (less than 5 kilometers) south of the town of Newton in Middletown Township, Bucks County, Pennsylvania: "The purchase of a property was eventually made as well. I have no idea what it looks like, but given the situation I think that with regard to the land and from a political point of view, we can be very happy".[269] Two Studebaker cars in the name of the legation were delivered to Washington for Le Gallais to finally have them registered in the name of the Grand Ducal Government.

At the beginning of August, Le Gallais was in New York where, together with Schommer, he greeted the American chargé d'affaires and American Consul in Luxembourg, George Platt Waller, who had returned to the United States. The latter had been reduced to the role of Consul from July 1940 when he left Luxembourg on July 7, 1941 and joined the exodus of American Consuls expelled by the Germans from the occupied countries and were on their way to Lisbon to return home. The two Luxembourgers sent a glowing report to Bech following their meeting with the American diplomat who was soon to continue to work in Luxembourg's interest. Indeed, it was on Friday, August 8, 1941 that Le Gallais' counterpart was honored at the Luxembourg legation in Washington, where a reception was held for him by the Ambassador and Mrs. Le Gallais. Platt Waller's invaluable services to Luxembourgers were recognized at the highest level. The Grand Duchess, Prince Félix and Minister of State Dupong were present in Washington for the occasion. The sovereign's speech, which Le Gallais had prepared, was somewhat modified—to the displeasure of the diplomat who opened up to Bech in his report. Deputy Secretary Adolf. A. Berle Jr. also gave a speech. A transmission of the speeches of the Grand Duchess, Mr. Berle and Mr. Waller took place via NBC. In the broadcast immediately following the reception, the poet Browning, who lived opposite the house where Hugues and Pisana were married in Venice, was quoted as saying: "But a man's reach should exceed his grasp, or what's a Heaven for?" President Roosevelt was described there as the "Liberator-to-be". Platt Waller said at the end of his speech: "My task has not been hard, because I loved it. I shared the love and trust of a noble people, their sorrows were my sorrows and their hopes were mine. I come forth inestimably richer for the experience. If the people of Luxembourg are in the valley of the shadow; if the sunlight of Liberty and Independence has been taken from them. Nevertheless, Ma'am, like our blessed dead, they wait in sure and certain hope of a glorious resurrection!"[270] Later, Waller would again demonstrate his devotion to the Luxembourg Government in exile, as he provisionally agreed to assume the presidency of one of the Review Committees that examined the cases of persons wishing to leave for the United States.[271]

Six days later, Le Gallais welcomed in the most glowing terms the joint statement by President Roosevelt and Prime Minister Churchill, and in particular the following element of this attempt to lay the foundations of a new international policy known as the Atlantic Charter: "They wish to see sovereign right and self government restored to those who have been forcibly deprived of them." The document, signed by the two leaders, was at the origin of the United Nations Charter, whose drawing up Le Gallais was to witness a few years later with Bech.

On August 12, 1941, Le Gallais met with Berle to thank him for his speech at the reception four days earlier at the Luxembourg legation. In it, he touched upon the major topics of the day, such as the future association of nations and future international structures. It was great international politics for an activist who, at times, was motivated by the dissatisfaction at not being listened to in a systematic manner (especially in relation to his proposal for the speech at the reception on August 8). He did not realize, however, that his enthusiasm (like his assessment that the speech given by the American representative on August 8 could be a first outline of an American peace plan) could also do him disservice. Thus Bech, always moderate and reserved, after several exchanges in August and September on this subject, recalled the course of action he himself had adopted since he became President of the Government in 1926. Bech tried to reason with Le Gallais and to lead him in the right direction, taking into consideration a more global outlook that Le Gallais was somewhat lacking in Washington. This is what Heisbourg describes rather well, considering that Le Gallais, sometimes simplifying things, did not have Bech's detachment and more general view. Nevertheless, on September 27, Le Gallais replied to his Minister quite eloquently, revealing his approach to his profession, which was much more sensitive and complex than it seemed, especially in those troubled times:

"The contents of this document will certainly be of invaluable assistance to me in the performance of my duties, and I shall not fail to be inspired by it. I hasten to say that I share your concern for the reserve that we must impose on ourselves, but on the other hand, as the Grand Duchy's representative in the United States; I am always looking for what we could do to improve our position here. Our means of action are very limited, our colony in the United States being small and the sums of money placed at our disposal do not allow us to do much."

Having the means to match one's ambitions and the formulation of a coherent foreign policy in times of exile remained prominent issues for Le Gallais during the war years.

To Le Gallais' great displeasure, the sovereign's presence on American soil now came to an end. At the end of August 1941, on the advice of Prime Minister Pierre Dupong, the Grand Duchess and her husband flew to the British capital, only to return to the United States on May 22, 1942. This second separation was much longer than that of 1940.[272] The princely children remained in the custody of their grandmother and Guill Konsbruck.[273] Bodson and Schommer arrived in London by seaplane at the same time as the Grand Ducal couple.[274] The Crown Prince and the Head of Government remained on the American continent.

On September 12, 1941, the Hereditary Grand Duke, Dupong, Le Gallais and Konsbruck travelled to Chicago, Aurora, Dubuque, Luxembourg, Remsen, Milwaukee, St. Paul, Minneapolis and Port Washington. The tour lasted until September 22, before they all returned to Washington.[275] During this "Goodwill Tour" they were accompanied by the Luxembourg Consul in Chicago and by Fred A. Gilson,[276] the chancellor of the Consul in Chicago. André Wolff, the Grand Duchy's Information Commissioner in the United States, also took part in the trip.

From October 1941, the Le Gallais family took up residence in a small flat in the Wardman Park Hotel in Washington. The hotel is located on Connecticut Avenue at 2660 Woodley Road, NW in Washington and is not too far from Massachusetts Avenue. Even back then, the Le Gallais employed a "cook and the nigger who arranges the garden and does some work around the house" who earned $18 and $4.25 a week respectively. He apparently did not really know what to do, as Mrs. Le Gallais only brought "the maid, who is going to be our cook".[277] A week later, Le Gallais wrote to Georges Schommer: "There is nothing very new here, except that the day after tomorrow Mr. Konsbruck and his family, HRH Grand Duchess Marie-Anne will arrive a little later[278] and there will soon be a small nucleus of Luxembourgers in Washington." In the absence of the sovereign, Le Gallais must have been pleased to see those of the exiled who remained in America reunited with him.

In October 1941, Konsbruck and Schaus corresponded on the subject of the participation of Princesses Elisabeth and Marie-Adélaïde[279] in the "Women's International Exposition of Arts and Industries" at the "Women's Arts and Industries Institute" at the Grand Central Palace in New York on October 28. They were accompanied there by Mrs. Le Gallais and Guill Konsbruck.[280] Subsequently, the organization of this princely participation seems to have given rise to certain misunderstandings and clarifications between Konsbruck and Schaus[281] on the need for prior information of members of the Government and the role of the aide-de-camp in relation to the Government.

In October, Le Gallais, together with Minister Krier, who had come especially from London, attended the International Labour Conference in New York. The two representatives were received at the White House. Le Gallais wrote a laudatory report to Dupong about the work and reputation of the member of the Luxembourg Government that he could accompany. The Labour Secretary Perkins had apparently given him a particularly warm welcome.[282] On December 1, the two Luxembourgers met Mrs. Perkins, as Le Gallais reported to Dupong. The American Minister had apparently been moved by the description of the situation in Luxembourg.

In November and December 1941, Dupong and Bodson continued the debate on the sovereign's stay and the residence of the head of Government. On November 12, Le Gallais explained to the Grand Duchess his point of view, this time similar if not identical to that of Dupong. He pleaded, however, for a rapid return of the sovereign to the United States, due to American sensitivities, and to the character and personality of FDR and his much greater power than that of the King in London. "In foreign policy, I firmly believe that one must be realistic, always be wary and never let slip an opportunity to put one's cards on the table... I would suggest that a date when Madame might consider returning here, without attaching political importance to it, would be Christmas; the family reunion of three generations would be very pleasing to the American people..."[283] All wanted the sovereign to be as close as possible to their field of action and, as reported above, much ink had been spilled over this. Around the same period, Dupong and Bech expressed somewhat different visions with regard to diplomatic representation, the former fearing the cost of extending this network, the latter arguing for proper Luxembourg representation in London.

Through notes and communiqués, Le Gallais regularly reported on his activities and those of his authorities. During the war, this was, along with the action of the highest Luxembourg authorities, a means of ensuring that the American leadership did not forget Luxembourg. From time to time, Le Gallais received unflattering appraisals from certain members of the Government. This was particularly the case at the end of 1941. In his memoirs, Minister Bodson mocked the diplomat somewhat, because

"In his letters Legallais [sic] claimed to know the Japanese Prime Minister well enough to know that he would never enter the war. By the time the letter arrived, Pearl Harbor had already taken place.[284] We were amused at the gullibility of our ambassador. We never thought he was very clever. He was kind and helpful and had an excellent education. He was the son of the Liberal MP and the grandson of Legallais [sic] who came from the Isle of Guernsey [sic] to our country to build bridges. The Bissen Bridge,[285] for example, is his work. He was a great engineer. Our ambassador was of English descent [sic] and his wife belonged to a noble family of Venice called Pisani [sic], a family which had lost its fortune. At last it was a makeshift solution. Le Gallais was not a career diplomat."[286]

This unflattering assessment contrasts with the description Georges Schommer gave on his arrival in the United States in early September 1940:

"I met in my interlocutor a knowledgeable, fully informed man with a prudent and balanced judgment. Our chargé d'affaires in Washington only gives an opinion, puts forward an opinion, after having thought it over. This is a very serious quality for the delicate position he occupies. If we add to this first quality various others, among which we should mention the desired and self-effacing modesty of the man, his distinguished and simple, therefore natural manners, the smiling and spontaneous helpfulness he shows, a thorough knowledge of the customs and habits of the Anglo-Saxon world, a perfect sense of American psychology, from the mundane relations that the visit of Monseigneur [sic] the Prince of Luxembourg in 1939 amplified, a certain consideration in Washington governmental and diplomatic circles, it can be said that the Grand Duchy could not be better represented in a position which is, along with London, currently the most important and vital for our country."[287]

It remains that despite his error of judgment on Japan's entry into the war with the attack on Pearl Harbor on December 7, 1941, the following day Le Gallais attended the session during which FDR asked Congress to acknowledge the existence of war between the United States and Japan. The Luxembourg Minister reported to Bech that he had been seated for the occasion next to the Chinese ambassador who, having been received by FDR the day before, had made him understand "how unexpected in high places Japan's attack in Honolulu had been".[288] Le Gallais was therefore not the only one to have made a mistake. Two days later, after the declaration of war by Germany and Italy, FDR asked Congress to recognize the state of war. Le Gallais was once again received by the President, this time with several colleagues from the countries at war with Germany. A reception attended by representatives of Belgium, Denmark, Greece, Iceland, Norway, Poland, Czechoslovakia and Luxembourg was held at the

White House on Saturday December 27, 1941, in the presence of Churchill and his Ambassador Lord Halifax, with the intention of having these countries sign a "declaration of purposes" to supplement the Atlantic Charter of June 1941. Le Gallais added three *considerata* to the report on the speeches of Roosevelt and Churchill:

"1) That the President, in mentioning the word 'Canada' when referring to the seat of one of the Allied Governments, made a direct reference to the Grand Duchy of Luxembourg. Let us not forget that for the Government of the United States, it is the United States Minister in Ottawa who is accredited to H.R.H. Grand Duchess. 2) that as far as war operations are concerned, we will have to be part of the group that has to discuss these problems in London. 3) that the President expanded on the case of San Salvador to indicate that no country is to be considered too small to declare war on the common enemy ... I would like to add a personal impression that the President seemed to be speaking to me on several occasions last Saturday and I am convinced that the President feels himself to be the special protector of the only country that has seen its sovereign and government (in part) take refuge in this hemisphere".[289]

On the first day of 1942, the Minister signed the so-called United Nations Declaration. Thus the representatives of 26 states fighting against the Axis Powers proclaimed their support for the Atlantic Charter. This was the first time that the term "United Nations", suggested by Roosevelt, was officially used. All the participating nations promised to put all their military, economic and other resources at their disposal to defeat the Tripartite Pact and not to conclude a separate peace with the aggressors. For Le Gallais, the year 1942 began as the previous year had, at the hotel. The Grand Duchess and the Prince were in London at

27 Wilton Crescent. The princely children were at the Eldorado Farm, where they also stayed from July 1941 to June 1943, at least for the holidays.

On January 5, Le Gallais met Sumner Welles and again raised the question of the seat of the Government. Welles believed that the Government could do what it wanted and that it could sit in London or Montreal as well as in Washington.[290] Despite this American position, which could have satisfied all the Luxembourgers, the issue of headquarters continued to keep the main actors who had very different views on the subject in suspense. However, in 1943 Washington accredited a successor to Moffat, who had died on January 23, 1943. Diplomat Ray Atherton, accredited to Canada from 1943 to 1948, who succeeded him, saw his mission come to an end soon due to the transfer of the Luxembourg Government to England on October 14, 1943.[291] Dupong, who had arrived from New York to Washington, first met Vice-President Wallace and then Secretary of State Hull.[292] On January 14, 1942, at 12:15 AM, the Prime minister of Luxembourg, Pierre Dupong, and the Minister of Luxembourg, Hugues Le Gallais, were received by Roosevelt[293] before a War Council was held and the President hosted a luncheon for Churchill. The latter spent three weeks in Washington and Florida and remained in the White House as a houseguest. Dupong made it clear that the memo informing the American Government that the Luxembourg Government considered itself in a state of war with the Axis Powers was in preparation. The effect was apparently excellent, with Secretary of State Hull visibly satisfied. After much procrastination between Dupong in Washington and Bech in London with the sovereign on the appropriateness of handing the note to Moffat in Canada, as advocated by the Minister of State and Le Gallais, or through Le Gallais, the official handover took place in Washington on September 8, 1942.[294] In May

1941, Prince Félix and Le Gallais had already held talks with the Brazilian ambassador to examine the possibility of Brazil's representation of Luxembourg interests.[295] With regard to the diplomatic representation of Luxembourg interests with Vichy, let us also note the intervention, in September 1942, of Le Gallais in relation to the American availability in this regard, an intervention which became immaterial following the occupation of the entire continental French territory in November. In Washington, in addition to the President, Dupong met Cordell Hull, Platt Waller, the Apostolic Nuncio, the Russian ambassador and Le Gallais' friend, Georges Brasseur. Reports of their interviews were sent by Dupong and Le Gallais to the Grand Duchess and Bech.[296]

The birthday of the sovereign, absent from Washington, however, was nevertheless commemorated on January 23, 1942 with an official luncheon held at the George Washington Hotel in New York in the presence of Dupong, Krier and André Wolf. The Vice-President of the American Federation of Labor, Matthew Woll, an American born in Luxembourg,[297] also attended and took the floor. The Hereditary Grand Duke had celebrated his 21st birthday a few days earlier. To celebrate January 23, 1942, the Crown Prince went to Montreal for a mass and reception with the Luxembourg community and other guests. The idea of seeing the Grand Duchess travel even further across the United States and connect with as many Americans as possible from all walks of life has been developed. On January 21, Le Gallais wrote to the Prime minister informing him that "the American President expressed the desire for the Grand Duchess to travel through the United States" after reporting that a formerly isolationist congressman had declared isolationism dead and that senators and representatives should be influenced by public opinion in their state on the long and hard task to convince members of Congress of the opportunity for a new United Nations. The Grand Duchess' Goodwill Tours—to Chicago, Philadelphia and Boston in 1941 and New Orleans in 1943—would contribute to the propaganda and effort to convince Americans to participate in the collective struggle against Nazi Germany.

In April, Dupong had briefly come to Washington to meet Sumner Welles, with Cordell Hull being on leave.[298] In particular the situation of young Luxembourgers in unoccupied France was discussed. As Heisburg recounts, Dupong and Bech were sorting out the task of informing the American and English authorities. Le Gallais, in turn, had to gradually come to the realization that action in London was also essential.

Just as January 23, the Grand Duchess' birthday, May 10, the date of the German invasion, provided an opportunity for Luxembourgers to draw the Americans' attention the situation in their country, which had worsened significantly. A draft speech for Crown Prince Jean was again prepared by Guill Konsbruck and Léon Schaus for May 10, 1942. This time, the Minister in Washington wished to contribute, as evidenced by a letter from Konsbruck to Schaus from April 20: "Mr. Le Gallais immediately made his [speech] with great brio and did so well with Colonel Donovan's Services[299] that he compelled me to deliver one too, subject: Our Grand Ducal Children, Their Life, etc., intended to be broadcast on May 10." Le Gallais, with little experience of the American special services, had apparently intervened on complex terrain, to Konsbruck's obvious displeasure. Links, or at least a certain benevolence, therefore existed within the Office of the Coordination of Information, which examined and processed information coming from all American military and civilian services. In June 1942, given the scale of the wartime crisis, it was transformed into the Office of Strategic Services (OSS), the ancestor of the CIA, and its objective became to coordinate the actions of the Allied special services and to bring them material assistance. This office was headed by Major General William Joseph Donovan, a veteran of the First World War who was familiar with Europe, having been there several times on mission. He was also a personal friend of President Roosevelt.

Shortly after, on May 22, 1942, the Grand Duchess and Prince Félix, like Joseph Bech, left London to go by clipper to New York. This was the first time Minister Bech had set foot in the United States. The New York Times of May 23, 1942 wrote that they were welcomed there by two brothers-in-law of the sovereign, Prince René of Bourbon-Parma and Prince Adolf of Schwarzenberg, as well as by the chargé d'affaires Platt Waller. The sovereign said on her return to the American soil: "We are all in the same war, against the same enemy." Le Gallais recalled on this occasion that the steel production of Luxembourg, the sixth steel producer in the world before the war (2 million tonnes), had been reduced by 25%. We can note here the reflexes of a former representative of the Luxembourg steel industry. Everyone then went to Washington where, two days later, on May 24, 1942, a third meeting of the Grand Duchess, accompanied by Prince Félix, took place with President Roosevelt, who offered tea to the Luxembourg couple. Bech, who was due to stay until September 3, first went to see his family in Canada after 20 months of separation. He then returned to Washington to meet, with Le Gallais, his counterpart Hull, who apparently gave him a particularly warm welcome. The Secretary of State had praised Le Gallais, and said that he "had won the sympathies of everyone he contacted in the State Department." Two weeks later, on June 5, 1942, Bech and Le Gallais were received at the White House with, this time, the Belgian ambassador, Count Robert van der Straten-Ponthoz, who accompanied his Minister of the Colonies

De Vleeschauver.[300] The subject of the future of Germany was broached there by Roosevelt, who at that time was in favor of a split and a larger European arrangement. Le Gallais wrote a long summary (concluding that "all our hopes are placed in Uncle Roosevelt")[301] of this interview taken up by Heisbourg, as well as the one which followed with specialists in economic affairs from the State Department, Pasvolsky[302] and Feis.[303] Le Gallais, in his report, was intransigent towards the Germans whom he considered responsible, while others argued for a responsibility limited to the principal leaders.

"The undersigned considers that the plan consisting in economically and not politically detaching certain German states [sic] from the Reich, could, if carried out, create great injustices ... In our opinion all Germans deserve the same fate, to live locked up in their homes [sic] for at least thirty years until the German youth are no longer able, neither to wage war, nor to corrupt the youth of other countries with Hitler's ideas ... The undersigned is of the opinion that it is necessary to destroy in Germany, or to remove and transport elsewhere, all the metallurgical installations producing cast iron, steel and transforming these products into finished products... this radical model will prevent Germany from secretly recreating weapons of war and, incidentally, will not stop the economic life of the country ..."[304]

In opposition to this attitude, Le Gallais, in a note of June 19, 1942 about his conversation with Sumner Welles, describes himself as a tolerant man while considering that "The system of keeping the Germans in a vacuum for an indefinite time being admitted, the undersigned developed the project of having an immense 'clearing house' established at the League of Nations..." after having affirmed that he "began by exposing what his personal relations with the Germans had been since his childhood".

The report culminates with the observation that Sumner Welles once again said that this idea of Le Gallais "seemed excessively interesting to him and that it deserved in-depth examination", the Under-Secretary of State having "warmly thanked the undersigned for a very fruitful exchange of ideas, he says."

At the beginning of June, the Grand Duchess was again in New York, while Bech had remained in Washington. In front of the Foreign Affairs Committee of the American House of Representatives, the Luxembourg Minister of Foreign Affairs had declared, in a completely visionary manner and demonstrating profound European conviction, two days before this meeting: "In my view Europe is ready to unite—at least economically [...]. But there is another fact which cannot but have an influence on the co-operation of the European nations. There is Germany and Germany cannot be excluded from the European Community. Even disarmed, and if possible split up".[305] Subsequently, Bech also met with Vice-President Wallace and several Senators.

The first United Flag Day, June 14, 1942, saw the organization of ceremonies and processions in major American cities, Le Gallais attending the one in Boston along with Krier.[306] On the occasion of Flag Day 1942, President Franklin D. Roosevelt launched an international United Flag Day, celebrating solidarity among the Allies of World War II. Bernard J. Cigrand,[307] born in Bourglinster in the Grand Duchy, is considered to be at the origin of the celebration of Flag Day in the United States. The day before, a meeting of Luxembourgers who had emigrated to the United States had taken place in New York with regard to the reconstruction of the statue of *Gëlle Fra*. Le Gallais traveled to Baltimore with most of his colleagues from the Allied countries on June 17, 1942,[308] at the invitation of the United Nations Committee for Maryland where Sumner Welles delivered a speech. With Dupong in mind, Le Gallais did not forget to mention that during the dinner hosted by the Governor of Maryland he "extemporaneously" spoke of the situation in Luxembourg following the German invasion, on which the Under-Secretary of State Welles would have "congratulated him on my address by telling me: It was admirable, to the point and just what the people wanted to hear." Quoting his impromptu speech and mentioning that he was applauded, and not without his usual modesty, Le Gallais added at the end of the report: "I am giving you these details because eventually this experience may be useful."

Le Gallais had made contact with a compatriot in Brazil, Louis Ensch,[309] who had become general manager of Belgo-Mineira, a branch of Arbed, as early as 1936. The idea of a visit by the Luxembourg authorities to this immense country of Brazil was developed by Le Gallais without him taking part in it. From June 21,[310] to July 8, 1942, the Hereditary Grand Duke, who returned to the United States, and Guill Konsbruck left from New York via Miami for Rio de Janeiro, São Paulo and Belo Horizonte. The official reception of the Brazilian Government, like that of the compatriots, led by Louis Ensch, was described as touching and enthusiastic. The general manager of Belgo-Mineira, who had created and built the factories, as well as other managers and engineers had ceded, since the invasion of their native country, 25-35% of their monthly salary to a fund transmitted to the Government in exile via the Belgian embassy. A statement from the legation in Washington made this Grand Ducal visit public.[311] The Brazilian excursion was a success from all points of view and was to have major implications for the Grand Duchy and for Arbed. Based on the success of this visit, Le Gallais even considered an additional trip for the Grand Duchess, which was never to take place. He remained in contact with Ensch who needed American material subject to license and who provided generous donations, via the Belgo-Mineira and in a personal way, later, to the *Oeuvre de Secours Grande-Duchesse Charlotte*.[312] Ensch had everything to please Le Gallais. The correspondence between the two men shows a certain familiarity and connivance. Le Gallais at one point qualifies Ensch as "a friend of mine".[313]

An amusing story made the rounds of the Luxembourg community during the summer of 1942. On June 8, Schaus wrote in a letter to Guill Konsbruck in Montreal: "The other day Mr. Dupong received a letter from our excellent friend Hugues in which he addresses him as Royal Highness. As this unjustified designation infringes the prerogatives of the Court, you will want to examine the case more closely and tell us if, in your capacity as Grand Marshal ff. you want disciplinary action against the Pillar". And Konsbruck replied to Schaus on June 11, 1942: "The story of Hugues and the Highness amuses me a lot; he claims that Mr. Dupong is very 'loose' with him lately and as he probably cannot claim the same with regard to his relations with the gods (G) who make lightning and thunderstorms,[314] he will have transplanted his favors and entire admiration to his Minister of State". The two Luxembourgers were referring to a momentary error of the Minister Le Gallais, one of many clues allowing us to better understand the dynamics of relations between the Grand Ducal family, members of the Government and officials who, during these trying times, certainly experienced tensions, but also moments of conviviality and intimacy.

In July, the attention of the small Luxembourgish community focused on New York, where Grand Duchess Marie-Anne had to undergo surgery. In various letters sent from Scarsdale, New York, where the Prince and Princess of Schwarzenberg lived, the Countess of Lynar informed Mrs. Maloney about the situation of the Dowager Grand Duchess Marie-Anne and the operation she was to undergo a few days later. On July 31, 1942, the Dowager Grand Duchess Marie-Anne, Infanta of Portugal, died at the age of 81 at Doctor's Hospital East End Avenue at 78th Street in New York following "an operation undergone on June 29 for an abdominal ailment."[315] She was buried in a crypt in the Catholic chapel in the New York cemetery of Calvary in Queens run by the Archdiocese of New York. For the occasion were gathered, in addition to the eight members of the Grand Ducal family, the third daughter of the deceased, Hilda, Princess of Schwarzenberg; the Duchess Maria-Antonia of Parma, sister of the deceased and mother of Prince Félix; two brothers and a sister of the latter, the Princes René and Gaëtan of Bourbon-Parma as well as Zita, the last Empress of Austria, accompanied by two of her sons, the Archdukes Otto and Félix of Habsburg.[316] Le Gallais had been to Detroit and Buffalo with Bech between July 18 and July 24.[317] According to Heisbourg, Le Gallais was with the Grand Ducal family, along with Wolff and Staudt at the time of the funeral. FDR sent a telegram to the Grand Duchess, as did, unexplainably, the head of the Vichy regime, Marshal Pétain. Le Gallais contented himself with sending an acknowledgment of receipt to the French ambassador in Washington.[318] In any case, the disappearance of the Dowager Grand Duchess was going to have consequences on the availability, from September,[319] of 2200 Massachusetts Avenue for Le Gallais and his family. The Countess of Lynar also stayed there, at least temporarily, pending another solution for this faithful friend of the late Grand Duchess. Other representatives of the community, as well as probably the Le Gallais, were often unaware of events affecting their loved ones on the continent occupied by the Nazis. As we have seen above, the Le Gallais were somewhat lonely and now felt even more isolated in Washington. Pisana seemed to have maintained a bond with her father and sister who remained in Venice, while Hugues did not have many people to confide in in Luxembourg since his father's disappearance.

After the summer, a fourth meeting of the Grand Duchess with the President took place on August 25, 1942. The entire Grand Ducal family was invited to lunch at the White House.[320] According to Heisbourg, Le Gallais was at that time on vacation in Massachusetts, which explains the lack of report.[321] Joseph Bech left New York on September 3,[322] with a fond memory of his first trip to the United States and having, again, according to Heisbourg, become closer to Le Gallais. Less than a week later came the news of the repressions of Nazi *Gauleiter* Gustav Simon in Luxembourg following the general strike triggered by the forced enlistment of young Luxembourgers born between 1920 and 1924 into the German army. On August 31, 1942, the people of Luxembourg rose up against their young men being forced to serve in German uniform. The Luxembourgish work stoppage constituted a challenge for the Nazi occupant who believed the Grand Duchy to be part of the Reich. While in September 1940, the Government in exile had protested against the "unjust and criminal" occupation, this time everyone rose up against German repression following this act of Luxembourg bravery. A little over a week after these events, on September 8, 1942, Luxembourg's diplomatic representative in the United States stated that while the Grand Duchy had never formally declared war on the German Reich, it "considers itself in fact at war against the Axis powers".[323] Putting aside its obligations as a neutral and disarmed country, Luxembourg was considered a de facto belligerent. Neutrality had just received its deathblow[324] and the strike was to constitute a high point in national history and the Luxembourg speeches and interventions that would follow. The Government in exile, and Le Gallais in particular, not only took an early interest in the issues of post-war reorganization, but also remembered the courage and determination of those left behind. The Grand Duchess and members of her Government, in very close consultation, protested via messages against the atrocities of the Nazi occupier.[325] In a letter of September 8, 1942,[326] Le Gallais informed the Secretary of State about the measures announced in Luxembourg by *Gauleiter* Simon, forcibly enlisting young Luxembourg men who were between 22 and 26 years old. The diplomat demanded that Cordell Hull, following a note of protest from the Luxembourg Government to allied and neutral Governments, publish a personal message that Platt Waller, the former US chargé d'affaires in Luxembourg, could broadcast. Le Gallais also informed the State Department that the Grand Duchess was coming from Canada to the United States to address her oppressed people by shortwave radio. On September 12, the Secretary of State, following the example of what had notably been undertaken by the British authorities in London, published a text regretting the German measures that were followed by a strike in Luxembourg and expressing his confidence in the indomitable will of the Luxembourg people. Minister Bodson broadcast a radio message on this tragic episode in Luxembourg history from Washington on September 14, 1942. Hugues Le Gallais has left a trace of it in his archives. Shortly thereafter he himself gave a speech on September 29, 1942, at the United Nations Night War Bond Rally at the Capitol Theater in Washington and on October 8, 1942 at the Atlantic Coast Network.

On October 6, 1942, Prince Félix and the Hereditary Grand Duke Jean left New York for London[327] where they enlisted as volunteers in the British army. According to Heisbourg,[328] Le Gallais had this time not pleaded for entry into the American army, but explained in a letter to Bech that "the main argument in favor of entry into the American army lies in the very useful propaganda that would result for our country in the United States… an entry into the English army which could be of great importance for the future." For Le Gallais, if FDR's advice was sought, it should be followed. On November 29, 1942, Prince Jean enlisted into the Irish Guards.

In October 1942,[329] Le Gallais also inquired about "the possibilities of sending vitamins and condensed milk to Luxembourgish children" following a letter of Bech on the "general problem of supplying our population". Carrying only two products, vitamins and condensed milk for children would make transport to Luxembourg much easier, according to Le Gallais. He took the opportunity to explain to his Minister that the sovereign should address President Roosevelt and not Sumner Welles

"in a matter so serious for the future of the country. When her children are hungry, a mother intervenes directly at the source that can help and she does not ask a nanny to act for her. A sovereign is never more in his role of head of state than when he asks another head of state for food for the children of his country and he has no need for hesitation or scruples; these latter factors fall within the governmental framework and I admit very well that the Grand Ducal Government does not want to address such a delicate question directly. Let's also remember that the conversation between the sovereign and President Roosevelt must be special and there is no need for its subject to be known. The goal is to get the President to remind the State Department of his desire for children in occupied countries to receive vitamins and condensed milk under the auspices of the Red Cross. Let's even admit that there may be leaks; it is not what will make the Allied Nations lose the war. However, if we are successful, the positive for the future of our people will be immense".

It looks like Le Gallais wished to explain democratic principles to his Minister, as he concluded this letter in relation to another thorny question just as imbued with constitutionalism and legalism, the state of war: "Referring to the last paragraph from your letter concerning the Secretary of State's note of September 30 on the subject of the 'state of war', I see with great pleasure that in this matter at least our views are in agreement." Previously, Bech had been of the opinion that for Luxembourg the situation was different from the other occupied countries, because

"In the eyes of the Germans, our population is German just like the people of Gau Moselland. The Prince told me that Mr. Sumner Welles demands a guarantee that food, etc., will only be distributed to nationals of occupied countries. Even if it was impossible for Germany to give the Red Cross this promise, we will never be able to say that we believe it. How, moreover, can the Germans be prevented from allowing their compatriots, established in large numbers in our country since May 10, 1940, to benefit from the advantages granted to Luxembourgers? In good faith, neither Mr. Dupong, nor you—I am not speaking of the Grand Duchess, because it is not the role of the sovereign to meddle in such a delicate matter which perhaps might earn her a refusal—will not be able to approach Mr. Sumner Welles without explaining to him in detail the considerations which I have just outlined... "[330]

As for the highly unlikely feasibility of this operation, Bech was right. Le Gallais, enthusiastic, had tried to do his best while hoping to be able to play, and have the sovereign play, a role in accordance with his design.

The Grand Duchess was in New York from October 19 to 20, 1942. On October 24, 1942, she and her eldest daughter, Princess Elisabeth, as well as Guill Konsbruck[331] were in Washington for a privileged and exclusive meeting with FDR. The Grand Duchess had meetings in the American capital with the Swiss ambassador,[332] during which she and the Le Gallais met the Vice-President and Mrs. Wallace,[333] the ambassador of Brazil, Sweden, Senators Green (Democrat) and Tom Connally (Republican),[334] etc. The spontaneity of this summit meeting was described by Guill Konsbruck on October 26:

"I still have to mention a pleasant moment concerning a telephone call between the President and Madame the Grand Duchess. Last Thursday evening in New York, Princess Martha of Norway[335] telephoned from the White House to Princess Margaret[336] with whom she was invited for the coming weekend with the President. As Princess Margaret had just left, our Grand Duchess picked up the earpiece and talked with Princess Martha; the President next to her, hearing the name of 'Lotty' spoken, took the device himself and shouted: 'Hallo child. How are you… I hear that you are coming to Washington, I will expect you on Monday any time of the day…'"

then, after signing, Guill Konsbruck marked "turn" and, on the next page: "The President having insisted, Her Royal Highness will spend two days with him at the White House, alone. She will be going there at 6 o'clock this evening." This is direct testimony to the cordial relations between the Luxembourg and the United States heads of state.

The Grand Duchess was thus invited, alone, by President Roosevelt to the White House from October 26 to 28, 1942. Le Gallais made a confidential report of it, mentioned by Heisbourg without indicating the origin of his information.[337] During the tête à tête between the Grand Duchess and Roosevelt, the future of Luxembourg, about which the report states, apparently following an agreement between FDR and Churchill, that "as it is, is too small, and something better, bigger will have to be found, creating in its place a larger 'Pufferstaat'". A grandiose future therefore seemed to be sketched out by FDR for a sovereign and her country who did not ask for so much. The President invited the sovereign to keep him informed if necessary. The meeting between the two heads of State supposedly ended, according to the report by Le Gallais, with "And now let me tell you that you are a very dear child, and that, if you want something, you can always come to me; and please let me know your plans."

On November 20, 1942, the Grand Duchess was received with great honors at the International Exhibition on Women, held in New York.[338] She attended with Le Gallais and delivered a speech. On the radio to the Americans ending with "May Almighty God grant them (the great American nation) Victory".[339] From November 23 to 25, 1942, the Grand Duchess, coming from New York, accompanied by the Prime Minister Dupong, Captain Konsbruck, the Le Gallais (Hugues having gone there two days before the visit) and Miss Sinner,[340] went to Boston at the invitation of the Governor of Massachusetts, Leverett Saltonstall, who had already welcomed the Queen of the Netherlands. In October of that year, Under-Secretary of State Sumner Welles had informed Le Gallais of a desire for the Grand Duchess attend. Le Gallais kept praising him, notably in a report to Bech and using subsequent press coverage of this trip described as a success with unexpected results: "Sovereign won all hearts; very favorable press noting simplicity and genuinely democratic manners; governor and mayor in their speeches noted rights to independence small countries and expressed their admiration for the spirit of resistance of the Luxembourg population; the governor said that Luxembourg has proved to the world that the latter needs such a country regardless of size."[341] Le Gallais had also reported on the visit to Sumner Welles who, according to the Minister, had observed that "there was no more effective means of propaganda than this kind of visits and which he appreciated keenly the collaboration that our sovereign wanted to bring to this work of rapprochement and better understanding between Europe and the United States. Mr. Welles then considered aloud in which state the next visit might take place and he considered one of the southern states, either North Carolina or Louisiana." Le Gallais was not going to rest in his efforts to bring the Luxembourg authorities there and to make people talk about his still occupied and oppressed country. We saw in discussing Le Gallais' personal bond with the sovereign that even the latter might have the impression that he was going too far and had placed her in front of a *fait accompli* in relation with the visit to Louisiana. He apologized for this by assuring her that "I love Madame deeply".[342] It should be noted in passing that the only downside for Le Gallais had consisted in the fact that the Grand Duchess' aide-de-camp had not, on the occasion of this visit to Boston, worn the uniform like the American officers. In fact, Le Gallais had wanted for some time that "the only Luxembourg officer in the United States" to have a military occupation. He simply recommended appointing Guill Konsbruck as military attaché to the legation in Washington. He had imagined that Konsbruck could spend a week per month in Washington and continue to be the Grand Duchess' private secretary. A refusal was to be communicated to him by the prime minister, Prince Félix not being in favor either. Bech also got involved in this idea of Le Gallais and saw himself somewhat abused in a letter from the latter to the sovereign: "Mr. Bech's arguments do not seem very serious to me".[343] In this letter, Le Gallais, excusing himself for having tried to strengthen his legation, also stated "my only excuse is to want to play Madame's game for the best and to have wanted to play the Konsbruck card." In the end, the visit to Boston, with a dinner in the company of some 50 personalities, a reception by the mayor and a visit to the university, had been crowned with success and was one of the suggested Goodwill tours[344] to the Luxembourgers by the President himself. A photo remains of the reception of the Grand Duchess, Messrs. Dupong, Le Gallais and Konsbruck by James Conant, the President of Harvard,[345] who received the Luxembourg delegation at the university on November 24, 1942. Let us mention here the efforts of the Government to raise awareness of the complex situation of the country held by the Nazis with the publication, from 1942, of *The Luxembourg Gray Book: Luxembourg and the German Invasion, Before and After*. On almost forty pages, the Government published in London news of its activities and that of the exiles with a preface by Joseph Bech. Le Gallais forwarded a copy of it to the Secretary of State.[346]

After these memorable visits by the sovereign, alone to the White House, to New York and to Boston, Le Gallais continued of course to brief his Minister on the activities that kept him in suspense. Thus, he wrote[347] to Bech in London about a meeting organized by the owner of the Washington Post: "Mrs. Eugene Meyer is back; ten days ago she gave a reception for Thomas Mann after a talk by the latter on his books: *The Joseph Novels*. At this conference in the Bookstore of Congress, the Vice President of the United States, Mr. Wallace, introduced Thomas Mann and I saw the Vice President at Mrs. Meyer again. Without question Mr. Wallace is one to be admired as a human being. Besides, he worries me a little because I'm afraid that his overly beautiful and idealistic conceptions of a future world will suffer the same fate as President Wilson's ideas. It seems to me that each of these men was, or is, ahead of his time and it is to be hoped that President Roosevelt will do the part because his good sense of realities and of what one can reasonably ask of the people, will avoid throw the latter again into the arms of the isolationists." A fine description of the most prominent political figures of the American capital, but also an intellectual encounter thanks to a bond forged with the banker and press man Eugene Meyer,[348] who was very influential in Washington. Meeting the German writer, winner of the Nobel Prize for Literature in 1929, who had lived in the United States since 1938—first in Princeton and, from the following year, in California, must have been to the liking of the Luxembourg diplomat who did not however dwell on the personality of this illustrious man.

Towards the end of 1942, the Grand Duchess, surrounded by her children, found herself without her husband and her eldest son at Chemin St-Louis Bergerville, Sillery, in Quebec. Chemin St-Louis is the main artery leading to Quebec City and is located a short distance from Laval University, which the Hereditary Grand Duke had attended. In 1943, the official residence of the Grand Duchess was still 809 Sun Life Building in Montreal.[349]

In early 1943, Le Gallais traveled to New Orleans to finalize preparations for the visit of the Grand Duchess, who was invited this time by the Governor of the State of Louisiana. At the end of January, Le Gallais had sent to the New Orleans authorities a copy of the *Luxembourg Gray Book* and a speech by the Minister to the Foreign Affairs Committee of the State House of Representatives. Le Gallais had received in return two pages on Louisiana, Baton Rouge and New Orleans. The visit was also part of the Goodwill Tours. The Grand Duchess was accompanied by Dupong, Mrs. Bech as lady of honor, Captain Konsbruck and Hugues Le Gallais. Arriving from Washington, the Grand Duchess spent three days in Louisiana, where Prime Minister Dupong delivered a speech. Following this journey, a clarification was made by the Luxembourgers. The Minister sent a letter to the editor via the New Orleans Chamber of Commerce following an editorial (*The Duchess' Visit*) recalling that it was a Goodwill mission to contribute to the best understanding of the two peoples of the United Nations which was supposedly misinterpreted in the editorial as political propaganda. Most of the cost of the visit that would have been borne by the State Department was also contested by Le Gallais. He said the US Foreign Office only reimbursed the costs incurred by the special agent in charge of security for the Grand Duchess. On this, the newspaper replied:

"we are happy to comply with Mr. Le Gallais' request to publish his letter and appreciate the opportunity of doing so. We think there isn't much difference in this case between a 'Mission of goodwill' and 'political propaganda'. Our information that the State Department paid the bills came from someone who certainly should know. We are not at liberty to reveal his identity. He may have misunderstood our question, or we his answer. Strange things happen in this World. – Editor, the Item."

On February 3, a dinner for 500 was hosted by the community, a citizens' committee chaired by New Orleans Business Association President Stuart Seelye. After New Orleans, the Luxembourg delegation went to Baton Rouge and returned to Washington, where the Grand Duchess arrived by train at 7 AM.[350]

On Saturday February 6, 1943, the Grand Duchess met for the sixth time President Roosevelt in Washington. On the sidelines of this visit to Washington, the sovereign also agreed to meet Mr. and Mrs. Sumner Welles for a lunch at the legation, and to receive two senators "provided that these arrangements do not interfere with the schedule of her visit with the President. HRH has once again made it clear that she would like to return to New York that same evening."[351] At the Luxembourg legation, the sovereign and Dupong broached with Sumner Welles, just like Dupong would do alone three days later, the subject of the post-war situation and the country's foreign policy, but also that of the Atlantic Charter and a map described as mysterious by Heisbourg.[352] The sending, a few days later by Le Gallais to Welles of an *Ensch plan* on the economic future of the Grand Duchy, with, in particular, a reflection on Alsace-Lorraine or the post-war political regimes in Germany, gave rise to an admonition from Bech who, sending his regards anyway, wrote by encrypted cable on April 19 to his representative in Washington:

"I formally disapprove communicating the Ensch project to Welles, even as a private individual. I have already warned you by cable of February 6 to refrain from submitting to Welles memoires and maps concerning our borders by drawing your attention to the dangerous precedent of the publication of Belgian documents concerning Luxembourg during the last war. In its political and historical considerations the Ensch project is really too simplistic and contrary to our traditional policy. From an economic point of view the Ensch project is only possible with the agreement of all our neighbors. This whole question of regional organization is the subject of an in-depth study in London among interested neighbors. Disclosure of the Ensch Project to a foreign government by our diplomatic representative without our Government's review and approval risks causing harm to the country."

The one Le Gallais considered a friend, Louis Ensch, had poured out a project for a European economic confederation, the choice of means not having been in line with Bech's aims. In the end, Le Gallais also had to justify himself against Dupong by calling the communications confidential and private. Dupong begged

Le Gallais to remind Welles of this at the earliest opportunity.[353] And here is Le Gallais once again, after the call to order of September 1941, having departed from his dutiful reserve. The private action of a diplomat always affects his diplomatic quality, and Le Gallais seemed to have ignored it again. In the archives of the Grand Ducal House[354] a letter from Le Gallais to Sumner Welles was found with extracts from the report in French ("extract from a report") and in English ("remarks on the eight states economic union project; general considerations on the future status of Germany") and reports of Le Gallais' interview in April 1943 with Sumner Welles and Serge Rips[355] of the Board of Economic Warfare. The somewhat incongruous nature today of the initial idea and the discussions led by Le Gallais on this subject only suggests that the latter took the matter seriously to the point of informing the sovereign before being called to order by his superiors.

In February, the Grand Duchess went to New York where a lunch of the "Friends of Luxembourg" was held.[356] In a letter of January 31, 1942 from Le Gallais to Joseph Davies, the Luxembourg Minister had proposed that the former ambassador in Luxembourg become the first President of the "American Friends of Luxembourg" that he wished to constitute. He had suggested that the following persons be invited to become members of an honorary committee of this association intended, according to its terms, to launch a propaganda campaign in favor of Luxembourg: the former American ambassador to Belgium Theodore Warburg, the former ambassador to Italy William Philipps, former ambassadors to Belgium and Ministers to Luxembourg Dave Hennen Morris and Joseph Davies, Platt Waller, John Gade, Matthew Woll, Ben Zimmer, and William Corcoran Eustis, but also the Chancellor of the University of New York, Chase National Bank of New York Vice-President Cornelius Vanderbilt, etc. The "Friends of Luxembourg" was also mentioned in a letter from Léon Schaus to Guill Konsbruck on October 28, 1942. Mr. Woll wrote to Prime Minister Dupong relating to this project to bring together the friends of Luxembourg in the broad sense, and Schaus also spoke about a project by André Wolff on this subject. Ultimately, Dupong attended this event in early 1943 in New York City. The formal inauguration or establishment took place at the Metropolitan Club of New York over lunch on February 24, 1943, in the presence of the Grand Duchess and Dupong. President Roosevelt and John D. Rockefeller sent messages but did not come. The mayor of New York, Fiorello Enrico La Guardia, photographer Edward Steichen[357] and Herbert Hoover[358] were among the founding members. The aim was to support the restoration for the benefit of the Luxembourg people of the right to self-determination and autonomy. During the summer the Grand Duchess Relief Fund and the American Friends of Luxembourg merged under the chairmanship of Matthew Woll and the vice-presidency of Fred Gilson.[359]

Then preparations began for the Grand Duchess' trip to the West Coast, which Konsbruck described to Le Gallais:[360]

"…I allow myself to offer you a personal consideration which I think is quite important and useful. In recent months, and especially in recent times, we have seen propaganda films in New York and others also dealing with successive invasions in Europe; we see maps showing all the countries except Luxembourg; we talk about everyone except us; is it on purpose or is it an oversight; anyway, given the intensified propaganda of recent times there would be a very great opportunity to mend this oversight on the trip to Los Angeles, spending a night in Hollywood; personal contact with the masters of the cinema industry, the film strip of this visit by the Grand Duchess, intended to be shown for weeks in all American cinemas in the news, would constitute incomparable propaganda and would be worth if it was only for the trip; I think this is a unique opportunity for our cause. Holland, Belgium and Norway have special films to show on the heroic conduct of their occupied countries; we are small, have neither material nor capital, but an absolute chance right now to fill the gap."

The result will be some pretty spectacular photos of the Grand Duchess with Hollywood stars. Finally, after the sovereign's visit to Canada, the visit took place from March 24 to April 5, 1943. The Grand Duchess was accompanied by Dupong, Mrs. Bech, Le Gallais and Konsbruck. They went to the states of Washington (March 24, 1943, to Seattle and Olympia), Oregon (March 26 stopover in Portland for the launch of the *Liberty Ship George L. Baker*), and to California and Missouri for a new "Goodwill Tour".[361] The Grand Duchess' visit to San Francisco on March 28 and 29, 1943, should normally have started with a dinner hosted by San Francisco Mayor Angelo R. Rossi and the San Francisco Chamber of Commerce. Governor Earl Warren[362] also delivered a speech on this occasion at the Bohemian Club in San Francisco, referring to the last stanza of the Luxembourg national anthem: "Let Freedom's sun in glory glow, for now and evermore". And finally, the Luxembourgish visit to Los Angeles on March 31 coincided with that of Mrs. Chiang Kai-Shek. The latter was entitled to a parade and a public ceremony while the Grand Duchess was visiting a war weapons production site, the reception having taken place when the Grand Duchess was visiting the Metro-Goldwyn-Mayer. At the beginning of May, Hugues Le Gallais wrote to Governor Warren who had sent him a copy of his speech: "Your kind words will long be remembered by all of us. The friendly reception extended by the people of California to the Luxembourg party will always remain one of my most pleasant memories". He subsequently had correspondence about the photos of the Grand Duchess with Hollywood stars and their copyright. This time around, an autograph request from the Grand Duchess in photos showing her with Greer Garson, Mervyn LeRoy, Spencer Tracy and Joseph Pasternak was added to the usual correspondence between Le Gallais and local actors having contributed to the success of the visit. Finally, they visited Kansas City on April 2 and St. Louis, Missouri on April 5. From April 7-15, 1943, the Grand Duchess was in New York. There followed a letter from Konsbruck to Prince Félix in London in which he openly criticized Le Gallais, describing him as "ambassador in spe, anxious to defend his point of view" who acted contrary to the Prince's wish that this "Goodwill Tour" was to be the last. Le Gallais has also reportedly inappropriately invoked the need for the Grand Duchess to "rest", while with the presidential elections approaching it would simply be better not being overzealous. Konsbruck even qualified Le Gallais' as: "to engineer that Mr. Sumner Welles, or even the President asks Her [Grand Duchess] to do such and such a thing, how could she resist."[363] Lots of diplomatic sensibilities and courtesies that Le Gallais did not always take into account, especially when pursuing goals he deemed indispensable in the interests of his diplomatic posting. Dupong even wrote, on April 13, to Le Gallais the following clarification: "As for the question of knowing whether you must seek approval from Mr. Bech to act, you are wrong. It is the President of the Government who is competent to decide where he wants to place the seat of his activity. On the other hand, I cannot fail to point out that you have not always been so anxious to seek the advice of the Minister of Foreign Affairs before taking steps of a more dubious nature than the one we are talking about." Decidedly, the grievances were substantial, and in normal times the career of Le Gallais would have been compromised. Dupong had preceded these lines with an interesting constitutional consideration:

"The concomitant transfer [sic] of the official residence of Her Royal Highness would not pose a different problem, as long as it is not a question of fixing this residence in Washington. Because the Grand Duchess is part of the Government. She herself is concerned only with having the same immunities that She has here and that we will seek if necessary for the personnel of the Government, of which I am. You surprise me when you say that the American federal government would have jurisdiction only in Washington. However, it was not the New York state government that granted tax immunity to Mr. Theunis and his staff and our New York officials. The President should be informed as a courtesy, by letter. Yes. But that is also indicated, I believe, if the Grand Duchess is in fact resident in the United States."[364]

A whole exchange of letters with constitutional, legal, protocol and financial considerations shows that Le Gallais always knew how to argue with his superiors and embellish his actions. While trying to remain faithful to his interests, he annoyed almost all his Luxembourgish interlocutors from time to time. On May 12, 1943,[365] from London, Bech had also set the record straight and had been uncompromising:

"The negotiations which you have initiated at the request of Mr. Dupong, in view of the establishment of the Montreal office in the United States, tell me nothing of interest. I don't need to tell you that neither the Grand Duchess nor my colleagues here in London, recognize the existence of a Luxembourg government headquarters on the American continent. In agreement with the Grand Duchess, I declared officially and from the start that the sovereign's residence and the seat of government were in London. Nothing is more dangerous for a small country than to practice duplicity or better to allow misunderstandings to be created. I hardly dwell on this issue, being sure that any arguments I might repeat would not change it. So I wash my hands of it. But the day I would be opposed here in London either to an official declaration from the State Department or to information from the American newspapers that the seat of the Grand Ducal Government is in Canada or in the United States, the situation of my colleagues and mine in the Government would become critical."

In May 1943, the Grand Ducal family rented a property in Meadow Spring, Glen Cove, Long Island under the name *de Clervaux*. From a letter of May 21, 1943 from Guill Konsbruck to the owner, Jackson A. Dykman of Brooklyn, New York, it appears that the Prince had to make a lease on the property of Glen Cove and wished to avoid publicity and, therefore, appearing by name on the contract, which was drawn up in Guill Konsbruck's name instead, and not to have his telephone number made public. On May 13, Prime Minister Dupong wrote from Montreal to Konsbruck who was at the "farm" to clarify the views regarding the establishment of the Grand Ducal family on Long Island:

"Under these conditions I believe that you have to take some additional precautionary measures. In my opinion, the transfer of the residence of the Grand Duchess should be presented as follows: The Grand Duchess wants her children to attend American schools during the following school year. Under these conditions for reasons of personal convenience she would like to transfer her household, under the benefit of a 'visitor's visa', to the United States in order to be closer to her children. However, she retains her official residence in Montreal, Canada. ... On the other hand, it would be useful if the Grand Duchess personally informed the President of her intentions."

Hugues Le Gallais asked the Minister of State on May 12 "for precise instructions on the content of the steps to be taken at the State Department" and affirmed that "Sumner Welles seems to fear discussions of a fiscal nature with the State of New York". And to recommend that the Grand Duchess visit Roosevelt to explain the situation to him, because "in all my communications concerning President Roosevelt, I have always insisted on the susceptible side of his character, and I cannot recommend that he be in this case faced with a *fait accompli*." He continued with a footnote, saying that "it was not smart that HRH only spent one day in Washington on the return from her trip to Louisiana (in February)". In the end, the President was informed by letter but did not apparently give a response, which the Luxembourgers were awaiting to get everything under way. On June 2, still in connection with this planned change of residence, Guill Konsbruck sent to the Prime minister "to complete the aspects and studies on the tax problem of HRH, the response of Mr. Dykman to my letter of May 27 and a detailed study on the same problem by Mr. Harf,[366] who specializes in tax matters... Our whole situation is therefore based on obtaining a visitor's visa for one year while remaining a resident of Canada... May I beg you not to speak to Mr. Le Gallais about this note yet, as the Prince, for one reason or another, is very touchy about changing the names of these accounts." It was another sign that, from time to time, neither trust nor transparency reigned among the main Luxembourg exiles.

On May 22, 1943, the Grand Duchess returned from the United States to Canada, having encountered difficulties on the border at Niagara Falls.[367] She was still there on June 11, 1943 with Konsbruck who prepared the move, and according to a letter of May 21 to Mrs. Maloney who, as was often the case, seems to have been alone at the embassy, taking care of everything, "to go down with the Grand Ducal family who will spend the holidays on the farm". On June 18, 1943, the Grand Duchess and five princely children left Quebec for the United States. This new move, described by Konsbruck to Le Gallais in his letter of May 8, 1943, also involved Eugène and Joséphine Niclou, Alice Sinner, Justine Reinard and Lucie Hansen. Konsbruck concluded: "Confused by so many disturbances and the interminable index of things to be settled, I present to you, dear Mr. Le Gallais, all my apologies, and only express my ardent wishes that, for your salvation and mine, this move may be the very last." There was thus much coming and going to keep the minister plenipotentiary in suspense.

On July 17, 1943, the embassy in Washington announced that the Hereditary Grand Duke and Guill Konsbruck had traveled from Washington by train to Miami, then to Rio de Janeiro for three days before continuing the visit for two days in São Paulo and eight days in Sabará, a town near the capital of the state of Minas Gerais. Louis Ensch, Managing Director of Belgo-Mineira in Brazil, was part of the trip. As the previous time, Hugues Le Gallais was not in the game. A month earlier, however, the embassy had to intervene: "Mr. Ensch's change of plans is painful to say the least ... we had relied so strongly on Mr. Ensch to carry out our placements under his watch, eventually under his supervision." Le Gallais had informed his authorities on June 12 that Sumner Welles had been asked to issue a visa to Mr. Ensch. The latter had shown an ardent patriotism and proved to be a strategic asset not only for Arbed, but also, in the absence of a diplomatic representation in South America, for contacts with the Brazilian authorities.

Another way for Le Gallais to draw attention to his country was through stamp collecting. The American Postal Service issued a five-cent stamp with the Luxembourg flag. On August 10, 1943, Le Gallais was received at the White House by President Roosevelt to commemorate this event. A photo shows the President holding a sheet of Luxembourg stamps in the presence of Ambassador Le Gallais and Assistant Postmaster-General Roy North. The Luxembourg Minister read a message sent by the Grand Duchess to her "Dear and Great Friend" and welcoming with "deep appreciation" this event in these times of Luxembourgish resistance against the Nazi oppressors. On the same day, Andrew Wolff, Information Commissioner of the Grand Duchy in New York, delivered a commemorative talk in connection with the commemorative stamp in Washington together with representatives from Poland, Czechoslovakia and Norway. Wolff retraced the history of Luxembourg and of its philately in particular, asserting that the Luxembourg leaders, Dupong and Bech, upon taking office, recognized the value of international philatelic interest. In January 1945 and May 1947, the State Department was informed of the intention of the Luxembourg authorities to issue postage stamps in honor of the United States, the United Kingdom and Russia, respectively, and two years later, of General Patton.[368] For the latter project, Le Gallais had approached the War Department and Patton's widow.

On September 22, 1943, the Grand Duchess was received by President Roosevelt for lunch for a seventh time, this time in Hyde Park.[369] On September 28, 1943, it was Minister Bech's turn (who had also seen Cordell Hull three days earlier) and Hugues Le Gallais to be received, separately, by Roosevelt. In this last interview, the issue was raised of the transfer of the post of Minister of the United States accredited to the sovereign in Ottawa to London. The Lend-Lease operations were also discussed, as was the bond of friendship that bound Roosevelt and the Grand Duchess.[370] After these meetings, what

US President Franklin D. Roosevelt holding a sheet of Luxembourgish stamps in the presence of Ambassador Le Gallais and US Assistant Postmaster-General Roy North, August 10, 1943.

had earlier been raised by the sovereign was confirmed at the political level, more or less regularly. This gave Hugues Le Gallais several opportunities to approach FDR, considered to be the supreme representative of the country which was most capable to contribute to the liberation of Luxembourg. Since the turn of World War II in favor of the Allied forces after the Battle of Stalingrad, the first sketches of a new order began to materialize. It was not until October 21, 1943 that Le Gallais communicated to the Treasury Department the financial agreement of the three Benelux countries, something which was to have favorable consequences for the post-war period and set out the principles of free economic relations to serve as a basis for closer economic cooperation after the conflict. It affirmed, announcing with several decades in advance the European monetary union: "The Netherlands Government on the one hand and the Belgian and Luxembourg Governments on the other have signed today a financial agreement which they believe will have a favorable influence on the development of trade in the post war period... Appreciating the importance of monetary stabilization, both parties have agreed upon a stable exchange rate between their respective currencies, which is identical to the rate prevailing before the war." On November 1, 1943, Le Gallais welcomed via communiqué the conclusion of the Moscow Pact and the inclusion in it of the unconditional surrender of all Axis Powers. The Grand Duchess now left American soil for the second time. For Le Gallais this meant the end of his direct contacts with his sovereign, whom he had very often been able to meet and advise in America without going through intermediaries. The Grand Duchess was not going to return to the United States until her state visit of 1963.

LE GALLAIS AFTER THE GRAND DUCHESS' DEPARTURE FOR LONDON

On October 13, 1943, the Grand Duchess, accompanied by Minister of Foreign Affairs Joseph Bech, left for London. After a year of separation, she was to meet her husband there. The following day the final transfer of Government to the British capital took place. A week after the sovereign, Princesses Elisabeth and Marie-Adélaïde as well as Mrs. Bech and her daughter also went to London. After the departure of their two older sisters for London, Princesses Marie-Gabrielle and Alix were sent to Mary Mount School in New York where they found their brother Charles who was a pupil with the Jesuits.[371] The Prince and the Princesses, who remained in the United States, were under the custody of Konsbruck and indirectly of Le Gallais. Pierre Elvinger, who was to be appointed, in May 1944, to the post of commercial adviser to the legation in Washington with residence in New York,[372] was to remain one of the last Luxembourg officials in Canada where Mrs. Dupong and her daughter Jetty and Mrs. Schommer still remained. Now Le Gallais was truly alone in Washington. His privileged bond with Sumner Welles was not to continue in the same way with Edward Stettinius who had succeeded Welles at the end of September. He was to be promoted Secretary of State following the departure of Hull in 1944.

At the beginning of December 1943, Mrs. Le Gallais took part in the Luxembourg stand at the Christmas bazaar at the United War Relief Center.[373] This led to correspondence from her husband with the President of the Government about the purchase of earthenware from Septfontaines and the reimbursement of certain related expenses. The Minister's entire family was active in promoting the interests of Luxembourg. So, Norbert was invited to sing on NBC. Photos, one of the 10-year-old child alone, and one with a picture of the Grand Duchess in his hands, bear witness to the recording. Like other children of diplomats, Berty took part in a program called "Kids interview children from embassy and legation" which described how these children "learn how to do their part for United Nations War Effort".[374] The only child of the Le Gallais' seems to have spent a quiet childhood during the war. Isolated, he had a Cocker Spaniel called Nicky to keep him company.

For the Le Gallais couple, the celebrations marking the end of 1943 took place in Washington without the Grand Ducal couple, now based in London. On December 28, 1943, Prime Minister Dupong left Montreal for London to return to the United States for "the Monetary Conference in March or April 1944".[375] It was on February 17, 1944 that Léon Schaus left Montreal for London aboard a bomber, followed, on March 20, 1944, by the former Minister of Justice René Blum and Dr Cerf. Almost all the main officials had now left North America. Dupong wrote at the start of 1944 to Le Gallais (who had already intervened and was going to continue doing so in other cases),[376] asking him to inquire about three Luxembourg prisoners of war in American hands who were "not to be recommended". While in his letter he considered it essential to be careful about these prisoners, in general he writes that: "The issue of prisoners of war in the American prison camps still concerns me. The British seem to cooperate more with our Government in this matter than the Americans." Decidedly, a lot of mistrust reigned within the exiled community. During 1944 and also the following year, Hugues Le Gallais was far removed from the measures that were going to be undertaken in Luxembourg in relation to the refugees, the forcefully enlisted, the non-compliant, the resistance fighters or the Jewish community.

On Sunday, January 23, 1944, the traditional reception took place at 2200 Massachusetts Avenue which all Washington attended. That of the previous year had been canceled in order to cooperate with the policy of the war effort; that of the following year was also to be canceled because of the Battle of the Bulge. This time, in attendance were the Chief Justice of the Supreme Court of the United States, the representative of the American Government appointed to the Grand Duchess in London attached to the Eisenhower staff, the delegate of the French Committee of the National Liberation, and Mrs. Hoppenot.[377] There was also Archduke Otto of Habsburg, while two Princesses and Prince Charles were in New York where celebrations had also been organized, as was the case in Montreal.[378]

As planned, Prime Minister Dupong left London on March 25, 1944 to return to New York. In fact, Dupong had returned to Canada to liquidate the office in Montreal and come to Washington from April 10 to 15. The Minister of State had met Louis Ensch there again who had arrived from Brazil in early March.[379] In the American capital, Dupong met various persons during three dinners organized by Le Gallais. He had various interviews with, among others, Secretary of State Hull, his deputy Berle, and representatives of the Ministry of Finance. Mainly economic and financial questions were discussed this time. Dupong finally left for London on May 5, writing to his minister plenipotentiary: "It remains for me to say goodbye to you. I have full confidence that you will best safeguard our interests in this hemisphere. The position you have acquired and the tact and knowledge you have shown in your business are the guarantees thereof. Thank you once again for all the service you have consistently rendered to me personally over the past four years and the dedicated collaboration you have extended to me whenever the opportunity arose".[380] A fine testimony of gratitude contrasting somewhat with the recent skirmishes with Bech who, in January of the same year, had further annotated a report by Le Gallais on his first interview with Stettinius and his appreciation of the change at the State Department, as an "untimely step which I disapprove of".[381] In March 1944, Dupong had already congratulated Le Gallais for an "adequate and timely development" following an American leftist publication to which a Catholic weekly replied by quoting Le Gallais who had defended the clergy of his country,[382] In June of this year, and while the Government had recognized the provisional Government of the French Republic, Le Gallais had expressed to Bech the dissatisfaction of the American authorities, which the latter acknowledged with: "In any case, we don't have to apologize for it and you will take all the care, I am sure, not to offend French feelings." Relations between the Minister in Washington and his President of the Government and his Minister of Foreign Affairs were, therefore, always complex and sometimes divergent.

Le Gallais had recorded a broadcast in Luxembourgish and English on the BBC on May 18, 1944 and broadcast on May 21 by the BBC in Luxembourg via London, in a way out of the loop and away from the main actors in exile. He also sporadically informed of developments relating to the exiles now regrouped in London at 27 Wilton Crescent. The main theater of action of the exiles was no longer in America. Thus, the SHAEF, the Military Mission to the Supreme Headquarters Allied Expeditionary Force, now had Prince Félix as its chief, while Guill Konsbruck had become its deputy chief and executive officer.[383] A bit in the same vein and accentuated by the fact that the Allies now acted from London, Guill Konsbruck wrote to Le Gallais on June 26, 1944: "Here everything works; we work like convicts, but it's okay. Soon we will be home", and, on August 1: "My work here is inexhaustible and extremely varied, but allows me to be in touch day and night with my great American friends. Luckily, I've been to Charlottesville (U.S. Army School of Military Government at the University of Virginia), you have no idea—or rather you had—how that simplifies things. I think that we will have with us in Luxembourg an allied Civil Affairs Group, the leader of which will be American and an excellent friend. So despite the pain and worry, it works, and especially if one thinks that in 2 to 3 weeks we will be home."[384]

Before the liberation of the country, the signing of the American-Luxembourg agreement concerning "civil affairs" in the presence of Prince Félix, Pierre Dupong, Alphonse Als and Guill Konsbruck, was announced for July 28, 1944 in London. Another, more operational, piece of news delighted Le Gallais who wrote on August 3 in a letter to Konsbruck: "I learned with great pleasure that HRH the Prince and you were now attached to the General Headquarters of the invading army…"[385]

Le Gallais said that he was right to be optimistic when he said earlier that "soon we will be back". Prince Félix, who had been Honorary Colonel of the Luxembourg Armed Force before the war, joined the combat units after the landing and accompanied them in their progress on the continent. Via Paris and Verdun, he reached Luxembourg, where he arrived on September 10, joined by Crown Prince Jean alongside Brigadier General Oliver, whose 5th armored division had just liberated the capital.[386]

On September 5, the signing of the Benelux treaty took place in London. A month later, on October 11, 1944, Guill Konsbruck, head of the Luxembourg military mission just appointed by the Government Commissioner for Supply and Economic Affairs of the Grand Duchy, sent Washington his first impressions of Luxembourg:

"From the beautiful capital, I hasten to send you and Mrs. Le Gallais all my most cordial memories. The city has hardly changed; people have changed a bit, given that for the moment they are quite divided, accusing each other of collaboration or of greater or lesser passivity towards the *boche*; but all that will pass… The supplies are good. The general situation is improving more and more … The position of the Government seems quite good; it is difficult to determine it before our deported families have returned. The position of the Grand Ducal Family, including Mgr. [Monseigneur] is fantastic."

And to continue by affirming that young Luxembourgers wished to go to the United States to study there and to ask Hugues Le Gallais to find out, in particular from the Rockefeller Foundation, about possible opportunities: "Love for this great country is all that is most pure and perfect, like my own… that says it all." This effort carried out in Washington was going to give birth to the exchange of young Luxembourgers in the program of the International Youth Farm Exchange. The young women and men often visited Massachusetts Avenue before continuing their American journey which would lead them during several months to live with American families active in the agricultural sector. Three weeks after Konsbruck, it was the turn of Minister Bech to inform Hugues Le Gallais by ciphered telegram of October 31 of his impression of things in Luxembourg, indicating that the

"Government was warmly received (in) Luxembourg. Our situation is undisputed, no one asks for a meeting of the Chamber, which, moreover, is no longer in number and of which half a dozen members from all parties have engaged in uncivil behavior. The atmosphere is not favorable for politics. … Material needs and purification dominate across the board. … The food situation much better than in Belgium France and is ensured for at least 3 months. Coal is our grave concern. … but we have been promised by the Americans and Belgians to receive it despite the even more precarious coal situation in Belgium … The rest of the country has hardly suffered. We believe that the front remains stabilized for weeks to come, the Germans occupying the heights on their side of the valley and the Americans on ours. Our police and armed force are rebuilding themselves with difficulty. The various resistance movements have come together in a union which collaborates with the Government as in France and Belgium in the form of a militia which is only partly armed. There is a tendency towards apolitical union and against political parties, refusing to admit into its midst the communist party, which is very active on the propaganda front. The Union[387] carries out sweeps and arrests in each village without always avoiding arbitrariness and conflict with the Prosecutor's Office. 2,500 persons are locked up according to Bodson, the same fate awaits 3,000 to 5,000. … The atmosphere of unease and suspicion in the country created by the unthinking mass membership of the population and above all almost all civil servants in the VDB[388] under almost irresistible German pressure. There is much cowardice but also many magnificent acts of courage and solidarity between peasants and workers. The situation of the Grand Duchess whose portrait with the Prince and children is in each window store is incomparable. The military authorities, the Government and the population agree that the Grand Duchess will not return until the country is fully liberated; the front is still so close. … Thank you for your interesting letters and reports. Regards. Bech".[389]

Thus, Le Gallais was informed by different sources and learned slowly and always with a certain delay the news about the country and about his old acquaintances. In a letter Bech sent to André Wolff (who was having difficulties with Elvinger),[390] he writes: "you will want to collaborate with Le Gallais to organize the return of our refugees. Anyone who is able to afford their repatriation costs, except Government employees and their families, will pay their return costs. For the officials, to the contrary, you and your family, Heuertz and his wife, Mrs. Blum, Mrs. Schommer, the Bodson family, the Government will advance the repatriation costs." Some details still remained to be settled, but the bulk of the business that had kept Le Gallais in suspense for four years was coming to an end.

Remaining isolated in Washington, while the war in Luxembourg was coming to an end was a turning point in the life of Hugues Le Gallais, and a photo shows him hoisting the flag on the legation building. The liberation of the Grand Duchy, and in particular of its capital, on September 10, was the occasion for an article in the *Evening Standard* published in London on Tuesday September 12, 1944. Under the title "Luxembourg Legation is First to Celebrate Recovery of Countries", it was said that Luxembourg would be the first to see the return of its representatives approved by the State Department, France having expressed its dissatisfaction with the absence of such an approval. It was also mentioned that the representatives of Romania and Bulgaria were in doubt about their status and that the Swedish legation assuming the affairs of the Romanian Government and Switzerland assuming those of Bulgaria had not been informed of any change by the State Department. The Belgian ambassador had a Te Deum celebrated on the occasion of the liberation of Brussels, which his Luxembourg counterpart did not consider appropriate. The chief of protocol shared his point of view "given that there were few people at this [Belgian] ceremony and that I did not consider appropriate to disturb important persons at this time." The Grand Duchess had sent a message via Le Gallais to FDR which had, on Monday September 11, broadcast a text following the liberation of Luxembourg. The text ended with the words "the American people salute the brave people of Luxembourg." Secretary of State Hull had also made a declaration.[391] Le Gallais had accomplished his mission among the exiles and other challenges now awaited him.

At the end of 1944, Le Gallais and Konsbruck once again exchanged views about the future of their country. On December 22, Le Gallais wrote to the head of the Luxembourg military mission Konsbruck, who had explained to him the activities of his service and the idea of organizing a specific office, while specifying that he "knows from what point of view you are interested in our national economy". Le Gallais informed Konsbruck that he had explained to Dupong about ten days earlier (declaring himself personally in favor of the cartels):[392]

"that the United States would not participate in a steel cartel and that after the period of reconstruction we would find ourselves facing American competition in world markets. Consequently, it would be wise for our metallurgical industry to prepare now for the manufacture of specialties. In order to be able to monitor whether Luxembourg metallurgical factories follow these recommendations, I suggested to Mr. Dupont to appoint to Arbed, Hadir, and Rodange, a technical expert per group, who should keep the Government informed of the modernization plans prepared and the three should make arrangements to develop a comprehensive plan. Your grand plan to take up the idea of the Ourtal-Sperre seems excellent to me, and I hope the Government will adopt it. I do not feel that I can speak about it here until the Government has given me instructions to do so."

Le Gallais based his ideas on a grandiose vision for his country while showing himself nevertheless also concerned at a moment which was tragic for certain regions of Luxembourg. At the end of the year, the North of the country once again fell into the hands of the Germans and was reoccupied. It was the Battle of the Bulge.

1945 was going to be the year of reconstruction with a new role for the Minister in the United States, who was going to be active in the search for means to supply his country, which was hard hit between mid-December and mid-January by the return of German troops. In a press release, the Le Gallais couple announced with a certain regret, but nevertheless with the contingency of the circumstance that the traditional reception in honor of the birthday of the Grand Duchess on January 23, 1945 was not going to take place this year, unlike the previous year, in order to cooperate with Government policy promoting the war effort. Dupong had asked Le Gallais as soon as he moved to Massachusetts Avenue that receptions and other social activities take place exclusively there to avoid additional expenses. In general, during the war and also afterwards, the Le Gallais' lifestyle was different from that of the members of the Government. The latter, with the possible exception of Bech, born into a wealthy family, were not familiar with the splendors to which the scion of the Le Gallais-Metz family had always been accustomed. It was especially Dupong who had tried to keep it in check. From 1945 on, Le Gallais was once again able to give free rein to his sense of hospitality and social life.

The spring of 1945 was marked by two almost concomitant events: the death of the American President and the return to the country of the Grand Duchess. President Franklin Delano Roosevelt, aged 63, died on April 12 of a brain hemorrhage in his cottage in Warm Springs, Georgia. As soon as the news of his death was announced, messages of sympathy poured in from neutral countries and from allies of the United States, including those from the Luxembourg authorities that Le Gallais immediately transmitted. Roosevelt's remains were brought back by train to Washington, where his funeral took place the day before the Grand Duchess returned home. The late President was buried on April 15 in Hyde Park, New York. These days of mourning were marked by great emotion in the country and abroad. His state of health had been kept secret by those around him and by the doctors at the White House. Roosevelt had been in office for over twelve years, a tenure unmatched by any American head of state. It was Vice-President Harry S. Truman, sworn in on the same day, who became America's 33rd President. Roosevelt's disappearance was to be commemorated every year with a ceremony of remembrance and meditation at the grave of the American President who had done so much for the liberation of Luxembourg. For the first anniversary, April 12, 1946, Le Gallais attended the dedication at the "Hyde Park Estate and Grave", now a national memorial, in the presence of Eleanor Roosevelt, President Truman and Fala, FDR's dog. Le Gallais made a special trip to Hyde Park for the occasion. Franklin Delano Roosevelt was born in 1882 in this family estate in Springwood, which became the Franklin D. Roosevelt National Historic Site upon his death.

Two days after FDR's death, on Saturday April 14, the moment long awaited by the entire Luxembourg population, the return of Grand Duchess Charlotte from exile, finally arrived. She arrived aboard a C47 Dakota plane which belonged to General Eisenhower and who was accompanied by five US Air Force fighter jets. The sovereign and Prince Félix, accompanied by Prince Jean and Princess Alix, joined by Guill Konsbruck, were greeted by Prime Minister Dupong, the Ministers and authorities of the capital.[393] A few days later,[394] Princesses Elisabeth, Marie-Adélaïde, Marie-Gabrielle and Prince Charles returned to Luxembourg. They had left London on April 12 in a Red Cross ambulance convoy with Mrs. André Clasen, Mrs. Als and Mrs. Léon Clasen.

THE END OF THE WAR AND BEGINNING OF DIPLOMATIC LIFE AS MAIN LUXEMBOURG REPRESENTATIVE IN THE UNITED STATES

On May 8, 1945, World War II finally ended in Europe after the unconditional surrender of Nazi Germany, signed the day before in Reims, France. This global conflict, even more genocidal and atrocious than the previous one, made a deep gouge in the European consciousness and bled the entire European continent. The planetary conflagration had killed more than 50 million people, mostly civilians, among them 20 million Soviets, 7million Germans, 600,000 French, 400,000 Americans and as many British. The devastation in Luxembourg was considerable, with 5,700 deaths, corresponding to almost 2 percent of the population which, at the time, numbered less than 300,000 inhabitants. In addition to loss of life, there was extensive material damage, especially in the North of the country after the Battle of the Bulge.

The liberation of the country by the American army and the return to peaceful life in Europe, however, also meant the gradual and this time permanent departure of the persons to which Le Gallais had been attached. In the United States, Honorary Consuls and a Luxembourg community scattered throughout the Midwest remained. The small group of Americans of Luxembourgish descent no longer seems to have played the same role as in previous years when they had to be mobilized for the war effort. Le Gallais hardly spoke of them in his correspondence, likely leaving it to the Honorary Consul in Chicago to deal with them. Only a few of the Royal Highnesses whom he had served and frequented with relish during the war remained close to Le Gallais. Prince Félix's mother, the Duchess of Parma, and her daughter, Princess Isabelle of Bourbon-Parma, lived after the war at 239 Chemin de St-Louis,

Villa St-Joseph in Sillery, Quebec. A trip to Quebec by Prince Félix, accompanied by his two eldest daughters and his son Prince Charles, had to be postponed due to health reasons having to do with the Prince. After a two-week stay in Quebec, an unofficial visit to Washington[395] by members of the Grand Ducal family around March 20, 1948 should have enabled the Prince to see Le Gallais unofficially, as well as old friends and other persons. Le Gallais rejoiced and had offered two dinners and accommodation at his residence. Prince Félix's mother and sister returned to Europe a few years later and the Duchess passed away at Colmar-Berg Castle in 1959. The other sister of the Prince Consort, the former Empress Zita, resided in Tuxedo around New York before returning to Europe as well.

We have seen that the remains of the Dowager Grand Duchess Marie-Anne had been provisionally buried in New York in the crypt of the Catholic chapel of the Calvary Cemetery, until the end of the war made it possible to transfer her ashes to Luxembourg. This transfer was planned for October 22, 1947, when the remains of Grand Duchess Marie-Adélaïde, who died in 1924, were also to be repatriated from Hohenburg castle. In the presence of Hugues Le Gallais, on October 4, 1947 at 9 am, the coffin containing the remains of Grand Duchess Marie-Anne was removed from the crypt and placed in the nave of the chapel of the Calvary Cemetery, where Monsignor G. Erhardt, director of the cemetery, said a Low Mass attended by Empress Zita, accompanied by her daughter Archduchess Isabelle of Bourbon-Parma, Countess of Lynar, lady of honor of Grand Duchess Marie-Anne, Joseph Bech, Minister of Foreign Affairs, Hugues Le Gallais, Minister of Luxembourg in Washington, the Government advisor and Mrs. Elvinger, Bernard Zimmer, member of the Friends of Luxembourg, and his wife, Cornélius Staudt, Honorary Vice-Consul of the Grand Duchy in New York, and finally the Information Commissioner in New York and Mrs. André Wolff. At the end of this ceremony, the coffin was transported in a hearse on board the Belgian SS *Stavelot*. Consul Staudt accompanied the convoy. On Monday October 6 at 9 am, the *Stavelot* set sail for Antwerp, where it entered the port on October 14, carrying the Luxembourg flag at half mast. The remains were buried in the crypt of the cathedral with that of Grand Duchess Marie-Adélaïde.[396]

For Pisana's family who remained in Italy, World War II had started without the country being involved from the start. Mussolini had evaluated the offers on both sides. In June 1934, Count Giuseppe Volpi hosted the first meeting between Mussolini and Hitler in Venice. Rome was liberated on June 5, 1944. On April 28 and 29, 1945, the Allies entered Venice, which had been occupied by the Germans since 1943. Mussolini was shot on April 28. The Italian family, the Velluti and the Nani Mocenigo, were in good health and Pisana was looking forward to seeing them again soon. In Luxembourg, cousin and colleague Auguste Collart and his family had been deported to Leubus in Silesia and had suffered the fate of many Luxembourgers deported and imprisoned. Hugues' cousin described this stage in a book called *Aus der shroer Zeit*. The attitude of Hugue's sister, Rozel Reverchon-Le Gallais, has been harshly judged. Hugues Le Gallais asked Guill Konsbruck on October 26, 1946, for news of several acquaintances and relatives. He made a list of familiar names that his interlocutor reviewed in subsequent correspondence. After this terrible conflict, the fate of his family was close to the heart of the diplomat in Washington. From now on and despite the divisions and separations, it was necessary to renew links that were sometimes suspended during all these years.

Legislative elections had taken place in Luxembourg on October 21, 1945. They had been preceded two weeks earlier by municipal elections. The result belied those who in previous months had fiercely criticized the government: the men in exile—Dupong, Bech, Krier and Bodson—were elected first or second on their list. The Christian Social Party held on to power without any problem, the Socialist Party being defeated by a strong push from the Communist Party and the Patriotic Democratic Group. The old coalition, however, had a comfortable majority in the new parliament. Nonetheless, Dupong decided to take into account the broad sense of national solidarity that prevailed among the population after the ordeal of the war and attempted to form a Government of National Union in which all parties were represented. The Government of National Union remained in power for sixteen months and ended, as elsewhere in France and Belgium at the same time and for similar reasons, following the departure of the Socialists and the Communists.

At the end of December 1945, Le Gallais led to the altar Elisabeth Dorothy Le Gallais, daughter of the couple Norman Le Gallais of Victoria in British Columbia, who married in Washington Cathedral John Denis Walsh, son of Mrs. Ada Walsh of London. The Washington Post on December 23 described the ceremony, including details of the bridesmaids and church decoration. We also learn that the bride was educated in Canada, lived for two years in England, and worked for the war effort in the US capital for three years leading up to her marriage. The exact family link could not be established between Hugues and this branch of his family with the same name, but Le Gallais must have been flattered to have such a prominent role to play.

In Luxembourg, it is especially the death of Anne-Marie de Gargan, which took place on January 16, 1946 at the Villa Vauban that should have brought back many memories of a difficult childhood and youth, the relationship with this stepmother having been trying for Hugues, but also for his sisters.

On Wednesday June 5, 1946, Le Gallais was received at his request by President Truman for about fifteen minutes (as specified in the published presidential timetable), since he was to return to the Grand Duchy the next day. A day earlier, Le Gallais also had a conversation at the State Department with the Secretary of State before starting his trip to Luxembourg.[397] Finally the possibility of reconnecting with Luxembourg had arrived. In March 1945 Le Gallais had remained in Washington to attend to a pending matter.

It was the end of an era and the opportunity for a new start for Pisana and Hugues in Washington. Le Gallais' role had become somewhat that of a classic diplomat, namely to be an expert on the country to which he was accredited and to explain the trends encountered there, even though the members of the Government in exile all had their own experiences of American reality. At the same time, it was (and still is) about representing and explaining one's own country. This must have been difficult, as Le Gallais had spent more than a decade in Asia before being separated from his homeland during the last five years of the war which had profoundly altered everything he had found upon his return from Asia only three years prior to his departure for Washington. Hugues would travel a lot to attend various international conferences. The United Nations having been set up, the desire to launch economic cooperation in Europe to prevent a new war would lead to the formation of European Communities organized around similar values, but also interests. Membership in international organizations has been a way for the Grand Duchy to make its voice heard and to channel the ambitions of its major neighbors towards a peace project. With its partners, Luxembourg was nested in a network granting it a status it had never enjoyed before. Le Gallais was at all the meetings laying at the origin of this new international cooperation, except those leading to the establishment of the European Communities in the 1950s. ✿

IV.

Diplomatic activities after the war and retirement in Venice

IMPORTANT INTERNATIONAL MEETINGS
IN THE 1940S AND 1950S

Armed with instructions from the Minister of Foreign Affairs and with more or less detailed directives as to the position to adopt on each occasion, Minister Plenipotentiary Le Gallais took part in various international meetings. Sometimes he was joined along the way by Minister Bech himself. During these meetings, the foundations of the international community, following on the one that failed in the 1930s, were discussed and adopted after lengthy negotiations. On many occasions the Washington Minister was assisted by an official from the capital. Most of the time he was in close contact with other diplomats and sent cables and requests for instructions to his capital. Important conferences have taken place at these times of renewal, when the representative of one of the smaller countries had to defend its interests and see far ahead. The positions and texts adopted in those days sometimes still have implications today. Called on to take the pulse of the international community, Le Gallais embarked on a journey that would take him to the most diverse places on the American continent. On behalf of his Government, he took part in several international conferences in America.

As we have seen, he had already participated with Minister Krier in the International Labor Conference in New York which lasted from October 27 to November 6, 1941.[398] In June and July 1942, Le Gallais had intervened on this subject in Washington, alone and with Bech, meeting Sumner Welles, the Assistant Secretary of State for Economic affairs Acheson, the policy adviser to Hull, Dunn. Later, Le Gallais was still going to work on this question, and even the President would be informed by Bech, but without success, "the absence of a loan-lease agreement will in no way prevent the Luxembourg Government from participating in time and entirely in the major multilateral economic and financial discussions".[399] Lend-lease was an arms program put in place by the United States during World War II to provide friendly countries with war materials without directly intervening in the conflict. Before the United States entered the war, this effectively put an end to the laws of the 1930s about American neutrality. With Belgium, an agreement was reached on September 24, 1946 on the basis of a provisional agreement of 1945 with a "reverse lend-lease" in relation to American forces in Belgium and Luxembourg. The latter was included because of its close economic relations with Belgium. The value of the materials sold by the United States to Belgium amounted to 159.5 million dollars. The fact that Pierlot[400] and Gutt had tapped into the Congo's uranium wealth to support the Allied war effort resulted in the Kingdom in 1944 having a credit account under Roosevelt's lend-lease system. Belgium therefore imported foodstuffs and raw materials on a massive scale without cutting into its gold reserves.[401] On January 6, 1947, Bech had asked Le Gallais to obtain information from the Foreign Liquidation Commissioner in Washington "To enable our Office of Mutual Assistance to meet its compensation obligations assumed under the aforementioned agreements ... if Luxembourg property during the war was the subject of requisitions by the American Government. If so, you will want to obtain a list of these goods and the related files to hand them over through my Ministry to the Office of Mutual Assistance." On August 13, 1947, Le Gallais informed Bech that "as a result of the settlement among the three (USA, UK and Canada) supplying Governments, it will now no longer be necessary for the Government of Luxembourg to maintain a reserve fund equivalent to 10 percent of the combined claims, as stipulated in the memorandum from the State Department to the Belgian embassy dated July 23, 1946."

As a delegate from Luxembourg, in May and June 1943 Le Gallais participated, along with the adviser and Secretary General of the Government Léon Schaus, in the Food and Agriculture Conference, which was held in Hot Springs,[402] and which lay at the origin of the United Nations Organization for Food and Agriculture (FAO) with headquarters in Rome. At the May 18 to June 3 conference in Virginia, forty-six Governments pledged to create a permanent food and agriculture organization. President Roosevelt delivered a speech there on June 7, 1943. Le Gallais, not to be outdone, issued a statement with his speech emphasizing the need for cooperation and trust. From this Food and Agriculture Conference in Hot Springs, Le Gallais reported: "I am still under the very strong impression of the spirit of cooperation and understanding which existed there... To my mind, no useful purpose can come out of international conferences or meetings of technical experts if all who sit at the same table are not fully imbued with the spirit that their fellow delegates are there gathered to help solve their problems. It is only by helping the single members that the whole machine can be kept running." A nice summary of what should, even today, form the basis of international cooperation and multilateralism. Le Gallais had already played a very active part in the work leading up to this conference, as recounted by Heisbourg, who added that his reports and his notes reveal that the conversations he had with the American, English, Belgian, French and Dutch delegates went well beyond the framework of the conference and concerned the future directions that the various countries were likely to give to their economic policy in general. Le Gallais had succeeded in appearing on the final editorial board of the conference alongside the most important, himself seeing it as "a compliment to our small country".[403] From mid-July, an interim committee charged with implementing the recommendations of the conference was established, and Le Gallais was authorized by Bech on March 18, 1944 to approve the draft constitution drawn up by this commission. During this conference, as later during the UNRRA conference, Le Gallais had raised the linguistic question. He pleaded in favor of French, the Americans asking him not to raise the question again.[404] It is thanks to the fact that Luxembourg has almost always been among the founding countries of post-war international organizations and to the presence of representatives like Le Gallais that the country has been able to act and defend its interests and help set up structures, most of which are still active. Thus, at the time, the establishment of standing committees, commissions, steering committees, etc. alerted the diplomat who noted on May 27 in Hot Springs:

"Mr. Clayton[405] amplified and said that he understood that the commission which is to meet in Washington before July 15 would designate what is called here a 'steering committee' of eleven people and that it is the latter which would hold the center of this world organization comprising all human activities. What a program! At the end of the dinner I told Mr. Clayton that I was afraid of his declaration that this 'steering committee' would consist of only eleven delegates, among them a few people so that small countries would have no delegates; or if we could admit that Belgium, the Netherlands and Luxembourg had a common delegate, we could not conceive of entrusting our interests to Great Britain, for example, which had all the concern for the interests of its Empire."

In Hot Springs, Le Gallais had once again mentioned Georges Brasseur. In a letter to Bech on May 23, he addressed a document his lifelong friend had sent him that he wanted to present to the conference before it was to be published. However, Schaus had asked that Minister Le Gallais submit the paper to Dupong who had changed his mind after a telephone call from Schaus "on the pretext that the Belgian expert found that the text of this memorandum, while being exact was not interesting enough to be published". Le Gallais therefore sent the document to Bech. He concluded, for once in a more than pragmatic way: "I am understandably disappointed in more than one way; on the other hand it's not important enough to make a big deal out of it and I take comfort in thinking that you've seen a lot more and yet you're still there."

Le Gallais also participated in the United Nations Relief and Rehabilitation Administration (UNRRA) conference in Atlantic City, New Jersey in 1943 and in Montreal in 1944 (this time assisted by Charles Heuertz).[406] UNRRA was created in November 1943 to help refugees fleeing from the aggression of Axis countries. After World War II, UNRRA worked to rescue millions of refugees displaced by the war and its aftermath. Food shortages around the world threatened millions of people, and the world had, as so often since then, looked to the United States for assistance and to try to eradicate the famine which threatened more than half a billion people left without resources. The founding agreement was signed at the White House on November 9, 1943 by 44 countries including those of the Benelux. Two weeks earlier, the three countries had signed a monetary convention. The day after this signing, Dupong, Le Gallais and Elvinger left for Atlantic City, where the first council session sat for three weeks.[407] Le Gallais wrote on several occasions that UNRRA funds made it possible to send food to Luxembourg, which the country was sorely lacking after the war. From Montreal, Le Gallais addressed Luxembourgers calling them *Léif Frënn* (dear friends), while welcoming the country's liberation in September. He addressed the supply problems in Luxembourgish and called on every Luxembourger to make American officers and soldiers understand how badly the Germans behaved towards their country during the war years.[408] The agency became a member of the United Nations in 1945 and essentially ended its activities two years later

In April 1944, Minister Krier from London, Le Gallais and Heuertz attended the 26th session of the International Labor Conference in Philadelphia. In a March 7 letter to Bech, Le Gallais estimated that it was not necessary for him to stay for the entire three weeks, his role being rather that of an observer.[409] The conference lasted until to May 12. On that day, a text in Luxembourgish translated into English was prepared for the closing of the conference, the Minister of Labor speaking via broadcast, on May 18, to Luxembourgers. Five days later, the signing by the delegates of the 41 member countries of the "Declaration concerning the Goals and Objectives of the International Labor Organization" took place at the White House.[410]

The Bretton Woods United Nations Monetary and Financial Conference was held from July 1 to 22, 1944[411] at the imposing Mount Washington Hotel near the ski resort of the same name in New Hampshire. Government representatives from 45 countries took part.[412] Le Gallais had received the following instructions from Dupong: "You will attend as an observer rather [than as a 'technical adviser'], which calls for an attitude of reserve. Keep in touch with the Belgian delegation."[413] Le Gallais had told organizers that he would be coming alone and planned to take the special train from New York to Bretton Woods, and did not require an office. Le Gallais was subsequently appointed deputy governor of the International Monetary Fund. On March 8, 1946, he attended the inaugural meeting, March 18 being the last day of the joint World Bank and International Monetary Fund councils in Savannah, Georgia. Belgium and Egypt obtained positions on the Fund's board there thanks to a liberal interpretation of the plans. In the *Savannah Meeting Echoes*, ten days later, Hugues Le Gallais was quoted as having explained that his country has not experienced a strike for 20 years, alluding to the work stoppages of 1917 and 1921. The management was to meet in May in Washington to elect a President of the Bank and a "managing director" for the Fund and begin work in the American capital. Belgian Camille Gutt was elected to this post on May 6, 1946 and held it for almost five years.

From Bretton Woods, Le Gallais had kept a telegram in Luxembourgish, Roosevelt's speech, as well as a document signed by Camille Gutt, Minister of Finance of Belgium, Charles Heuertz[414] and Goldsmith, giving Le Gallais credit for the very good text he delivered. A broadcast by Le Gallais was aired on July 4, 1944, following Gutt's broadcast the previous day.

A long report was sent on March 19, 1946 on the inaugural meeting of the Governors of the Fund and the Bank held in Savannah on March 8, 1946, at the headquarters of the Fund and the Bank (the United Kingdom having argued for New York, while the Americans finally imposed the seat in Washington) and on the function of directors and deputy directors. The Belgian Gutt was also present, even congratulating Le Gallais for the collaboration with his delegation, that is to say Frère, Ansiaux and barons de Gruben and Boël. While Hugues Le Gallais wanted to attend a UNRRA conference, the Belgians asked him to stay and support their position, which quite flattered the Luxembourg diplomat. Le Gallais was appointed a member of the "by-laws" committee and attended other committees, notably on the remuneration of the Managing Director of the Fund and President of the Bank. Assistant Secretary of State for Economic Affairs William Clayton was also present, and supported Le Gallais' suggestion that the name of the governor of one of the countries with small quotas be added to the list so that the interests of such countries could be defended. After the conference, proud of the results he had achieved, in a letter written in Bar Harbor on August 18, 1944, by Minister Le Gallais considered that

"I have defended our interests well at Bretton Woods (it remains to be seen if we can find a satisfactory formula to the question within the framework of the Economic and Monetary Union). ...as regards the question of the bank of issue, I think I remember that one says 'or such other Institution which a Government might indicate'. Our savings bank or the International Bank may be able to help. As for the question of gold, the gold held by Luxembourg companies must, it seems to me, be used primarily to ensure our participation in the fund and in the bank. This is a matter of general national interest and our societies should immediately agree. Our independence in the economic and financial field is nowadays the only consideration which can count. I trust you."

The institutions arising from Bretton Woods, seeking to establish multilateral governance and to promote the free movement of goods, were closely followed by Le Gallais. By Grand Ducal decree of March 30, 1946, Dupong was appointed governor and Le Gallais deputy governor with the International Monetary Fund. Prime Minister Dupong was in Washington from September 26 to October 2, 1946 to attend the first annual meeting of the Board of Governors of the IMF and the International Bank for Reconstruction and Economic Development. Thus began the tradition of regular visits by Luxembourg leaders coming to the American capital to participate in meetings of various international financial institutions.

Le Gallais also participated in the International Civil Aviation Conference in Chicago in late 1944. In response to the invitation of the United States Government, representatives of 54 nations met from November 1 to December 7, 1944 in order to "arrange for the immediate establishment of provisional global air routes and services" and "constitute an interim council to collect, record and review data relating to international aviation and make recommendations for its improvement". The conference was also invited to "discuss the principles and methods to be followed in view of the adoption of a new aviation convention". During the opening, President Roosevelt proclaimed that the United States aims to open the skies for all.[415] When the conference concluded, 52 countries signed the new Convention on International Civil Aviation.

Le Gallais' participation, with his Minister of Foreign Affairs, in the Conference on the United Nations in San Francisco in 1945 was one of the highlights of his career. Minister Bech had come especially in May and June to participate in the founding of this organization, when the Minister of State in Luxembourg was about to resign due to constant criticism and the unpopularity of the Government. Dupong intended to organize elections which would ultimately take place in October.[416] During the major Allied conferences which established the United Nations, Luxembourg intended to secure its place within the new international organization, which was being born. Participation in the UN had serious consequences for a country like Luxembourg, which had already been a member of the League of Nations before withdrawing from it on August 30, 1942. Although it was planned to limit the country's military contribution to right of passage and the provision of infrastructure to international troops, these measures were incompatible with the status of neutrality.[417] A neutral and disarmed country before the war, the Grand Duchy was to put a definite end to its geopolitical vulnerability in 1949 with accession to NATO and the official abandonment of neutrality.

Forty-six countries were first invited to the San Francisco conference. These were, in addition to the four countries under whose

Hugues Le Gallais with the Minister of Foreign Affairs Joseph Bech and the minister's chief of staff, Alphonse Als, May 11, 1945 in San Francisco.

aegis the conference opened, all the countries which had declared war on Germany and Japan and signed the United Nations Declaration at the beginning of January 1942. The adoption of the Charter unanimously took place on June 25 when representatives gathered for a final plenary session at the San Francisco Opera. Lord Halifax, who was presiding over the international meeting, submitted the final draft Charter saying: "In our whole life we could not vote on a more important question than the one on which we are now going to vote." Given the historic significance of the ballot, Lord Halifax proposed that the ballot be taken not, as usual, by a show of hands but by roll call. All the delegates rose one after the other. Then the whole audience, some 3,000 people, also stood up. A huge ovation was heard when the President announced that the Charter was adopted unanimously. The next day, June 26, therefore, delegates gathered in the Veterans Memorial Hall to sign the two historic documents: the Charter and the Statute of the International Court of Justice. China, the first victim of aggression from an Axis power, had the honor of signing first. President Truman, having succeeded Roosevelt only on April 12, said in his closing remarks: "The Charter of the United Nations which you have just signed is a solid foundation on which we can build a better world. This historic act honors you. Between victory in Europe and final victory over the most destructive of wars, you have achieved victory over the war itself. ... Thanks to this Charter, the world can begin to see the time when all human beings can live a decent life as free men". Le Gallais said at the closing of the conference:

"Taking into account the current political situation in the world, the Grand Duchy of Luxembourg is fully satisfied with the Charter of the United Nations in its present form. The reasons are as manifold as they are obvious. Small nations desire peace, small nations want large ones to come together and discuss their issues together in order to find common ground, small nations desire to be able to bring their own issues to the world forum or to a small council that has the power to act according to the requirements of each case... While admitting that from a theoretical point of view a better document could have been drafted, the Luxembourg delegation will give its full support to the Charter of the United Nations and will do everything that is in its power to obtain ratification by the Chamber of Deputies in Luxembourg. The Luxembourg delegates are fully convinced that this ratification will take place, knowing that their compatriots love peace, that they have suffered a lot during this war and that they are ready to face the realities of life".[418]

The *Luxembourg Bulletin* published in Montreal on June 1, 1945 reported Minister Le Gallais' thanks to the Americans in San Francisco, by publishing extracts from his *Victory Day Broadcast*:

"I wish to express the heartfelt thanks of the Luxembourg people for the magnificent material aid which they have received and are continuing to receive from the American army of occupation. Their thanks also go to the factory workers, the farmers, and to all those in the United States who have made victory possible... Now that victory is won in Europe, my prayers are joined with yours in thanksgiving, in the hope that the war against Japan will soon be over, and let us not forget to pray also that the delegates to the San Francisco Conference will be successful in establishing an international organization which will ensure a lasting peace."

The participation in these historic days in California represents a truly unique episode in the memory of the Luxembourg representative. He brought back a beautiful and precious wooden box from this memorable event. Two letters written in testimony of his commitment deserve to be mentioned. Thus, Peter Fraser,[419] the Prime minister of New Zealand, who governed the country during most of the Second World War, wrote on June 26, 1945 to Bech, who was already gone: "He gave his great ability and experience to the task of Rapporteur, and his report to the Commission was excellent. It was a splendid summary of not only the work of the Commission but of various points of view expressed. As you had to leave, you could not possibly have left anybody better in your place than Mr. Hugues Le Gallais." The President of the Chamber of Commerce of San Francisco also had to flatter

Hugues Le Gallais a year later, by writing to him, on April 25, 1946, that

"we of San Francisco have followed the development and the work of the United Nations organization during the last year with deep interest, aware of the magnitude of the undertaking and appreciative of the unselfish efforts of those who assisted at the creation of the Charter which will take its place along the monumental documents of history. The important contribution you made as a delegate to the Conference will be long remembered by our citizens."

This participation in the San Francisco conference and its results were the basis of a multilateralism that the Grand Duchy had always wished to be effective, based on the rule of law and the sovereign equality of states. The United Nations gradually became the frame of reference, the embassy in Washington trying for many years and in the absence of a separate representation in New York, to defend Luxembourg's interests there and to promote its values at the international level.

At the first session of the conference of the Food and Agriculture Organization (FAO) in Quebec, Canada, from October 16 to November 1, 1945, Hugues Le Gallais participated as Member of the Interim Commission on Food and Agriculture, with a deputy in the person of Alphonse Schwinnon (Schwinnen), advisor at the Ministry of the Economy in Luxembourg. This time Le Gallais was not alone and dependent, as so often, on statements and the positions of his Belgian or Dutch partners.

In April 1946, Le Gallais traveled to Cleveland for the International Labor Conference, which ended without result on the 28th of the same month. An article was published that day in the *Cleveland Press* in which the Luxembourg representative again claimed that there had not been a strike in Luxembourg for twenty years. This argument aimed at presenting the Grand Duchy as a stable country without too much social protest had already been used. Le Gallais also made a tour of steel plants in the Cleveland area.

In the early spring of 1946, Le Gallais attended the first meeting of the World Economic Council in Washington. This was a follow-up to the Hot Springs conference three years earlier and took place in the framework of FAO.

In 1946, Le Gallais was also to take part in the United Nations General Assembly in London, where Bech had been present since October 12 with, in addition to Le Gallais, Albert Calmes,[420] member of the Superior Council of the Belgian-Luxembourg Economic Union, Pierre Elvinger, Government advisor at the Ministry of Foreign Affairs, as well as Pierre Pescatore, Secretary. That same year, another General Assembly was held at Flushing Meadows in New York. Le Gallais participated in it, as he did in 1947 and 1949. In 1948 and 1951, the conference took place at the Palais de Chaillot in Paris. Le Gallais does not seem to have been part of those meetings.

The International Telecommunications Conferences in Atlantic City in 1947 lasted from May 16 to October 2, with an International Convention adopted on the last day in the presence of Hugues Le Gallais. It should be noted in this context that in September 1944, at the time of the liberation of the Grand Duchy, the Luxembourg Government in exile signed an agreement with the United States allowing it to use the Radio Luxembourg transmitter. SHAEF's Psychological Warfare Division broadcast programs intended to demoralize the Germans until the end of the war. In July 1945, the radio came under the control of the Office of War Information before, on November 11, 1945, the Americans returned the station to the Luxembourg Broadcasting Company (CLR). At the time,[421] this was the second most powerful station on the Continent, shortly becoming the official transmitter in Europe of the United States. As with Arbed, the Americans had extended their control over a key sector of the Luxembourg economy.

Le Gallais was also present at the signing of the act of the North Atlantic Treaty Organization (NATO) in Washington, on April 4, 1949, by a committee chaired by the director of the Office of European Affairs of the West, Theodore Achilles, and to which the Director of the Office for European Affairs of the State Department, John D. Hickerson, made a significant contribution, following discussions at the Pentagon between March 22 and April 1.[422] Twelve Western countries have thus established a political and military alliance in order to ensure their collective security. The treaty was intended to ward off an attack from the Soviet Union, and the mutual defense clause was invoked for the first time until 2001 after the attacks on the World Trade Center and the Pentagon as part of the Operation Eagle Assist. Among the twelve signatories of the founding countries were, for Luxembourg, the Minister of Foreign Affairs Joseph Bech and Hugues Le Gallais. As the event was indeed historic, the Luxembourg minister plenipotentiary was standing when Minister Bech signed the treaty. The photo of this memorable moment appeared on the cover page of the Luxembourg illustrated publication *Revue* of May 7, 1949. Le Gallais had a paper framed with the signatures of all those who had dined at his house on this occasion. This paper featured prominently with Le Gallais. The treaty entered into force on August 24, 1949 after the deposit of the instruments of ratification of all signatory states. Hugues Le Gallais had obtained a beautiful solid silver box commemorating his participation in these intense days, as he preserved the one he had obtained in 1945 in San Francisco and that, in wood, in memory of his friends who had played bridge with him. A few months later, in Washington, the United States signed a mutual defense treaty with each of the NATO member countries. It was not until January 27, 1950 that Hugues Le Gallais signed the treaty in Washington, together with Secretary of State Dean Acheson, with the United States concluding separate agreements with Belgium, Denmark, France, Italy, Luxembourg, the Netherlands, Norway and the United Kingdom, where these nations pledged to defend each other in the event of a military attack.

The minister plenipotentiary also participated in the Conference for the Settlement of Peace with Japan in San Francisco. The treaty was signed on September 8, 1951, during the Korean War. Among the representatives of 47 allied nations, there was the Luxembourg Minister who arrived from Washington. A photo was taken as Hugues Le Gallais gave a speech on behalf of his government, recalling as we saw in the part about his years in Japan, his experience and best memories of the Japanese people.

In addition to NATO's activities, the project for a European Defense Community was one of the subjects that captured Le Gallais' attention in Washington. Minister Bech, faced with the demand for a speedy ratification of the European Defense Community, argued that Germany and France had to do it before Luxembourg could do it, at the same time as Belgium because of the Economic Union. Bech had shown considerable skepticism about the possibility of ratification by France before the following spring. The introduction in Luxembourg of the twelve-month military service had already been hard to impose because of the participation of the Socialists in the Government and the latter's electoral pledge not to accept it. Bech had also said that industrialists had been opposed to the Schuman plan. Finally, Luxembourg approved by

LETZEBURGER
7. Mai 1949
5. Joerg. Nr. 19 ILLUSTRE'ERT *Revue*

Aussenminister Bech
unterzeichnet den Atlantikpakt

Clichés exécutés par la Photogravure Lemaire Frères, Liège

„*Sentier de l'Alzette*"

I. Artikel der interessanten Serie: Schöne Promenaden durch unsere Heimat

Aus dem weiteren Inhalt: Die Oeslinger in Kanada :: „Gemeinde" Rollingergrund :: Fromme Häuser-frauen der Hauptstadt :: Zur Oktave :: Vögel lernen singen :: Die Welt der Frau :: Horoskop usw.

The front cover of the Revue of May 7, 1949, with Minister of Foreign Affairs Joseph Bech signing the North Atlantic Treaty with Le Gallais at his side. (Photo: Revue).

a law of April 24 the treaty establishing the European Defense Community (EDC) and its annexes. The EDC never entered into force as, at the end of August 1954, a majority of French deputies withdrew their confidence in the Mendès-France Government and thus de facto rejected the EDC.

It is interesting to note that a case deemed confidential has been appended to it. On April 16, 1954, the State Department asked if the sub-committee called "select committee to investigate the incorporation of Lithuania, Latvia and Estonia into the USSR" could carry out its investigations in Luxembourg, a city located in the heart of Europe where it was considered that it would be easier to bring in foreign persons whom one wanted to interview than elsewhere. The Le Gallais paper is simply checked off by Bech, as so often, but a confidential cable from Bech of May 13, 1954 put an end to the project:

"Reference your letter of April 16 on the Congress Committee to inform you that on May 10, I spoke to the Minister of the United States of America. By authorizing the committee to operate in the Grand Duchy we would endanger the lives of prisoners at a time when the anti-Communist speech provoked by the CED ratification debate has irritated Moscow; this danger being among other reasons the main cause which obliges us to give a negative answer to the American request."

Thus, fell into oblivion a rather spectacular idea recounted rather quickly by Le Gallais, without being made public. Bilateral relations remained nonetheless marked by unconditional Luxembourgish recognition for the liberation of the Grand Duchy on two occasions and aid for reconstruction.

RECONSTRUCTION OF THE COUNTRY AND INTERVENTIONS IN VIEW OF ITS PROVISIONING

A third of the country was in ruins, and the embassy in the United States was called upon many times to check whether shipments of basic necessities could be organized to the Grand Duchy. Le Gallais and other diplomatic and economic representatives not only worked to defend the political and economic interests of the country, they also excelled in finding solutions to help their compatriots in need. Very soon, it became clear that it was better to be represented by one's own nationals and to have an efficient and loyal network. To do this, the Luxembourg diplomatic network had to be strengthened. From Guill Konsbruck's letter to Hugues Le Gallais on May 12, 1945 it follows that the Government appointed Léon Clasen in London as Industrial Advisor to the Luxembourg Government with the Columeta apparatus at his disposal. "He will also be the Luxembourg industrial representative in the committees that will be set up in London in the future…" Similarly, Konsbruck considered "it would be useful to have the same kind of representation in America". He had mentioned the usefulness of this with Minister Bech,

"and I had spoken to him about Mr. Bohler, Mr. Schilling and Mr. Staudt with Amerlux to help us, respectively to defend Luxembourg's interests if necessary. Mr. Dieudonné[423] of Columeta, to whom I referred, was in turn in complete agreement with this solution. … We realize that it will almost always have to be done by the Belgian Economic Missions, but on the other hand we think it would be extremely useful from all points of view to have in parallel just a semblance of personal representation."

It is in a way a prefiguration of the Consulates General or even of the Board of Economic Development set up later. In the meantime, Luxembourg representatives, whether in Washington or London, were also invited to find solutions to supply their country with basic necessities.

In June 1945, Le Gallais was once again in contact with his former colleague in Japan, Tony Rollman, now a delegate in Brussels with the Kronacker mission.[424] The mission was named after the Belgian liberal politician, who had been the Belgian Government's military attaché in London and had headed numerous missions in the United States and Canada in connection with Belgian procurement. Konsbruck sent two reports by Rollman to Le Gallais on June 23. This is a note on "civilian imports during directed periods" which also answers questions from the Information Commissioner in New York André Wolff about the trade negotiations initiated on behalf of Luxembourg in the United States. Due to the Belgian-Luxembourg Economic Union, all imports, except those from Belgium, had to go through this Kronacker mission. Le Gallais was very interested and sent Rollman's reports to Wolff for transmission to Bohler.

Concrete cases of fund allocation are legion, and afterwards we will simply review some of the cases in which Le Gallais intervened from Washington.

In May, June and July 1945, correspondence was conducted between Le Gallais, Guill Konsbruck and Auguste Bohler, director of Amerlux Steel Products Corporation of New York, on the shipment of spectacles to Luxembourg. Mr. Wolff from New York was to bring them to Luxembourg. In other cables between Washington and Luxembourg, the transport of children's shoes was also discussed.

Other orders were placed through Le Gallais and on Konsbruck's behalf with the Inter-Allied Combined Food Board in Washington (to obtain 4,500 tons of potassium salt)[425] or with UNRRA (15,000 lbs of used clothing and shoes; UNRRA Canada threw in 7,500 lbs; then other lots were proposed and accepted by Konsbruck). In the spring of 1946, correspondence with Washington from the Minister of Supply and Economic Affairs still revolved around UNRRA's allocation of used clothing to a project to have the Marion Steam Shovel Company manufacture in Luxembourg. Le Gallais' friend, Georges Brasseur, had contacts in April 1946 with the chairman and the commercial director of this company.[426] On April 25, 1946, Le Gallais, who was in New York, set out the conditions for "fundamental bases for the realization of their project", of another project to manufacture mining equipment. However, a month earlier, Bech had been quoted as estimating that there was a lack of manpower in the Grand Duchy.[427] Le Gallais also was informed that the skilled labor force was quite restricted, so that at the beginning only relatively easy parts and pieces could be manufactured.[428] In September 1946,[429] Konsbruck sent to Le Gallais, in preparation for the exhibition which was to open on October 1 in the presence of the Secretary of Agriculture, the list of "shortage of food per normal consumer kg/year" listing consumption in 1939 and 1945 and summarizing in percentage terms the shortages, especially those of meat, milk, cheese, rice and fish.

At the end of November 1945, Le Gallais and Konsbruck exchanged information on "the interest of the Grand Duchy in seeing American industry create a medium-sized industry here rather than in Germany" and on "the idea of setting up a factory in Luxembourg for the manufacture of agricultural machinery". André Wolff and A. Burks Summers,[430] who at the time was a financial and economic consultant and who was to be American ambassador to Luxembourg between 1960 and 1961, were involved in the latter project.[431] On September 4, 1946, the embassy in Washington communicated to Konsbruck that Burks Summers had sent him a letter that the Globe Wernicke Company was no longer willing for the time being to open a manufacturing plant in Europe. Indeed, as Gilles Regener noted:[432]

"In the aftermath of the war, Luxembourg's minister plenipotentiary in Washington, Hugues Le Gallais, contacted Allingham Burks Summers, President of General Credit Inc. in view of possible collaboration. The latter is interested in the investment of American capital and patents, and also maintains important contacts with numerous industrial companies. Burks Summers is to identify American industrialists wishing to establish themselves in Luxembourg. The companies to be contacted must meet three conditions: use iron and steel as raw materials; hire a satisfactory number of workers; and produce for the Luxembourg, European and international markets. The results of this initiative are very modest and the few companies—Deen & Company, Maguire Industries, Globe-Wernicke Company and Wil-Lys Company—that are approached by Burks Summers have, according to him, 'serious hesitations to establish themselves in Europe because of the unstable political situation'. A few months after Goodyear's decision to erect a branch plant in the Grand Duchy, the Consulate General of Luxembourg in New York drafted a memorandum in March 1950 to provide 'information about these essential factors of significance to specific industries considering the establishment of a branch plant in the Grand Duchy of Luxembourg'. Unfortunately, the addressees of this memorandum are not known, but it can be assumed that it was rather an isolated action that went relatively unnoticed. It was only towards the end of the 1950s that the Luxembourg Government embarked on a campaign to promote the Grand Duchy's economy and industry with the creation of the Board of Industrial Development (BID)".[433]

In addition to the Luxembourg representative in Washington, the representative in New York was also active in the field of economic diplomacy. Already on March 5, 1946, Mr. Wolff asked for clarification on the developments of Luxembourg's trade treaties with France, as this question would often be put to him, as France had a reputation for being very protective of its production. And Hugues Le Gallais in turn asked on March 14: "if you have an idea of what French policy will be towards the Belgian-Luxembourg Union, and what the payment facilities will be." André Wolff from New York gave a report on his activities to Konsbruck with a copy to the Minister of State and the ambassador in Washington: meetings with the president of General Electric, Clark Minor; contact with Deca Records, etc. Mr. Wolff also suggested to the Luxembourg Government to maintain the office in New York, which was due to close on June 30, and that the commercial attachés be linked to the Luxembourg legations. Wolff recalled that Luxembourg had benefited during the last six months from 300,000 dollars of material aid from the United States, which will have to be increased by an additional 100,000 dollars during the coming year. As a result, the Luxembourg Government could and should invest at least 10% in return for the creation of Government commercial offices.

From Savannah, where he attended the inaugural meeting of the joint board of the World Bank and the International Monetary Fund, Le Gallais added at the beginning of this note, on March 10, 1946: "H.EXC. M. J. Bech: For information Boël says that it is a mistake to want to create new factories in our country because we lack manpower. Can we better employ our workers by creating new industries? I cannot answer that question. But this answer is an important factor in judging the appropriateness of the NY office." One may wonder whether this is the position of Le Gallais in Washington, who takes a dim view of the actions of his Luxembourg "competitors" in New York. In any case, the establishment of Goodyear in 1949 and DuPont de Nemours in 1962, companies that were actively coveted in order to diversify the economic fabric of Luxembourg, were not to prove him right.

With unfailing constancy, the Luxembourg authorities were grateful to the Americans for the support they received during these troubled and difficult times. Thus, following a request addressed by Le Gallais to Konsbruck on May 25, 1945, a message from the Grand Duchess for the "National clothing collection for overseas War Relief" was published in which she expressed her thanks and gave her first impressions of the situation in her country following her return a few days earlier.

In August 1945, the purpose was to answer questions from the United Nations War Relief Inc. and to provide information via the embassy in Washington about the food situation in the Grand Duchy. In a speech given by Guill Konsbruck as Minister during the August 30, 1945 visit to Luxembourg of members of the House of Representatives Select Committee on Post-War Economic Policy and Planning,[434] he concluded: "We are most grateful and happy that America, under the enlightened guidance of its President and Congress, has selected Luxembourg for its cultural centre; we feel confident that the same interest which promoted this choice will eventually extend to the economic field."

A note from Le Gallais of December 5, 1946 reports on a conversation with the head of the division for Germany at the State Department Riddleberger to whom he had given a memorandum on Luxembourg's claims against Germany, which had found prior agreement with France. A Luxembourg claim concerned a series of German villages and the surrender of German territory up to a depth of 1 to 5 kilometers, with the border being brought back to the ridge line, in particular in order to build a dam on the Our River.[435] Similarly, a memorandum was transmitted on June 18, 1947 by Le Gallais following the Secretary of State's statement of June 5 on the improvement of the economic and financial situation in Europe. The aim was to keep the Americans informed and interested in the development of the Grand Duchy.

In order to increase the attention of his government, Le Gallais also sometimes qualified as "Top secret" a statement by Secretary of State Anthony Eden before the House of Commons on relations with Soviet diplomats following the factual separation and the growing gulf between East and West ("forbidding chasm"). Undated, the document refers to an article of Sir David Kelly in the Sunday Times of December 2, 1951. In any event, it is difficult to judge the extremely confidential nature of this communication.

In addition to these specific cases of intervention by Hugues Le Gallais for the benefit of his country, there was his decisive action in relation to Arbed and the chairman of its board of directors, Aloyse Meyer.[436]

INTERVENTIONS FOR ARBED
AND POST-WAR FILES

During the war, Hugues Le Gallais was involved in Arbed's finances, which were highly complex due to the legal situation of investments in the most diverse countries. He had also tried to bring Gaston Barbanson to the United States. This relative had taken up residence in Mougins in the South of France in the so-called free zone. The leader of Arbed was saddened by the death in battle of his son Jean during an attack on his base by Luftwaffe bombers on May 10, 1940.[437] Le Gallais recommended that he come to the United States and corresponded with Brabanson,[438] particularly about the suspicion by the Arbed leader of being expropriated in some fashion, something against which he protested energetically. He was reassured that the Belgian and Luxembourg Governments, contrary to what had been the case for the Dutch, would not resort to this measure and seize funds blocked in the United States that were owned by Luxembourg companies or individuals.[439] In July 1942, an investigation by Sumner Welles had revealed that there were no longer any objections to the business relations between the companies Belgo-Mineira and Amerlux. One month later, Amerlux New York and Amerlux San Francisco were placed under the supervision of the Alien Property Custodian. When in August 1943 the Custodian appointed two American directors to replace two Luxembourgers at the Amerlux shareholders' meeting, Dupong was "unpleasantly surprised at the turn this affair took" when he had asked Le Gallais to formally oppose it and delay the matter until he arrived. The diplomat could not always succeed in everything according to the instructions he was given, even if he did his best and understood what was at stake.

Barbanson's attitude during the war, which he spent partly in France and Switzerland, tended to preserve his interests as chairman of the board of Arbed and as one of its largest shareholders. Thus, he wrote to Le Gallais on November 18, 1942:

"I think I must tell you that you would do well to think twice before you get your hands on the assets of our Company in New York. There is no doubt that this will come to light and that there will be no hesitation in Europe to take retaliatory measures which could have the greatest consequences for our Society which, in the future, will make your Government responsible for any damage which may have been caused to it on that occasion. I therefore urge you to make your Government aware of this matter and not to take any decision lightly."

The desire to transfer to the Government in exile the ownership of Luxembourg capital invested in the United States and thus to shield it from enemy control created a complex situation for the former Arbed employee.[440] In a letter urging Barbanson once again to come to the United States, Le Gallais had written on March 28, 1942: "It is, moreover, up to you alone to take part in this attempt of protection, which I have been trying to make you understand for many months. ... I really don't know why I am taking so much trouble to convince you, instead of leaving you in peace, as you wish. Family links probably and because by instinct I am attached to the steel industry and that I imagine that you are better here than there".[441] Even to a recalcitrant Barbanson, Le Gallais was not all-powerful.

Le Gallais would again come into contact with Arbed's leaders after the Second World War, but this time with the successors of the founding fathers, who had more or less ousted his father and who no longer belonged to the Metz and Tesch families such as Félix Chomé and Tony Neuman. Thus, he was going to work closely with Arbed representatives to defend the wartime stance of Luxembourg's industry leaders. Aloyse Meyer, Arbed's managing director before becoming chairman of the board of directors from April 1947 to 1952, had seen his reputation called into question, just as the United States raised certain grievances against his management of the company during the war. Arbed, and Meyer in particular, had been somewhat roughed up by the Americans, who accused him of not taking a sufficiently firm stance against the German occupiers. In close contact with Deputy Managing Director Guill Konsbruck, whom he had got to know in exile and who had joined Arbed in mid-October 1946 after serving in government, Le Gallais in Washington tried to settle the matter quietly. The Meyer affair was brought to a final conclusion in May 1947. This was to become a story with many twists and turns, with contacts in Washington being reported to the political authorities, to Arbed in Luxembourg and sometimes even commented on by the media in Luxembourg.

It should be pointed out that Bech had already defended Meyer in May 1943:[442] "The note on your conversation with Rips interested me very much. Although it is difficult to judge from afar, I cannot accept that A.M. [Aloyse Meyer] is a collaborator. Following the fact that, for example in Belgium, industrialists who are supposedly collaborators in the eyes of the general public are considered by insiders to be active patriots, I say that this fact makes me very cautious in my judgments." From a note recounting a conversation between Le Gallais and Rips on April 19, 1943,[443] it emerges that at the time the State Department was already "particularly concerned with Luxembourg and that the time was approaching when Luxembourg factories and communication routes in the Grand Duchy would be bombed." From a three-page report by the German government representative attached to Arbed and available to the State Department at the time, Rips was informed that the latter considered that: "*Meyer ist ein guter Freund aber man muss vorsichtig sein*".[444] And again: "It would appear from Mr. Rips' statement that some people believe that Mr. Meyer 'is a collaborator'. On the other hand, Mr. Rips himself finds it difficult to pass judgment in such cases." A few years later, the case was taking a new turn for Luxembourg and Le Gallais was going to do his utmost to get his country out of a very complex situation.

On April 27, 1946, the *Luxemburger Wort* published an article entitled *Die luxemburgischen Guthaben in Amerika deblockiert*,[445] following an invitation to the press by the chargé d'affaires George Platt Waller the day before, to announce the good news that the Luxembourg assets would be released (from "foreign funds control") in the United States in accordance with the procedure provided for in License 95 which does not automatically free the assets (those of Arbed continued to be subject to a special blocking regime), but allows nevertheless to foresee a positive outcome of the issue, something that had been of concern to the Luxembourg representative for quite some time. This was likely a coincidence in time.

But that didn't mean that everything was settled. The State Department sent an aide-memoire to the Luxembourg government on June 7, 1946, the same day that Ambassador Alan G. Kirk[446] delivered a letter regarding Arbed's assets in the United States. Le Gallais also submitted a Luxembourg memorandum. He spoke of "my Memorandum of June 21, 1946 on Luxembourg's special position—history of the activities of the Arbed and the General Directorate during the war years" which he drafted following:

"the notification by the Extraordinary Envoy and Minister Plenipotentiary Alain G. Kirk to the Grand Ducal Government that as from 26/8 April, the general license will be applied in Luxembourg ... and that from then on, the assets which are the property of natural or legal persons, domiciled in the Grand Duchy, are released from foreign fund control after certification. The benefit of this administrative measure is nevertheless denied to the assets of Arbed in Luxembourg which continue to be governed by the administrative measure, modified on August 20, 1945 by the Federal Reserve Bank to the Guaranty Trust Company in New York and under the terms of which these assets are subject to a special blocking regime; in other words, any act of disposition of these assets remains subject to prior authorization by the Treasury Department."

From Le Gallais' interview with the Treasury and State Departments on June 21, it follows:

"What are the criticisms made of ARBED: a) Mr. A. Meyer's problem; the sole person of the Managing Director is confused with the entire company. b) History of the activities of ARBED and the General Management during the war years ... From the discussions that followed my presentation, the following conclusions emerge in summary and very clearly: 1) The Treasury says that Mr. Meyer's case is a Luxembourg case to be decided by the Luxembourg judicial authorities. 2) What is of exclusive interest to the Treasury is to obtain that 'Luxembourg Government issues certification that there is no enemy interest in ARBED and that there is no enemy interest in ARBED's assets in the US. The Government in addressing this certification to the Guaranty Trust Co. of NY (and copy to the Treasury) should state that this assurance is based on a full examination of all ARBED books and files'."

On June 22, 1946, Le Gallais sent the Minister of State and Konsbruck a report on an interview the previous day at the Treasury Department and the State Department in connection with Arbed's frozen accounts in the United States.

In September 1946, an American newspaper[447] had added fuel to the fire by publishing an article entitled "The Washington Merry-Go-Round" denouncing Arbed as a "famous Nazi steel cartel" and again:

"After the last war Woodrow Wilson et al. ordered ARBED to become a French and Belgian outfit. However, the Germans, through secret stock purchases, by 1926, had rebuilt control of their giant, far flung steel-mills. ARBED operated from Argentina to Brazil, but has headquarters in Luxembourg. Thus when Hitler came into power, ARBED was all set for his munitions program. It went to town in a big way. ...certain wire-pullers are lobbying to get its funds unfrozen. It has a lot of cash tied up in the USA, and the Treasury has been ahead to unfreeze them." [...] Aloyse Meyer was described in it as 'district Führer for the entire steel industry' or 'one of the many plants the Nazis arranged in foreign countries'."

On this point, despair set in again among the main Luxembourg actors after efforts to mediate this delicate problem with, in particular, a visit by Konsbruck in June and, before November 1946, by the Minister of State (accompanied by Mr. Verelst who had previously pleaded to sell part of the Belgo-Mineira portfolio rather than take out a loan, which Le Gallais had advised against) in Washington.[448] Konsbruck wrote to Le Gallais on November 2, 1946: "I myself no longer understand anything about it. All the very great trust and friendship I have for this noble Nation has been shaken quite a bit by the results of Mr. Dupong's interviews in Washington." Afterwards, Konsbruck sketched, without hesitation, the history of the problem. He was

"personally of the opinion that the evil genius behind this affair is Mr. Markx ... who, when he learned of the net, favorable result which went against his intentions, he mobilized public opinion: New York Times. Drew Pearson[449]... By pursuing ARBED, the Treasury is doing the Luxembourg economy the greatest harm and one wonders what are the real reasons behind all this attitude? It is possible that the Treasury is applying 2 different measures to blocked funds of various Belgian Cies which are in an identical, even more negative position than ARBED and to Mr. A.M. [Aloyse Meyer] or even by him and his company. It is true that ARBED is one of the most important businesses in Europe and is solidly established in the world, especially in Brazil (!). Does one want to take advantage of this opportunity to harm it, to ruin its moral prestige, its position in a word. Does one want to oust a harmful competitor? Are our successes in Brazil looked down on by the USA, which does not forgive an intruder. In the end we come to all sorts of conclusions. One really wonders how the USA, which has shown us its effective friendship so many times, which defends the rights of small nations all over the world (is this just theory or is it simply a matter of defending political rights?), how they can treat us worse than the Swiss companies collaborating with Germany!"

Le Gallais was therefore aware of the thoughts of the Luxembourg officials and kept them informed in return, as a diplomat should.

In connection with the Meyer affair, Le Gallais reported on November 21, 1946: "... I saw Mr. Clayton and submitted to him the text of the Mandate which it is desired to entrust to the Swiss Trust Company... I told Mr. Clayton that I knew Mr. Meyer well enough to be able to assure him 'that he was no cloak[450] for enemy interests'. Mr. Clayton agreed that there should be no further requests." It should be noted that in July, in his correspondence with Konsbruck, Le Gallais had already described his interlocutor as a very good friend.

At the end of the year,[451] a meeting took place in Luxembourg between Guill Konsbruck and the American ambassador in Brussels Kirk, in the presence of Mr. de Munk, vice-governor of the Société Générale and director of Arbed. Kirk stated that the report of September 9, 1947 of the Swiss Trust Company and the Belgian-Luxembourg Foreign Exchange Institute in Brussels, commissioned on July 27, 1946,[452] was not complete and requested an audit, which Mr. Meyer accepted by handing over all his documents and account statements to an expert. As to the makeup of Arbed's capital, Konsbruck repeated that the maximum would be 3,625 (German) shares, i.e. not even 2% of the capital, which moreover is in the hands of the Luxembourg government through the Office des Séquestres. And Konsbruck specified that:

"Already at this moment we are one and a half years behind schedule for our re-equipment. Orders are being placed in the USA to purchase installations directly for an equivalent value of 800 million francs; we are unable to confirm the orders due to our unavailable funds. The whole reconstruction of Europe is affected. The refuge we were able to find for our money in the USA has become fatal for us in the meantime. In addition, you are certainly aware that all our Belgo-Mineira assets are permanently frozen."

We also learn that the Minister of State had to see the Attorney General to "implore him to conclude his files ... Mr. and Mrs. Meyer's health is very shaky and Mr. Meyer's morale is low".

At the beginning of December 1946, Le Gallais sent a brochure entitled *Prevent World War III* which contained an article directed against Mr. Meyer. Konsbruck called it "disgusting" and said he had "decided to react to this infamy".[453]

On January 11, 1947, Konsbruck informs Le Gallais that "the favorable settlement of the case of Mr. A.M. [Aloyse Meyer] ... the examination of his books begins on Monday January 13 and as the bulk of the work has already been done, we hope that everything will be ready around January 20." Le Gallais has been kept regularly updated on the situation in the country. Thus, in the same letter, he learns that "the supply of fuel to Luxembourg in general and steel coke in particular has been excessively precarious since December [1946]. We have had to close the Esch plant and Hadir and Rodange have had to shut down their blast furnaces since January 1. You can see that the small economic boom we've enjoyed since the middle of 1946 is slowly beginning to crumble."

Overcoming the Meyer issue was to take much longer than expected, despite the dismissal of the case on January 8, 1947 by the Luxembourg State Prosecutor and a second report commissioned on January 3, 1947 and completed at the beginning of April. Le Gallais discussed the problem again with Under-Secretary of State William L. Clayton at the State Department.[454] During the meeting, the Luxembourg representative, while specifying that his country was opposed to German rearmament, requested an exception in a very important case for Luxembourg, namely the modification of the Allied provisions on the decartelization, socialization and nationalization of German companies in the Anglo-American occupation zone employing 10,000 and more people in favor of two subsidiaries of Arbed. The document entitled *Décartellisation* dated February 18, 1947, summarizes the issues at stake: "American decrees affect the two German subsidiaries of ARBED; serious matter for Luxembourg, wants an exception made; Luxembourg utterly opposed to rearming Germany."

Finally, at the beginning of April, when the experts had finished checking Meyer's books, the sky seemed to have cleared and Konsbruck wrote to Le Gallais on April 2, 1947:

"This famous problem of unblocking is now more important and vital than ever. Indeed, everything has been finalized with regard to the order for the sheet rolling mill for Dudelange. The order is ready to be placed, but it can only be placed when we can freely dispose of our assets with the Guaranty Trust. When placing the order, we must make an initial payment of 30%. You will see that the problem is no longer just an ARBED problem, but a national problem, because it is a question of re-equipping the country's largest industrial company."

On March 29, 1947, Konsbruck had written (in French and specifying that the request was to be considered "strictly confidential, from friend to friend") to Dan Grant, Vice-President of the Guaranty Trust Company of New York, asking him "to kindly let me know if the Guaranty Trust Co. is willing to issue the letters of credit in question, starting directly with the first 4 steps, amounting to 25% of the total amount of the order, i.e. approximately $2.5 million. Given the importance of the ARBED funds on deposit with you, I am sure that you will be able to help us in the requested direction." The proceedings between the State Department and the Treasury Department were still to take some time before finally, on June 10, 1947, the representative of the Treasury Department at the American embassy in Paris, Delbert A. Snyder, informed the Minister of State in Luxembourg that there was no longer any obstacle to the certification of Arbed's assets in the United States. The fact that in the middle of the Cold War, five days earlier, George Marshall had presented his plan to help certain European countries to Harvard, was probably not without significance in this change of attitude and the outcome of the matter.

On July 11, Konsbruck thanked Le Gallais "wholeheartedly, both on behalf of the Executive Board and on my own behalf, for the great dedication and readiness you have shown at all times to support us in our endeavors". In order to carry out the project, on July 12, 1947, Messrs René Schmit,[455] Gonner and Reiland (clectrician) and Mr. Victor Buck[456] flew to New York, accompanied by Mr. Auguste Bohler. In a very personal way, Le Gallais welcomed, on August 7, the fact that "a satisfactory arrangement had been reached between the Government and Arbed in connection with the Grand Ducal loan from the International Bank for Reconstruction and Economic Development", which allowed Arbed to "retain a good part of its gold, which is also in the national interest. I feel to some extent the author of our participation in the International Bank for Reconstruction and Economic Development and I am happy to have been able to do a service to a society to which I have family and sentimental ties. I have not forgotten the beautiful years I spent in the service of Columeta in Japan." On August 30, 1947, Le Gallais informed Konsbruck that "the contract for our loan has been signed and that we have obtained 2 million dollars in Belgian francs and 10 million dollars in dollars. I see the fruit of my work at Bretton Woods, which I am very happy about." A week later, Konsbruck congratulated him "very warmly on the magnificent result".

The Meyer affair therefore seemed to be settled, even though "on January 9, 1948 a circular was issued by the Society for the Prevention of World War III, repeating its slanderous and untruthful attacks against Mr. Aloyse Meyer". The Society had already sent a telegram to President Truman in August 1948. Konsbruck concluded[457] that "we no longer allow ourselves to be spat in the face and forbid anyone to sully our honor".

On the subject of the collieries belonging to firms from Allied countries in Germany, correspondence was conducted in parallel to the Meyer affair with a memorandum from Luxembourg dated November 27, 1946 submitted to the Allied Council of Ministers in New York and a memorandum dated February 1, 1947 submitted to the Council of Deputy Ministers responsible for Germany meeting in London on February 7, 1947, the latter requesting that the production of the *Eschweiler Bergwerks Verein* be considered as Luxembourgish production. Similar steps were taken at the beginning of March 1947 in three capitals. Le Gallais intervened on the basis of his Government's instructions with the State Department. Under-Secretary of State for Economic Affairs Clayton replied that the requested report on Mr. Meyer's activities was awaited and that, if this could be arranged, the atmosphere would be better. A note was submitted on February 18, 1947 by André Clasen to the Foreign Office following certain measures recently adopted by the authorities of the military Government in the Anglo-American zone to implement the policy of decartelization and public administration of industry in Germany, and in certain operations, the transfer of control and executive responsibilities to production committees of officials and representatives of management and workers or trade unions. It was in London that this was to be considered. In Berlin, Representative Albert Wehrer met the head of decartelization Mr. James Martin,[458] who had arrived in Luxembourg with his deputy on March 22 and 23, 1947. During this meeting, probably on the instructions of General Clay, the Governor General of the American zone in Germany, they were given a memorandum by Konsbruck. During the meeting, public opinion in the United States confused the International Steel Agreement with Arbed, perceived as "the instigator, the linchpin, the embodiment of the EIA".

In this context, the Benelux partners were a source of concern to the Luxembourgers:[459]

"...Part of our coal concessions are being claimed by the Dutch. ... Holland is looking for German coal... In the attached note we talk about the Dutch intrigues (territorial and economic claims about which a note was circulating in New York...),[460] our Belgian friends are even more worried about the tricks used to steal our very substance. Indeed, the Laura and Willem Sophia collieries, which are Belgian companies with Belgian capital, are constantly approaching the English authorities to obtain permission to exploit our subsoil. On this point we are fighting back directly and energetically."

The mining concessions on the left bank of the Rhine were in question and it was necessary to fight against the wishes of the Benelux partners.

On August 30, 1947, Le Gallais reported that he had (again) "on August 27 handed over to the State Department a note concerning the Allied collieries in Germany and one concerning the Eschweiler collieries". A week later, Konsbruck thanked him for this, while considering that "the reaction of the British and American military authorities themselves is not very encouraging, but we nevertheless remain hopeful that through our joint action with France and Belgium our interests will be recognized and safeguarded...'. In September 1947 members of the Congressional Investigative Committee of the Smith-Mundt Congress[461] composed of four Senators and four members of the House of Representatives visited Luxembourg, as well as a committee (Select Committee on Foreign Aid) known as Herter Committee.[462] Konsbruck had in the meantime written on October 9 to the staff consultant Henry F. Holthusen from New York, who accompanied the first delegation, to inform him of the situation in Luxembourg. Let us remember that the "material damages caused by Nazi occupation amount to a total sum of 20,000,000 Luxembourg francs i.e. about 500 million US dollars". The reply of the State Department dated October 22 "deeply frightened me... because at the same time when we were expecting American food aid, the American note only mentions deconcentration and decartelization...", as Konsbruck reported to Le Gallais on November 7, 1947, and announced an official *démarche* that Foreign Affairs was going to mandate Le Gallais to undertake. This was followed by a note from the State Department on November 14, 1947.[463]

In December 1948, Amerlux encountered difficulties in freeing itself from the grip of the "Alien Property Custodian", which had been under the control of the Department of Justice rather than the Treasury since September 1948. Following a letter from Auguste Bohler to Konsbruck on December 15 explaining the subject (Amerlux was incorporated on December 1, 1925 with a capital of 10,000 dollars), the latter estimated that "either one is blaming Columeta, the theoretical owner of Amerlux, or Arbed, the actual owner". At the end of the year, Konsbruck also met in Luxembourg with the new American chargé d'affaires, Mr. West (who discussed this issue with Mr. Bech) and asked Le Gallais in Washington to make a *démarche* to the State Department. Konsbruck also considered contacting the Washington lawyer King, a former claims officer in Luxembourg familiar with the case. The case appeared to be settled in February 1949, and Konsbruck again thanked Le Gallais for his mediation.[464]

On October 21, 1949, Konsbruck wrote to Le Gallais about Arbed's interests in Austria, a subject that Bech discussed with the minister plenipotentiary during his stay in Washington in early September. These new difficulties arose during the discussion of the Peace Treaty with Austria and in connection with safeguarding Allied interests in that country. Arbed's indirect majority interests in Austria were at risk in different companies (Felten & Guilleaume in Vienna and Kleedorf, Pohlig, and Flüggen). Konsbruck therefore asked Le Gallais to "approach the American, the British and above all the French elements with a view to drawing their attention to the danger for Allied interests and insisting that a formula be adopted for this special article of the Peace Treaty with Austria safeguarding the Allied direct and indirect majority interests in Austrian companies".

In September 1951, the Managing Director of Felten & Guilleaume Carlswerk in Cologne, which had been in the group for 25 years, Dr Joseph Horatz,[465] went to Washington to discuss certain problems in connection with submarine cable telecommunications between the United States and Germany.[466] Le Gallais met Dr Horatz who obtained an order for Nordenham (a city in Lower Saxony, Germany).[467] In the same vein, Konsbruck announced that, after having visited several American industries, he might also travel to Washington in the second half of November to attend the Congress of European Industrialists. Finally the two men met again on the occasion of Konsbruck's visit to Washington from November 30 onwards.[468] Arbed's American problem seemed to have been solved once and for all.

OTHER CASES HANDLED IN WASHINGTON

Hugues Le Gallais and Guill Konsbruck discussed several subjects related to bilateral relations or of a personal nature. The diplomat tried to help his government, but also his acquaintances and friends and to open doors. Through Le Gallais and thanks to his in-depth knowledge of the American continent and an extensive and diverse address book obtained thanks to good "networking", many cases were settled more easily. He tried to pursue a policy of industrial diversification and prospecting abroad, with the United States as a priority.[469]

In 1946, the German architect Otto Bartning thanked Mrs. Mayrisch for the "Care Paquets" he had received from Hugues Le Gallais.[470] The CARE (Cooperative for American Remittances to Europe) parcels were sent to Europe after the end of the Second World War as part of American aid programs. A hundred million CARE parcels were distributed in Europe. Almost ten million parcels reached West Germany between 1946 and 1960, three million of which reached West Berlin, particularly in 1948/1949 through the Berlin Airlift. In March 1950, in relation to a question raised by Le Gallais on behalf of a mutual friend about shipping Akron products via LRP transport Inc. NY, Konsbruck intervened with the managing director of Goodyear-Luxembourg, Mr. H.C. Pownall, assuring him that the transport company would be considered for tenders and that it would probably be able to handle part of the transportation of machines destined for Goodyear-Luxembourg.

The same was done in September and October 1954 in response to a request from Dr Aloyse Willems, an otorhinolaryngologist in Luxembourg, who had developed and perfected a new method for operating on laryngeal cancer. As President of the American-Luxembourg Society, Konsbruck approached Le Gallais to ask him to examine why the work of the Luxembourg doctor did not meet the fate it deserved in the United States, as an article by the expert had not been published in the American Medical Association's journal *Archives of Oto-Laryncology*. The article was finally published in December.

Le Gallais continued to attend the most diverse meetings and to represent Luxembourgers who were unable to travel for the occasion. In September 1950, Konsbruck was invited by the Administrative Director Mr. Everett R. Clinchy to attend as the Grand Duchy's representative at the meetings of the World Brotherhood and the National Conference of Christians and Jews which took place in Washington on November 9 to 11, 1950. This meeting dealt with "the program of activity in the field of employers' and workers' organizations and the financing of the program". A request to attend was addressed to Minister Bech. As the Minister for Foreign Affairs was attending the ordinary session of the UN General Assembly, a request was sent to Konsbruck on September 22, asking him to take the floor. President Truman was due to speak at the closing lunch. Secretary of State Acheson was also expected to attend the meeting. However, as neither Bech nor Konsbruck was finally able to make the trip to Washington, Konsbruck asked Le Gallais on September 27, 1950 to judge the advisability of appointing a member of the Luxembourg delegation that was in America to represent the Grand Duchy at the "important events with regard to world union". Le Gallais annotated the written request, suggesting that the matter be referred to the Luxembourg diplomat Pescatore. On October 13, 1950, he informed Konsbruck that he was willing to attend the World Brotherhood dinner on November 9 at the Mayflower Hotel, being prevented from doing so for the rest of the time because of conferences, in particular of the FAO. In the autumn of the following year, similar correspondence between Konsbruck and Le Gallais was exchanged concerning the Luxembourg representation, Le Gallais having agreed, this time, to give a speech on November 9, 1950, which was broadcast to the "Board of Sponsors for World Brotherhood". In order to enable the Luxembourg diplomat to prepare himself, Konsbruck sent him, on October 27, 1951, a short documentation on the organization, including his speech of June 1950 in Paris.

On October 30, 1950, Le Gallais and Colonel Aloyse Jacoby, Chief of the Army Staff, were received at the White House by President Truman on the occasion of the meeting of NATO Defense Ministers.

We should also mention Le Gallais' voluminous correspondence with charities, but also Jewish organizations. At least a dozen organizations representing Jewish interests contacted the Luxembourg Minister after the war.[471] From a letter dated March 9, 1949 from Bech, Le Gallais learned that Luxembourg recognized the State of Israel and that he was authorized to notify the American Zionist Emergency Council of this. In June 1944, a Committee representing the Jews of the Grand Duchy of Luxembourg to the World Jewish Congress had just been set up. Le Gallais duly informed Dupong and Bech, in accordance with the request of the committee's president, Dr. Frank J. Mayer, and its secretary, Sigismund Leib. Dr. Serebrenik, Louis Ackermann, Nathan Hertz, Charles Learsy and Otto Wolff were members of this committee, which had offices in Broadway, New York. In the embassy's archives, there are many traces of correspondence with a dozen other Jewish associations and organizations after the war.

There are always new cases to learn about while trying to further them in the interest of Luxembourg and for the benefit of bilateral relations. Le Gallais was made for this job, which allowed him to satisfy his passions and ambitions. For example, he did everything possible to be accredited in the two countries neighboring on the United States, as well as in Cuba and Brazil.

ACCREDITATION TO MEXICO AND CANADA

On March 11, 1948, Le Gallais presented President Miguel Aleman of Mexico with his letters of accreditation as envoy extraordinary and minister plenipotentiary. On April 24, 1950, he presented them to Viscount Alexander of Tunis, Governor General of Canada.

Two years before being accredited to Mexico, on February 23, 1946, Le Gallais had already prepared the ground and considered that "thanks to better diplomatic relations between the Grand Duchy and Mexico, we will undoubtedly be able to count one day on an additional vote to our advantage within the United Nations organizations. Furthermore, if I go to Mexico it will allow us to examine whether there is a means to find a way to increase trade between that country and the Grand Duchy." Finally, precedents are cited in this letter, as "for example, the Haitian ambassador to Washington has returned from Mexico, where he presented his letters", and, to top it all off, "As you know, I have good relations with the Mexican Minister of Foreign Affairs, Mr. Castilla-Najera, the former Mexican ambassador to Washington." How would it be possible to refuse to follow up on such a strong desire of the Luxembourg representative in the United States to go to Mexico to represent his country! The Luxembourg Minister in London had also pleaded in favor of this accreditation. At the beginning of February, he reported that the Mexican ambassador in London, before his transfer to Paris, had raised the issue of diplomatic relations between the two countries. This ambassador had renewed his statements of attachment to Mr. Bech and confirmed that his Government was willing to accredit Le Gallais. In this case, Mexico would accredit its ambassador in Paris to Luxembourg.

The Grand Ducal decree is dated March 1. A typo had crept into its wording since the letters had originally been addressed to the predecessor of the Mexican President in office (decree of September 3). The letters of credence to be presented to the President of Mexico had finally arrived in Mexico City at the last minute on the day of the presentation. Accreditation to Mexico had to be postponed, Le Gallais regretting that he was unable to present his credentials, as proposed by the Mexican authorities, between February 19 and 29, 1948, as he had to travel to Lake Success on Long Island near New York for the "small Assembly of the United Nations". He finally travelled to Mexico by train, staying for ten days at the Hotel Geneva and meeting with the President. The delivery of the letters to President Aleman finally took place on March 11, 1948.[472] Le Gallais pointed out that ministers are received in the private residence of the President, ambassadors in the National Palace. As the president was receiving the Uruguayan ambassador that day, Le Gallais was, like the latter, received at the Palace, which gave him a certain satisfaction, with the regret, however, that only the Uruguayan colleague was entitled, as an ambassador, to a military band playing the national anthem. The rest of the two-page report consisted of a description of the ceremony, meetings and interviews that each newly accredited head of mission sent to his or her capital. Le Gallais specifically mentioned that his wife had accompanied him and had met with the minister's wife and that of the Chief of Protocol. He went to see the Dean of the Diplomatic Corps, ambassadors and a number of ministers, although he did not meet the Spanish chargé d'affaires, "who represents the Republican Government". Three days earlier, on his arrival in Cuernavaca, after a train journey of 3 days and 4 nights that he described as tiring, he sent a four-page handwritten letter to his "dear Mr. Bech". He wrote from this sublime city, with such a rich cultural heritage and located near Mexico City, where he had come to seek some rest. Le Gallais first complained of a bad night on his arrival in the Mexican capital located at 2,200 meters of altitude. He described the climate of Cuernavaca as ideal and began to dream, describing "the beautiful landscape, hills, plains and mountains in the background". He noted a great resemblance between this beautiful place and Italy, but with one drawback: "what misery from the border to Mexico City, reminiscent of China". He met the Secretary of State Jaime Torres Bodet, who had just received a decoration from Bech. He affirmed that the situation was serious and that the Russians will maintain the pressure on all fronts. The most critical places would be Greece, and the one with the greatest potential for danger, Palestine. Le Gallais also met his Dutch and Belgian colleagues Kielstra[473] and Ruzette,[474] who offered a lunch and dinner in honor of the new Luxembourg minister. Finally, Le Gallais pleaded for the use of a means to flatter his colleagues' egos: the presentation of honorary distinctions. Even though many people claim not to know what it is all about, they are nevertheless still fond of honors and being decorated for supposed merits. Le Gallais therefore suggested to Bech to decorate Kielstra who would have done more than Ruzette, the latter having "dropped the remark that you [Bech] had spoken of a decoration for him".

As often in life, patience is of essence, but Le Gallais knew how to insist and remind people of his arguments. In the end, most of the time, he won with those to whom he was generous in his compliments. This time, however, between the application for approval in May 1946, the sending of the first letters of credence in October of the same year and the handing over in March 1948, a great deal of time had passed.

Le Gallais had long argued for accreditation not only in Washington and Mexico City, but also in Ottawa. Thus, in a letter to Minister of State Dupong dated March 29, 1948, he had asked "to consider whether it might not be appropriate for you to discuss with Mr. Bech the question of my appointment as Minister in Ottawa. I would remind you that you took a first step in this direction and that I made other attempts in the same direction, the last of which was successful in February 1947. Mr. Pearson,[475] Under-Secretary of State, informed me that if the Grand Duchy made a request, it would be favorably received." And it is a piquant, not to say fallacious, point to begin with a personal argument in favor of this accreditation: "To a certain extent it can be explained that we have not yet done anything because it can be said that I wanted to wait for the right season before going to Ottawa." And Le Gallais developed after these considerations no less personal arguments invoking the embarrassing situation he might find himself in relation to his Canadian counterpart in Washington with whom he had discussed the subject, to finally consider "that it is in the interest of the country to consolidate our friendly relations with a state like Canada". How to resist such a plea any longer? Accreditation to Canada from Washington was again initially refused in April 1948 by Minister Bech himself, citing "financial reasons". Although he had been designated, by Grand Ducal decree of July 4, 1949, as an extraordinary envoy and non-resident Luxembourg Minister in Ottawa, Le Gallais did not deliver his letters until April 24 of the following year.

The delivery of the letters in Ottawa to Governor General Viscount Alexander of Tunis was described in a handwritten letter to "dear Mr. Bech" on the letterhead of the Chateau Laurier, a majestic Ottawa hotel, dated April 25, 1950. Le Gallais recounted in much better handwriting than the notes addressed to Mrs. Maloney that he and his wife had a good lunch the day before, and added that "my wife was the conversation starter". In more detail, he wrote:

"The governor came back from the American maneuvers very impressed with the novelty of the recoilless guns (France also has some, which shoot with a remarkable precision and are excellent against tanks, he said). He witnessed 35 different aerial maneuvers carried out in 55 minutes and admired the precision of the bombardments with big bombs . . . Alexander, answering my question frankly, said that a war within 5 years seemed likely to him unless something was done. This means arming ourselves so that the Russians cannot believe in certain victory. He added that even if they doubt the outcome that is not certain to stop them. He fully supported the idea of trying to make the Politburo members understand that the US does not want to attack the USSR and he believes that the plan of his friend Churchill to talk again with Stalin is a good one: I said that when Stalin was no longer there an agreement might be more difficult, to which he replied yes, adding that the latter had a certain sense for compromise, unlike Molotov, as for Vishinsky there is no trust in him, that is to say that he would become a bourgeois again if his interests so required (conversation between the two of us after lunch). Yesterday evening dinner at du Parc,[476] Ambassador of Belgium, a hunter friend, in the company of the Ambassadors of the Netherlands, Italy and France, very good, excellent wines, very pleasant. This morning visit to van Royen,[477] who understands my plan of attack. The director of the European division, Mac Dermot, agrees, summing up: 'try to get it through that the U.S. does not want to attack the USSR by making use of the Atlantic Treaty'. Mac Dermot would like to know our views on the German problem and he hopes that in London it will be decided to centralize information on this issue and that it will be shared; to judge and decide it is necessary to know, he concluded. I warned him against the Germans saying 'they must earn their way back'. He agreed, and then he said 'some must be reasonable'. Beware of too much wishful thinking."

He continued his account on April 27:

"Yesterday, lunch offered by Heaney—Under-Secretary of State to about ten diplomats and civil servants, including Pearson—sitting next to Ritchie, the Deputy Under-Secretary, who seems rather reserved towards the French proposals to set up a new co-ordinating body. (This attitude has since been confirmed to me—

it is hard to understand why not use the working committee in Washington). Visited the dean that you know: Sakellaropoulo.

Dinner at the van Royens with the Pearsons, etc. (Appointment with the latter on May 2) continue the visits today but I won't be able to finish them before I leave and I say everywhere that I will come back at the beginning of October. Luncheon in our honor in Parliament offered by the Claxtons;[478] sitting to the right of Mrs. Claxton and St. Laurent to her left, the latter very kind—I told him about the decoration for Mr. King[479] because it requires an authorization; he said he would arrange it and that they were very happy with our gesture—the Claxtons very eager and grateful for your welcome; a short speech on his part to express satisfaction at my appointment, thanks to Grand Duchess etc. The Grand Duchy is very well regarded here and we did well to open a legation.

Last night after dinner Pearson admitted that Cordier had come by plane to bring him a note that Lie was sending to Moscow. He said that we should propose to the USSR that the 1951 meeting of the United Nations be held in Moscow—he himself is in favor of Delhi but he thinks we should choose Paris."

Le Gallais resumed the May 1 missive with a lot of information deemed useful for his superior: "Visit to St-Laurent[480] this morning. Canada does not produce enough steel and did not receive enough from England and hopes that we could provide some steel and a courtesy visit to European colleagues and not the chargé d'affaires, including that of the USSR."

He finished his concise and expeditious report to Minister Bech on May 4: "Great dinner on May 2 at the French embassy for 36 people followed by a concert for other guests, magnificent modern embassy; May 3 dinner almost as big at the Pearson's offered to the van Royens; May 4 lunch described as very successful offered by the Le Gallais couple."

Aside from Hugues Le Gallais' suggestion to point out this potential market to the Luxembourg factories, he also raised in his report the opportunity to award a decoration to MacKenzie King. The latter was Canadian Prime Minister for almost 21 years and had participated in the creation of the United Nations in 1945. He received the Grand Cross of the Order of the Crown of Oak on May 4, 1950, just before his death on July 22 of the same year. The report on Le Gallais' Canadian escapade later stated that the dean of the Diplomatic Corps would also like to receive the decoration, a "*grand cordon* that he did not get because of the war." Le Gallais specified that he is said to be neurasthenic. This idea may never have come to fruition, even though Le Gallais always justified the awarding of honors.

He then concluded the account of this Canadian journey: "I am tired and happy to leave, but I don't think I am exaggerating when I say that this trip has been useful and that we are leaving a good impression of our country here. We did more than my colleague from Ireland who only stayed for five days. Ritchie spoke to Pearson who laughed and said he would tell you: I got my instructions. Since she has been here my wife is finding Washington better!" Always satisfied with his own prowess, Le Gallais did not hesitate to let everyone know.

Le Gallais and his wife were also in Canada in April 1951[481] during the visit of the French President and Mrs. Vincent Auriol, whom they had also met a few days earlier in Washington.[482] The French ambassador had given a reception for 1,500 people, and in the social column of the Evening Star it was mentioned that the Luxembourg Minister had worn his uniform.

Le Gallais would return regularly to Canada, for the NATO Council of Ministers on September 15, 1951 in Ottawa among other things. However, he informed his Minister that he would not return to Canada in 1953 as he did every year, given that "... in Washington there are a lot of people to get to know. And lastly, if I can save money, so much the better". This heralded a financial dispute as Le Gallais should have known all about Washington after thirteen years and been happy to be able to leave the American capital for a short while.

New credentials were issued at the change of reign in the United Kingdom which directly affected the recipient of such credentials in a Commonwealth country. Hugues Le Gallais was finally able to present his adapted credentials on October 8, 1952 to Thibeaudeau Rinfret, President of the Supreme Court of Justice and Deputy Governor General of Canada. However, an error also seems to have crept into the writing of the letters to Queen Elizabeth II, who had been on the throne for only a few months following the death of her father, King George VI, in February, since the Canadian Government had preferred to use the formula "Canada" and not "Dominion of Canada". The Canadian Minister in Brussels should have drawn this to the attention of the Ministry in Luxembourg. Neither Le Gallais nor, above all, the department seemed to have paid too much attention to it. Corrected letters were sent by post in May. An insert in the Canadian press with a photo in support certainly gave the ambassador, who was keen to publicize his country, but also his actions and his person—the greatest pleasure.

For some time, Le Gallais had been developing more pronounced aspirations to be accredited also to Cuba and even Brazil. In December 1944, he had already written to Bech: "I find it opportune to take up with you the thesis that has already been presented several times over the past two years: That the Grand Duchy of Luxembourg should have a legation in Brazil. Our Minister accredited there could at the same time be accredited in other South American countries".[483] Accreditation from Washington could indeed have led to other interesting journeys or even to participation in spectacular ceremonies or even the presentation of decorations. For example, for the installation of the new president of Brazil Kubitschek, Guill Konsbruck had travelled to Brazil from January 28 to February 12, 1956 to attend the event on January 31, 1956. Announcing his trip in a letter to Le Gallais on January 27, 1956, the latter wrote back on February 10, 1956: "I congratulate you on having been appointed to represent H.R.H. at this inauguration. I hope that you will come back with a beautiful Brazilian decoration, but from here it is not certain. Indeed it seems to depend on the individual customs of these countries. I have been to similar inaugurations in Cuba[484] three times without receiving a decoration, but I was nevertheless happy to go". Often magnanimous, Le Gallais here revealed a certain bitterness at the successes of others, even if in this case it was merely an honorary distinction. Prior to these ceremonies, Le Gallais had also arranged for President-elect Kubitscheck to travel to Luxembourg on January 12 from London.[485]

TRIPS TO CUBA

Although he was never accredited to Cuba, Hugues Le Gallais was able to visit it twice, as an article in the *Evening Star* in 1948 and a note in 1955 show.

In October 1948,[486] Hugues and Pisana Le Gallais travelled to Cuba for the inauguration of Carlos Prío as President. Like several other colleagues from Washington, the couple had attended the festivities and ceremonies in Havana.

At the beginning of March 1955, Le Gallais was able to travel there for the inauguration of President Batista. The country, described as the pearl of the West Indies, was heavily dependent on sugar cane production and exports to the American market. Rubén Fulgencio Batista y Zaldívar[487] had returned to power following a coup in 1952, and was elected unopposed in 1954 after the withdrawal of former president Ramon Grau San Martin, who called for a boycott to protest against the corruption of the regime. The influence of the United States was such that its ambassador was considered the second most important personality of the regime.

Hugues and Pisana travelled together to Havana. According to their son, this was apparently the only opportunity for Hugues' wife to take a plane, so the trip was a discovery for the couple, who were used to long journeys by train and boat. On March 4, Le Gallais reported to his Minister, who, again, had become President of the Government a year earlier:

"I am pleased to be able to inform you that my wife and I returned from Cuba the day before yesterday in good health. Your prompt acceptance of the Cuban Government's invitation for the Grand Duchy to be represented at President Batista's inauguration made things easier, since of the 51 heads of mission, I was number 9 and was able to march quite quickly. As three heads of mission before me were not accompanied by ladies, my wife had the seat number 6 at the big presidential dinner and there was only the Vice-President and the Spanish ambassador between her and the President. To her left she had the President of the Senate, Mr. Alliegro, whose family is of Italian origin, so the conversation was very lively. On my side, I was sitting between the Greek ambassador, Mrs. Melas, and the wife of the Minister of Justice of Cuba. After dinner we were able to have a pleasant conversation with the new Minister of Foreign Affairs and his wife, Mrs. Saladrigas.[488] On another occasion we met the former Minister of Foreign Affairs, Mr. Campa,[489] who is due to come as ambassador to Washington; he is very good but the choice is rather curious given that he does not speak English. In other words, we were quite prominent thanks to your quick response since the place depended on the date of arrival of the acceptance."

On the face of it, it was a nice combination of circumstances. In fact, Le Gallais was pursuing an ultimate goal: that of seeing the legation elevated to the status of an embassy. He would admit it openly, as he continued:

"If I've gone into a little bit more detail on this question of placement it is to show you that there are advantages to functions of this kind not to be at the end of the table as is the case for us at the White House dinners where we have the number 68 while being here for 15 years. This observation leads me to ask the question if our country has not now acquired a sufficiently established international position for us to consider elevating our respective legations to the rank of embassy and vice versa. Objectively speaking, I think it can be said that this would be a compliment to the country and consequently also to you as President of the Government and Minister of Foreign Affairs. That Luxembourg, by its will, continues to consider itself, or at least to place itself, which is the same vis-à-vis third parties, in the international arena on a lower level than that of Liberia for example, is, when you think about it, quite surprising. The same could be said of other countries such as Costa Rica, El Salvador, Honduras, Saudi Arabia, Finland, etc. Once all these countries have been placed on an equal footing with Great Britain and France, for example, is it in our interest to stay out of the movement. To the objection that an ambassador should have a secretary and be better paid than a minister, I will answer why, the work remains the same. I am telling you this not only because of the events in Havana, but also because the Swiss Minister told me just before my departure that Bern had asked him for a list of embassies in Washington. He added that he knew from the Finnish ambassador that the Icelandic Minister was very keen to see his legation raised to the rank of embassy and Mr. de Torrenté[490] concluded that it might be possible to envisage that for all three countries—Iceland, Luxembourg and Switzerland— the change could take place at the same time. I answered evasively but I wonder whether it would not be good if you could give me some indication of what I should say if it is asked again."

For the occasion, Le Gallais sent the report to the home of the Minister of State at 34, avenue Monterey. He addressed his superior more than insistently, calling him "dear Mr. Bech". Le Gallais had to wait until September 10, 1955 before the Luxembourg legation was granted embassy status.

Less than four years after this event, Fidel Castro would, on January 1, 1959, overthrow Batista's authoritarian regime and Le Gallais was never to return to this Caribbean island again. In the meantime, as was his custom, he was enjoying life, spending time in exquisite and exclusive places. For Le Gallais, the extraordinary was barely sufficient to "be well seen" and shine like no other Luxembourg diplomat could.

DREAM PLACES
TO HAVE A GOOD TIME

A certain curiosity and his temperament predisposed Hugues Le Gallais to make the most of the good moments of diplomatic life, which he exercised with allure and dignity. In addition to the very representative residence on Massachusetts Avenue rented by the government to the Grand Ducal Court, he had at his disposal stately and exclusive places where he could receive guests with the interpersonal skills that characterized him.

In Seal Harbor, Maine, the villa called *Rocco Pisana* was part of the Le Gallais' annual program. The resort is located on the southeastern portion of Mount Desert Island in Hancock County near Acadia National Park. Numerous sailboats, yachts and lobster boats anchored at Seal Harbor, adding to the seaside atmosphere. The quaint and chic little village with beautiful and peaceful views had become the summer favorite for many rich and famous Americans such as the Rockefellers. In 1958, Hugues Le Gallais made it clear long before he left the United States that the house was neither for sale nor for rent. However, Le Gallais later disposed of it. In his memoirs, banker David Rockefeller described his family's home in Seal Harbor and the 24-hour train ride to get there. The future president of Chase Manhattan Bank described Seal Harbor as quieter and more conservative than the more rowdy Bar Harbor. The Le Gallais had therefore chosen the ideal and exclusive location in more ways than one.

In Italy, the Le Gallais were welcomed with open arms at the Nani Mocenigo in Ca' del Duca. They also had the opportunity to enjoy a chalet in Cortina d'Ampezzo which actually belonged to Pisana's sister, Countess Katy Nani Mocenigo, and her husband, Count Marino Nani Mocenigo. The Le Gallais often took

Hugues Le Gallais and his wife Pisana and their son Norbert.

Undated photo of Hugues Le Gallais with his wife Pisana and their son Norbert.

advantage of this facility to recharge their batteries. The ski resort in the North of Italy is situated at an altitude of 1,210 m.
The Olympic Games were held there in 1956. It took two hours
by car and about five hours by train to get from Venice to the
southeastern pre-Alps in the heart of the Dolomites. The sister
of Pisana and her husband also had a house in Lido di Jesolo
and a fabulous estate in Dolo, also near Venice, which the family
could enjoy.

Another holiday project, this time in the South of France, was not
going to materialize. In a letter dated January 31, 1957 to an estate agency, Mrs. Montagne Taylor c/o John Taylor & Co located
on the Croisette, Hugues Le Gallais expressed interest in a prop-

Hugues Le Gallais with his wife Pisana and their son Norbert on a boat.

erty investment. This was followed by a request and details of the number of bedrooms, bathrooms, etc., desired. The villa should preferably be in the vicinity of Cannes, but Beaulieu and Villefranche could be considered. Le Gallais said he was in no hurry, but added photos of villas that could match his wishes and "we don't want a big property, but with enough land for some flower gardens. We do not want a pretentious villa, but a comfortable one in good taste." A lot of wishes, but without giving any idea, on two pages, of the price he was willing to pay for the object he was seeking. In an additional letter, Hugues Le Gallais specified in February that "when I speak of a beautiful view, I mean of the sea. Friends of mine ... told me that several new villas were for sale just below 'Philippine' (California, property of Princess de Ligne). I would very much like to have some information regarding these villas as well as quotations in French francs as I have funds available in France." The agency contacted responded to the enquiries with a selection of properties and an idea of the prices. As there was no rush, it was recommended to meet on the spot when the ambassador next came to the South of France. We don't know if a follow-up was reserved for this idea or if a trip was made following this request. In any case, Le Gallais wanted, as always, to be housed as well as possible and close to respectable people.

As for most diplomats, their often excessive residence in the American capital was finally a tool allowing Le Gallais to approach and retain certain individuals. As the exclusive social contacts of the Le Gallais can testify, the welcoming at Massachusetts Avenue has always been very refined.

Hugues Le Gallais and his wife Pisana in the salon of the legation in 1953.

SOCIAL AND OTHER ACTIVITIES OF
THE LE GALLAIS COUPLE AFTER THE WAR

The Le Gallais have left a considerable and appreciated mark in their community and beyond, their social life having been rich and varied. Pisana could not speak English when she arrived in the United States, so she had to make efforts to acclimatize. At one point, her husband suggested in correspondence that she was not always happy in the United States. At the end of his career, Hugues wished, perhaps also for this personal reason, to be appointed to his last post at the embassy in Rome. However, this post, opened in 1956, was occupied by a colleague of Le Gallais, Pierre Majerus.[491] The same year, former Minister of State Emile Reuter was appointed non-resident Ambassador to the Vatican. The two diplomats therefore had to meet Hugues Le Gallais from time to time, especially during his visits to the Italian capital. This embassy would have been a great reward for the woman who had always faithfully supported and accompanied him. It would have meant for Pisana to be able to return to her native country through the front door without having to return immediately to Venice. Hugues' wife considered that city too small and had left it, following Hugues without too much hesitation some 25 years earlier.

In the meantime, the memory of the war faded somewhat and social activities resumed in earnest at 2200 Massachusetts Avenue. As was to become customary after the war, on January 23, 1948, the Le Gallais hosted a reception on Massachusetts Avenue that was even the topic of the social columns of some newspapers. Evelyn Peyton Gordon wrote under the title *Little Nation, Little Legation—Minister and Mme. Le Gallais are the works for Luxembourg*: "One very satisfying thing about the legation of Luxembourg is that when you have met the Minister and Mme. Le Gallais you've met the staff! And you're never again bothered trying to figure out the difficult names of dozens of counselors, attachés, military and naval aides who clutter up other embassies and legations to the point of overdoing." In this flattering article, the journalist had reviewed the history of the country and of the Grand Ducal family, and described in a truly laudatory way the Le Gallais couple and their activities. The celebration of the Grand Duchess' birthday was the first reception since 1946 at which the most prestigious officials from Washington would have attended the legation.

On the Grand Duchess' birthday, on January 23, 1947, Le Gallais made a broadcast on the National Broadcasting Company (NBC) and, in 1952, on Voice of America with a reception for 600 people at the legation on the latter occasion. A description of an undated reception on the Grand Duchess' birthday was given in a letter to Mrs. Maloney from the Evening Star Broadcast Company. The festivities in Luxembourg, but especially at the legation are described as follows:

"a reception at the legation from 5:30 to 7:30... the popular Le Gallais have been here since 1940 and have many friends who will attend, in addition invited... according to the ambassador's secretary, Miss [sic] Eleanor Maloney, the Ambassador and Mrs. Le Gallais will receive in the hall upstairs until the crowd gets too large, then will receive downstairs... Mrs. Le Gallais, who is of Italian birth, will wear a strapless Dior taffeta dress with full skirt, oblique stripes of blue, brown and gold...with an Oriental scarf of blue and gold."

And another national touch: "Luxembourg is noted for its roses ... you may have seen the 200 Luxembourg rose bushes in front of the legation that bloom 8 months of the year... too bad they're not right now in bloom...". The celebration of the sovereign's birthday on January 23, 1952 must have been particularly successful with no less than four newspaper articles cut out for the *Scrapbook*. Thus in the *Washington Daily*, Evelyn Peyton Gordon gave the Grand Duchess "Her Majesty" with the headline *Popular Embassy Opens Doors*, while Mary McNair of the *Washington*

Post spoke of Pisana's fashionable hair, comparing it to that of a Titian portrait. She also mentioned the absolute "necessity" of seeing the dress of the mistress of the house, the whole reception being the equivalent of a fashion show. Achsah Dorsey Smith of the *Washington Times Herald* and Betty Beale[492] had not been more restrained in their descriptions of the magnificence and luxury put forward by the Le Gallais. The previous year, Mary McNair had, in a similar article entitled *Everyone—but Everyone—came*, stated that Mrs. Le Gallais had worn a red satin dress by the couturier Jacques Fath for the occasion. Her terribly "glamorous" destiny sometimes led her to be perceived as the ideal classical beauty born to play the great worldly bourgeois ladies. In January 1951, an article in the *Evening Star*[493] on the Luxembourg reception must not have pleased Mrs. Maloney: "Incidentally the annual reception given by the Luxembourg Minister and Mme. Le Gallais is invariably one of the best parties of the year—draws nearly everybody of any importance in the Capital's official set under one roof. The Le Gallais' perhaps do not need a social secretary as many of the ambassadors here do."

In August 1953 a report on the couple Le Gallais and the embassy appeared in a Luxembourg magazine, the *Revue*.[494]. Also mentioning Mrs. Maloney's activities, the article focused on the historic events that had taken place in recent years at 2200 Massachusetts Avenue, enabling the country to attain the place on the world map as President Roosevelt had wished. In addition to a photo of the building, five shots depict the dining room, the couple sitting in their living room, the entrance to the legation and Le Gallais as well as his Secretary, the latter taking notes under a mirror above a fireplace decorated with baroque stucco and under a portrait of the Hereditary Grand Duke Jean.

In addition to their busy social life, the Le Gallais family also took part in a number of charitable activities. In 1943, an insert entitled "The lovely lady of Luxembourg at home with her son" appeared in an American newspaper with a large photo of Mrs. Le Gallais and her son sitting by the fireplace in an embassy drawing room. In fact, it was scheduled to be made public on May 15, when the legation would be opened to assist the Home for Incurables in Washington by means of an annual tour of many mansions. Le Gallais did not fail to inform, albeit briefly, his Minister of State of the arrival of 2,000 people who had passed through its salons: "One may consider that this also constitutes a kind of propaganda for the Country",[495] in a way similar to the effort undertaken for some years by its authorities. In April 1950,[496] Goodwill embassy Tours organized by the Goodwill Guild brought other visitors to the Luxembourg legation.

The photo of Hugues Le Gallais in ambassador's uniform also dates from this post-war period. Le Gallais, as we shall see, knew how to combine form and substance, sometimes playing on one and sometimes on the other. Rather ostentatious, more rational than emotional, he had taken the law of June 30, 1947 on the organization of the Luxembourg Diplomatic Corps and its implementing regulations literally. By the way, Bech and some of his colleagues, such as the diplomats Als, Wagener, Reichling and Reuter, had done the same. For example, the texts of the law provided for the obligation for an agent of the diplomatic corps, whatever his rank, who proposes to enter into marriage, to obtain the prior authorization of the Minister of Foreign Affairs, which will assess in particular whether the future wife possesses the personal qualities required to assist her husband in the fulfillment of his social obligations. Authorization to enter into marriage with a person who did not possess Luxembourg nationality was only granted if special circumstances justified an exception. A Grand

Ducal decree specified one year later: "The official costume of envoys extraordinary and ministers plenipotentiary is that provided for by the Grand Ducal royal decree of April 10, 1855." Le Gallais and a few other diplomats had therefore acted in accordance with the texts that suited them and which placed them on an equal footing as their colleagues from other countries who had been proudly wearing their uniforms for ages. One or the other diplomatic uniform was supposedly bought second-hand.[497] This was certainly not the case for Le Gallais. For the visit of French President Auriol in March 1951 to the United States, it had been noted that: "the Minister of Luxembourg in gold braided, diplomatic uniform complete with sword, escorting his wife, Mme. Le Gallais, whose handsome jade necklace topped a starched white net picture gown".[498]

The 1950's were a prosperous time for the couple, who was settling into a familiar routine and spending several weeks, or rather months, on holiday in the United States and, especially, in Europe. Thus, in 1950, the couple boarded the French line from New York to Le Havre on June 8 and was back only on September 15. That summer, an international driving license was issued by the sub-prefect of Le Havre on June 13 for Hugues Le Gallais residing at Place Vendôme 8 and Massachusetts Avenue 2200. An international automobile certificate was issued in Le Havre the same day for a green 1950 Cadillac Sedan. The Le Gallais couple had thus become more mobile and knew how to travel comfortably throughout Europe and the United States.

BILATERAL VISITS IN THE 1950S

After the war, several bilateral visits kept the head of post in Washington, and his counterpart in Luxembourg, in suspense. The rich heiress and socialite Perle Mesta[499] was sent to Luxembourg by President Truman in 1949. It was now difficult for Le Gallais to compete with his more flamboyant and omnipresent counterpart, who did everything to attract the attention of Luxembourg dignitaries.

The visit of Eleanor Roosevelt, the president's widow, to Luxembourg[500] took place on June 21 and 22, 1950. She went to see the American military cemeteries at Hamm, Ettelbruck and Clervaux, where a visit to the castle of the de Lannoy family was also planned. There, as during the visit to the medieval castles in Vianden and Wiltz, she heard many stories about the Second World War. Mrs. Roosevelt considered that the Marshall Plan had helped to rehabilitate and rebuild the country—a task which she felt was two-thirds accomplished. She also went to Bastogne to see the monument commonly called *Mardasson* erected in memory of American soldiers by the Belgian-American Association. On her return to Luxembourg, a reception was organized by Mayor Emile Hamilius and a pleasant half-hour visit was paid to Joseph Bech's house before a dinner, hosted by the American Minister Perle Mesta, took place at the American legation. Mrs. Roosevelt was always in the company of Mrs. Mesta, who left a positive impression on the widow of the former President. The visit had been important in many ways. Wishing to be present at the reunion of his superiors with the former American First Lady, Le Gallais had taken time off in view of this visit, but also to be able to attend, a little later, the wedding of the youngest daughter of the Grand Duchess, Princess Alix of Luxembourg.

Hugues Le Gallais in his ambassador uniform.

As Commander-in-Chief of the NATO armies from 1950 to 1952, General Eisenhower visited Luxembourg again after his September 1946 visit. He came to Luxembourg again in January 1951 to meet the Grand Duchess, the Prime minister and the Minister of Foreign Affairs. He also went to Luxembourg to visit his friend Perle Mesta and to play golf. Shortly afterwards, on April 26, 1952, the General paid an official farewell visit to Luxembourg where he was received with full honors. Together with Minister Joseph Bech and Ambassador Perle Mesta, he went to the *Gëlle Fra* monument to lay flowers in honor of the soldiers who died during the war. A visit to the Hamm cemetery, as was the case in 1946, was a must. A few months later, on January 20, 1953, Hugues Le Gallais was to attend the inauguration of Eisenhower as the 34th President of the United States. Despite his seniority and the fact that the legation did not yet have the rank of an embassy, the Luxembourg Minister had made sure that he could take part in this great event, which is repeated every four years on January 20, with large balls and the swearing-in of the new head of state below the Capitol, often in the coldest weather. The re-election of the general four years later was to be the last of a president that Le Gallais could follow closely, this time as a fully fledged ambassador.

Other Americans were to find their way to Luxembourg, such as Matthew Woll, of Luxembourg origin, who, as vice-president of the American Federation of Labor, visited Luxembourg on November 20, 1949, or Senator Theodore Green of Rhode Island on December 10, 1951, as reported in the *Journal d'Esch*. The new Secretary of State, who was appointed in 1953 by Dwight D. Eisenhower and remained in office until 1959, Foster Dulles,[501] was in Luxembourg for a brief visit in February 1953. Le Gallais kept all sorts of traces in his *Scrapbook* of all these visits to his native country, with a stopover at his counterpart's house. He was probably a bit disappointed as many dignitaries visited Luxembourg while only a few visitors like Bech came regularly to New York for the United Nations General Assembly. The visit of Foreign Minister Bech in 1952 gave rise to a description in the *Evening Star* of November 18 that is worth repeating in part:[502]

"Foreign Minister Is Entertained On Visit Here; The Luxembourg Prime Minister, Mr. Joseph Bech, who is in Washington for a few days during a lull in the operations of the Political and Security Committee of the United Nations of which he is chairman, was honored at dinner last evening. The hosts were the Luxembourg Minister and Mme. Le Gallais, who will entertain for him again this evening. Guests last evening included the Canadian ambassador and Mrs. Hume Wrong, Associate Justice and Mrs. Felix Frankfurter, the Director of the Veterans' Administration and Mrs. Omar N. Bradley, the Chief of Protocol and Mrs. Stanley Woodward, Lady Wilson, wife of Field Marshal Sir Henry Maitland Wilson; Mr. and Mrs. Wayne Chatfield Taylor, Mr. and Mrs. Andre Visson, Mrs. Edwin M. Watson and Mr. Edward Nash of the State Department. Mr. Joseph E. Davies, former United States minister to Luxembourg and ambassador to Belgium, entertained at a stag dinner Sunday night at Tregaron in honor of the Foreign Minister."

This was a lot of socializing for Hugues Le Gallais, who liked to show himself to Luxembourg visitors and prove to them how well he has settled in a dozen years, a stay that was longer than usual but which was to last even longer.

In Washington, Hugues Le Gallais had the opportunity to meet some of the greats of this world. Thus, the Luxembourg Minister had been invited in November 1949 on the occasion of the visit of Reza Pahlavi, the Shah of Iran. During the visit of the Iranian sovereign, Betty Beale had described one of those scenes of diplomatic life, which today may seem futile. She reported in detail that the Belgian and Luxembourgish ambassadors had exchanged their decorations. The journalist concluded the episode on the honors exchanged by asking whether the ladies should curtsy and what decorations the gentlemen should really wear for the occasion, thus embodying all the dignity they had been given. Le Gallais had also been invited to a reception at the French embassy during Vincent Auriol's visit to Washington on March 30, 1951. The French President had travelled to Mount Vernon in early April to deliver a message, emphasizing the loyalty and gratitude for American assistance in the defense against Communism to which France would contribute, and for this reason nothing could come between the two countries. Seven months later, in early November 1951, the British Princess Elizabeth and the Duke of Edinburgh were also in attendance, but Le Gallais did not keep a record of them in his *Scrapbook*, probably because he had not been invited to the event. Le Gallais had been reunited with one of the royals in exile only a few years earlier, on April 23, 1952, during the visit to Washington by Prince Bernard of the Netherlands, with dinner on the occasion of the National Aeronautics Meeting. A nephew of the Grand Duchess, Prince Heinrich of Bavaria, and his young wife, Baroness Anne-Marie de Lustrac, whose parents had a house in Norfolk and who apparently wished to settle in New York, were in Washington on February 11, 1952 for a brief stopover without us knowing whether they met the Luxembourg diplomatic representative, who nevertheless kept a record of it in his *Scrapbook*. In September 1953, Imperial Prince Akihito visited the United States for the first time. Some eight years earlier, his country had been occupied and transformed into a democracy, as his own father had lost much of his political power. The heir to the Japanese throne, whose existence Le Gallais had followed since his birth in 1933, a few months before the Le Gallais' son, spent two days in

Washington and Mount Vernon. A photo shows Le Gallais reverently greeting the future Japanese Emperor. It was a high point, after his Japanese experience of about ten years in the 1930s and two years after the signing of the peace treaty with Japan in 1951.

CULTURAL DIPLOMACY

In addition to his tireless diplomatic efforts, aimed at dialogue, negotiation and persuasion, the Luxembourg Minister was also active in the field of cultural diplomacy. As a connoisseur and collector of oriental art, he did not, however, look down on classical works. He knew how to promote Luxembourg culture in the broadest sense, as the country did not have any real treasures for having been quite poor before the steel boom at the end of the 19th century, in which the Le Gallais family had played a large part. While less than a century earlier, a third of the population had emigrated, mainly to the American continent, Luxembourg was now booming economically, and Le Gallais was proud to contribute to the development of Luxembourg's cultural heritage.

An exhibition of "Art privately owned" at the Corcoran Gallery in Washington from February 10 to March 30, 1952, with a cover page from the *Washington Post* on January 20, would allow Le Gallais to make people talk about a "16th century Italian polychrome wood carving of St Anthony". 352 works of art, belonging to 161 persons from the Washington area, were shown there. These included a representation of Benjamin Franklin by the 18th century French painter Joseph-Siffrein Duplessis, a work donated by de Gaulle to Truman, and a bronze statue by Ernst Barlach

Hugues Le Gallais with the statue of St Anthony from his collection.
(Photo: Corcoran/Washington Post).

representing a boy singing. Le Gallais' contribution, along with
that of four other persons, appeared on the cover page of the most
influential newspaper in the American capital. In a photo taken
on this occasion, the haughty and phlegmatic Le Gallais was sto-
ically facing St. Anthony in this picture. He had the good taste
to pretend not to take himself seriously, whereas usually, he was
known as one of the most posh and prominent individuals in all
of Washington. Sometimes giving the impression of an unbearable, even ceremonious and somewhat conceited type, Hugues Le
Gallais, always dignified and rigorous, shows himself in this photo
in a funny and sympathetic light. A catalogue was published un-

der the title of *Privately Owned: A Selection of Works of Art from Collections in the Washington Area.*

Several other activities with cultural connotations were undertaken to make the Grand Duchy known in the United States. For example, a press article of September 27, 1953 relates a week-long exhibition organized by the American chain of department stores Jordan Marsh Company, based in Boston, "to pay tribute to Belgium and Luxembourg".

A major retrospective was organized the following year. The Smithsonian Institution Travelling Exhibition Service presented the painter Pierre-Joseph Redouté on a itinerant basis. Both Walloon and Parisian, this official artist of the Court of Versailles in the 18th century was born in 1759 in Saint-Hubert in Wallonia, about a hundred kilometers from Luxembourg City, then part of the Duchy of Luxembourg. The Belgians and Luxembourgers were therefore somewhat at odds with each other. A retrospective with 37 works by the artist was to travel throughout the United States and be displayed in several cities. It was shown in California, Texas, Kentucky, New York and Washington from January 15 to February 2, 1956 at the National History Building on 10th Street and was a great success. The opening in New York by Hugues Le Gallais at 1130 Fifth Avenue, headquarters of the Audubon Society Art Show, on April 7, 1954, was the starting point for the presentation of works made available by the Musée d'Histoire in Luxembourg, Hugues Le Gallais himself and other private collectors. The historian and journalist Hans Roger Madol[503] and the English poet and essayist Sacheverell Sitwell[504] published an album about the painter and his works in 1954, printed by Collins in London. At the inauguration, Hugues Le Gallais expressed the predilection he had always felt for this master whose character and art are so characteristic of the Ardennes. The opening took place in London on September 9, 1952 in the presence of the diplomat Hans Roger Madol, who had known the Grand Duchess and Bech before the war and had placed numerous articles on Luxembourg in the media.[505]

Doubts remain as to the date of Le Gallais' first meeting with the Luxembourg-American photographer and painter Edward Steichen. Born in Bivange in Luxembourg 17 years before Hugues, Steichen came from a completely different background than that of Le Gallais. Steichen's family had left Luxembourg when the future artist was only one year old. He was a specialist in specific artistic fields that were not so familiar to the connoisseur of oriental art the Luxembourg diplomat was. Steichen was, from 1947 to 1961, Director of the Department of Photography at the Museum of Modern Art in New York and was the originator and curator of the collection *The Family of Man*. The two men probably met as early as 1943 in New York. Edward Steichen travelled to Luxembourg around 1952 to meet Ministers Bech and Frieden without the latter apparently having informed Le Gallais specifically or to ask him to ensure any follow-up.[506] The exhibition *The Family of Man* was shown in 1955 in New York and in Washington.[507]

Heritage days and other open door days would allow ordinary people to get an impression of Embassies, often narrowly perceived as a place of power and influence or even of a supposedly golden life. In May 1952, Mrs. Maloney wrote that, with some 300 visitors, there were fewer on the special day than in previous years. In 1953 and 1954 there were requests for Goodwill Tours of the legation for the end of April. All this helped to spread knowledge about Luxembourg, which was often, then as now, completely unknown and sometimes even confused in the United States with the Principality of Liechtenstein.

DEPARTURES AND ARRIVALS

From time to time, old acquaintances also left the world of Le Gallais, while others came to join or visit him. Most of the time, the Luxembourgers came to Washington on business, as mass tourism had not yet become part of everyday life. The city was the capital of the world's leading power and was therefore also a must because of the international financial institutions and the proximity to the United Nations headquarters in New York.

In a letter dated May 6, 1952, Mrs. Maloney reported the death of the engineer and steelmaker Aloyse Meyer on May 3, 1952, at the age of 68. We do not know whether the two men had any personal ties, but we have seen the extent to which Le Gallais and Konsbruck had intervened on his and Arbed's behalf. An engineer in Dudelange and then, after the First World War, technical director at the head office, Meyer had been General Manager since 1920 and had therefore already most probably been in professional contact with Hugues' father.

Another departure, this time undoubtedly in accordance with Le Gallais' wishes, was that of Countess of Lynar, who took the train to New York on June 26, 1952.[508] Le Gallais did not attend this departure as he was on holiday in Europe, and one may suppose that he was somewhat relieved.

In the summer of 1952 Prince Antoine de Ligne, husband of Princess Alix, arrived in the United States. The Prince, a Belgian national, was to work at the Belgian embassy as a military attaché. At the end of August, with the Minister still absent, Mrs. Maloney reported that two Princesses, one of whom was Princess Alix and the other bearing the name of Princess of Bar (pseudonym of an Archduchess of Austria), had arrived on their turn. This gave rise to inquiries by some journalists, which Mrs. Maloney tried to avoid, reporting only that the Prince and Princess de Ligne were going to reside at the "farm" near Trenton and occupy a flat in Washington. In addition to this news, Mrs. Maloney reported on August 20 that Dupong and Werner would arrive on the *Nieuw Amsterdam* on August 30 and reported on the state of the embassy's cash till. Le Gallais must have been delighted to have a member of his Grand Ducal family and his Minister of State with him again for a while.

THE FUNCTIONING OF THE EMBASSY

The cost of running embassies varies from country to country, with the United States, and Washington in particular, always being expensive. In the early days of Luxembourg diplomacy, nobles and bourgeois with sufficient means were chosen to take on these more or less well-paid functions. When the material situation became somewhat secure, the government reimbursed the expenses incurred. We have seen that at the beginning of the war, Le Gallais had been invited to ask for advances from his acquaintances in Washington. He had pleaded for an increase in the budget of the legation on several occasions and had been reproached for an excessively lavish lifestyle. Let us simply recall a letter addressed to the Minister of State on April 7, 1941 with a view to increase the budget which he considered insufficient: "In the present times, we must not appear to be a small country... I firmly expect the Grand Ducal Government to support, by all the means at its disposal, the efforts I am making to be present everywhere and to ensure that we are not forgotten".[509] It was especially during the war that the functioning of the embassy and Le Gallais' visions of a dignified presence were, as we have seen, a point of friction between the diplomat and his direct superiors. As Dupong reported in his report on the years of exile of the government at the Constituent Assembly meeting of March 20, 1945 in the Chamber of Deputies, during the war £50,000, or $266,000, was spent on legations and consulates.[510] Subsequently, in the archives of the embassy, the cost of operation was regularly the subject of notes and documents, as we shall see by way of a few examples.

It was not only the lifestyle of Le Gallais that was scrutinized, but also the expenses incurred by all those who were, more or less directly, at his service. As early as the early 1950s, the embassy's accounting system was so difficult that Bech himself wrote in October 1950 that the second servant, the chef de cuisine Ennio Petrucci, should be included in the embassy's accounts and that the driver's allowance should be included in separate accounts in the legation's funds. In July 1951, the calculations of the allowances relating to the civil servants' state of service were considered "often incomplete and sometimes inaccurate". For the legation, the following were included in the statement: Mrs. Maloney and her replacement, the driver René Cettolin and Ennio Petrucci; for the New York Consulate: Mr. Staudt, Mrs. Loesch; for the Chicago Consulate: Mr. Gilson, who received a monthly allowance; for the Information Office in New York: Mr. Madol, who also received an allowance. The following year, Le Gallais asked that the matter be reconsidered, as "it would be fair to increase the gratuities gradually each year to reach a ceiling of one month's salary. I see no reason why indigenous staff working for a foreign Government should be treated as if they were working for private industry." From a budget proposal for 1953 we know that the ambassador received a salary of $16,092, while his assistant received $3,600 plus $125-$150 per month in bonuses. The driver and the chef received $2,370 and $2,030 including gratuities respectively. The total proposed expenditure for the staff of the embassy in Washington, D.C., including allowances and gratuities, was almost $25,000 in 1953. This was in addition to about $6,500 for building maintenance and $2,550 for office expenses, including $500 for newspaper subscriptions, etc., which were paid by the embassy. Travel costs were estimated at $7,420 and entertainment costs (divided between large diplomatic banquets and receptions) at $4,500. A total of $42,897 was proposed, plus $12,770 for the New York Consulate, $1,050 for Chicago and $1,185 for the stipend of the Information Commissioner in New York, Mr. Madol.[511]

On June 24, 1952, Eleanor Maloney wrote to Hugues Le Gallais: "I hope to have prepared a letter about the accounts for you to view when you are in Luxembourg. It means, I have come to the conclusion going over the 1950 Accounts. I may have to get an expert accountant, but I know you will agree that it will be worth it in order to settle once and for all the situation of our accounts for seven years." In July, a firm of accountants did the bookkeeping, and Mrs. Maloney even reported that an accountant reviewed the accounts and set up a system to keep the books. As he had done this for free, the secretary took the liberty of offering him two bottles of scotch. Le Gallais later agreed to give additional bottles, but specified that if Mrs. Maloney could not explain a difference of $194, he would have to reimburse them from his personal account and that: if you made a mistake in giving the figures for 1950 no harm can come from admitting it but it Must be explained". For Le Gallais, managing a legation or embassy involved a financial and accounting aspect for which he was not overly prepared and which he faced only with some reluctance, preferring by far the other social and worldly aspects that were much more pleasant and entertaining.

HOLIDAYS AND OTHER AMENITIES
OF DIPLOMATIC LIFE

Many fantasies exist about the life of diplomats. However, behind the myths, there are always real men and women. The Le Gallais couple certainly led a busy life in Washington, where they stayed at most nine months out of the year. Numerous trips, and especially over two months off in the summer, came to brighten up their sumptuous daily life in many ways. The summer period being particularly humid and unbearable in the American capital, civil servants and diplomats have always fled to the open sea, returning to work on the eve of the Indian Summer, which is one of the most beautiful seasons in North America, with its natural gilding and multicolored foliage. This way of life, with the head of mission and his family taking time off when no one had any idea of the internet and instant communications, is today perceived as absolutely out of proportion. During those days, absences from work were always presented in writing to the minister before being confirmed by Grand Ducal decree.

In his youth, Hugues Le Gallais had played bridge brilliantly. Around the age of 40 he suddenly stopped playing, feeling that he no longer had a good enough memory to do so. As a token of his attachment to bridge, his companions gave him a beautiful silver box. For her part, Pisana played canasta, notably with the Walter Lippmann couple,[512] who were very popular in Washington. The journalist in the *New Republic*, the *World*, and the *New York Herald Tribune* had notably written a laudatory article on the Le Gallais couple and the Grand Duchy. The couple's passions and predilections have allowed them to make their way in the most diverse circles and the highest Washingtonian spheres. Tennis, hunting and fishing were other hobbies they shared with Washingtonian friends.

The Le Gallais knew how to entertain and went out of their way to leave the best impression on their guests. Thus, the eldest son of Prime Minister Dupong, who was at Harvard during the war, was received at 2200 Massachusetts Avenue and was very impressed to see the precious metal plates used to receive the Le Gallais guests. The staff would have warned Lambert Dupong[513] not to mention that they were saucers that were part of the silverware of the Grand Ducal family, so as not to tempt potentially dishonest guests.

Even during the war, and especially before the Americans joined in the conflict, social life was intense in the American capital. Newspapers relayed the slightest deed and gesture, so that a regular agenda could be traced from the publications that now seem very superficial. Thus, in February and March 1941,[514] the President's wife "heads the list of patronesses for the benefit fashion show and tea which will be given in Anderson House... The proceeds will be shared by Relief for French Refugees in England, Inc., of which Mrs. George Barnett is chairman, and Refugees of England. Inc., of which the Countess of Abingdon is chairman," and "heads the list of patrons for the lecture". These events were attended by the whole of Washington, and the Le Gallais could not fail to attend. In October 1941[515] followed a "supper party in the Chinese room of the Mayflower Hotel followed the final Good Neighbors' concert at the Pan-American Union last night when Vice President Henry A. Wallace, delivered an address over the short-wave program." In August 1942,[516] it was the turn of a "Noted Patrons Rally to Aid Children's Hospital Benefit" with a performance of the opera Carmen at the Water Gate by the San Carlo Opera Company, which was back in Washington in May 1944 with the Le Gallais still present.[517] The funds raised by the "Newspaper Women's Club" were to be handed over in full to the "fund inaugurated seven years ago by the club for the maintenance of a bed in Children's Hospital for seriously ill little tots who otherwise would not receive the specialized hospital care they so much need". In November of the same year,[518] the newspapers reported the presence of the Le Gallais couple at the concert of the National Symphony Orchestra for the benefit of the "Community War Fund" from which many foreign support groups were to benefit. Other more or less unusual activities followed during the war years, such as in May 1943[519] the "United Nations' Doll Festival" organized by the "Dollology Club" for the benefit of "Goodwill Industries". This time, the event did not attract the minister, only the wives of diplomats making the trip. At the beginning of June 1943,[520] the Le Gallais couple opened the doors of their mission to the Chamber Music Guild. This was an event that was a little more original compared to the many dinners and receptions that can not be mentioned in detail. This commitment to the Chamber Music Guild dates[521] from the Grand Duchess' reception at the White House, and the Le Gallais attended various events organized by this association throughout the 1940s, willingly granting their patronage.

At the concert with "Prominent Patrons" on November 16,[522] the wife of the Belgian ambassador, Countess van der Straten-Ponthoz, was among the "patronesses for the concert which will be given by the noted soprano, Grete Stueckgold at the Statler Hotel", while Mrs. Le Gallais was mentioned along with various other patrons of the event. Other dinners, receptions and even teas are mentioned in the social columns of the American capital's newspapers, for example, in May 1944,[523] a tea for the "Luxembourg day at the United War Relief Center".[524]

Le Gallais' son was also to lend his assistance and made appearances on various occasions,[525] such as in December 1944, when the daughter of the Under-Secretary of War and Mrs. Robert P. Patterson, Virginia, aged 7, sent a message of hope and peace for

Christmas, imitated by many other children of illustrious Washingtonians.

"Her message will be sent December 22 in the 10th International Children's Christmas Broadcast ... and will be broadcast through the co-operation of the Blue Network Co. There will be a coast to coast hookup and the program will be heard locally ... and carried to foreign lands by short wave. Invitations have been extended to 43 Embassies and legations to select a child of one of the members of the staff who will send a message from children of their native land to the children of the United States... Thirty children of diplomats representing 25 foreign countries have accepted the invitation of the committee to take part in this fitting ceremony during the Christmas season. ... Many of the children will send their greetings to their home land in their native tongue and repeat it to the children in this country in English."

After the end of the war in Europe, the couple's social activities resumed with renewed vigor. The second half of the 1940s and the 1950s were for the Le Gallais a prosperous period, with events often reported by the fashionable press of the American capital. Without wanting to be exhaustive and based on a search engine made available by the Library of Congress, here is a summary of the activities of which a report in the written press remains. At the beginning of March 1945, Mrs. Le Gallais "wore a black satin frock under her black coat and a narrow brimmed hat ornamented with tiny gold dots" when she was in Congress to listen to President Roosevelt's assessment following his meeting in Yalta in February 1945 with Churchill and Stalin.[526] The Le Gallais were also present in September 1945[527] "when diplomatic, official and residential society gives itself over to sharing that which it has with the little ones who have it not. The occasion will be the opening performance of 'Dinner at Eight' given for the benefit of the Save the Children Federation by the British Players, who have volunteered their services as a token of their appreciation of the work done by the American branch of the federation to save the children of Great Britain during the German bombings." In December 1945,[528] Mrs. Le Gallais had to be there when President Truman's wife honored the United Nations War Relief Christmas Bazaar with her presence, being greeted by the United States Marine Band. Two months later,[529] Mrs. Truman was, like Pisana Le Gallais, present at a dinner given by the Washington Branch of the American Society for Russian Relief in honor of Mrs. J. Borden Harriman. In November 1947,[530] Le Gallais was in Congress with his Minister of Foreign Affairs, who was visiting Washington and attending the United Nations General Assembly in New York, to listen to the President's ten points ("plea for legislation to aid suffering nations across the seas and to bolster domestic economy"). In February 1948,[531] Pisana Le Gallais attended the luncheon offered by Mrs. J.M.W. Koning Hamilton at the United Nations Club in honor of former directors of the United Nations War Relief. The Washington premiere of *The Tales of Hoffman*, a film in Technicolor, took place at the Play House on April 18, 1951[532] under the patronage of Mrs. Truman and was sponsored by the British ambassador and Lady Franks. The event was in support of the National Symphony Maintenance Fund. It was attended by a brilliant audience, including the dean and several members of the diplomatic corps. Mrs. Le Gallais, along with other Washington social leaders, attended the French Fashion Show and Luncheon on October 11, 1951,[533] at the Mayflower Hotel, to benefit the Thrift Shop. Le Gallais also attended, in October 1951,[534] at the invitation of the Indian ambassador, Mrs. Vijaya Lakshmi Pandit,[535] the premiere of the film *The River*. The presentation was made by the Theatre Guild. The film had been produced in India by Kenneth McEldowney, directed by Jean Renoir, based on the autobiographical novel by Rumer Godden. A few days later, they were at Constitution Hall for the New York Philharmonic Orchestra concert for the benefit of the Children's Fund of Queen Frederika of Greece.

A November 3, 1953 an article in the *Washington Post* by Mary McNair on a dinner in honor of the American Minister in Luxembourg Wiley Buchanan[536] was entitled "This game is that's tries men's minds!" deserves to be quoted in full:

"The minister produced an ancient Japanese scroll which looked like nothing more than a splash of gray paint and a few scattered brush strokes. Then he gave everyone a slip of paper with instructions to write their interpretation of the painting. The responses were varied—amusing, mystic and perplexing. Not one of the more than 20 people present had the right answer. Some said 'a tiger', a 'lake and village'. The clew was in three almost microscopic strokes of the paintbrush. It was a 'bursting chestnut'. And then to show how accurately the artist had reproduced nature, M. Le Gallais showed a photograph of a bursting chestnut taken from a newspaper. However, before they were given the answer, guests were asked to sign the guest book, each writing along with his name, an interpretation of the printing. Looking through the pages of names distinguished in the arts, politics and diplomacy, I could find only one with the correct answer. That was the Japanese ambassador, Elkich Araki. The two prettiest women around the dinner table that night were the hostess and the guest of honor. Mme Le Gallais wore a gown of turquoise blue shining satin with a generous stole of cherry red satin. Ruth Buchanan's gown by Dessés combined chiffon and velvet, made a ruffled bustle and a velvet stole in the same shade of dusty pink."

The Buchanans were to succeed the famous and fanciful Perle Mesta at the legation on Boulevard Emmanuel Servais in Luxembourg.

They were about to leave, accompanied by their three children, Diane, Barnie and Wiley Jr. called Bucky, by boat from New York a few days after a dinner at the embassy. Press articles on this subject, with photos, have been carefully preserved in the *Scrapbook*. Already in December articles were published on the installation of the new American diplomatic couple in Luxembourg. The Buchanans left no doubt as to their intention to do just as well, if not better, than their ingenious counterparts in Washington.

Another prestigious dinner at the embassy on the occasion of the departure of the Australian ambassador and Lady Spender[537] was also described in the *Evening Star* of January 6, 1958: "the entire table was decorated with the most beautiful lacquer vases, and stands bearing little figures of the Japanese No dancers". The "four piece Sidney orchestra" played music for the 60 people present. There was Chief Justice Earl Warren, State Department adviser Frederick Reinhardt, Assistant Secretary of State Andrew Berding and, as so often, the Walter Lippmanns.

The diplomatic and social life of the Le Gallais' thus became both a spectacle and a witness to the great Washingtonian theatre. The Le Gallais couple's enriching and exciting evenings were appreciated and always full of encounters and exchanges. The diplomats knew how to have fun and did everything possible to attract the Gotha of the political and financial life of the United States concentrated in the District of Columbia. With panache, Hugues and Pisana Le Gallais, whose personalities were dissimilar but complementary, knew how to entertain and were not concerned about managing their image, even if laudatory comments were always welcome and were carefully included in the *Scrapbook*. Skillfully, the couple knew how to wait for the right moment to advance the Luxembourg cause on a parquet floor overflowing with all kinds of social events.

A clarification by Minister Bech in February 1950 on Le Gallais' request for leave, which had been pushed a little too far, set the record straight for once:

"Any agent on duty abroad may, if the needs of the service permit, be granted thirty days' leave each year... A staff member who has not been granted annual leave or more than one year's leave may be granted such leave on the occasion of subsequent leaves up to a maximum of three months. Travel time, both outward and return, shall not be counted as leave. As the leave you are requesting exceeds the duration of 30 days, please let me know what previous leave, if any, you intend to use to apply for leave of approximately 2 months and 20 days that you have not taken."

Le Gallais requested leave from June 8 to September 15, 1950, while he did attend the annual conference of the Governors of the International Monetary Fund and the International Bank in Paris from about September 6 to 14, 1950. Finally, he rectified the situation somewhat by only asking for leave from June 22 to August 22, at least this is what was retained in the traditional and compulsory Grand Ducal decree.

In 1951, Le Gallais apparently did not take any extended leave. As he had given up his traditional summer trip to Europe that year, it seems that Le Gallais missed the famous Beistegui ball in Venice. On September 3, 1951, Charles de Beistegui[538] gave on the Grand Canal, at the Palazzo Labia, famous for its frescoes of Tiepolo, the famous costume ball known since then as the "Ball of the Century".

In 1952,[539] Le Gallais asked for leave from July 4 to September 4 and was absent from June 11 to September 10. He took the opportunity to visit the island where his paternal grandfather was born. From Jersey he wrote twice to Mrs. Maloney, on June 19 and 21, from the St. Brelade's Bay Hotel. An airport has existed there since 1937, but as always, Le Gallais preferred to travel by train and boat to return to the island of his ancestors, a return almost to his roots which seemed to bring him a certain peace of mind: "Jersey is a lovely place and the weather is fine." Then he went to The Hague where his cousin Collart was accredited and, at the end of June, to Luxembourg where he gave a speech at the American Club attended by 190 people. In July, Venice and Cortina were on the program. Berty began his studies at Harvard in the fall.

At the end of August 1952, Le Gallais was back in New York. At the end of September, he was in Washington. During the absence of the head of mission, Lucien Margue, director of Hadir, Henri Stein, chief engineer at Arbed Esch, and Henri Welter, chief engineer at Arbed Belval, went there on business. On September 15, 1952, Hugues Le Gallais was in New York to have lunch with Messrs Dupong and Werner, and the following day to attend a lunch organized by Consul Staudt for Luxembourgers in New York. Bech was due to arrive in New York on October 13. Prime Minister Pierre Dupong, whose trip across the Atlantic was one of the last before his death a little over a year later, had left in the meantime on board the liner Queen Elizabeth. The voyage was memorable: on arrival in Cherbourg on September 22, 1952, Charlie Chaplin, who was also on board with his family, had just learned that he was suspected of political activism, he would not be able to return to the United States, where he had been living for several years. He therefore gave a press conference denouncing this witch hunt. The media reported that the turmoil caused by Charlie Chaplin's presence on the Queen Elizabeth overshadowed the presence of other distinguished passengers on board, such as King Faisal II of Iraq and Prince Regent Abd al-llah, Polish pianist

Arthur Rubinstein and the Prime Minister of Luxembourg. Le Gallais left no written record of this memorable return of "his" Minister of State.

In 1953, there were no travel expenses, and Le Gallais did not attend the wedding of the Hereditary Grand Duke with Princess Joséphine-Charlotte of Belgium. For this ceremony, on April 9, 1953, he did not make the trip. He had organized a reception at the legation to mark the royal event. He had had to insist somewhat with the Belgian ambassador Sylvercruys, who would have liked to do something at home, but the latter had finally given up. Le Gallais was right in both form and substance, and had thus scored a fine diplomatic victory for Luxembourg with no major consequences, apart from the cost of the reception.

In Luxembourg, the political situation changed following the sudden and unexpected disappearance of the Minister of State. Prime Minister Pierre Dupong having died on December 23, 1953, Le Gallais wrote in a telegram sent to the new President of the Government, Joseph Bech, on January 8: "I read with great emotion the text of your speech on the day of the funeral, I too have lost a great friend; all we can do now is to carry on as he would want us to do." On the eve of his letter of January 8, 1954 following the funeral of the former Prime Minister, on January 7, the Le Gallais couple had nevertheless organized a dinner in honor of the Secretary of State and Mrs. Dulles, attended by the French ambassador Henri Bonnet and his wife, the Belgian ambassador and Baroness Silvercruys, the Under-Secretary of Commerce and Mrs. William, the Deputy Under-Secretary and Mrs. Murphy, etc. Not being very sensitive to the national mourning decreed and feeling of loss in Luxembourg, Le Gallais had taken the liberty of recommending to Bech "to have an opinion published in the Luxembourg press as there are important guests". Le Gallais went so far as to report that "the dinner was very successful as company and as a meal... Mr. Dulles enjoyed our white wine and champagne but he did not drink Bordeaux and he ate a lot so I hope he will give you a good report next time he sees you." Reading this story in the light of the national mourning in Luxembourg, one thinks one is dreaming with regard to Le Gallais' insatiable need to make a name for himself. He has regularly sent notes to the Ministry with information on his meetings and even on the movements of the American authorities and has added many press articles on American and international news.

From time to time, Le Gallais' health also gave rise to concern. Thus, there was "a serious setback" and he waited for the results of a cardiogram in September 1946, with Bech wishing him a speedy recovery by telegram of September 20. Similarly, on March 24, 1954, the Honorary Vice-Consul of New York, Corneille Staudt, J.-P. Kremer, delegate to the United Nations, and Roger Madol were received by Eleanor Roosevelt while Le Gallais was ill. On the ninth anniversary of FDR's death, Staudt read a message on his behalf and laid a wreath of flowers on the grave of the President, who died on April 12. They were received for lunch at the cottage of the widow of the former President. Other members of the Luxembourg Society accompanied them on their journey, but not for lunch. Le Gallais must have regretted not being able to attend.

Le Gallais, now recovered, was most complimentary of Bech in a letter of April 19, 1954: "I saw Mr. Douglas MacArthur yesterday at a reception and told him that I read in a Luxembourg newspaper that President Eisenhower had expressed himself in flattering terms for Mr. Foster Dulles and that he had told friends that in his opinion the only other diplomats of equal standing were Adenauer, Robert Schuman and yourself. Mr. MacArthur replied that indeed the President had a very high opinion of you." Already during the war, Le Gallais had written to Bech during his absence in March 1943: "We will do our best here without you, but I do not hide from you that your absence will be a handicap in maintaining the interest of leading American political figures in problems affecting our country".[540] Or again, in June of the same year: "General Watson[541] asked a lot about you, saying that you had a very good mark with the President and that he was mentioning you favorably. He added that you were 'a very smart man' and that there should be such men at the Peace Conference." Always friendly and considerate, Le Gallais knew how to seduce and, if he thought it appropriate, to soften his world.

And the worldliness continued happily with, for example, a dinner on April 29, 1954, described as the last of the season, in honor of Mr. Joseph W. Martin Jr., Speaker of the House. The following were among those present: Mrs. Davies and two guest houses, Lady Brabourne[542] and Lady Birley,[543] the curator of the National Gallery, the Walter Lippmanns, etc.

In the summer of 1954, Le Gallais was on official holiday from July 13 to September 12 and absent from July 1 to September 21. Pisana and her son left New York for Genoa via Lisbon on June 15, 1954, where they attended a prestigious dinner at the Guggenheims' house. From August 1 to 17, 1954, Le Gallais was in Cortina d'Ampezzo and then in Venice, from 24 August, before returning to New York. A certain routine characterized the course of these prosperous years for the Le Gallais couple.

ECONOMIC DIPLOMACY AND
DIVERSE ENCOUNTERS

From time to time, Le Gallais would summarize various conversations he had had with members of the administration, other ambassadors accredited to the United States or American diplomats returning to the US capital.

In these times of renewal, Le Gallais was led to witness how transatlantic relations could be developed—first of all multilaterally, as we have seen, but also bilaterally with the negotiation of agreements laying the foundations for a closer relationship between the United States and Luxembourg. Thanks to these agreements, the foundation was laid that would later be used for American investments in the Grand Duchy, and increased trade and air links were finally made possible. During the 18 years of his presence in Washington, Le Gallais was more or less directly involved in the conclusion of a dozen agreements or other instruments or even their amendments or modifications in fields as diverse as the Memorandum of Agreement between the United States of America and Luxembourg respecting the arrangements for civil administration and jurisdiction in Luxembourg territory liberated by an allied expeditionary force signed by Luxembourg on July 27, 1944; the Economic Cooperation Agreement between the Grand Duchy of Luxembourg and the United States of America (done at Luxembourg on July 3, 1948); the Agreement on Aid for Mutual Defense between the Grand Duchy of Luxembourg and the United States of America (done at Washington on January 27, 1950); or the Agreement for the Establishment of a Permanent Cemetery of World War II in Hamm (1951). Also signed or amended in the 1950s, were the Agreement for the Financing of a Cultural and Educational Program, the Reciprocal Agreement on Pension Insurance for Private Employees, and the Agreement on Offshore

Purchases and the Reciprocal War Damage Compensation. An exchange of notes on "the reciprocal war damage agreement with Luxembourg" was discussed in June 1954 and recommended for signature. This agreement "extends the benefits of the war damage laws of Luxembourg with respect to property, losses of American nationals on a basis of equality with Luxembourg".[544] Similarly, measures necessary for the application of the provisions of the Refugee Relief Act or the guarantees of currency transfer and expropriation provided for in the Mutual Security Act of 1954 were negotiated and signed.[545] Several documents from the end of 1949[546] on a "draft treaty of friendship, commerce and navigation between the US and Luxembourg" were fulfilled well after Le Gallais' departure,[547] with the Luxembourg Government seemingly dragging its feet on the proposal. In November and December 1949, several documents had to do with the proposal for an air agreement and a direct route between Luxembourg and the United States.[548] This agreement does not seem to have been fulfilled in a concrete manner until much later (1980s), although memoranda explaining the political and economic arguments had been submitted. Difficult negotiations had been conducted as early as during the time of Le Gallais. The Americans had not really been interested in concluding it, despite Le Gallais' insistence.

A few Luxembourgish visitors came to the American capital and Le Gallais welcomed them appropriately and accompanied them to appointments with the American administration. Thus the Minister of Justice, Victor Bodson, was in Washington in September 1951, returning with Le Gallais from a NATO ministerial meeting in Ottawa, before travelling to New York.[549] On April 8, 1952, Minister Bodson and Lambert Dupong, the son of the Prime Minister who had become a director at Luxair, held discussions at the State Department on an air agreement that Washington refused to negotiate with the Grand Duchy. The Luxembourg representatives, accompanied by the Minister, pleaded in favor of such an agreement which had been conceded to all the member countries of the Atlantic Alliance and even to such "non-important" ones like Iceland, Lebanon and certain Caribbean countries. Bodson even went so far as to speak of discrimination, fearing that Luxembourg would become "an island stranded in the middle of Europe", also citing the 3 million tonnes of steel produced in Luxembourg with exports totaling between $500 and $600 million, those to the United States having disappeared. The Luxembourg delegation spoke not only of national legislation, but also of absolute necessity, because (among other things) an airport had been built at the cost of between 2 and 3 million dollars and which would now be overgrown with grass. How could the Americans give Germany what they refused Luxembourg? The Americans would stand firm, while recognizing that Luxembourg was fully pulling its weight within NATO, believing that there was no economic or political justification for a transatlantic service between the two countries. There was also talk at that time of Seaboard & Western, which had a substantial investment in Luxair and was in fact its operating agency. Less than two months later, Le Gallais was back at the State Department to see how far the negotiations, to which Bodson had committed himself energetically, had progressed. For this, the diplomat felt he had to apologize in a way, given that his Justice Minister had been "a little too insistent in his presentation, which could have been damaging to the case". His American interlocutor replied that, on the contrary, he preferred someone who argued in Bodson's style. Le Gallais further argued that the Luxembourg press could take up the case and that Luxembourg would not be able to benefit unilaterally from its freedom of movement. Without success, the Americans invoked that Congress would not approve such an agreement and that the United States could be prevented from concluding such agreements in the future and would be obliged to conclude treaties, subject to a two-thirds vote in the Senate. As the negotiations lasted three years, the Luxembourgers, believing themselves to be accepted and respected allies, were more than ever discriminated against and embarrassed.[550] Reports from the American legation to the State Department in May 1952, still on these negotiations, spoke of "rather crude tactics" following the *Luxemburger Wort* publication, which was judged severely: "The tone and anti-American bias of the article is most unusual for Luxembourg".[551]

Numerous affairs therefore had to be dealt with in Washington, but also in New York, where Le Gallais was Luxembourg's representative to the United Nations There he had support from Luxembourg to assist him in his missions, whether to the General Assembly or to various UN committees.

LE GALLAIS AT THE UNITED NATIONS

Having been present in San Francisco with his Minister for the negotiation and signing of the United Nations Charter, Le Gallais later travelled regularly to New York to follow the activities of the United Nations.[552] While the organization had 50 member states in 1945, this figure had doubled by the time Le Gallais retired. The Permanent Representation of Luxembourg would grow in importance over the years. Young diplomats such as Pierre Pescatore,[553] or Pierre Wurth,[554] were delegated to New York to follow the General Assembly and the committees. It was only in

1961, several years after the departure of Le Gallais, that the post in Washington was separated from that in New York.

Before beginning to examine the positions adopted by Luxembourg in one or other United Nations matter, it is interesting to note that in the mission's *Scrapbook* is an article from October 1953 when the young Henry Ford made his debut there.[555] Entitled *No country can do it alone,* it relates the fact that the heir of the American automobile dynasty gave an interview explaining his activities and describing an open American policy "interested in mutual advantages ... not exploiting anybody", the United States having committed itself to give 60 cents for each 40 cents given by others, which would amount to a "sound investment" of 15 million USD. This kind of message and these various reports were to be used by the Luxembourg diplomat to distil one or another comment of a political nature in Luxembourg where they always ended up, without intermediary or censorship, on the desk of the Minister of Foreign Affairs, if not the Prime Minister.

In connection with the Korean War, in which Luxembourg had participated in 1951 under the United Nations' flag as part of the Belgian contingent, Hugues Le Gallais adopted a position that deserves to be examined. The Geneva conference from April to July 1954 was to lead to a peace treaty. Representatives of the United States, Great Britain, the USSR, France, the People's Republic of China (for whom this was a first on the diplomatic stage), the two Koreas, Laos, Cambodia, Vietnam and the Viet Minh met. The conference dealt first with Korea, then mainly with Indochina. Hugues Le Gallais asked for instructions on Luxembourg's participation, recommending participation "in order to show our interest in the restoration of peace".[556] Finally, Minister Bech participated in April 1954. The following episode was certainly one of the highlights of the minister plenipotentiary's sporadic presence in New York in connection with the United Nations.

On August 24, 1953, Le Gallais stated that his country did not request to participate in the conference on Korea. The Luxembourg Minister in the United States renounced this request at the First Committee of the United Nations, eloquently invoking that

"his delegation, lacking the 'third eye of Buddha', and facing two varying points of view, would abstain on the invitation to India. He hoped, however, that some formula could be found to permit the participation of India. Luxembourg is one of the cosponsors of the joint draft resolution of fifteen member States which recommends that 'the side contributing armed forces under the unified command in Korea shall have as participants in the (political) conference those among the member States contributing armed forces which desire to be represented, together with the Republic of Korea'".[557]

Shortly afterwards, diplomats again turned their attention to the financing of the Secretariat. At Belgium's request, it was clarified that these were only the costs arising from the conference on Korea, not the Indochina conference. The United States maintained that it would bear 50% of the costs, along with France and the United Kingdom, and that the rest would be shared equally among the other members. While the Netherlands opted for a solution on the scale of the entire United Nations, Le Gallais said that under no circumstances could Luxembourg accept the American proposal and that his country only pay the costs of the Korea conference. The United Kingdom and the United States were opposed to this statement, especially as America had never paid more than a third of the UN costs. Upon leaving the room, Le Gallais explained to the assistant of Secretary of State Dean Rusk, a certain Young,[558] that his country cannot pay a quarter of what the United States pays. Rusk's deputy, Young, was understanding and promised to look into the problem. Notwithstanding his statements, Le Gallais sought to find a compromise. He consulted with his Dutch colleague De Beus,[559] and considered adjusting the entire United Nations scale so that America paid only one-third. De Beus promised to make the calculations based on this assumption. Le Gallais called him the next day: the figures being considered satisfactory, so De Beus proposed to bring this solution forward under the auspices of the Benelux countries. Le Gallais therefore presented it the same day to the State Department. Canada, the United States and the United Kingdom did not reject it. Although the proposal was less favorable to the British and Canadians, Le Gallais believed that an agreement on the Benelux formula would be reached. Once this discussion on the theoretical allocation was over, the heads of mission reflected on the actual costs. Young estimated that the joint secretariat would cost a maximum of $100,000 per month. Le Gallais deduced that his country's contribution would be $150 per month according to the Benelux proposal instead of $3,850 as per the American suggestion! Common expenses such as heating and electricity were divided among the nineteen conference participants. Young estimated them at $20,000 per month, which was about $1,000 for the Grand Duchy. Even if this figure seemed high to him, Le Gallais did not wish to question it. By doing so, he would have forced the United States, France and the United Kingdom to renegotiate a new distribution with the Communists.

Bech attached some importance to the Benelux formula being adopted and to his country only paying for the conference on Korea. If Le Gallais was unable to impose his point of view and it proved impossible to separate the costs of the two conferences, the Minister was prepared to send a telegram to the State Department.

And he did! He recalled the reason for the Grand Ducal presence in Geneva—solidarity—as he refrained in any case from intervening in the general political settlement of Asian issues. The conference was disproportionately important for Luxembourg, which wished to withdraw its participation, unless the State Department invoked reasons of major interest. By chance, for unknown reasons, this telegram never reached its destination! At the same time, Bech telephoned Le Gallais to ask him to remind the head of the United Nations at the State Department, Ward Allen, of the Grand Duchy's position. The diplomat did so without delay on April 16 and again made it clear that Luxembourg had participated in the Geneva conference in a spirit of solidarity and that it should therefore bear the resulting costs within reasonable limits. Allen was understanding and expressed the conviction that the Benelux formula was increasingly being used. This conviction seemed to be confirmed: the French embassy called Le Gallais to inform him of its approval of the Benelux formula and to thank him for having proposed it. The embassy promised to convey his position to the United Kingdom. Le Gallais speculated that the United Kingdom would also accept the Benelux project, as it could reduce its financial participation. Indeed, England joined the Benelux position shortly afterwards. This meant that the matter could be definitively closed.

Whether at the United Nations or in other forums, Le Gallais and the Luxembourg government, with Prime Minister Dupong and Minister Bech in the lead, always thanked the United States for the liberation, emphasizing the small size of the Grand Duchy and hence the need for a great ally. The growing antagonism towards the Soviet Union was also often mentioned. Despite the lukewarm nature of his convictions in some of his letters, Le Gallais' determined views were reflected as a common thread in some of his speeches. Like his minister and mentor, Joseph Bech, Le

Gallais remained true to himself. Both were born into high circles and had eclectic tastes. What set them apart was above all the old sense—so typical of Luxembourgers at the time—of moderation, which Bech practiced all the time and everywhere. Le Gallais was more ostentatious, not to say convinced that pomp and a certain unmatchable and at times spectacular affectation could not harm the Luxembourg cause. Thus Bech had written in a long eight-page report to Dupong on January 8, 1941 about Le Gallais, who had invited him to the United States to make a presentation to the Congressional Foreign Affairs Committee. Bech's assessment was masterly: "I have somewhat the impression that he [Le Gallais] is letting himself be tempted by high diplomacy. It is an excessively slippery ground for the representative of a small country."[560] It is nevertheless unfair and false to see in the determined and skilful Le Gallais a man devoid of political sense when he gives, at least in the clichés of the time, the image of an impenetrable sphinx. Despite his weaknesses, there are many points for which he deserves justice. The prolonged distance from his native country and his extended family did not make his analyses of the pivotal post-war period any less relevant.

RELEVANT VIEWS ABOUT THE INTERNATIONAL POLITICAL SITUATION

Le Gallais' activism and panache served the country well. His way of doing things opened doors to persons in the United States who have since become more difficult to approach and influence. An undated excerpt from a speech by Belgian ambassador Sylvercruys sums up the attitude that his Luxembourg counterpart must also have had after the Second World War.

"The two countries, the United States of America and Belgium, had in recent years to clear their accounts, provide for the restoration of the national economy, deal with food first, then re-equipment, play their part in the European recovery effort, accept and continue a military effort that was all the more painful as we were emerging from a conflict whose legacy weighed on the treasury, and finally assume new responsibilities in terms of collective defense and Atlantic and European unity."

On May 31, 1947, at the Luxembourg legation, Le Gallais had presented the Grand Cross of the Order of the Crown of Oak to the Belgian ambassador, Baron Silvercruys, in the presence of the US Under-Secretary of State for Economic Affairs and Mrs. Alan G. Kirk, the Managing Director of the International Monetary Fund and Mrs. Camille Gutt, the owner of the *Washington Post*, Mr. and Mrs. Eugene Meyer, and other guests. Le Gallais knew how to surround himself with people and maintain contacts that could be useful.

As complex as ever, the world had indeed become smaller, and a country like Luxembourg needed all the more allies, especially influential ones, as Le Gallais himself had described in an undated speech to members of the American-Luxembourg Society and Alumni of American Universities:

"I am not the first—undoubtedly not the last either—to remark that the World has grown smaller since I was a boy. Distances today are not greater than the speed of the latest plane. It used to be our fellow countrymen who emigrated to the United States scarcely ever thought that they would see their native land in their lifetime, now hundreds of ex-Luxembourgers and Americans of Luxembourg origin drop from the skies each summer day after a comfortable journey of some hours. Almost every edition of that staunch little newspaper published in Chicago, the Luxembourg News of America, lists the names of travelers en route or planning visits to the Grand Duchy".[561]

On this occasion, he also mentioned the exchange of young Luxembourgers within the framework of the International Farm Youth Exchange (IFYE), academics and the visit of a junior American Red Cross in Luxembourg.

The Manichean vision that was current among many leaders at the time quickly turned against Russia. Not only politicians, but also the media gave a most threatening image of the Soviet Empire with Churchill's Iron Curtain and the Marshall Plan as key words in rallying democracies against this evil force. In a carefully guarded article by Le Gallais in the *Evening Standard* of January 7, 1950, it was explained how to survive in the event of an atomic bomb blast. On February 10, he was interested in an article on the Acheson Homily, which advocated not taking a new approach to Russia. Any suspicion of good faith evaporated from relations between the West and the USSR following the latter's acquisition of the atomic bomb.

As the President of the French Republic recalled in his speech of May 30, 2018 at the opening of the OECD ministerial session chaired by France: "Those years were marked by the renewed multilateralism of the post-war period, the effort to rebuild Europe preceding the 30 glorious years and the transatlantic link strengthened thanks to the Marshall Plan and NATO. It was an invention of those men and women who had understood that past conflicts would not happen again if dialogue and joint reflection replaced ultimatums and sometimes the clash of arms." Luxembourg's leaders of the time could base themselves on the solemn affirmation of the right of small nations to exist, which had been the subject of the Atlantic Charter agreed upon by Roosevelt and Churchill on August 14, 1941. The document had brought together a series of principles to be used in the maintenance of international peace and security.

Let's take a look at some of the speeches or texts in order to better understand Le Gallais' vision in the 1940s and 1950s. On August 9, 1941, the day after the reception held at the embassy in honor of Platt Waller, Le Gallais wrote to his Minister: "I feel that Her Royal Highness the Grand Duchess and His Excellency, the President of the Government, find it difficult to detach themselves from the pre-war idea that Luxembourg is purely a small country. There are no small countries at the moment (...), we are all equal in our determination to defeat the enemy and we all have our responsibilities and duties towards each other." Nine months later, in the first issue of the *Luxembourg Bulletin* published by the Government in exile in Montreal and New York,[562] the Minister of State agreed with the position outlined by Le Gallais.[563] Inspired by each other, the diplomat and the politicians pleaded the same cause.

Then there was the speech at the Metropolitan Opera on January 30, 1943 on the occasion of an event organized by the Metropolitan Opera Guild[564] on the "part of the Luxembourg people in the fight against Hitler, whose repression had struck almost all Luxembourg families". Le Gallais' three-page draft speech to Dupong[565] contains one of Le Gallais' rare references to God and, as so often, a Manichean world divided between friends and enemies and good and evil:

"the world wars which in less than thirty years have twice ravaged humanity and have taught it a terrible lesson. May God wish that lesson to be understood. The people of Luxembourg have high hopes for the American nation. In the pursuit of war, it deploys material and moral resources which are admired by its friends and terrorized by its enemies. If, as we firmly hope, its effort is equal for the establishment of an international peace regime based on Law and Freedom, the game will be won".

At the end of the speech was the unshakeable hope for a better world thanks to the Americans. For once, a comment by his prime minister in the margin of the speech, which is only three pages long, seems rather laudatory for the diplomat: "will be translated into English somewhat shortened. P.D." [Pierre Dupong]. This is another example of the idea that Le Gallais had been able to use as a basis for further developments by his government.

Two speeches delivered in February 1943, one by Joseph Bech in London and the other by Pierre Dupong in Louisiana, are worth recalling in order to better understand the position that Le Gallais could adopt. Thus, Minister Bech gave a lecture at the Belgian Institute in London under the title "Small nations in Europe after the war" demanding for the future United Nations to have an international army capable of imposing respect for the law, a skepticism that the Cold War and peaceful coexistence would justify. And as the historian Gilbert Trausch continues to state in his biography of the Luxembourg politician with almost 30 years of political life behind him: "for Bech, Europe will have to organize itself with respect for small nations or, to quote the famous speech by Bech in London: With or without a League of Nations, Europe will have to organize itself".[566] For his part, Minister of State Dupong expressed the same sentiments at the beginning of February: "This (Luxembourgish success) seemed too much for Hitler. On May 10, 1940 he ordered his armies to invade and occupy peace-loving and thriving Luxembourg. Since then he rules over Luxembourg in a satrapian manner through a deputy-Führer. The 30th of August 1942 our Country was formally incorporated to the Reich. Our boys of military age have been forced since that day to don the hated German uniform, to fight against their allies and die for their oppressors." Or, in the same speech by Dupong: "But our right is equal to that of any nation in as much a right is not to be measured by all." And to finally quote the great French poet Lamartine: "*Adore ton pays et ne l'arpente pas, Ami, Dieu n'a pas fait les peuples au compas*" [Love your country and do not survey it, Friend, God did not make peoples using a compass].

And always, there is the reference to the small country that has the right to exist and to be considered equal to the others and the call to lay the foundations of a new world order for the post-war period. This is why this text is quoted extensively, even though it was not pronounced by Le Gallais. Ideas might have been his own, and no doubt he used them in his explanations throughout his career to call on the United States to give his native country a dignified and appropriate place after the war:

"We have therefore the right to ask… what principle, with avowable interest could justify the suppression of such a country. Because, perhaps, we are a small country. It is a dangerous concept for all countries to base the right of a nation on the space it occupies or the number of people who live in it. Every nation might encounter one stronger than itself, or one that believes itself stronger, which amounts to the same thing. To base the rights of peoples on such relative values as territorial space or population would be playing into the hands of Hitler who established the same principles in his political bible, although he called it by the more ruthless name: Force. This would be to base international relations on a principle which would provide any aggressor nation with the simplest and most brilliant pretext to attack weaker nations. The impression of human nature will prevent the scourge of war from disappearing from the face of the earth. But one should not multiply its germs by advocating theories which would legalize it. Does this mean that after the war is over we should simply restore the world to its previous status? I am not of this opinion. When speaking of small countries one generally has their size or their population in mind. But a country may have immense area and still play only a minor role in world politics, because of its small population. Another country with a larger number of inhabitants may have no influence in world economy because it lacks natural resources. Nor is it difficult to list vast spaces, blessed with all riches of the earth, which have been transformed into colonies and are treated as such for the very good reason that their people are too backward to enjoy political independence. All of which proves that in objectively estimating the international value of a country, one should not consider solely its territorial area, or the number of its inhabitants, nor even the combination of these two elements. To these elements one must add cultural and educational standing. Culture, in most cases, is the result of a century-long evolution, a composite of tradition, collective experiences and individual realization."

In London on March 11, 1942, Grand Duchess and Bech addressed the National Defense Public Interest Committee in London. Bech gave a speech on the place of one of the smallest Allied countries in Europe. He presented his views there, just as, on May 1, in front of the Iron and Steel Institute. Heisbourg described them as premonitory ten years before the creation of the European Coal and Steel Community and fifteen years before that of the Common Market.[567]

Basically, Luxembourg's foreign policy has not changed much since then, and the position so often adopted by Le Gallais to defend the interests of a small country in the most influential country in the world is still valid.

Another excerpt from a letter of June 11, 1943 from Le Gallais to Bech following the proceedings of the Hot Springs conference and his meeting with the Under-Secretary of State should be noted:

"Mr. Welles replied that what we had told him had been very instructive and interesting, that he shared our views on the situation of the small countries if good understanding and peace were to reign in Europe, and that he could say that we had correctly interpreted the views of the American Government, with the reservation, however, that in the military field the large countries would have to provide 'the world police'. (We reserve the right to ask in a future conversation which are these large countries?)."

Le Gallais went on to exaggerate when he said: "I am very pleased with this conversation because I feel that you should now (with the help of this letter and the related report) be able to formulate very clear views on what US foreign policy will be like in the next few years." Although he has again exaggerated the contribution he has been asked to make as a public servant, it is undeniable that Le Gallais has had a strong influence on his leaders' vision of the United States and the world.

After having already recorded messages for BBC broadcasts, Le Gallais, on August 8, 1944, made a broadcast on the WWDC station on the equal treatment of large and small nations, on Bretton Woods and the United Nations, entitled "Treatment of Small Nations at the International Conference". He recalls a discussion between Bech and Secretary of State Hull before leaving for Hot Springs for the United Nations Agriculture and Food Conference, in which the American Secretary of State said that when he went to the first Pan-American Conference in Montevideo, he would have acted on the principle that all nations represented there should be considered equal, and added that this principle was upheld at subsequent conferences. Luxembourg should be accorded the same treatment, according to Hull. These very wise words on the part of the Secretary of State would have given Le Gallais food for thought as to their implementation in practice. Indeed, the representatives of little Luxembourg would have realized that the principle of equality of nations represented would have prevailed during this conference. At no time was an attempt made to prevent a delegation from expressing its opinion. On the contrary, the presidents of all sections and committees took great care to ensure that each speaker had sufficient time to explain his or her point of view. For Le Gallais this approach was the basis of any relationship between democratic partners and allies.

Another example of how to enhance and present the Grand Duchy from a historical point of view took place on Sunday September 17, 1944. Le Gallais and his wife were present in New York[568] for the ceremony of the Luxembourg Freedom Charter commemorating the 700th anniversary of the franchise letters granted to the city of Luxembourg by Countess Ermesinde which took place at the City Hall in the presence of the Mayor of New York, Fiorello Enrico La Guardia.[569] Also present were Matthew Woll, President of the American Friends of Luxembourg, and André Wolff, Commissioner for Information. A speech was delivered by the latter, Hugues Le Gallais reading a message from the Grand Duchess to the Mayor of New York. This was followed by a presentation by Prince Charles of copies of the Freedom Charter to the Mayor of New York, with a very long speech by Matthew Woll, Vice-President of the American Federation of Labor, and messages from Minister Krier and La Guardia. Princesses Marie-

Gabrielle and Alix were also present for the event. A message from FDR could not be published due to the short time available and probably also due to the fact that a statement welcoming the liberation of Luxembourg had been issued by the President less than a week earlier.

At the United Nations Consultative Assembly in New York, Minister Bech had declared on August 9, 1945: "It will be our pride and our salvation, that from the first draft of an allied collaboration, our small country was able to join in the common work ... if our independence came out of this war intact, it is because we defended it as belligerents alongside the Allies...".[570] After the first United Nations draft was prepared during a conference held in a Washington mansion called Dumbarton Oaks in the autumn of 1944, Bech introduced himself at the inaugural session as "a representative of a small nation whose voice must be humble in the concert of nations, it would be impolite of me not to follow the advice the President gave us this morning, namely to keep our speeches to a minimum".[571] The recognition of the small Grand Duchy in relation to its liberators and the hope that with the establishment of the United Nations the world would maintain peace were also the *leitmotif* of Minister Bech's speech to the United Nations General Assembly in New York on January 16, 1946. There he described himself as the representative of the smallest member State and expressed his confidence that the emergence of the United Nations had made war less likely. Some seven months later, on August 26, 1946, an article appeared in the *Luxemburger Wort* entitled "Luxembourg Finest Little Country", based on the recent trip to the Grand Duchy by journalist Walter Lippmann, who not only praised his friends, the Le Gallais, in Washington, but also expressed his admiration for their little country he had just discovered.

On the other hand, the journalist William Attwood wrote one of these articles in the New York Herald Tribune on February 2, 1947, which a Luxembourg diplomat does not appreciate: "Luxembourg an Island of Luxury in Midst of Struggling Europe", subtitled "Thanks to rich iron ore vein and industry free of war damage, citizens have warm homes, English tweeds, US fruit, French wines". Luxembourg is described as an "island of comfort and luxury... because they have to pay taxes for the first time in anyone's memory, but they do not mind footing a 380 million $ bill for reconstruction of the devastated northern regions..."

This would not prevent, six months later,[572] Luxembourg from receiving a $12 million loan from the World Bank in Belgian currency, while $20 million had initially been requested.

Le Gallais regularly transmitted news gleaned in Washington from the most diverse interlocutors. Thus, on April 22, 1946, he sent

"information that may be of interest to you. It seems that it is true that the Russians withdrew about 100,000 troops from Romania, but they sent the same number to Bulgaria and 150,000 to Hungary. On the other hand it is true that the United States are reinforcing its air force in Germany. The impression here is that on May 25 a poker game will begin in Paris during which the participants will have revolvers on the table. Mr. Byrnes[573] leaves Washington rather pessimistic. A few days ago I sent you a newspaper article indicating that Mr. Byrnes is considering a separate peace with Italy if no agreement can be reached in Paris; this indiscretion obviously has a purpose. On the subject of this conference, please find enclosed an interesting article by André Visson.[574] I would like to point out that in Washington it is reported that Mrs. Cornu, Mr. Bidault's secretary,[575] is Communist and that Moscow receives confidential information through this channel within forty-eight hours. Quite recently the Russians have indirectly informed the Turkish Government that the question of the provinces on the Iranian side could be forgotten for the time being, but we would like to see the Turkish Government admit two Ministers who are friendly towards the USSR; this corresponds to the usual policy of gradual infiltration. I have also learned that the French have been rather annoyed that Poland has presented the Spanish case before the Security Council. They say: 'They've cut us off...' It was only later that it was made clear in Washington that the French Socialist Party and public opinion wanted to intervene against Franco and in the note handed over to the State Department asking for diplomatic relations with the Spanish Government to be broken off and for a fuel embargo, it was stated that if this was not satisfactory, the matter would have to be brought before the United Nations Security Council. Finally, I would like to point out that in the Security Council things are not going so well, even though the press says otherwise. The French are seeking at all costs to obtain what they call 'our own policy', but their efforts to reach a compromise between the Anglo-Saxons and the Russians have unfortunately so far not produced any results".[576]

It was a lot of news that only an insider could put into context and, like Bech, perhaps use in his contacts on the international scene.

The Marshall Plan,[577] also known as the European Recovery Program, was announced on June 5, 1947 at Harvard University. The American program of loans granted to the various states of Europe to help rebuild the cities and infrastructure bombed during the Second World War was to have a considerable impact on Luxembourg and Western Europe. The loans were conditional on the import of an equivalent amount of American equipment and products. The *Luxemburger Wort*, in an article dated June 18 of the same year, reported that the Luxembourg Government had asked Hugues Le Gallais and the Belgian and Dutch ambassadors to indicate to Washington that Luxembourg was ready to consider any new suggestions that could help improve the economic situation in Europe. Two years later, Hugues Le Gallais gave a speech on June 5, 1949 at the Carlton Hotel at a dinner hosted by the 16 Heads of Mission from OECD member states in honor of General Marshall. In it, he reiterated that he had acted as the representative of the smallest country accredited to the United States, the Icelandic Minister noting in his personal speech that "to my friend and distinguished colleague, the Minister of Luxembourg, I owe just one remark. Let Luxembourg and Iceland both be great in their smallness, the degree of which will never become an issue, because we in Iceland are also most desirous that General Marshall may continue, many, many years to come, to enjoy health and happiness at home." The Luxembourg representative noted on that occasion that steel production had increased in 1948 by 43%, something that would not have been possible without the Marshall Plan. For Le Gallais, the relationship with this Secretary of State,[578] whom he had already met in San Francisco in 1945, would intensify. The bond forged by Le Gallais with Marshall was to last and develop personally with the sending of Luxembourg roses to the general, an episode to which a note from Marshall, who had been in charge of American defense for only ten days, testifies: "It would be much pleasanter to be discussing or even planting roses." An exchange of kind letters of December 1953 also exists on the import, two months earlier, of rose plants. Nor did Le Gallais fail to congratulate Marshall by telegram when the latter was awarded the Nobel Peace Prize, which was presented in Oslo in December of the same year, to which the recipient replied: "it was very thoughtful of you to think of me, and your gracious words add much to the richness of the Award." Marshall, who had autographed a photo showing him with the ambassador, was to die the year after Le Gallais left Washington.

When the Peace Treaty with Japan was signed on September 8, 1951 by Secretary of State John Foster Dulles signed (he would leave this post a few days later) and representatives of many other countries, Hugues Le Gallais delivered a speech in English. In San Francisco, Le Gallais recalled the good and peaceful Japanese people he had known until "after 1931 the people let themselves be led by those of a more adventurous spirit". That was the understatement of the day. Hugues was nevertheless to savor this return to his own history with a banquet offered at the Palace Hotel with the presence not only of the Secretary of State, but also of Dean Acheson and Japanese Prime Minister Toshida. We have seen that for the Luxembourg Minister, being able to greet Crown Prince Akihito during his visit to Washington two years later was an honor.

The American Government's international radio and television broadcasting service, which has been in existence since 1942, was used to make the Grand Duchy known. Mrs. Le Gallais also addressed the Americans via the Voice of America in April 1950, recalling the sacrifices of Luxembourg women and mothers, the American losses and the graves of American soldiers which would always be honored in Luxembourg. He also thanked the Americans for the benefits of the Marshall Plan. In the embassy files is a text from that year's Voice of America program welcoming in French and English the appointment of General Dwight D. Eisenhower as Supreme Commander of the Integrated Defense Forces in Western Europe.

In 1950, at the legation in Washington, the 28th Infantry Division of the American Army was awarded the Croix de Guerre 1940-

1945. This division, which was involved in the liberation of the country in September 1944 and in defending the territory during the Battle of the Bulge, was honored in the presence of former ambassador Davies and Perle Mesta, the Assistant Secretary of Defense and the Assistant Secretary of the Army, the Assistant Chief of Staff and the Assistant Chief of Staff of the Army, a member of Congress and many high-ranking American military officers. André Wolff, the Grand Duchy's Information Commissioner in the United States, mentions Le Gallais for once: "during the entire ceremony, which was conducted with great dignity and grace by our Minister." However, in the compilation of speeches and events in which Wolff participated and which he organized in New York, Le Gallais is hardly mentioned. At the end of the Wolff memoirs, the Minister in Washington is thanked for his welcome at the legation: "…extended the most friendly and reassuring cooperation on each of my visits to the Capital."

Various organizations and institutions have again mobilized the Luxembourg Minister. Thus, on November 9, 1951, Le Gallais gave a speech to the World Brotherhood Organization at the Mayflower Hotel in Washington, D.C., recalling the economic union with Belgium, the Benelux, the Council of Europe, the Marshall Plan and the Grand Duchy's efforts in social matters from the beginning of the 20th century. The World Brotherhood is a private transnational civic movement created in 1950 in Paris "by men and women who believe in the spiritual interpretation of the universe from which they draw inspiration to promote justice, friendship, understanding and collaboration among people of all races, nations and religions". Active mainly in the 1950s, there was also a Luxembourg section. That said, Hugues Le Gallais' view of the world was characterized more by material than spiritual aspects. He himself seemed more a follower of *Realpolitik* and had no illusions about the place of a small country like his own without the support of great allies.

In a speech on May 11, 1952 at the Hudson View Hotel in Cold Spring, New York, to the American Luxembourg Society, which had been originated by Mr. Madol first in England and then in the United States, Le Gallais recalled that of the 75 accredited Heads of Mission, Luxembourg was the smallest country, at least in terms of area. Once again, a comparison was made with Iceland, which would have a smaller number of inhabitants than Luxembourg. He also recalled, on May 10, 1940: "some of us, active participants in world-shattering as well as world-mending events", stressing that "twelve years ago today—May 11, 1940—I had accepted an invitation to be with the Luxembourg Colony in New York to mark the anniversary of the Treaty of London which was signed May 11, 1867, but the nefarious events of May 10 caused plans to be changed and there was no celebration in New York." We have seen that Le Gallais had been rather distraught, if not lost, at the time of the German invasion, but gained confidence to defend the interests of his country during the war years.

Le Gallais appeared in a thirty-minute radio program on The Europe Show on May 24, 1953. Following a request at the end of March 1953, he agreed to answer a wide range of questions from Bill Costello, CBS' White House Correspondent. Minister of Foreign Affairs Bech had encouraged him, even sending him his latest budget speech as a useful input for answers on financial matters. The topics covered were the maintenance of independence, European unification, self-sufficiency and industrial production, military affairs, the Benelux countries and the expansion of Communism. Le Gallais addressed subjects that are still topical, such as subsidiarity in the face of a pooling of sovereignty or the unity of the precursors, the Franco-German duo. In his answers, the head of mission gave his knowledge of diplomacy and his assessment of the international situation:

"In the world today, no nation, no matter what its size in territory or in population is completely sovereign in the true sense of the word, for the interdependence of states obliges each to take into consideration the interest of other countries ... if Europe is to become a living reality, some surrender of sovereignty is indispensable. It is obvious that these renunciations must rest on the principle of complete reciprocity and equality of rights between the various states. That which is called 'little Europe' isn't really so little after all, since it's six countries represent 150 million people of a very high political, economic and cultural level."

After listing the United Nations, the Brussels Pact, the Organization for European Economic Cooperation, NATO and the Council of Europe, the ECSC, Hugues Le Gallais stated that

"the Grand Duchy is also in favor of a European Political Community, provided this does not abolish individual states and preserves the autonomy necessary for their internal administration. In other words, the supranational should only take away from the national that which is absolutely necessary to make more effective the principle of European Integration. Evidently it would be desirable for other countries to join the six states united under the Schuman Plan – this would only strengthen European unity.

If France and Germany were united by common interests the repetition of the catastrophe provoked by their secular antagonism in the world would be avoided.

The Franco-German problem is the keystone of European unity – on its resolution rests the fate of all of Europe and the unification of the little countries will not bear fruit unless France and Germany unite their destinies.

The cost of the various government services is met by tax receipts. The question of supporting the government apparatus presents no special financial problem for my country. To a certain extent tax revenues have been used during the past few years to meet extraordinary expenses such as reparation of war damages. The national debt in 1951 was $210 per capita.

The Marshall plan was the deciding factor in the fight against Communism. Although Luxembourg benefited only slightly in direct economic aid, it is certain that Luxembourg profited widely from the amelioration of economic conditions which the Marshall Plan produced in Europe, and prosperity is by far the best antidote to Communism.

The rising of the standard of living of all classes has been the constant care of the Luxembourg Government.

It is a Fact that Luxembourg needs military rather than economic help..."

Following Stalin's death in March 1953, Le Gallais added:

"It is obvious that in regard to foreign policy there has been a change in tactics on the part of the Soviets after the death of Stalin. In my opinion it is still too soon to say if this change in tactics means a real reversal of policy. As it has been said so often lately: after the words of appeasement coming from the East, one must now wait for deeds in order to decide if they mean a change in tactics only or in strategy.

Europe must be united politically, economically and military-wise. If military aspects have assumed a special urgency, it is solely because of the serious threat to Western Europe by excessive Soviet rearmament. I see no valid reason to renounce a Treaty which was signed more than a year ago[579] and governs a matter which sooner or later would have to be dealt with in the framework of a united Europe.

To sum up, I believe there are two principal means to assure the world, if not complete harmony, at least an atmosphere of peace in which the cold war would be eliminated as far as possible: First, a Europe from which Franco-German antagonism is banished – hence a Europe including a free democratic Germany; second: the balance of military power between the East and West to be re-established – when this is accomplished in reality and not only on paper, the peaceful co-existence of the Communist and Western Worlds will be possible. This evidently does not constitute the true peace to which the world aspires, but the absence of war which, after two world wars, seems to me to be a great achievement; also this state of affairs would permit the re-establishment of normal economic and political relations with the Eastern European countries and would furnish the basis of true understanding."

This statement by Le Gallais reflects the influence of McCarthyism, also known as the Red Scare or the witch hunt. The strong anti-Communist sentiment that had developed in the United States in the context of the Cold War extended precisely from 1950, with the appearance of Senator Joseph McCarthy at the forefront of American politics, to 1954, with the vote of no confidence in McCarthy, who was reprimanded by the Senate. Apart from a very pronounced anti-Communism shared with his authorities, we do not know what Le Gallais' attitude was towards this phenomenon that wreaked great havoc in the United States.

Le Gallais' speeches are always short, usually no more than half a page. Le Gallais had a good sense of language, especially with regard to his colleagues on the occasion of their departure from office. It's always a wrench for budding friendships and, what's more, hard on spouses, often confined to a comfortable but complex diplomatic system. This is evidenced by a dinner offered on April 13, 1953 on the occasion of Mrs. Hellé Bonnet's birthday[580] in the presence of René Pleven, French Minister of National Defense, followed on June 10, 1954 by a dinner at the home of ambassador Bonnet, his colleague of almost ten years, when Le Gallais, often so reserved, said: "We have always been on the same side of the barricade." Then, in the same way, during the French ambassador's farewell dinner, with always this sense of the right formulation: "We are downright sad that they are leaving." And: "However, I must not end on this note and so I will add only that when the memories of diplomatic life begin to fade (much later on, let us hope) one of them will stand out always, and I am sure it will be the same with Bill Burden,[581] these delightful hours spent with Henri on fishing trips." Let us also mention the departure, in January 1953, after almost ten years, of the Italian ambassador Alberto Tarchiani[582] who had been editor of *Corriere della Sera* before the Fascist era and a non-professional diplomat like Le Gallais: "I am sure that when he looks back, he can do so with the feeling that he has done well for his country and I would like to use the expression 'il a beaucoup de plumes à son chapeau'—but hesitate to do so because he never wears a hat!" Or the one of January 15, 1954, during a lunch on the occasion of the departure of the British ambassador Sir Gladwyn Jebb[583] to Paris. And another speech (probably in 1957) to say goodbye to Maurice Frère[584] who had been general manager of the National Bank of Belgium in March 1946 in Bretton Woods, Governor of the National Bank of Belgium from 1944 to 1957, President of the banking commission from 1938 to 1944 as well as Vice-

President of the Bank for International Settlements in Basel. In fact, the two friends would often meet in Venice. These are all testimonials of good manners and loyalty to colleagues known for many years.

On June 5, 1953, during a luncheon for about a hundred people held at the Carlton Hotel in honor of the six representatives of the European Coal and Steel Community (ECSC) in the presence of Jean Monnet, President of the High Authority established in Luxembourg, Franz Etzel, Vice-President, and Dirk Spierenburg,[585] Le Gallais chaired one of the four tables of about thirty people with Monnet himself. In his speech, Monnet described the unification of Europe as indispensable in order to create lasting peace. He informed that "the Community's parliamentary assembly has drawn up a treaty for a constitution which the Governments are currently discussing and which will combine the will of the peoples with the transformation of Europe into a political community." A long road indeed, and still relevant!

In the *Financial Post* of May 22, 1954, another reference to the small size of his home country caught the attention of the Luxembourg diplomat: "Small in size but big on steel— Tiny Luxembourg boasts world high per-man output" or the article by Dorothy Mc Cardle on the temporary return of the ambassador to Luxembourg Wiley Buchanan in the *Washington Post* of December 12, 1954: "Luxembourg is a Story Book Land" describing a sojourn without traffic jams in one of the smallest countries in the world. The times were very different and the ties were more personal and varied.

The letter of November 18, 1955 retraces the dilemma and indecision of the Luxembourg diplomat in Washington, swinging between two gaps in preparation for his meeting with the American President announced for later, probably early 1956:

"Anything we say to the President now could be interpreted in different ways; for example, if we tell him too much about his farm (in Gettysburg) and what he has accomplished over the last three years, it could be interpreted as an induction that he will not present himself [for reelection]. On the contrary, if too much emphasis is placed on the excellent appearance of his health and the future development of the world situation the interpretation could be that we think he will represent himself. Under these conditions I believe that what we say will have to be weighed very carefully and I wonder if it would not be appropriate for me to say the following: I have advised my sovereign and the President of my Government that you would receive me today and Her Royal Highness the Grand Duchess has asked me to convey to you Her very best wishes for a speedy and complete recovery. Mr. Bech has requested me to join his wishes and also those of the Luxembourg people. Because of your and Mr. Bech's friendship, I suggested to him that you might like to hear what are his views on the present political situation in Europe, and he replied as follows: ... I will learn by heart the text you want to send me."

Always careful, trying not to offend anyone, trying to sell himself and to (re)present his country as well as possible, this is the art of Le Gallais. A lot of hesitation and prevarication for little in the end, even if, when it comes to accreditations, a certain protocol must be respected and the words weighed as best possible.

Most of the speeches testify to a global and committed vision of Le Gallais, even if he does not show excessive determination when he had finally become, two months earlier, and ambassador of the Grand Duchy of Luxembourg.

ELEVATION TO EMBASSY STATUS
IN SEPTEMBER 1955

On September 10, 1955, the Luxembourg legation was granted embassy status. Le Gallais' power, somewhat regal and often illusory but substantial in spite of everything, had reached its peak. Even though Le Gallais remained the same, his appointment allowed him to shine even more brightly. It must have been one of the happiest days of his life.

This appointment had given rise to an exchange of letters between Le Gallais and Bech and was also to become the subject of correspondence between Le Gallais and Mrs. Maloney due to Le Gallais' absence from a trip to Turkey and Greece. After spending some time in Turkey, the Le Gallais couple was to travel to Greece, Hugues considering in a letter to Mrs. Maloney that one feels more at home in Greece: "Greece incredibly beautiful and much better than I expected; the mosques in Turkey are beautiful too but one feels more at home in Greece." Mrs. Maloney congratulated the ambassador in a letter dated September 9 following a call from the Swiss ambassador and an announcement from the State Department. Le Gallais[586] took care to inform Mrs. Maloney that: "You may have heard that I am to be appointed ambassador some time this month I believe; don't mention it as it is not official. Mr. Werner told me that Mr. Bech had asked him to tell me." Le Gallais and Mrs. Maloney expressed their joy at this long-awaited recognition. This change led to the printing of new business cards for ambassador Le Gallais, a subject about which Mrs. Maloney had been writing about at length in several letters. Were the new business cards to be printed like those of the Belgian ambassador: "Ambassador Extraordinary and Plenipotentiary of H. M. the King of the Belgians" or "The Luxembourg Ambassador", as some countries did, or "Ambassador of Luxembourg"? On August 11,

Eleanor Maloney asked the ambassador: "I have prepared two replies to Mr. Bech's letter. For I was struck by the use of both 'Excellency' and 'honorable'. I called the State Department and talked to Mrs. Nicholson, Assistant..." A difficult choice that she finally preferred to let the ambassador make himself after his return.

An article by "Star society columnist" Betty Beale in the *Washington Star* on September 9, 1955 entitled "Little embassy raised to ambassadorial status" had made the case public and must have pleased the ambassador. The journalist argued that in addition to increased prestige and rank, there is no difference in the salary of the head of mission and concluded her elucubrations about the change in quality of the head of mission by saying that "No matter how able or senior in service a chief of mission might be, if he's a minister he sits below the dumbest, least contributory ambassador."

This good news was not going to prevent Le Gallais from making the most of his holidays and only returning to Washington on October 6 after spending two days in New York.

The title of ambassador was awarded on September 28. The credentials received at the White House on November 8, 1955, could not be presented to President Eisenhower immediately. The solemn act was delayed, according to a letter from Chief of Protocol John F. Simmons, due to the health of the President, who was going to receive Ambassador Le Gallais as soon as he resumed his normal schedule in Washington. *The New York Times* on October 15 had raised the dilemma of the American authorities in the face of the President's prolonged illness, as a delegation of powers had not been arranged in favor of Vice-President Nixon. The article made no mention of the accreditation of Le Gallais as ambassador. It was an unforgivable oversight.

AMERICAN DIPLOMATIC REPRESENTATION
IN LUXEMBOURG

Because of the parallelism of forms, so important in diplomacy, Wiley T. Buchanan was appointed first ambassador of the United States in Luxembourg also on September 9, 1955, after having been minister plenipotentiary since 1953. In Luxembourg, the United States was also represented after the war—as it had been from 1931 until 1941—by chargé d'affaires George Platt Waller. The chancellery acting as a consulate was located at 99 de la Grand-Rue. Shortly before Waller's departure, in June 1948, the former embassy of Nazi Germany on Boulevard Emmanuel Servais was acquired for the embassy of the United States. Then President Truman appointed Mrs. Perle Mesta as American Minister in Luxembourg in 1949. Still known as the "Widow of Oklahoma" or "The hostess with the Mostes", she resided on embassy premises until 1953. At the time of Le Gallais, the following heads of mission were also accredited in Luxembourg: Wiley T. Buchanan, Jr. from 1953 to 1956 and Vinton Chapin from 1957 to 1960.

Even more than Hugues Le Gallais, Perle Mesta[587] had a gift for putting herself in the limelight. She seems to have somewhat annoyed the Secretary of the embassy in Washington. In the *Scrapbook* are kept articles marked in red on a few diplomatic deviations of the "socialite" posted in Luxembourg. Let us mention here the unfavorable appreciation of Le Gallais towards his counterpart. On May 6, 1949, on the occasion of her appointment, he wrote: "I am afraid that we can only say yes", and once the appointment had been made official, he added: "There has been much discussion about the appointment of Mrs. Mesta and my colleagues are envious of us. They feel that having a Minister who can correspond directly with the President is a huge advantage and they believe that Mrs. Mesta will do her best to ensure that her mission is successful and that Luxembourg can only benefit from that." In the same missive of June 10, 1949, Le Gallais reported vilifications, according to which Mrs. Mesta had never read a book and that she would not spend her money in Luxembourg, concluding that "this is not the perfect choice, but in general it is thought that Luxembourg can be very satisfied with this appointment". In spite of these reported hesitations and rumors, it remained that the elevation of the status and the independence of the Minister from the American embassy in Brussels was also a step forward for Le Gallais, who was hoping for a future promotion of his own mission in the United States. The fact that Perle Mesta had excellent links with the press and was going to get a lot of press coverage could only move things in the right direction and in the end only suit Le Gallais. On June 23, 1949, before the congressional hearing, Le Gallais had written that "Mrs. Mesta will bring us a lot of publicity to an audience that is interested in what she is doing, but is not interested to the same degree in the North Atlantic Pact". A few days later, Le Gallais again took the opportunity of a meeting with Secretary of State Dean Acheson to express Luxembourg's appreciation to him on the occasion of the appointment of a Minister who would reside there and that people were "very happy with the appointment of Mrs. Mesta".

Irving Berlin's musical "Call me Madam" about the activities of Perle Mesta received a mixed reception, with Deputy Secretary of State Acheson forbidding his diplomatic representative to attend the premiere. Le Gallais wrote in a confidential cable dated November 15, 1950 to Bech that Mrs. Truman had confided to him during a dinner at the White House that she had not liked the play because it made too much fun of her friend. On the other hand, Le Gallais mentions in the same note that he told the President, during a "conversation between gentlemen" after dinner, that during the procession from the cathedral to the Grand Ducal Palace on August 15, Mrs. Mesta had been the only diplomat to be applauded, which apparently amused Truman.

An article in the *Washington Star* of February 2, 1950, "Perle's pace panics Luxembourg", had been included in the *Scrapbook*, stating that Perle Mesta had had to solve few pressing problems in Luxembourg. The population there would enjoy the highest standard of living and would traditionally love the United States and therefore also Perle Mesta.

During a 48-hour visit by American Senators (Elmer Thoma of Indiana, John L. McClellan of Arkansas, A. Willis Robertson of West Virginia), they were so enchanted by the welcome they received at the American legation that they went so far as to proclaim: "she is the greatest lady in the world", while she went so far as to confess: "I have put Luxembourg on the map." It was enough to make Hugues Le Gallais a little jealous. All that remained for him to do was to keep in the *Scrapbook* the article published in *La Meuse* making public one of Mrs. Mesta's blunders. The front page of this newspaper of November 8, 1949 must have particularly offended Mrs. Le Gallais and even Mrs. Maloney, who had circled it with a double red dash. Perle Mesta affirmed without hesitation under the title "*La classe féminine au service de la diplomatie*" that she dressed "at Dessés but finds that European women still have to evolve". In the same way, articles criticizing her style and published in the United States were kept by Mrs. Maloney. Thus, the *New York Journal* of January 29, 1952 stated that "the social conduct is politically grotesque and a discredit to our diplomatic service".

At the end of Perle Mesta's term of office, Le Gallais reported in a politically inaccurate manner on March 31, 1953, following his interview with the Assistant Secretary of State for Administrative Affairs Mr. Lourie who had asked his opinion on having a woman as diplomatic representative: "I replied that Mrs. Mesta is very popular throughout the Grand Duchy, but that on the other hand one can hardly have an in-depth conversation with her on matters of international politics." After she left, Bech sent a coded message asking Le Gallais to seize the opportunity without approaching the State Department officially to tell them that "our preference is for a career diplomat and not a woman despite Mrs. Mesta's success due to an unusual combination of circumstances". In other words, opinions were divided, even and especially among Luxembourgers. Relations between Le Gallais and his counterpart were not to be the best, their styles being too different, even if they had a certain glamour in common.

LAST YEARS IN WASHINGTON

Hugues Le Gallais often worked in the shadows, emerging only occasionally and leaving the spotlight, most of the time and at least in Luxembourg, to his government, Minister of State Pierre Dupont and, since the latter's death in December 1953, to Joseph Bech. Always acting with a clear conscience and in good faith, the ambassador could also be conscious of his achievements and even, from time to time, a little snobbish and vain. However, Le Gallais never failed to underline the precious role he played in one or other of the affairs of the moment and went so far as to write that he felt that his intervention in the negotiations on Luxembourg's place in the Bretton Woods financial institutions was well worth a decoration. He was usually discreet, especially in relation to the Luxembourg media, where at most half a dozen times his person or his intervention was mentioned. He made up for this in some way by asking Mrs. Maloney to keep any article about him and Luxembourg that appeared in the American press. There was enough to fill the *Scrapbook*. In a premonitory manner, Le Gallais tried with the assurance and allure that was his to describe, advise and influence the authorities of his country, his vague misjudgments not belying the common sense of his appreciation of the true interests of Luxembourg. His contacts with important people in the United States were very well followed up, as were those with his colleagues and representatives of the presidential administration and Congress. Le Gallais frequented both the Rockefellers and the Guggenheims, to name those two families.

Art was a means of access to the highest spheres of American society. Mr. and Mrs. John D. Rockefeller 3rd,[588] for example, had one of the largest collections of Asian art in the United States, consisting of only 300 objects, but of the highest quality. John D. Rockefeller 3rd had founded the Asia Society in 1956 and considered art to be an indispensable and integral means to achieve better relations between Asian countries and the United States, especially through education and better mutual understanding. John and Blanchette Rockefeller really began their collection in the early 1960s, but it seems that their shared affinity for Asian art had connected them with the Le Gallais much earlier. The Luxembourg diplomat also had ties with the other Rockefeller brothers, such as Nelson, who had taken on various responsibilities under the presidencies of Roosevelt, Truman and Eisenhower and became Governor of New York in 1959, and David, of the Chase Manhattan Bank, also avid collectors and philanthropists. Their father and mother, who died in 1960 and 1948, were very much involved in the art world. Abby Aldrich Rockefeller was a socialite and philanthropist and the driving force behind the founding of New York's Museum of Modern Art (MoMA) in November 1929. We do not know whether Hugues Le Gallais was a true lover of this New York institution or of modern and contemporary art in general.

Links with the Guggenheims also seem to have been established as early as the mid-1940s.[589] Thus, in a letter of August 18, 1944, Le Gallais reported meetings with members of one of the wealthiest families in the United States: "I am writing to you from the countryside ... we are at the home of friends, the Guggenheims, by the sea until the 31st and very happy to be away from Washington in this terrible heat wave ... I have met my friend's uncle, who is eighty-three years old, while remaining remarkably active and lucid. His fortune is estimated at a hundred million dollars; it is indecent." Although the rest of the letter is missing from the archives, Le Gallais has for once been a little more critical of one of the most eminent personalities in this country, now the world's leading power. He was going to remain linked to certain members of this eminent family. About ten years later, an invitation in 1955 for a winter week of quail hunting at Poco Sabo (meaning "little unknown"), forty miles from Charleston, South Carolina, had been sent by Meyer Robert Guggenheim.[590] Guggenheim had been a colonel in the US Army and had served in France during the First World War. He was active in the family business and served briefly as ambassador to Portugal in 1953 and 1954, just one year before being recalled following certain *faux-pas*. Robert Guggenheim was an influential contributor to the Republican Party, and his contributions to Eisenhower's election campaign had earned him the posting. Pictures were kept of wilderness and a colonial house where hunters were to meet to discuss business and politics. Robert and his brother Harry owned Poco Sabo and

Cain Hoy's farm and hunting grounds respectively. These were ideal places to relax, retreat and enjoy life in the great outdoors, away from the family business. In *The Guggenheims—a Family History*,[591] we learn that "like Harry, he (Robert) used it (Poco Sabo) as a lodge for his grouse and partridge shooting and for frolicking with male cronies." In memory of his visit to Poco Sabo, Hugues Le Gallais kept photos of the imposing estate and the enchanting nature. The Guggenheims lived in Firenze House on Rock Creek Park and were part of the Washington social scene, active in charity work and sponsors of the National Symphony Orchestra. Later, Le Gallais would frequent Peggy Guggenheim, a wealthy heiress who bought a Venetian palace in 1949 close to the Le Gallais family and lived there until her death 30 years later. There she exhibited her collection of works of art that she had acquired from 1938 onwards from the greatest artists of whom she was a patron. Le Gallais did not even try to compete with her and confined himself to preserving his works of art of another kind.

We have seen that Le Gallais maintained cordial links with most of his colleagues accredited in the United States and even in the two neighboring countries he visited sporadically. Collaboration with colleagues from the Benelux countries seems to have brought a certain increased visibility to Luxembourg. Le Gallais seems to have willingly lent himself to this lifestyle, as was the case on April 10, 1956, when the Belgian Chamber of Commerce organized a Benelux lunch at the Waldorf Astoria. On this occasion a US-Holland brochure was published with the biographies and photos of Hugues Le Gallais and Honorary Consul General Bernard Zimmer on the cover with their respective counterparts. A huge guest list was kept with the biggest names of the political and economic world of the time.

All this—maintaining social ties and keeping the chancellery and the ambassador's accommodation in the same state—cost money. Increasingly, there were discussions between the ambassador and his secretary about the functioning and financing of the embassy. On June 21, 1956, Mrs. Maloney drew the attention of her boss to the financial situation of the embassy: "It is plain to see that this last credit is not sufficient to carry us through another month. This is true regardless of how many extra months you took. My reason for concern that we have now placed two more orders with the Department of the Army." And to continue with similar indications about the finances on July 17:

"About the cash situation and the deficit ... I started again where I left off two summers ago and think I have uncovered two credits which were not counted and perhaps one refund never received. Please give me some more time ... the confusion is due to 1) the way the books are kept and 2) to the juggling around of expenses (by the Government) incurred for Foreign Affairs, other department and Government in Exile. Often we could receive a transfer without saying for what purpose, that is just in the beginning, not within the past. Also I find we never actually wrote that we did not accept Mr. Wampach's figure; we always wrote (provisionally) after the figure of the Government in Exile…"

The summer of 1956 was used at the embassy in Washington to carry out painting work, install a hot water heater and buy a new car.[592] In June 1956, Eleanor Maloney informed the ambassador about the importation of one hundred and fifty rose plants at 12 francs each, which were subject to quarantine and import permission from the Department of Agriculture, to which were added fifty roses as a gift for the Secretary.[593] Le Gallais could be generous and grateful.

Fortunately, he was able to escape his baser material concerns by spending holidays in Seal Harbor and Europe. In Venice, several visits were made to the recently acquired Ca' Contarini Michiel Palace, visits to which we shall return: the Bech and Truman couple registered on May 30; the Buchanan couple on August 19 and 20, the Franks couple from August 19 to 26;[594] the Werner couple from August 30 to 31, 1956. In any case, the ambassador was absent from June 27 to September 18, with a leave of absence of two months between July 10 and September 10. On July 5, Le Gallais was at the Hotel Bristol in Luxembourg and dined with the Bech couple to watch his film about Venice. Le Gallais had promised that he would be back in Washington for the IMF sessions. Le Gallais seems to have been absent on September 22, 1956 when the Werner-Pescatore couple arrived with René Franck who was having discussions in Washington on claims at the State Department, the three of them staying at the embassy.[595] Then Bech came in November to the United Nations and was expected with his wife in Washington.

At the end of March 1957, Hugues Le Gallais carefully noted the signing in Rome of the treaty laying at the origin of European project. Washington followed with interest the developments on the European continent which, since the ECSC and the failure of the EDC, had gained new impetus.

A little later, the declaration on paper dated June 11, 1957 signed by Hugues Le Gallais affirmed that he "had given Mrs. Maloney copies of all the letters sent to the Government which he held and that he no longer possessed in his private flats any official documents. The undersigned also declared that henceforth all official documents would remain in the chancellery." As mentioned above, this document remains difficult to interpret, even if a joke between the two protagonists seems the most likely explanation, all the more so since, as of June 25, 1957, correspondence resumed as normal, a letter from Mrs. Maloney being received by Le Gallais in Seal Harbor.

In late June and early July 1957, Mrs. Maloney's letters to her boss at Seal Harbor related to the state of health of Corneille Staudt who had been Honorary Vice-Consul in New York while Bernard Zimmer had been Honorary Consul General there since December 1946. Mrs. Loesch had requested advances to help Staudt who appeared to be very ill and suffering from cancer, and concerns were expressed regarding Staudt's accession to the 'Government Account' in the event of his death. Active preparations for the funeral are discussed in a letter of August 26, 1957. *The New York Times* of October 6, 1957 reports that Corneille Staudt died at the age of 62. On November 12, 1955, Le Gallais had offered a lunch in New York on the occasion of the 25th anniversary of Corneille Staudt's entry into the consular service in which Le Gallais stated: "Luxembourg could not have found a more local and industrious man. With his devoted wife the Consul has brought together the Luxembourgers and strengthened the ties among them. He is the right man in the right place." On this occasion Le Gallais had conferred on Staudt the Grand Officer of the Order of the Crown of Oak.

Despite everything, the summer of 1957 looked joyful, with escapades at the end of June in Seal Harbor and also in mid-August, when Hugues was joined there by his wife and their son. During the summer of 1957, Mrs. Maloney wished to visit her daughter in Vermont as well as in Rehoboth Beach at the end of August. Thus, the embassy was unoccupied for a while, which seemed to bother no one.

From time to time, high patronage was requested from the embassy by American charities or through other Embassies. For these events, Mrs. Le Gallais had some valuable jewelry at her disposal. Thus, in March 1954 the jeweler Edward E. Ayre of Washington wrote to the insurer R. P. Lepowski an evaluation of a "pair of ear-shaped emerald drop ear-rings" valued at more than 17 thousand dollars with the precision "On the side of the mounting of each of the hexacut diamonds is stamped Boucheron-Paris". In February 1957, an insurance policy of 20,000 dollars for a ruby brooch was taken out with Lepowski. There is also a declaration of loss of a small diamond from Mrs. Le Gallais' flower earrings.

On September 18, 1957, Hugues Le Gallais was back in New York for the lunch of the Benelux Chamber of Commerce with the presence of the Dutch Minister of Foreign Affairs, Joseph Luns, future Secretary General of NATO.[596]

A princely visit to the United States took place before the last Christmas and New Year's Eve celebrations for the Le Gallais couple. On November 5, 1957, Le Gallais accompanied the younger brother of the Hereditary Grand Duke, Prince Charles, to Monticello to visit the house of President Thomas Jefferson. A luncheon was hosted at Kenwood by Mrs. E. M. Watson, widow of Major General Edwin M. Watson, who had served as Military Advisor and Secretary to President Roosevelt, before both returned to Washington. Although other meetings are not mentioned, Le Gallais must have spent a few pleasant days with the Luxembourg Prince, known for his joviality.

Le Gallais also never failed to congratulate Bech by using a tone of preciousness for such and such a speech or to mention that such and such appreciated the idea contained in the positions taken by the Luxembourg Minister of Foreign Affairs, who, after the death of Dupong, became Minister of State and President of the Government once again.

As detailed above, from time to time Le Gallais has continued to write policy briefs, give his opinion on international current affairs and report on American views. Sometimes he also received indications or even instructions on Luxembourg politics. Thus, on February 24, 1958, a three-page note[597] from Minister Bech thanked the ambassador for the information he had received "concerning opinions expressed by politicians on the question of the seat of the European institutions" and then, for Le Gallais' personal information, gave indications on the policy followed and a summary of the positions of the other Community member states. Bech also mentioned "that the question of the seat of the European institutions is of great importance for our country, both from a political and a purely material point of view" and that "the Luxembourg Government has never hidden its reticence towards too much centralization and it still believes that the so-called 'regional concentration' solution, for example between Brussels, Luxembourg and Strasbourg, would better respond to the possibilities that exist at the moment to achieve a fair result." He concludes that the Government will not accept the hypothesis of the ECSC's departure under any condition and that it is premature to talk about the choice of a European capital.

In March 1958, health problems seem to have preoccupied the ambassador and his wife. Le Gallais accepted an invitation alone to the Douglas Dillon house,[598] his wife having had a strong flu and not having gone out for three weeks. He himself reported in the same letter to Bech that he "is not well either believing he was disturbed in the head the other day at a cocktail party by a glass of bad whisky which then went to his stomach." The day before, he was in bed with a fever, also stating that he thought he "would have to cancel the dinner the next day at the French embassy where our mutual friend Robert Schuman will be present", which he deeply regretted. He also announced that Mrs. Maloney would be absent from March 31 to April 21, preventing him from writing "confidential letters, at least typed ones". Finally, he again made it clear to Bech that he had taken a "wise decision by resigning as President of the Government", retaining the post of Minister of Foreign Affairs, "taking into account all that you have been able to do in the field of foreign policy and given the 1959 elections". This letter was sent to Mr. Bech's home at 34, avenue Monterey. Bech's departure may have given Le Gallais pause for thought as to the end of his own career.

In any case, summer was approaching with the traditional break which, this time, was going to correspond to a non-return, a definitive departure and even a farewell to many friends and countless acquaintances. In a letter of January 15, Le Gallais initially planned to embark in New York on June 18 to go to Paris, Luxembourg and Venice, where he would take his leave from July 1 and later leave on the *Queen Mary* on September 11 after a "short visit to Paris and the International Fair in Brussels".

However, on April 23, 1958, an exchange of cables between the ambassador and the minister reported details in connection with the departure from Washington. Le Gallais wrote at the end of the letter: "I thank you for your agreement, provided that I can embark on Wednesday May 7; we are taking the *Queen Mary* and should be in Paris on May 12, Hotel Bristol." A Grand Ducal decree of April 23 confirmed the holiday from May 20 to July 20, 1958.

The next day (Thursday April 24, 1958), Le Gallais again reported to his minister that the day before he had given a lunch in honor of Baron Hubert Ansiaux,[599] governor of the National Bank of Belgium from 1957 to 1971, stating that "the Belgian ambassador pointed out that he regretted not being able to present printed menus as I did with the names of the owners themselves sitting next to each other", a menu of which the ambassador also took care to send a copy to his minister. The ambassador had indeed served Wiltinger Kupp—Le Gallais—1955 and Château Haut-Brion—Dillon—1945. There was also the Undersecretary of the Treasury, Chief of Protocol Wiley T. Buchanan Jr. who had been Head of Mission in Luxembourg. On that occasion, the Deputy Under-Secretary for Economic Affairs, Douglas Dillon, discussed with Le Gallais the invitation to participate in an exhibition in Chicago and another on the Pacific coast the following year, considering

"that it might be appropriate to draw my Government's attention to the importance of the event in Chicago. Indeed, thanks to the improvements to the St. Lawrence River, the city of Chicago will become a seaport and the whole region behind it would feel the consequences. This part of the United States had always been the most backward in terms of international trade, and that we would help the State Department by making a special propaganda effort in Chicago. Mr. Dillon confirmed this to Mr. Ansiaux and I informed Baron Sylvercruys who thanked me."

Four members of the Luxembourg delegation who were in Washington for "talks with the International Bank", namely Messrs Franck, Hamer, Wehenkel and Leydenbach, were also invited. The day after the lunch at the Luxembourg embassy, Le Gallais attended a lunch given by the governors of the Federal Reserve for Mr. Ansiaux, who gave "a brilliant presentation on the economic situation in a number of European countries and also noted that the Common Market would need American capital."

On April 29, press clippings were sent to Luxembourg before, on the following day, Le Gallais began to take care of his archives and the embassy files and considered that "embassy documents should be reclassified according to a new system". To this end, he asked Ms. Sullivan, who replaced Ms. Maloney during her leave, to help with the classification. This recruitment at a cost of $75 was accepted and was to be charged to the staff costs account. Mrs. Sullivan began work on May 21, 1958 and had to work her way through all the paperwork that the ambassador was about to leave. Two weeks later, on June 8, the ambassador "found" that one week was not enough to tidy everything up, as additional days were requested. Le Gallais was thus concerned to leave some order and a trace of his activity in the embassy archives. Was it a premonition or a desire to leave his mark as he approached his retirement, scheduled for mid-May 1961, once he reached the age of 65? The fact that the departure took place some two and a half years earlier must be considered unexpected and unplanned, even though various elements ultimately contributed to this ineluctable precipitation.

A SOMEWHAT HASTY RETIREMENT

All in all, Hugues Le Gallais was to remain in office for eighteen long years. He had woven an unbroken thread of demanding work, even in the depths of doubt and war. He was, as we have seen, a multi-faceted character. He left his embassy on Monday, May 5, 1958, never to set foot there again. He ended his career as a diplomat on September 30, 1958. He bowed out unexpectedly and, in any case, if he had thought about it inwardly, he had kept the possibility of an early departure well in hand. As aging is in a way to give up, Hugues, after having been an unparalleled diplomat, not so attractive but able to convince, demonstrated that he knew how to do it with class. He also excelled in the last stage of his life, which was to be no less hectic than the one he was putting an end to. The reorganization of the diplomatic corps, but also a tax dispute, seem to have been at the root of this premature resignation. Le Gallais received half of his Arbed pension as a lump sum. He was going to go into a sort of chosen exile and take advantage of the waves and the favorable climate offered by Venice. Life was not at all restful, with many visitors, but left time for walks and visits to museums.

On April 30, Le Gallais advised his minister that he had informed the day before

"M. Torbert that I was leaving on holiday. He told me that his deputy, Mr. Service, had seen you in Luxembourg and had heard with joy the story of your conversation with the USSR ambassador in Luxembourg in which you put forward the idea that instead of adopting the Rapacki plan,[600] it was sufficient to demilitarize[601] the regions in question. We spoke of two hypotheses: either continue the two-by-two talks in Moscow or hold talks with six people and Mr. Torbert made me understand that the State Department was above all afraid of creating a precedent if the second solution was adopted, particularly at the United Nations."

Le Gallais also reported having met the German and Austrian ambassadors and having received at lunch Manilo Brosio,[602] Italian ambassador to the United States, and his wife as well as Charles Burke Elbrick and his wife.[603] Elbrick was Secretary of State for European and Eurasian Affairs and was due to meet Bech in Copenhagen in the next few days. There was a discussion on disarmament, the subject being further developed in a confidential note of May 2 (Friday) on a lunch for the heads of the European Coal and Steel Community mission at the French embassy. This is the last note from Le Gallais written from Washington, finally mentioning that "as I am leaving by Monday (May 5) I will no longer have the pleasure of writing to you. In New York I shall see Mr. Zimmer, who fortunately is doing better." And again: "At lunch yesterday I told your story of de-terrorism, which made everyone laugh." This was a somewhat amusing note to conclude eighteen years of activities in Washington as head of post.

The ambassador having been authorized to take leave from May 20 to July 20, and this again, as always, by Grand Ducal decree, as every year, the Le Gallais were absent, this time with the peculiarity that no one knew there would be no return. And as every year, even though Washington in the summer calms down due to the sometimes tropical humidity, the couple missed one or other social event, such as, on June 26, a reception at Marjorie Merriweather Post in her fabulous Hillwood home, this time with her fourth husband, Herbert May. Mrs. Maloney did not fail to point out that this was the fourth marriage for Mrs. Post. Hugues Le Gallais left Washington on Monday, May 5, and from New York two days later to go first to Paris and, from May 19 to 28, to Venice. On Monday May 5 it was Mrs. Maloney who, as usual when she was alone, sent press extracts on behalf of the ambassador, as she did a week later, with reference to the confidential letter of May 2, a copy of a note from the German ambassador and the appendix referred to therein. A trip by the Le Gallais couple from Venice to Luxembourg from June 3 to 10, 1958 for consultations was authorized. This seemed a departure from custom, but undoubtedly helped to clear up some matters.

On June 18, 1958, Le Gallais again sent a letter from Venice to Mrs. Maloney on Sotheby's and some belongings to arrive in

Venice in mid-August.[604] On June 20, there was a letter from Mrs. Maloney to Le Gallais on details of the management of the embassy and the roadmap and the question:

"Did you ask Mr. Schulté[605] when you were in Luxembourg how to write up the expenses for Europe? Will each page contain one step? Such as Washington-New York; New York-Le Havre; Le Havre-Paris; Paris-Venice etc? It is too bad you have to be troubled with these questions on your vacation. It does seem to me they are trying to make it as difficult as possible for us where the accounts are concerned. For example why in previous years didn't they ask for the items on petty cash to be signed?"

So far, the correspondence does not reveal the thunderclap that was to follow, reporting nothing but matters relating to the functioning of the embassy. In a handwritten letter dated June 24, 1958, Hugues Le Gallais informed Mrs. Maloney that he would not be returning to Washington and agreed with Bech that he would resign on September 30. He requested that the letter be typed by his secretary with orders to destroy the original once typed and a copy to be sent to Le Gallais and one copy kept by Mrs. Maloney.

In the margin of this note, Eleanor Maloney wrote "called June 30, 1958", suggesting that the two of them explained themselves orally on the latest developments and did everything possible to keep only an official record in the embassy archives. In the end: "I regret giving you so much trouble during the summer." And above: "My reason for not coming back at all is to avoid the numerous tiring parties departing diplomats must go through." This was an explanation that everyone understood and which meant that he had drawn a hardly glorious line under almost two decades of activity and untiring, hectic life in Washington.

And even higher, at the very beginning: "I gave Mr. Bech to understand that I wanted to resign September 30, 1958 and will confirm this to him when you send me back the 2 enclosed papers typed out. Should you have any remarks to make concerning the 'situation de caisse' or the yearly accounts please make two drafts, one as per enclosed and the other with your suggestions." It is not known whether Mrs. Maloney has taken the liberty of correcting the accounts of her dear ambassador in those last years; one thing seems obvious, namely that the somewhat loose management of public funds seems to have been one of the causes of the hasty departure of the Le Gallais couple from Washington. On July 29, Paul Schulté arrived in Washington to make detailed statements and review the accounts, it seems. This future ambassador was like Le Gallais, a faithful follower of Bech, but apparently a meticulous supervisor who had a lot of trouble with the Washingtonian accounts... All the correspondence between Mrs. Maloney and Le Gallais in the next few weeks was with regard to the return of Mrs. Le Gallais, insurance, packaging, the wine available at the embassy cellar, the staff, the successor etc., but not a word about the financial situation. Until August 5, 1958, when Le Gallais wrote from Cortina d'Ampezzo[606] "received your news about the accounts and my 'indemnité' [sic]. Your way of calculating appears right and so with the last 'indemnité' you will be able to pay the Seal Harbor tax bill. I have signed the 'décompte' and am returning it together with the old one."

Five years earlier, Le Gallais had asked Mrs. Maloney to type a letter of several scribbled pages which he corrected and completed on July 10, 1953 before sending a copy to the Prime Minister and the Minister of Foreign Affairs. It must be quoted in full to understand the atmosphere prevailing at the time:

"Answer by Mr. Hugues Le Gallais to the second memorandum of the Administration of Contributions (Luxembourg Inland Revenue) of June 24, 1953:

The Administration of Contributions having seen fit to return to the question of the personal objects of the undersigned by giving them the title of works of art, I have no objection to sending the Council of State a list of these objects with an indication of their value. I do so without any hesitation because I find it very difficult to believe that the Council of State, composed of men who have the general interest of the country at heart, would want to impose a capital tax on personal objects or works of art which at the moment serve, without any possible dispute, more the State than their owner. I hope that Mr. Pierre Dupong, Minister of State and Mr. Joseph Bech, Minister of Foreign Affairs, who know the legation's building very well, will be willing to confirm the above. I have just used the words 'personal objects or works of art', not knowing from the point of view of the Administration of contributions at what value a personal object becomes a work of art. The Administration of contributions mentions in its brief that I would have sold part of my collection to a museum in Washington for the sum of $15,000. Since these objects were still in my possession on January 1, 1946, I do not feel that I need to make a statement about a sale that occurred years later. [Addition requested by Le Gallais on July 10, 1953:] I wish to point out that in a spirit of correctness to the Government I have replaced the objects sold with a painting by Signac purchased for $2,000 (I have the invoice) and in addition I have paid $400 (I have the cheque) for a painting which is not worth that much and which I do not like (and my wife does not like at all) by a young American painter whose father is a great friend of former President Truman. I thought that one day this gesture might be useful and moreover later I asked the painter's father to intervene with the President in a matter concerning the Government. Mr. Dupong and Bech know what this is all about. It is with reluctance that I am giving these details but I think it is necessary for the members of the Council of State to know that if I am taking such pains to defend my point of view it is because I feel that I have acted correctly towards the Government from a financial point of view and that I cannot allow the Government to act otherwise towards me [end of addition of July 10, 1953].

The Directorate of Contributions notes in its memorandum that, as far as I am concerned, the pretexts given by the Government are vain and, moreover, absolutely irrelevant in the present case. I hope that the Council of State will be prepared to accept, when it hears these pretexts, that they are, on the contrary, relevant to the case. 1) If, instead of making my objects available to the State free of charge, I had sold them, I would have made a small capital investment which would have brought me income over many years. I have renounced this income in favor of the State. 2) If I had sold my objects, or if I had sent them to Europe to furnish one of my wife's personal residences, it would have meant that the State would have had to buy a certain number of paintings and tapestries to decorate the rooms in which we receive at the legation. By not doing so I obtained that the State did not have to use a certain amount of capital in a non-remunerative way i.e. I avoided a loss of interest. Consequently, by keeping my objects 1) I have renounced personal income and 2) I have made the State save money[607] and I can ask the question whether it would be fair for the State in addition to use and benefit materially and morally (artistic value) of the objects.

It seems to me that it has been established: 1) that my personal objects and works of art serve the State as long as I hold my present position. 2) that my wife and I had no other capital on January 1, 1946. 3) that I have spent in the interest of the country all that the

State has given me since 1940 and my wife her income until January 1, 1946. Consequently I can only find that at least financially I have done my duty to the State and that it would be unfair after the sacrifices made voluntarily that they would want to impose a new one on me. In these circumstances I ask the Council of State not to endorse the conclusions of the Directorate of Contributions".[608]

This argument by Le Gallais shows that five years before his retirement there was already a debate on financial aspects that played an undeniable role in the decision to end his diplomatic career in 1958.

Let's look forward in time to see how this case evolved. While most of the time his official role took precedence over his private life, he gave the impression in this case that he considered himself abandoned, if not simply dropped. The dispute had definitely not evolved in favor of the principal. In the Venetian isolation, as it were from the summer of 1958 onwards, Le Gallais showed a certain reserve, even though he sometimes said aloud what he had long thought in silence. Le Gallais was notified at a public hearing on January 21, 1959 that his appeal against the tax authorities in respect of the extraordinary tax on capital had been withdrawn, the costs imposed on the claimant party (so Le Gallais still had to pay, for example, lawyers' fees) and the case to be taken off the roll. Le Gallais had therefore lost on all counts, and the arguments and interventions at the highest level were of little use this time. In the recitals, we also learn that in the course of the proceedings, the claimant (again Le Gallais) acknowledged the unfounded nature of his appeal and simply withdrew it. A second recital clarifies that there are no public interest grounds to prevent this withdrawal and that it is therefore appropriate to acknowledge this and to impose costs on the claimant. The Litigation Committee of the Council of State had again heard the report of the rapporteur-counselor and the observations of the government delegate in order to rule *in absentia* in what must have been a slap in the face and a flagrant disavowal for the principal party concerned. All memories of the happy years were beginning to fade following this snub. While at the time ambassadors lived mostly on their own personal funds, times were changing and Le Gallais was no longer willing to let this happen, even though he eventually abandoned his claims.

Mrs. Maloney, having spoken on the telephone to her departed ambassador, still so dearly appreciated, only replied in writing on July 1: "I suppose I just wouldn't admit to myself the fact that you were not returning to Washington … What a relief you must be feeling; how light you must feel. … I have a kind of feeling 'the king is dead. Long live the king' for I keep thinking of the things to be done in preparation for another ambassador and at the same time a host of questions to ask you." It was a rather impersonal and pathetic answer to someone who is undoubtedly in a delicate and most difficult personal situation. Comparing the life of an ambassador to that of a sovereign may have been a consolation to someone who had to find himself quite alone in Venice, far from his homeland of Luxembourg and his workplace in Washington. Le Gallais had to think about all that he had to leave behind: a prestigious life and good friends and acquaintances, but also about how best to present things. Whether in Luxembourg or Washington, Le Gallais sought an honorable way out of the complex situation in which he had found himself, a sort of face-saving, acceptable to his authorities and credible to his many acquaintances.

On July 7, 1958, from Venice, Le Gallais, as unalterable as ever, wrote again to the private address of his Minister of State:

"I wish first of all to tell you how much I appreciated your understanding attitude towards my plans to retire on September 30,

1958 instead of waiting for the normal age of 65, which I should reach on May 15, 1961 if all goes well. You will remember that you made me aware that my pension would only start to run from May 15, 1961, which made me think, but on the other hand I learned that I had once signed a paper allowing me to receive half of my Arbed pension now in a lump sum. Now this capital spread over 30 months will allow me to have a decent pension while waiting for the state pension in 1961. Under these conditions, in agreement with my wife, I have decided not to change anything to the plans developed before you during my last stay in Luxembourg on which you agreed. I obviously regret not remaining in the service of the Government until the normal retirement age, but on the other hand I have the feeling that my departure now will make it easier for you to organize our representation in Washington as well as at the United Nations so that basically everything is for the best for everyone. Please let me know when you have made a decision about my successor. It might then be a good idea for me to come and see him and see what he wants to do about the servants. In my opinion vis-à-vis the representatives of the State Department in Luxembourg it would be best to say at the appropriate time that my state of health does not permit me to continue in the post or to undertake another trip to the United States. For my part I shall write to close friends (Mrs. Watson, Ben Zimmer and someone in Maine who is to help me with the sale of my house) that I have seen you, that I have told you that I get tired very quickly in Washington, that you have shown a great deal of understanding for this state of affairs and that under these conditions it may well be that I shall not return to the United States. This would allow me to give news of what I have not yet done and you could postpone the appointment until a time that suits you best. I will conclude that I intend to open a small museum of oriental art in Venice, which as an occupation should tire me far less than diplomatic life in Washington and provide me with a not uninteresting end to my career. My wife intends to embark on the

SS Queen Mary on September 11 for New York and to leave on the *Vulcania*[609] for Venice on October 4. It can therefore be assumed that the embassy would be at the disposal of my successor from October 6. Mrs. Maloney is aware of this since she typed this letter. If for administrative reasons I have to write you an official letter concerning the above, may I ask you to send me an appropriate text. To conclude, I would like to say how much I am pleased every day to have had such a clear-sighted and understanding leader since March 1940 and I thank you wholeheartedly for the many expressions of confidence you have shown me and for what you have done to facilitate my task. Please accept, dear Mr. Bech, the expression of my sincerest and most grateful sentiments."

Attached to this letter is a note concerning the change of ambassador in Washington. The note largely repeats much of what is stated above, beginning:

"I will write to Mrs. Maloney and ask her to pass on the following press release to the society column in about a week's time on July 16, unless she receives a phone call asking if it is true that I am resigning and then she will communicate immediately: ...

It seems to me that thanks to this last remark ('he will be able to give them a personally conducted tour as was the custom after dinner at the Luxembourg embassy') I remain kind until the end. You will see that I have crossed out the words 'it may well be' to tell it like it is. This saves me from having to write new letters later and it is not because I am resigning that you have to appoint my successor immediately.

I have found that I have had to write about twenty personal letters which I will send tomorrow: Elbrick, Buchanan, Acheson, Frankfurter,[610] Sumner Welles, Mrs. Meyer, Mrs. Astor, Mrs.

Grew, Theodore Green,[611] Guggenheim, Lippmann, Silvercruys, Brosio etc. Later as I am not making a farewell visit to Dulles I will prepare a letter to be written by Mrs. Maloney which I will sign, the same for Warren. I will send a letter by hand to Mrs. Herter.[612] I had not thought it necessary to write to my colleagues in Luxembourg but having received a letter from Schaus[613] saying that he is temporarily leaving our diplomatic corps I think I should write to them."

Le Gallais does not seem to be overly bitter or frustrated and has little feeling of revenge. He expresses neither forgiveness nor too many regrets. He was not tempted to erase the past but did everything he could to open the way to the future with a new life in Venice. In the city where his wife was born, Hugues seems to have continued to charm his world. His wife remained faithfully at his side, even if it was not always easy. He was grateful to her, and their complicity seems to have increased over the years, both of them more than ever willing to lead a dream life and to receive friends and acquaintances from the society that was theirs. As always, he continued to make efforts to keep in touch with his relations in the United States and Luxembourg.

On leaving his post, Le Gallais made suggestions regarding the change of ambassador in Washington and was concerned about the fate of his staff. He described them in great detail, praising their qualities, as in the case of

"Rino Cettolin, 45, chauffeur serves at table when there are many guests—gardener; $260 per month, 12 years of service; Ida Cettolin, 41, excellent chambermaid, can sew, can prepare a good big dinner, but does not wish to be a cook; $50 per month, 12 years of service ; Salvatore Amari, 41, cleans the embassy, serves at table, gardener, some cooking; $190 per month; 6 years service;

Elsa Amari, 34, kitchen helper, washes and irons; $100 per month; 13 months service and who was pregnant at the time of the change of ambassador and gave birth in April 1959; Karoline Jensen, 61, cook, cordon bleu, particularly good for pastry and fish; $70 per month; 14 months service."

The first four were Italians, the last one was Danish. The salaries of the driver and the cook were paid by the government. Each servant had half a day off per week and half a day on Sunday every fortnight. At one point there was an excellent cook named Ennio Petrucci, but he was not related to the teacher who had made Hugues love oriental art. In addition to these employees, local recruits in the service of the ambassador in Washington, the embassy had to look after the representatives in New York, the consul and the members of the mission to the United Nations, but also the Luxembourg honorary consuls scattered throughout the United States.

On a date impossible to determine, perhaps July 21, 1958, Le Gallais wrote to Mrs. Maloney: "I received today a very nice letter from Bech accepting my resignation and complimentary too, which gave me great pleasure; he adds as a p.s. that he is proposing as my successor Mr. Georges Heisbourg[614] who will also be our permanent representative at the UN; everything is for the best; George Marshall sent me quite a nice letter without me writing to him; I very much appreciated." He always had a certain ability to turn and present in a positive way certain less glamorous or sumptuous aspects of his life. It is true that he seems to be able to count on Bech's support, but the fact remains that he is desperately lonely and hardly ever spends moments of rest or personal satisfaction. To George Marshall, who wrote to him on July 17, "it might be that we will never see each other again, but whenever I look at the roses you so kindly sent me several years ago I will remember our association and your many kindnesses

Hugues Le Gallais and US Secretary of State George Marshall.

to both Mrs. Marshall and me", he handwrote in his most legible handwriting on July 22: "That you and Mrs. Marshall should have thought of writing to us is deeply appreciated both by my wife and myself. We will never forget your kindness and if we have no roses, I have next to me the ash tray with your name, which you so kindly gave me and the colored photo of you and Mrs. Marshall in your garden."[615] Everything is said there, or almost everything, and Hugues seems to regret, more than he admits, the good old days in Washington. This exchange also proves that personal relationships can be established. Diplomats like Le Gallais can leave excellent memories and even regrets.

The unexpected announcement of the ambassador's non-return was the subject of numerous press articles and was widely commented on in certain circles. For example, Betty Beale's article of July 14 in the *Evening Standard* under the heading of her column "Exclusively Yours": "Hugues Le Gallais retires: diamonds dazzle at supper", stating: "With the departure of Le Gallais go probably the finest privately owned oriental art collection in Washington—the ambassador's: the prettiest Titian haired braids in town—his wife's and a respected and well-liked couple." The next day, Evelyn Peyton Gordon reported in the *Washington Daily News*: "Le Gallais leaving is quite a surprise", adding: "he has had a bad bout with the flu last winter" and describing Mrs. Le Gallais as "Titian haired noted for her wit and her unusual gowns usually fashioned of fabulous oriental fabrics acquired during years in Far East. Or, on the same day, Mary McNair who wrote in the *Washington Post*: "Town topics: Envoy Le Gallais invites Capitalites". This journalist wrote that the news of the ambassador's retirement came from their Venice holiday spot and that the official end of the mission was September 30, as the ambassador was not returning to Washington due to health problems. There was also talk of the Nani-Le Gallais collection to be shown the following spring and the ambassador's hope to see his friends in Europe again. The article states that Le Gallais should have succeeded the Norwegian ambassador Wilhelm von Munthe af Morgenstierne as dean of the diplomatic corps, who served from 1942 to 1958.[616] The fact that Luxembourg had only a legation until November 1955 had prevented the Luxembourg diplomat from taking up this honorary post. His hasty departure finally proved to be his ultimate disadvantage. From then on, none of this was really important.

While at first Hugues Le Gallais hoped that a certain amount of time would pass before his successor was appointed, this was not the case. The question of the chargé d'affaires and problems with signing visas arose during the interim; some documents had to be signed by the Belgian consul. Within a month, Bech appointed Georges Heisbourg, aged 40, as future ambassador in Washington. Le Gallais' successor was married to Hélène Pinet from France. They had three children: Janine, 12, Pierre, 12 and a half, and François, 9. In a letter of August 5, 1958 from Le Gallais to Eleanor Maloney, mention is made of a dinner with Heisbourg at the home of Le Gallais in Venice on August 8. Mr. Heisbourg then went alone to New York for an emergency United Nations session before mid-August and then to Washington around the weekend.[617] He wished to check on the situation at the embassy. The Heisbourg family left Luxembourg by train on October 1 for Paris and took the boat the next day. Mr. Bech and Mr. Pescatore took the same boat to come to Washington for the meetings of the international financial institutions. Ambassador-designate Heisbourg flew to New York, where he arrived on October 3, before coming to Washington with his family. Luxembourg diplomatic life resumed its usual course without the Le Gallais couple.[618]

The material situation of Hugues Le Gallais was comfortable, with a monthly pension from the "Caisse de pension des employés des Arbed" in Dudelange, which informed him by letter of August 28, 1958 that his pension would be 1,692 francs from October 1. From September 26 to 30, 1958 he was at the Hotel Brasseur in Luxembourg, then a few days in Paris. He wrote that he had seen Mr. Werner, Mr. Schulté and Mr. Heisbourg and that: "there were no questions; everything seems in order." Decidedly, the waves that were to be expected were not yet unleashed, even though life, as Hugues Le Gallais noted during this hectic summer, is not a long quiet river.

Pisana Le Gallais had to return only once to the United States. She was in New York and Washington from September 11 to October 4 to settle certain matters and supervise the move. Her husband had given precise instructions on the amounts available to his wife. Similarly, on the inventory, he gave endless instructions and details. The same was the case of his personal effects, works of art, furniture, books and costumes included, whether it was their value to be declared to the insurer or their packaging. The Security Storage Company also drew up a list, with 237 and 146 items respectively, as well as several boxes of books, in September 1958. Finally, in those September days, and still from the European continent, Hugues Le Gallais took care of the amounts due to the embassy staff. He also wished to leave the piano at the embassy and hoped, for once a bit old-fashioned, that his successor would be interested in taking it over, as well as a certain part of the wine cellar. In the end, the piano of Le Gallais was sold to a nephew of Mr. Sokolov[619] after an attempt to sell it to Heisbourg. Le Gallais also asked that the list of dinner guests, menus and seating plans be left with the Heisburgs, as they would prove more useful to his successor than to himself. It was a fine gesture on the part of the departing person towards his successor, who often finds himself without the institutional memory of the embassy, apart from that of the locally recruited staff. In the embassy's archives[620] there are countless lists of the most diverse guests, with also requests from news agencies and other news services to add them to the lists of the Luxembourg embassy. The collection of several hundred 78 rpm records has been bequeathed to the embassy. The successor was to find in the cellar six cases of wine of twelve bottles each from the state's vineyards.

Mrs. Le Gallais left Washington after packing her personal belongings, including those sent from the holiday home in Maine[621] to take the boat to New York the next day. The boat with the ambassador's belongings was scheduled to leave Baltimore on

October 16 and arrive in Venice around November 15 on the American Export Line.[622] Now that all the couple's personal belongings had been moved from one place to another, he felt as though he was naked, waiting to find the few things he really cared about. Most of the belongings had memories, stories and anecdotes that ultimately made them irreplaceable because they were often unique. During this time, Hugues Le Gallais went to Paris where he stayed at the Hôtel Raphaël, located on rue Kléber. He found himself on the same train with the Heisbourg family on their way to Washington. According to him, the Heisbourgs had "charming children".[623] Without hard feelings towards his successor, Hugues joined Pisana in Venice.

There were still a few matters to settle anyway. On November 16, 1958, Le Gallais was delighted that the embassy's count was in his favor to the tune of $372.25. On November 20, 1958, Mrs. Maloney wrote that she had completed the cash situation promised to Mr. Schulté. The detail of the cash situation gave her a lot of work. She was delighted with the draperies installed in the embassy's library and a new carpet in the first-floor hall, as well as contemporary paintings of Luxembourg giving a touch of color to the embassy. All of this was far away now and no longer really concerned Hugues. The main thing was that the embassy's financial dossier had been settled for good. As Le Gallais abandoned his appeal to the Council of State on January 21, 1959, it was only on February 13, 1959 that Mrs. Maloney sent Le Gallais the account for signature and thus the financial file relating to the management of Le Gallais was closed. A ministerial decree of December 1, 1958 granted Mr. Hugues Le Gallais an honorable resignation from his position as Alternate Governor of the International Monetary Fund. He had been appointed to this position by Grand Ducal decree of March 30, 1946 with Dupont as Governor. It was Government Councilor Pierre Guill who replaced Le Gallais in this position. As Mrs. Maloney recalled in a correspondence, Le Gallais had declined the invitation to attend the annual meetings of the Fund and the World Bank in New Delhi in October of that year.[624] Everything was over now, and a new life began.

RETIREMENT AT THE CA'CONTARINI MICHIEL ON THE GRAND CANAL IN VENICE

Sometimes, retired ambassadors can be recognized as they sit in the back left side of their car, forgetting that there is no driver at their service anymore. This was not the case for Le Gallais, who had consciously and after careful consideration chosen Pisana's hometown to settle. There they had a palazzo allowing them to continue to receive their friends with dignity. As a perfect gentleman, Hugues tried not to realize, or at least not to show too much, that he missed the extraordinary life in Washington. Around Christmas 1958, Pisana and Hugues Le Gallais were for a month in Cortina d'Ampezzo in the middle of the Dolomites in northern Italy.

To get to Venice and make themselves at home there, the Le Gallais had again taken the boat and the train. In the year in which Pisana and Hugues celebrated their silver wedding anniversary, they found an island town that no longer corresponded to what Stendhal had described as an overabundance of the beauty of Italian art, which had bewildered Ruskin by degradation and complacency, and which was no longer the historical place of excellence, open to the world, that Pisana had known in the first three decades of her existence. The lagoon city offered what the couple, who had been accomplices for so long, really wanted. They no longer really wished to discover far away places. The city of the Doges provided them with calm and voluptuousness, all the guarantees of happiness and serenity. Hugues knew how to appreciate works of art and learned everything about Titian, who had brought Venetian painting to maturity, the most original and prolific Venetian painter Tintoretto, Veronese, retracing the life of the patricians of the Renaissance, and Canaletto, meticulously describing the City of the Doges and more particularly the Grand Canal in the 18th century. Also, for this last stage, Le Gallais had preferred a daily city life surrounded by water rather than isolating himself in nature or the countryside.

Pisana and Hugues Le Gallais therefore chose the Ca' Contarini Michiel on the Grand Canal for their Venice retreat. In the 15th century, the Contarini owned the largest number of palazzi in the city. The Ca' Contarini Michiel Palace was used to receive friends and relatives from August 22, 1954 when Pisana's sister received the first entries in her guest book. While Hugues had only spent a few weeks there in the summer, Venice was the birthplace of his wife, the *gentildonna veneziana* Pisana Velluti. But it seems that she did not like to come back to Venice very much. The place she had wished to leave in the 1930s still seemed provincial and upper-crust to her. With the help of his sister-in-law, Countess Caterina Nani Mocenigo-Velluti, Hugues set up a collection of Far Eastern porcelain and art in the *Ca' del Duca* in San Marco 3051. The official address was as follows: Museo Cà del Duca Nani Mocenigo—Le Gallais San Marco 3051; 30124 Venezia. For possible friends intending to visit him in Venice, the ambassador left instructions in Washington to go to Palazzo Contarini Michiel at 2794 San Barnaba. There he said that it is important that the first contact with Venice should be by gondola and therefore to tell the gondolier to go to Pontile Ca' Rezzonico. To get from the Le Gallais' property to San Marco, one can go on foot via the Academia, the main museum of paintings, or take the *vaporetto* or the *traghetto* gondole which will pass on the other side of the Grand Canal. The residence of the Le Gallais family was located opposite Palazzo Grassi, which was spread out around an imposing inner courtyard with access to the first floor via an imposing staircase. These noble residences of a different scale were the apogee of the *Serenissima*'s majesty which had declined at the end of the 18th century. The Le Gallais' palace was separated by an alleyway from a residence with a Moorish flair that was to become the Hotel Stern. Baroness Ernesta Stern, a member of a Venetian family ennobled by Emperor Franz Joseph of Austria, had lived here until her death in 1926. This French collector, writer and woman of letters was allied with the Murat, Baron Lambert and the Rothschild families. Next door is the house of an antique dealer and collector and then separated by the Rio S. Barnaba, the Ca' Rezzonico. This famous massive double-storey noble palace, after having been occupied by a family of the former nobility of the city and later by the famous poet Robert Browning (who died in 1889, a commemorative plaque has been affixed) and the musician Cole Porter, became a private palace bought in 1935 by the city of Venice to house the Venetian 18th century Museum.[625] The Le Gallais were located very close to the Accademia Bridge and therefore not far from the house where Pisana was born. Not really the most beautiful house in this magical spot on the Grand Canal, the Ca' Contarini Michiel has one of the most extraordinary views of the incessant coming and going of the canal that crosses Venice in the shape of an S. Four floors overlook the quay of Ca' Rezzonico, and next to the palace of the same name are distributed on the ground floor with a large hall and paintings of muses. The windows on the first and third floors are small and irregularly recessed in a façade where the eye is focused on the second floor balcony with three windows with two columns separating them, giving the whole a classical look. It was a welcoming home with an eclectic and unique atmosphere. The open spaces of this Palladian house made the atmosphere clear and warm, to the delight and pleasure of their many foreign friends. After having given its titles of nobility to Luxembourg diplomacy, at least in the United States, Le Gallais was about to set the stage once again, this time in the majestic setting of the Grand Canal. Le Gallais' collection of oriental art was not the only one in Venice where the one of Prince Henri of Bourbon-Parma,[626] uncle of Prince Felix, had been exhibited at Ca' Pesaro. It was suggested to Hugues Le Gallais that he merge his collection to that of the Prince, but he politely declined, preserving his collection well away from prying eyes. However, Hugues had witnessed major and generous donations, just as philanthropy was well established among some Americans. He was aware of the altruistic gestures of members of the Rockefeller, Carnegie, Guggenheim and other families, but did not let himself be tempted and was not inspired by them. He did, however, keep in his *Scrapbook* an article on the 1954 donation by the family of former diplomat Truxtun Beale of Decatur House, a prestigious house on Lafayette Square opposite the White House, which was to become the guest house at the presidential residence in Washington. To explain and publicize his own collection, a booklet was commissioned by Hugues Le Gallais with a survey, a preface by Giacinto Auriti,[627] who had been Italian ambassador to Japan in the 1930s and a word of explanation on the history of Ca' del Duca by Guido Perocco,[628] who had been director of the Museum of Modern Art at Ca' Pesaro in Venice. An expert from Rome had carried out a scientific survey of each work. Le Gallais claimed that his high-quality collection, although reduced in number since the auction of a significant part in 1958, was "academic", that of the Prince of Bourbon-Parma being "characterized by its quantity rather than its quality".

Before their retirement, Pisana and Hugues had welcomed in their Venetian palace, or sometimes left it to Katy to do so in their absence, Barbara and Oliver Franks, former colleagues and acquaintances in Washington such as Germaine and Maurice Frère, Archduke Carl and Archduchess Yolande of Austria, born Princess of Ligne, whom they had known in the United States, Shirley and Stanley Woodward, Chief of Protocol under Roosevelt and ambassador to Canada under Truman.

On May 30, 1956, a major event must have been the passage in Venice of the former American President (1945-1953), Democrat Harry S. Truman, and his wife Elisabeth, known as Bess Wallace Truman.[629] Truman's presidency had been marked by his decision to drop the atomic bombings of Hiroshima and Nagasaki. There were thus many subjects to discuss with such a prestigious interlocutor!

Another prestigious American visitor came to Ca' Contarini Michiel in the person of former Secretary of State Dean Acheson, accompanied by his wife Alice. They signed the guest book on September 21, 1959.

We should also mention the couples Joseph and Georgette Bech-Delahaye (May 30, 1956), then Pierre and Henriette Werner-Pescatore (30-31 August 1956), Henri Bonnet, the Buchanans (19-20 August 1956). The Hereditary Grand Ducal couple, Princess Marie-Adélaïde and Prince Charles, were visiting on September 2, 1956, while Princess Marie-Gabrielle of Luxembourg, since 1951, married to the Danish Count Knud of Holstein-Ledreborg, came to see the Le Gallais on September 14, 1960. Princess Eugenie of Greece and Denmark and her daughter, Princess Tatiana Radziwill, were also present during the visit of the Luxembourg princely couple.

Then the Brosio's, former Italian ambassadors, preceded the de Lustrange and the de Saint Just. Princess Aspasía of Greece signed the guest book on June 3, 1959.[630] This Princess of Greece and Denmark lived in Venice in the Garden of Eden, a villa famous for its park, located on the island of Giudecca. She was followed by others, such as the Baldissera and the Mocenigo, relatives of Pisana.

In August 1960, according to a letter to Mrs. Maloney, the following contacts were maintained in Venice: "Shelan and Cowan (former class mate) motoring in Europe"; Virginia Bacon[631] had come; the George Kennans,[632] ephemeral American ambassador to the USSR in 1952, the American diplomat Elbrick. The director of the Freer Gallery of Art John and Annemarie Pope,[633] the dancer and choreographer Ninette de Valois,[634] the Russian dancer Valentina,[635] the Zimmers, Honorary Consul General in New York, engaged to come. For the month of September, Le Gallais was delighted that former ambassador Oliver Franks and Lord Harcourt,[636] who had been economic advisor to the British embassy in the United States, were expected to attend.

The Hereditary Grand Ducal couple travelled to Venice again on June 13, 1961. The two visits of the princely couple of Luxembourg five years apart did not go unnoticed, with an evening in a white dinner jacket and a guided tour by Hugues of the future sovereigns being documented photographically and an article being published in Italian.

Mrs. Maloney, accompanied by her sister Alice Cloran, came, as mentioned above, from 10 to July 14, 1961. Prince François de Hohenlohe Waldenburg Schillingfürst signed on August 21, 1961, followed by the del Posse, by Gabrielle de Cossé-Brissac. The Bonnets again, in July 1962, the Frère couple, Agnes E. Meyer in August 1962 and her daughter Katherine Graham and her husband Philip Graham with many other guests, Peggy Guggenheim and the Baldissera, on September 2, 1962, the Franks again, Olga de Cadaval de Robilant[637] on September 28, 1964. Another Princess, with the unusual name Urraca of Bourbon-Sicily,[638] a granddaughter of King Ludwig III of Bavaria, did so on on September 10, 1963. And for the last year of his life, no less than 70 signatures were counted in Hugues' guestbook. The last signatories were Adriana Rocca Winspeare on November 3, 1964, just before Le Gallais' death. She accompanied her brother, Vittorio Winspeare,[639] who had been Italian ambassador and Under-Secretary General of the United Nations.

Luxembourgers who passed through Venice were fewer: Christiane Rodenbourg-Loesch,[640] on May 11, 1962, the couple Manu and Thérèse Tesch-Laval,[641] a distant cousin on the Metz side in September 1962, the former minister and Ambassador Lambert Schaus on August 21, 1964. On August 26, 1958, cousins related to de Gargan via the Pescatore were in Venice: Gisèle and Juan

Le Palazzo Contarini Michiel on the Grand Canal in Venice.

de Liedekerke-de Malingreau.[642] As with the visit of the Werner-Pescatore, the memory of their relative, Hugues' mother-in-law, must have resurfaced from an unhappy youth and a buried past. Hugues' sister, Aimée, had come from British Sussex for an extended stay in April 1959. The daughter of Hugues' first cousin, Missy Rochon, was there in September 1963. Very often, Pisana's sister would sign the guestbook as she was a neighbor and very close to the couple. The Frère couple, who had bought a house in Venice in which they moved in the summer of 1960, the Franks and the Bonnets were the ones who passed by most often, as the links with their former diplomatic colleagues were followed and intense.

It was moving to see in the guestbook an inscription by Rozel Le Gallais, the sister with whom Hugues had somewhat loosened his ties given her overly complacent attitude towards the Nazis. In any case, Rozel hardly ever returned to the Grand Duchy, where her attitude was strongly reproached by her family. With her husband, she came to see her sister-in-law after the death of Hugues and wrote in the guest book on February 2, 1965: "Very sad and beautiful memories, I leave you dear Pisana, and thank you very affectionately." In Venice, the city of 500 bridges with only three crossing the Grand Canal, a kind of reconciliation had come about late, perhaps too late, but nevertheless with sincerity and affection.

Everyone enjoyed the hospitality of the Le Gallais couple in this city of imposing *palazzi*, gondola rides, sumptuous dinners, festivals and fancy dress balls. The string of palaces on the Grand Canal that could be admired from the balcony of Palazzo Contarini Michiel gave everyone a unique impression of home, sometimes pathetic, often fabulous. Hugues knew how to please his guests and, with Pisana in such a proud appearance, in addition to some long-standing friendships such as Maurice Frère or Georges Brasscur, had affinities with one or other of the ladies in their circle of friends chosen according to the hazards of life, but also according to the interests of each one.

We have seen that on January 23, 1959 the couple travelled to Luxembourg to attend the reception at the Grand Ducal Palace on the occasion of the Grand Duchess' birthday. It was a great opportunity to show themselves in public in the country where Hugues was born and for which he had worked for many years. Both of them showed up with big smiles on their faces after the unspoken and even tumultuous circumstances of their departure a few months earlier and acted as if nothing had happened. This was the best tactic in the face of adversity and the Venetian remoteness.

In 1959, Le Gallais seems to have taken a more detailed interest in the history of Italian-Luxembourgish relations and to have found pleasure in recalling a link to Baptista Nani,[643] ambassador to France of the *Serenissima* in the 17th century and who would have been considered a Luxembourger in his native country. To this end, Hugues Le Gallais, a retired ambassador, sent Bech (who remained Minister of Foreign Affairs until 1959), at the end of the 1950s, a copy of a letter in Italian from Daniele Varè[644] to the Italian ambassador in Luxembourg dated December 3, 1926. Difficult to solve the mystery, even though the Italian Daniele Varè was indeed a diplomat and author who had grown up in the United Kingdom and Italy before becoming a diplomat in China in 1912 and returning there as ambassador from 1927 to 1931. In Beijing, his collaborator was Ciano, later Italian foreign minister and son-in-law of Benito Mussolini. He was also posted in Geneva, Copenhagen and Luxembourg, hence a probable link with Le Gallais and even a meeting in Asia in the 1920s. Le Gallais was always on the lookout for a link he wanted to strengthen between his home country and the place where he was, whether it was Washington or now Venice.

The honorary ambassador also maintained epistolary ties with his former secretary. On February 5, 1963, Le Gallais lucidly noted: "I still believe that I retired at the right time ... The Heisbourgs' seem very clever at saving money and maybe they have the right attitude. Governments are not grateful. My excuse is that I thoroughly enjoyed the style of life I led in Washington. You can't eat your cake and have it..." He had remained a diplomat at heart, even though he had only entered this world late in life and had kept certain reservations about the demands of his job, which was more complicated and demanding than generally accepted. Contrary to popular belief, diplomacy is not the art of beating about the bush. A good diplomat is not someone who thinks twice before saying nothing, in the words of a former British Prime Minister. Diplomacy requires honesty and a good dose of outspokenness. Dialogue—and this lies at the heart of diplomacy and foreign policy—can only work when you are also prepared to say things frankly, clearly, and tell truths, even if they are sometimes embarrassing. Le Gallais was one of those. In a letter of May 30, 1962, he had confessed to Mrs. Maloney that "Washington is now far away", even though preparations for the Grand Duchess' state visit, originally planned for the end of October 1962 and postponed until May 1963, continued to interest him. On December 1, 1962, he wrote again from Brussels to Mrs. Maloney: "Mr. Konsbruck is going to Washington for the State visit and this can't be changed. I agree that 1800 people seems exaggerated." Le Gallais must have regretted not being able to attend this event, which is often considered the apotheosis of an ambassador's presence. This state visit to President John F. Kennedy was the last before his assassination in Dallas in November 1963. Grand Duchess Charlotte and Hereditary Grand Duke Jean visited Philadelphia, Chicago, Washington and Cape Canaveral from April 29 to May 4, 1963. Hugues Le Gallais confessed that he had considered taking part as chamberlain, but dropped the idea so as not to embarrass his successor. Quite philosophically, he concluded in his letter to his former secretary and confidante: "The past cannot return and the present is never the same." In these exchanges of letters with Mrs. Maloney, one can detect some regrets about no longer being involved in the diplomatic world. Le Gallais also speculated about the future occupants of diplomatic posts in Washington, Paris and Brussels.

In November 1963, the Le Gallais rented a flat in Rome at 10, Via Serfieri, with the intention of staying there for Christmas, while their only son was still in Brussels where he had met a young German woman who was the same age as him and whom he had introduced to his parents. Norbert had completed his Master's degree in Paris and intended to do a PhD in Geneva for two years. He entered the Common Market in Brussels as an attaché for six months, travelling to Strasbourg, Paris and Berlin for work.[645] Around this period his parents rented a flat at rue du Fossé, number 28, near the Théâtre de la Monnaie in Brussels. According to a letter from April 1963, Berty started working in a bank in Brussels for six months. In November 1963, Norbert Le Gallais intended to join the Common Market or to go to work in Milan, a project which did not come to fruition. All this was a source of satisfaction for Le Gallais, even though the world of industry and diplomacy was moving away from the field of action of this family, which remained attached to the Grand Duchy of its origins.

In January 1964, the Le Gallais couple was invited by the Hereditary Grand Ducal couple for a dinner at the Grand Ducal Palace. These were the preparations for the change of reign, with the Hereditary Grand Duke, whom the ambassador had seen grow and assert himself during the war, now having the responsibilities of Lieutenant-Representative and preparing to assume the throne a few months later. On November 12, 1964, for the abdication of Grand Duchess Charlotte, Hugues Le Gallais wanted to be in

Luxembourg at all costs. As Chamberlain, he had been invited and felt that his place was with the one he had served and advised for many years as a figure of the court and as ambassador. Against the advice of his doctor, he therefore travelled to Luxembourg one last time to attend, more than ever a patriot and monarchist at heart, the festivities and celebrations for the abdication of the Grand Duchess and the accession to the throne of her son.

After this grandiose event, Christmas was approaching quickly since his return from this final journey to Luxembourg. Perhaps Hugues was aware that his end was near, saying to himself along with Goethe: "More light, soon, but not all of it now". After all, a life of elegance and passion had to come to an end one day. The assessment that everyone makes more and more frequently with age seemed to him without any doubt positive and why not enchanting beyond expectation. For Le Gallais, life had been a constant struggle marked by the desire to take ownership of his history, allowing it to continue to function, to dare and to enjoy the best it had to offer. Like Jean-Jacques Rousseau, did Hugues Le Gallais meditate on his youth, the time to study wisdom, when old age had become the time to practice it? Or put another way: "if youth knew and old age could". All in all, and despite his legendary hospitality, Hugues seems to have often been lonely. Although he knew many people, he had also lost many friends; to him applied what is true of most diplomats: far from the eyes, far from the heart. Gently feeling his forces abandoning him, Hugues Le Gallais saw the end approaching, and after having experienced health setbacks for several years, he suspected that nothing on earth is eternal and that he would one day soon be swept away by a mirage.

Hugues Le Gallais died the day before Christmas Eve, on December 23, 1964, at the end of a full life, rich in diverse journeys accomplished without any oddity or lack of taste. The death "occurred quite unexpectedly, following a heart attack... at about six o'clock in the afternoon, without being preceded by any illness. The deceased had kept his lucidity until the last moment", according to the report of the ambassador of Luxembourg in Rome.[646] Before being buried in Susegana, Mass had been said in the church of Santa Maria dei Carmini, which had been the place where Pisana loved to pray with devotion. During his lifetime, Hugues had followed her there rather out of conscience. In this parish, Pisana frequented the patriarch Albino Luciano, the one who was to become the short-lived Pope John Paul I. An article tracing the important dates in the life of one of the Grand Duchy's most eminent ambassadors was published two days later in the *New York Times*.

Luxembourg's ambassador in Rome, Pierre Majerus, who had been mandated by the Grand Ducal Court to attend the funeral, left a description of the circumstances, mentioning that

"According to a wish expressed in his time by the deceased, the body was transferred in a gondola from Palazzo Contarini Michiel to the Church of the Carmini. It was raining non-stop on this second day of Christmas. The nave of the church was almost completely filled. Apart from many representatives of Venetian high society, I noted the presence of the Prefect of Venice, Mr. de Bernart, the French and Belgian Consuls and the Honorary Consul, Mr. Bellati. Mr. Maurice Frère, former Governor of the National Bank of Belgium, a great friend of the deceased, also attended the funeral with his wife."

The entire ceremony and the decoration would have been a great pleasure for the deceased, all the more so as "the two crowns with the initials of Their Royal Highnesses (the Grand Duke and Grand Duchess, but also Grand Duchess Charlotte and Prince Felix) flanked the catafalque."[647] Those for whom he had devoted himself for many years and his best friends had not forgotten him.

Hugues Le Gallais was buried in the tomb of his wife's family in Susegana in the municipality of Treviso, an hour from Venice. Pisana's parents had a country house in this small town of about 10,000 inhabitants with a melodious name. In the family chapel overlooking the cemetery are still buried, besides Pisana Le Gallais-Velutti, who died at the age of 75, Pisana's mother, her sister Katy, who died in 1983 at the age of 85, and her brother-in-law Marino, who died in 1953 at the age of about 70. Ambassador Majerus recounted:

"After the funeral service, the procession in which the next of kin, Mr. and Mrs. Maurice Frère and myself took part, travelled to Susegana, a village about 60 km from Venice, where the funeral took place at half past three in the afternoon, after a short funeral ceremony in the local church. The cemetery is set against a hill at the foot of the Low Alps. Facing south, it is in full sunshine during the good season. Mr. Le Gallais himself had long ago designated this place as his final resting place."

For this last stage, Hugues Le Gallais had remained true to himself, always valiant and choosing as always a most dignified place.

Pisana Le Gallais-Velutti survived him for about ten years, dying at the age of 75, and not 70, as some of her papers might have led one to believe, on October 16, 1975. After his father's death, Berty was to marry on April 24, 1965 in Uccle (Brussels) a young German woman from Hanover who, like him, worked for the European Communities. Rita Eckstein, born in Sonderhausen on September 21, 1934, had met her future husband's father. In 1966 and 1968, two children were born, Catherine and Hugues, who in turn perpetuated the family of Hugues Le Gallais. ❂

Appendices

GENEALOGICAL TREE SHOWING
HUGUES LE GALLAIS' 8 GREAT-GRANDPARENTS
AND THE LINK TO MESSRS MAYRISCH
AND BARBANSON

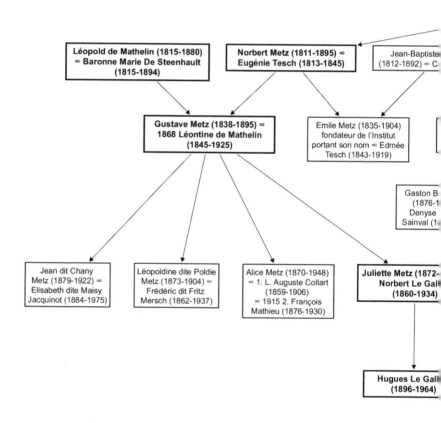

Léopold de Mathelin (1815-1880) ∞ Baronne Marie De Steenhault (1815-1894)

Norbert Metz (1811-1895) ∞ Eugénie Tesch (1813-1845)

Jean-Baptiste (1812-1892) ∞ C

Gustave Metz (1838-1895) ∞ 1868 Léontine de Mathelin (1845-1925)

Emile Metz (1835-1904) fondateur de l'Institut portant son nom ∞ Edmée Tesch (1843-1919)

Gaston B (1876-1 Denyse Sainval (1

Jean dit Chany Metz (1879-1922) ∞ Elisabeth dite Maisy Jacquinot (1884-1975)

Léopoldine dite Poldie Metz (1873-1904) ∞ Frédéric dit Fritz Mersch (1862-1937)

Alice Metz (1870-1948) ∞ 1. L. Auguste Collart (1859-1906) ∞ 1915 2. François Mathieu (1876-1930)

Juliette Metz (1872- Norbert Le Gal (1860-1934)

Hugues Le Gal (1896-1964)

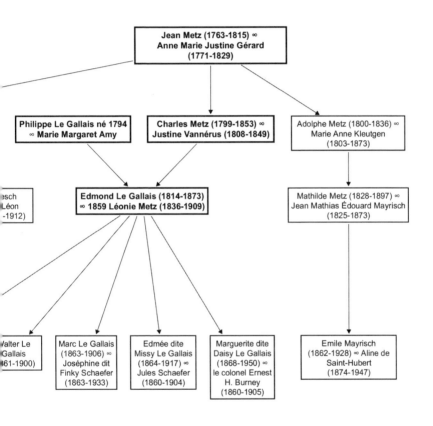

Jean Metz (1763-1815) ∞
Anne Marie Justine Gérard
(1771-1829)

Philippe Le Gallais né 1794
∞ Marie Margaret Amy

Charles Metz (1799-1853) ∞
Justine Vannérus (1808-1849)

Adolphe Metz (1800-1836) ∞
Marie Anne Kleutgen
(1803-1873)

esch
Léon
-1912)

Edmond Le Gallais (1814-1873)
∞ 1859 Léonie Metz (1836-1909)

Mathilde Metz (1828-1897) ∞
Jean Mathias Édouard Mayrisch
(1825-1873)

Valter Le
Gallais
61-1900)

Marc Le Gallais
(1863-1906) ∞
Joséphine dit
Finky Schaefer
(1863-1933)

Edmée dite
Missy Le Gallais
(1864-1917) ∞
Jules Schaefer
(1860-1904)

Marguerite dite
Daisy Le Gallais
(1868-1950) ∞
le colonel Ernest
H. Burney
(1860-1905)

Emile Mayrisch
(1862-1928) ∞ Aline de
Saint-Hubert
(1874-1947)

Prepared by Cathy Meder-Dempsey
with data furnished by Paul Schmit

425

ACKNOWLEDGEMENTS

This work on Hugues Le Gallais is essentially based on research carried out over the years thanks to many combinations of circumstances, but also and above all to the testimonies of a wide range of people whom I would like to thank without necessarily listing them all.

This book is also based on the work of various historians, predecessors and colleagues whom I have met in recent years and who have guided me with great professionalism and patience. The files of the Government in exile and those of the Luxembourg embassy in the United States as well as those of the Ministry of Foreign and European Affairs, which are largely preserved in the National Archives in Luxembourg, have been an enormous support.

I would also like to thank the following for their invaluable contributions and advice:

The members of the Le Gallais family, be they the son or the grandson of Hugues Le Gallais, Norbert and Hugues Le Gallais (Jr.) in Venice, a grand-nephew of Hugues Le Gallais, Jens Reverchon in Cape Town, South Africa, or even other family members such as Reginald Neuman or Rémy Viénot, who answered many questions and provided access to family archives and private photos.

At the Grand Ducal Court: Pierre Even, Director of the Archives of the Grand Ducal House, and Marie-France Kremer, Librarian-Archivist, who made letters clarifying Le Gallais' position in relation to his government available to me.

At the National Archives: Charles Barthel, Economic Section, scientific collaborator, and Corinne Schroeder, curator, Contemporary Section, who guided me with great patience and professionalism, particularly in the (re) discovery of the archives of the embassy in Washington.

Special thanks to the National Cultural Fund (FOCUNA).

In addition, many thanks to Professor Paul Dostert, former director of the Centre for Documentation and Research on the Resistance, and to Jean-Marie Majerus, seconded professor at the Robert Schuman Centre for European Studies and Research, who took great pains to guide me, to reread and correct the typescript and advise me in the research leading to the finalization of this biography. May they all be thanked for their unfailing support!

I would also like to thank the following persons, listed in alphabetical order :

Vincent Artuso, Luxembourg historian and author;

Véronique Dockendorf, Deputy Head of Mission at the Luxembourg embassy in Washington;

Tom Elvinger, grandson of Hugues Le Gallais' best friend;

Colette Flesch, former Minister of Foreign Affairs;

Germaine Goetzinger, former director of the National Centre for Literature;

Irma Hadzalic, postdoctoral researcher, Luxembourg Centre for Contemporary and Digital History (C2DH);

Paul Lesch, Director of the Centre National de l'Audiovisuel;

Wolf von Leipzig, head of Editions Saint-Paul, Luxembourg, for his tireless encouragement and valuable advice, without whom this biography would not have been published, and his team: Lydie Develter, graphic designer, and Jean-Marc Schmidt, reader-editor;

Dr. Robert Philippart, historian;

Heinrich von Spreti, Honorary President, Sotheby's Germany;

Victor Weitzel, publicist;

and all those who are no longer with us, such as Mrs. Maloney's daughter or Ambassador Georges Heisbourg, who had kindly received me before my departure for Washington in autumn 2001, at the very beginning of this adventure.

Without the incredible patience of my family and the encouragement of those close to me, this project would not have been possible.

A special word of thanks goes to the deceased Manuel Schortgen from "Editions Schortgen" who took over as editor in 2020 for the e-book, and without whom the English version would not have been possible.

To all those who gave me their moral and material support, I renew here the expression of my very sincere gratitude.

PRIMARY SOURCES

National Archives of Luxembourg:
Embassy in the United States fonds (ANLux-AE-AW)
Heisbourg Fund
Bodson Fund

Civil Status and Municipal Archives of the City of Luxembourg

Library of Congress

https://chroniclingamerica.loc.gov/

National Archives at College Park

State Department
Marshall Foundation
Archives Department of Foreign Affairs Canada

Private archives of the Le Gallais family (Venice)
Private archives of the family of Mrs. Maloney (Venice and Luxembourg)

BIBLIOGRAPHY

ALS, GEORGES, *Robert Als (1897-1991) au service de son pays. A la recherche du temps perdu.* Rapid Press, Luxembourg 2003.

ANSEMBOURG, GASTON, comte d'Au bon vieux temps. Editions Labor, Brussels 1947.

ARTUSO, VINCENT, *La « Question Juive » au Luxembourg (1933-1941). L'Etat luxembourgeois face aux persécutions antisémites nazies.* Rapport final remis au Premier ministre le 9 février 2015.

BAIER, STEPHAN ET DEMMERLE, EVA, *Otto von Habsburg 1912-2011. Die Biographie,* Amalthea Signum, Vienna 2012.

BARTHEL, CHARLES, 'Un aspect particulier de la culture politique internationale luxembourgeoise: Joseph Bech et l'art de concilier les Affaires étrangères avec la diplomatie du grand capital sidérurgique', in Schirmann, Sylvain (ed.), *Robert Schuman et les pères de l'Europe. Cultures politiques et années de formation.* Actes du colloque de Metz du 10 au 12 octobre 2007. Publications de la maison de Robert Schuman, vol. 1. P.I.E. Peter Lang, Bruxelles, Bern, Berlin, etc., 2008, pp. 235-256.

CARRIER, THOMAS J., *Washington, D.C.: A Historic Walking Tour (Images of America).* Arcadia Publishing, West Columbia, SC 1999.

Cerf, Paul, Die Juden in der Periode von Mai bis Herbst 1941. "Virun 40 Joer... Letzebuerg um Ufank vum 2. Weltkrich" – Bericht des Rundfunkgespräches von Radio-Tele-Luxembourg, organisiert vom Centre d'Etudes Libérales. Imprimerie Centrale, Luxembourg 1981.

COUTU, JEAN-CLAUDE, *La millionnaire de Mascouche: le manoir seigneurial de 1930 à 1954.* Editions SODAM, Mascouche (Québec) 2006.

DITTRICH, KLAUS, 'Selling Luxembourgian steel in Japan : Columeta Tokyo, 1925 to 1941', in *Zeitschrift für Unternehmensgeschichte,* 2 (2016), pp. 215-236.

DITTRICH KLAUS ; Buddhism, Business, and Red-Cross Diplomacy: Aline Mayrisch de Saint-Hubert's Journeys to East Asia in the Interwar Period. In: Fabricating Modern Societies: Education, Bodies, and Minds in the Age of Steel. Pages: 79–107. DOI: https://doi.org/10.1163/9789004410510_005

DOSTERT, PAUL, 'Norbert Le Gallais 1860-1934' in *400 Joer Kolleisch, Band II*. Editions Saint-Paul, Luxembourg 2003.

DOSTERT, PAUL, *Les finances du gouvernement luxembourgeois en exil (1940-1945); publication a l'occasion du 80e anniversaire de Gilbert Trausch.*

FEIGL, ERICH, *Zita de Habsbourg*. Criterion, Fondation pour l'Ecole, Paris 2014.

FLETCHER, WILLARD ALLEN AND FLETCHER, JEAN TUCKER (EDS.), *Defiant Diplomat: George Platt Waller, American Consul in Nazi-Occupied Luxembourg, 1939-1941*. University of Delaware Press, Newark 2012.

GISCARD D'ESTAING, ANTOINE, *Leopold III. Un Roi dans la tourmente*. Editions Racine, Bruxelles 1996.

GOETZINGER, GERMAINE (ED.), *La Grande Guerre au Luxembourg. Le journal de Michel Welter (3 aout 1914 – 3 mars 1916)*. Centre national de littérature, Mersch 2015.

GROSBOIS, THIERRY, *Les relations diplomatiques entre le gouvernement belge de Londres et les Etats-Unis (1940-1944)*. Presses Universitaires de France.

HAAG, EMILE, *Une réussite originale. Le Luxembourg au fil des siècles*. Editions Guy Binsfeld, Luxembourg 2011.

HAAG, EMILE AND KRIER, EMILE, *La Grande-Duchesse et son Gouvernement pendant la Seconde Guerre mondiale – 1940, l'année du dilemme*. RTL-Editions, Luxembourg 1987.

HEISBOURG, GEORGES, *Le gouvernement luxembourgeois en exil*. 4 volumes. Imprimerie Saint-Paul, Luxembourg 1986-1991.

HEISBOURG, GEORGES, '100 Joer Letzebuerger Dynastie', in *Collections et Souvenirs de la Maison Grand-Ducale. Edites par la Présidence du gouvernement*, Ministère d'Etat du Grand-Duché de Luxembourg. year

KAYSER, STEVE, *La neutralité du Luxembourg de 1918 à 1945*. Forum de juin 2006; Luxembourg 2016.

KOCH-KENT, HENRI, *Vu et entendu. Vol. 2 : Années d'Exil 1940-1946*. Imprimerie Centrale, Luxembourg 1986.

KRIER-BECKER, LILY, *Pierre Krier. Ein Lebensbild*. Edited by the Letzeburger Arbechter-Verband. Luxemburger Genossenschaftsdruckerei, Esch/Alzette 1957.

LESCH, PAUL, *Playing her part. Perle Mesta in Luxembourg*. American Chamber of Commerce, Luxembourg 2001.

LINDEN, ANDRÉ, 'Léif Lëtzebuerger ... dir dohém a mir hei baussen. The radio speeches of Grand Duchess Charlotte in exile', in *Ët wor alles net esou einfach. Questions sur le Luxembourg et la Deuxième Guerre mondiale*. Musée d'histoire de la ville de Luxembourg, Luxembourg 2002.

LINDEN, ANDRÉ, *Luxemburgs Exilregierung und die Entdeckung des Demokratiebegriffs*, Editions Forum, Luxembourg 2021.

MERSCH, JULES, *Biographie nationale du Pays de Luxembourg, depuis ses origines jusqu'à nos jours*. Imprimerie de la Cour Victor Buck, Luxembourg 1957.

PIMENTEL, IRENE AND RAMALHO, MARGARIDA, *O comboio do Luxemburgo*. Esfera dos livros, Lisbon 2016.

ROSSY, JEAN, *La Famille Dupong dans la tourmente de 1940-1945*. Edited by the Steinsel communal administration 2010.

RUBIN, NANCY, *American Empress : The Life and Times of Marjorie Merriweather Post*. iUniverse, Indiana 1995.

SCHOENTGEN, MARC, '"Heim ins Reich"? Die Arbed-Konzernleitung während der deutschen Besatzung 1940-1944 : zwischen Kollaboration und Widerstand.' *Forum*, February 2011.

SCHROEDER, CORINNE, *L'émergence de la politique étrangère du Grand-Duché de Luxembourg vue à travers le Ministère des Affaires étrangères (1945-1973)*. Unpublished thesis.

STRONCK, GASTON, *Le Luxembourg et le Pacte atlantique. De la neutralité à l'alliance*. Doctoral thesis in history presented at Montpellier 3 in 1991.

UNGER, IRWIN AND UNGER, DEBI, *The Guggenheims: A Family History.* Harper Perennial, New York 2005.

TRAUSCH, GILBERT, *Joseph Bech, un homme dans son siècle.* Imprimerie Saint-Paul, Luxembourg 1978.

VIALLET, PIERRE, *La Foire.* Editions de La Table Ronde, France Loisirs, Folio, Paris 1973.

VON BAYERN, IRMINGARD, *Jugend-Erinnerungen 1923-1950*, EOS Verlag, Sankt Ottilien 2010.

WEBER, JOSIANE, *Familien der Oberschicht in Luxemburg. Elitenbildung und Lebenswelten 1850-1900*, Editions Guy Binsfeld, Luxemburg 2013.

WEHENKEL, ANTOINE, *Histoire de la famille Pescatore-Dutreux. Deux siècles de relations franco-luxembourgeoises.* Familjefuerscher 62, Luxembourg 2001.

WEITZ, PAUL, *Charlotte von Luxemburg.* Editions Saint-Paul, Luxembourg 1988.

WOLFF, ANDRÉ, *Memories. A Mission in the United States.* Imprimerie Saint-Paul, Luxembourg 1950.

LINKS

FAMILY

http://www.geneanet.org/genealogie/fr/gallais.html

http://industrie.lu/legallais.html

http://www.eluxemburgensia.lu/BnlViewer/view/index.html?lang=en#panel:pp|issue:
1224212|article:DTL87

http://www.luxemburgensia.bnl.lu/cgi/getPdf1_2.pl?mode=page&id=18970&option

http://preview-mosel.vdp.de/de/winzer/steckbrief/le-gallais-63/

https://books.google.lu/books?id=6RtqIVTMzkkC&pg=PA281&lpg=PA281&dq=norbert+le+
gallais+1919&source=bl&ots=H4_ukSaAPH&sig=L9PvrCMJBLCQpsdg-CZcQol_ano&hl=fr&sa
=X&ved=2ahUKEwj_rI6n1bHeAhWPalAKHSykB-sQ6AEwBXoECAUQAQ#v=onepage&q=
norbert%20le%20gallais%201919&f=false

https://www.theislandwiki.org/index.php/Philip_Walter_Jules_Le_Gallais

https://gw.geneanet.org/edehults?lang=en&iz=2&p=jean+bernard+louis+frederic+leopold&n
=de+mathelin

http://www.galerie-mazarini.fr/category/peintres/pierre-thevenin/

http://mohr-rautenstrauch.de/Stamm_Boch.htm

http://onsstad.vdl.lu/index.php?id=242&tx_ttnews%5Bswords%5D=%23&tx_ttnews-%5B
scontent%5D=villa%20vauban&tx_ttnews%5Bauthor%5D=yegles&tx_ttnews-%5Byearfrom
%5D=1993&tx_ttnews%5Byearto%5D=alle&tx_ttnews%5Bback-Pid%5D=245&tx_ttnews%
5Btt_news%5D=1732&cHash=2d8b7c8df86c5a873e46b-2c3a3609e2c

LUXEMBOURG

https://industrie.lu/deMuyserTabouraing.html

https://sip.gouvernement.lu/dam-assets/publications/bulletin/1947/BID_1947_10/
BID_1947_10.pdf.

https://gouvernement.lu/dam-assets/fr/actualites/articles/2015/02-fevrier/10-bettel-artuso/
rapport.pdf

https://gouvernement.lu/dam-assets/fr/actualites/communiques/2007/07/27spoliation/
Spoliation.pdf

https://www.pressreader.com/luxembourg/tageblatt-luxembourg/
20180428/281509341799020

http://www.angelfire.com/realm/gotha/gotha/lynar.html

http://www.colpach.lu/data/aline_mayrisch_approches.pdf

http://e-gide.blogspot.com/2013/06/une-carte-de-la-bastide-franco.html

https://www.nytimes.com/1970/09/15/archives/bernard-n-zimmer-aide-of-luxembourg.html

https://www.forum.lu/wp-content/uploads/2015/11/7432_319_Schroeder.pdf

INTERNATIONAL

https://chroniclingamerica.loc.gov/search/pages/results/?state=&date1=1789&-date2=1926&
proxtext=le+gallais&dateFilterType=yearRange&rows=20&-searchType=basic&x=0&y=0

http://www.historic-structures.com/washington_dc/dc/townsend_house.php

https://www.nytimes.com/2006/03/05/magazine/it-is-what-it-is.html

https://www.nytimes.com/2002/01/04/us/benjamin-welles-biographer-and-journalist-is-
dead-at-85.html

https://books.google.fr/books?id=uaeD_etmGL0C&pg=PA263&lpg=PA2
63&dq=foster+dulles+luxembourg+brêve+visite&source=bl&ots=G50Ix-
GoKb&-sig=iumha2Hm9J9IX80lGpVUKf757bo&hl=fr&sa=X&ved=2ahUKEwiD-
PPnjcXcAhWlyIUKHYnbDzQQ6AEwAHoECAAQAQ#v=onepage&q=foster%20dulles%20
luxembourg%20brêve%20visite&f=false

http://www.fdrlibrary.marist.edu/daybyday/daylog/july-25th-1940/

http://www.fdrlibrary.marist.edu/daybyday/daylog/january-14th-1942/

https://www.cairn.info/revue-guerres-mondiales-et-conflits-contemporains-2001-2-page-167.htm

https://www.nytimes.com/1994/02/04/obituaries/c-s-vanden-broeck-investment-banker-74.html

https://www.lootedartcommission.com/bretton-woods

http://www.un.org/fr/sections/history-united-nations-charter/1945-san-francisco-
conference/index.html

Guerres mondiales et conflits contemporains 2001/2 (n° 202-203). DOI 10.3917/gmcc.202.0167.
https://www.cairn.info/revue-guerres-mondiales-et-conflits-contemporains-2001-2-page-167.
htm?contenu=resume

NOTES

1   Paul Mayrisch (1861-1915), son of Jean Mathias Edouard Mayrisch and Mathilde Metz, and brother of Emile Mayrisch.

2   Emile Mayrisch (1862-1928), husband of Aline de Saint-Hubert (1874-1947).

3   Mersch, Jules, *Biographie nationale du Pays de Luxembourg, depuis ses origines jusqu'à nos jours*, Imprimerie de la Cour Victor Buck, 1957.

4   Weber, Josiane, *Familien der Oberschicht in Luxemburg. Elitenbildung und Lebenswelten 1850-1900*, Editions Guy Binsfeld, pp. 131-137.

5   As he pursued the same diplomatic career as his cousin Hugues, he will reappear again in the book.

6   Interview with Anne-Marie Le Gallais-de Gargan's great-niece, Mrs. Dominique Charpentier, at the Château de Preisch, on June 18, 2018.

7   Emile Bian (1873-1918), director of the Eich/Dommeldange factory and the Emile Metz Institute.

8   Rozel Reverchon-Le Gallais states in her memoirs that she was eleven years old at the time.

9   Félix Bian (1870-1926), notary and deputy.

10   Panhard ceased its activities in 1967 and was taken over by Citroën.

11   From the speech delivered on July 17, 1979 at the European Parliament in Strasbourg by the oldest member of the parliament, Mrs. Louise Weiss. Source: European Parliament (ed.), Strasbourg, European Parliament 1979, pp. 15-23.

12   Goetzinger, Germaine, Ed., *La Grande Guerre au Luxembourg. Le Journal de Michel Welter (3 août 1914 - 3 mars 1916)*, Centre national de littérature, Luxembourg 2015, p. 463

13   Philippe Berthelot (1866-1934), French diplomat, Secretary General at the Quai d'Orsay from 1920.

14   Dr. Michel Welter (1859-1924), Luxembourg politician and leader of the Socialist Party, member of the Chamber of Deputies, Director General in charge of Agriculture, Trade and Industry.

15   Viallet, Pierre, *La Foire*, Editions de La Table Ronde, Folio, Paris 1973.

16   *Luxemburger Wort*, March 6, 1934, obituary and, a few days later, description of the burial, *Tageblatt* of March 8, 1934.

17   Robert Brasseur (1870-1934), politician (deputy from 1899 to 1925), lawyer and journalist, married in 1914 to Jeanne de Saint-Hubert (sister of Aline Mayrisch-de Saint-Hubert) who had been divorced since 1900 from her first husband, Xavier Brasseur, Robert's first cousin.

18   Interview with Jens Reverchon, grandson of Rozel Reverchon-Le Gallais, December 6, 2018.

19   ANLux, AE-AW; letter from Le Gallais, June 27, 1952.

20   *Indépendance luxembourgeoise*, obituary on February 10, and funeral announcement on February 16, 1928.

21   Interview with Jens Reverchon, December 6, 2018.

22   Anatole de Mathelin (1855-1923), son of Léopold de Mathelin and Marie de Steenhault, husband of Fanny Cornesse (1855-1923).

23   Camille Wolff (1894-1977) represented Luxembourg at the 1924 Summer Olympic Games in Paris.

24   In Luxembourg (Villa Vauban), in 1932 marriage of Edmond Reverchon (b. 1893) - Rozelle Le Gallais (b. 1903), but also in London: Registrar 28 Marloes Road in Kensington. Interview with Jens Reverchon, December 6, 2018, who stated that the marriage took place in London because Rozel was marrying a divorced man.

25   Edmond Reverchon (1893-1967), son of Alice von Boch (1860-1944) and Adrian Reverchon (1861-1923), had three sons, the two eldest of his union with Maria Brügmann: 1.1. Heinz Reverchon (1921-1999), soldier in the Wehrmacht (who married first Gretel von Suttner, and then Karin Davidson); 1.2. Günther Reverchon (1922-1944, killed in action); and from the second union: 2.1. Eddie Reverchon (1934), married to Margaretha so-called Nicole Nicolas.

26   This villa became the residence of the Belgian Ambassador, and was later destroyed to make way for the present Banque de Luxembourg.

27   Maurice Pescatore (1870-1928), son of the Pescatore-Nothomb couple, husband of Gabrielle Barbanson, Gaston's sister.

28   *Luxemburger Wort* of July 11, 1940.

29   The Villa Vauban. Symbol of culture and historical identity. *Ons stad* 93, p. 16-19.

30   Raphaël Petrucci (1872-1917), sociologist, art historian, orientalist.

31   Correspondence Aline Mayrisch, Centre national de Littérature.

32   Goetzinger, Germaine (ed.), *The Great War in Luxembourg. Le journal de Michel Welter (3 Août 1914 - 3 Mars 1916)*, Centre national de literature 2015, p. 360.

33   Elisabeth van Rysselberghe (1890-1980), daughter of the painter Theo van Rysselberghe and Maria Monnom, mother of Catherine Elisabeth van Rysselberghe (natural daughter of André Gide).

34   Correspondence André Gide - Marc Allégret, Marc Henri Noël Allégret (1900-1973), French film director and photographer.

35   André Gide (1869-1951), French writer.

36   Walther Rathenau (1867-1922), German statesman who served as Minister of Foreign Affairs in the Weimar Republic. He was an industrialist and writer who stayed with the Mayrisch family in Colpach. He was murdered by a right-wing terrorist group.

37   Pierre Masson and Cornel Meder (eds.), *Correspondence André Gide - Aline Mayrisch 1903-1946*. Gallimard, Paris 2003, p. 214.

38   Centre national de littérature (CNL), Mayrisch Fund, correspondence between Andrée Mayrisch and her mother Aline Mayrisch-de Saint-Hubert. Andrée Mayrisch (1901-1977), wife of Pierre Viénot, Member of parliament, she was one of three women members of a Government of the Fourth Republic.

39   Jean Schlumberger (1877-1968), German-French journalist and writer.

40   Paul Desjardins or Louis Paul Abel Desjardins (civil status name, 1859-1940), French professor and journalist. For thirty years he led annual meetings of intellectuals committed to freedom of opinion, the Decades of Pontigny.

41   Decades of Pontigny: in August, three Decades of ten days each were organized. These were the 2nd Decades of 1925. These Decades were held from 1910 to 1914, then from 1922 until the beginning of the Second World War in 1939. They were organized in Pontigny Abbey, a former 12th century Cistercian monastery in the Yonne department, bought by Desjardins in 1906 upon the separation of Church and State.

42   Pascal Mercier and Cornel Meder (eds.), *Aline Mayrisch - Jean Schlumberger: Correspondence 1907-194*, Publications nationales, Luxembourg 2000, p. 697.

43   Interview with Germaine Goetzinger, December 6, 2018.

44   Dittrich Klaus, "Buddhism, Business, and Red-Cross Diplomacy: Aline Mayrisch de Saint-Hubert's Journeys to East Asia in the Interwar Period", in Fabricating Modern Societies: *Education, Bodies, and Minds in the Age of Steel*, pp. 79-107. DOI: https://doi.org/10.1163/9789004410510_005, p. 86

45   Hugues Le Gallais signed the Livre d'or de Colpach in 1925, upon his return from Japan.

46   Aline Mayrisch - Jean Schlumberger, *op. cit.*, p. 697.

47   Letter from Aline Mayrisch to E.R. Curtis announcing her trip with Le Gallais to China. Ernst Robert Curtis (1886-1956), German philologist and specialist in Romanesque literature at the University of Bonn. Aline Mayrisch de Saint-Hubert, *Toute la noblesse de sa nature: recueil des récits publiés*, Cornel Meder. Editions du cercle des amis de Colpach, 2014.

48 Aline Mayrisch, *Approaches*, lecture given at Colpach Castle on January 19, 1997 on behalf of the Luxembourg Red Cross on the occasion of the 50th anniversary of Aline Mayrisch's death.

49 Galerie 30 (2012) no. 1, S. 101

50 Dittrich Klaus, "Buddhism, Business, and Red-Cross Diplomacy, : Aline Mayrisch de Saint-Hubert's Journeys to East Asia in the Interwar Period", in *Fabricating Modern Societies: Education, Bodies, and Minds in the Age of Steel*, pp. 79-107. DOI: https://doi.org/10.1163/9789004410510_005, pp. 89, 91

51 The 1933 visit is confirmed in the guestbook of Colpach. Aline Mayrisch added the names of Hugues Le Gallais and Pisana Velluti by pencil. Aline Mayrisch Fund, CNL-L-37. III. 3-1.

52 Correspondence Mayrisch - Schlumberger, p. 329.

53 Correspondence Mayrisch - Schlumberger, p. 342.

54 Information from Patricia de Zwaef, September 24, 2018.

55 As the couple remained childless, the house reverted to the heirs of Hugues and Pisana.

56 Subsequently, and for almost twenty years, the ground floor of the palace hosted Luxembourg's participation in the Venice Biennales until 2017.

57 Telegram of condolences from Doody to Gianni Velluti, Pisana's half-brother, dated March 22, 1957.

58 Mersch, Jules, ed., *Biographie nationale du pays de Luxembourg depuis ses origines jusqu'à nos jours*, Luxembourg 1972, fasc. 19, p. 68, Mémorial no. 51 of July 19, 1920, p. 764.

59 Victor Bodson (1902-1984), Minister of Justice from 1940 to 1947.

60 Heisbourg, Georges, *Le gouvernement luxembourgeois en exil*, 1942-43, p. 22.

61 War Department documents from February 1944 and March 1946 made available by the family of M. Brasseur (Tom Elvinger).

62 Robert Flesch (1882-1940), engineer, head of the rolling mills at the Dudelange plant.

63 Élie Decazes, 5th Duke Decazes (1914-2011).

64 Peggy Guggenheim (1898-1979), collector and patron.

65 The term *spats* can be translated as gaiters – a shortening of splashes or splash guards, a classic type of shoe accessory for outdoor wear, covering the foot and ankle.

66 Top hat that flattens and lifts up with the help of springs.

67 Most probably Gaston Barbanson.

68 Renée, known as Poussy Muller, daughter of René Muller and Jeanne Laval, wife of Jacques Neef de Sainval (Gaston Barbanson's brother-in-law) who went to work in Dublin when Hugues Le Gallais went to Tokyo in 1927, childhood friend of Andrée Mayrisch.

69 Correspondence Aline Mayrisch, CNL.

70 In 1976, Columeta was renamed Trade Arbed.

71 The Belgian writer Alexis Curvers, a friend of the Mayrisch family who took part in the Colpach meetings, erroneously called Le Gallais the "Ambassador of the Grand-Duchy of Luxembourg in Tokyo." See Aline Mayrisch-de Saint-Hubert and Marie Delcourt-Curvers, *Correspondance 1923-1946*, Catherine Gravet and Cornel Meder, eds. Luxembourg, Edition du Cercle des amis de Colpach 2009, p. 62. Albeit false, this label testifies to the strong overlap between industrial and diplomatic functions in interwar Luxembourg. Indeed, Columeta's role went far beyond the sale of steel products, see Gérald Arboit, "Un comptoir de vente particulier: Columeta," in *Les mutations de la sidérurgie mondiale du XXe siècle à nos jours/The Transformation of the World Steel Industry from the 20th Century to the Present*, Charles Barthel, Ivan Kharaba, and Philippe Mioche, eds. Brussels, Peter Lang 2014, pp. 199-221. Quote from Dittrich Klaus, "Buddhism, Business, and Red-Cross Diplomacy: Aline Mayrisch de Saint-Hubert's Journeys to East Asia in the Interwar Period" in *Fabricating Modern Societies: Education, Bodies, and Minds in the Age of Steel*, pp. 79-107. DOI: https://doi.org/10.1163/9789004410510_005, pp. 86, 99. Imaizumi Kaichiro (1867-1941), Honorary Consul of Luxembourg and businessman, said to be the "father of modern industry", founder of Nippon Kokan (NKK Corporation, now the JFE Steel Corporation, the second largest Japanese steel manufacturer.) and member of Japan's National Diet.

72   Correspondence Mayrisch-Schlumberger, p. 252.

73   Tony Rollman (1899-1986) worked in Japan from 1926 to 1935 and left Columeta in 1948 for the European Communities before returning to Arbed in 1950.

74   Albert Marie Léon Adolphe de Bassompierre, Baron (1873-1956), Belgian Ambassador to Japan from 1921 to 1939. See his memoirs: *Dix-huit ans d'ambassade au Japon*, Paris, Libris 1943.

75   Joseph Hackin (1886-1941), husband of Ria Parmentier (1905-1941), later curator and renovator at the Musée Guimet, his wife being his main collaborator. He died as a hero of France. In his volume on the year of exile 1941, Heisbourg describes the link between Bech and Hackin, whose disappearance he greatly regretted, all the more so as an invitation from the couple in October 1940 had probably saved the Luxembourg Minister from perhishing in a London bombing.

76   Pierre d'Espezel (1893-1959), archivist-palaeographer, curator in the Cabinet of Medals and Antiques at the Bibliothèque nationale, Paris, Secretary of the *Gazette des beaux-arts*.

77   Bourg, Tony, *Madame Mayrisch et l'Orient*. Letzebuerger Land of December 18, 1987, letter of December 13, 1932, Mayrisch Fund, ANLux.

78   Bourg, Tony, *Madame Mayrisch et l'Orient*. Letzebuerger Land of December 18, 1987, letter of July 31, 1932, Mayrisch Fund, ANLux.

79   Boy, Marie, *L'intelligence sensible du décideur: Relation, intuition, valeurs: des atouts pour développer votre potentiel de dirigeant*, Editions Dunod 2011.

80   Marunouchi means "inside the circle", in reference to its location inside the moat of the imperial palace. The district is the financial centre of Japan, the three largest banks in the country have their headquarters there.

81   Dittrich, Klaus, "Selling Luxembourgian Steel in Japan, Columeta Tokyo, 1925 to 1941", in *Zeitschrift für Unternehmensgeschichte*, 2 (2016).

82   This attack was planned by the Japanese to prevent the unification of China under the Kuomintang, which Japan perceived as a threat to its pre-eminence in the region.

83   Als, Georges Robert (1897-1991), *Au service de son pays: à la recherché du temps perdu*. Luxembourg, Rapid Press, 2003.

84   Guill Konsbruck (1909-1983), aide-de-camp to Prince Félix, Commissioner for Food and Economic Affairs. From February 23, 1945 to August 29, 1946, he was a member of the government, before being appointed director of the central administration of Arbed from October 15, 1946. In 1947, he became deputy general manager of Arbed and in 1959 general manager of Arbed Participations.

85   Alfred Loesch (1902-1982), lawyer, Grand Marshal of the Grand Ducal Court from 1947 to 1964.

86   See further under World War II.

87   AMgdL 1697, official correspondence Le Gallais to H.R.H., notes on official interviews in Washington, 1st category, letter from Hugues Le Gallais to the Grand Duchess, of February 12, 1943.

88   See further under World War II.

89   AMgdL 1697, official correspondence Le Gallais to H.R.H., notes on official talks in Washington, 1st category, four handwritten letters from Le Gallais to the Grand Duchess: December 22, 1942, before the visit to California and Missouri; December 12, 1942, following an invitation to visit Louisiana; November 28, 1942, on the subject of military representation and the rejection of Konsbruck's appointment as military attaché to the Legation; October 8, 1942, before the meeting with the President and on the formation of the Hereditary Grand Duke.

90   As these testimonies had little impact on the years spent in the United States, they are not included in the description of the 1940s. Le Gallais played on several fronts, and his long-standing and singular relationship with the head of state was not to be denied and went far beyond an honorary function.

91   Albert Wehrer (1895-1967), chargé d'affaires in Berlin from June 1938 until 1940 and after the war until 1950. Before May 10, 1940 he had been a Government Councillor, then Secretary General of the Government, and from May to October 1940 chairman of the Landesverwaltungskommission. In 1945 he became head of the Luxembourg mission to the Allied Control Council in Berlin. In 1950, he became Minister in Berlin, then, from October 1951, Minister Plenipotentiary in Paris, before being appointed, in April 1952, member of the High Authority of the ECSC.

92   Joseph Bech (1887-1975), President of the Government from 1926 to 1937, and Minister of Foreign Affairs after the 1937 referendum. He resumed the presidency of the government after the death of Pierre Dupong (1953), and remained in this post until 1958.

93   Pierre Dupong (1885-1953), Prime minister from 1937 until his death on December 23, 1953. At the time, the Prime minister was appointed Minister of State, President of the Government.

94   The original Siegfried Line (called the Hindenburg Line by the Allies) is a fortified line built by Germany in 1916 and 1917, during the First World War.

95   London: André Clasen, Chancellor of the Consulate in London from 1935 to 1940, Secretary General of the Ministry of Foreign Affairs from January 14, 1941, chargé d'affaires to the British Government on October 29, 1941 (for 30 years). He was the son of Bernard Clasen (1874-1941), representative of Arbed-Columeta, director of Columeta Export Company Ltd. in London, Honorary Consul General of Luxembourg in London in 1940. His brother, Léon Clasen, was director of Luxembourg broadcasts at the BBC.

96   Georges Schommer, called Menni (1897-1961), was appointed Information Commissioner in New York on November 7, 1940, before being appointed to London later during the war.

97   Paris: Antoine Funck, who became Minister Plenipotentiary by Grand Ducal decree of September 18, 1940.

98   Auguste Collart (1890-1978), Director General of Agriculture, Trade, Industry and Labour from 1918 to 1920 as an independent supported by the People's Party (*Volkspartei*), chargé d'affaires at The Hague from 1933, and ambassador after 1950.

99   Count Gaston de Marchant et d'Ansembourg, chargé d'affaires for Luxembourg in Brussels in 1940, son of Count Amaury who had been chargé d'affaires until 1927.

100   Schroeder, Corinne, *The Emergence of the Foreign Policy of the Grand Duchy of Luxembourg Seen through the Ministry of Foreign Affairs (1945-1973)*, unpublished thesis.

101   Pierre Krier (1885-1947), Minister of Labour from 1937 until his death.

102   Schroeder, Corinne quoting Heisbourg.

103   Trausch, Gilbert, *Joseph Bech, un homme dans son siècle*, Luxembourg, Imprimerie Saint-Paul 1978, p. 70.

104   William H. Hamilton, Honorary Consul General of Luxembourg in New York. Luxembourg Commissioner for the 1939 World Exhibition, attended by Princes Félix and Jean, accompanied by Guill Konsbruck.

105   Herbert Claiborne Jr., Pell (1884-1961), Democratic Representative of New York 17th District, 1919-1921, defeated in 1920, American Minister in Portugal, 1937-1941 and in Hungary, 1941-1942.

106   ANLux, Heisbourg Fund, AE-AW, Dupong file 1940-1941 (WD1-WD189), undated letter from Prince Félix written on stationery from the Waldorf-Astoria in New York City.

107   Testimony by Norbert Le Gallais in Venice, May 2018.

108   Carl Abbott, historian and author of *Political Terrain*, relates the development of the American capital.

109   David Brinkley, journalist, describes the development of the American capital in the book *Washington Goes to War*, New York, Knopf 1988.

110   *Washington Post*, May 27, 2004.

111   Raymond de Waha, baron (1877-1942), right-wing politician and member of the Reuter Government, ANLux, AE-03194.

112   ANLux, Heisbourg Fund.

113   Haag, Emile and Krier, Emile, *1940 L'année du dilemme*, p. 53.

114   811.111 Diplomatic/15136 (Feb. 29, 1940) - granting 3(1) visa, National Archives at College Park.

115   Heisbourg 1940, p. 197.

116   811.111 Diplomatic/15136 (Feb 29, 1940) - granting 3(1) visa, Central Files of the State Department.

117　AMgdL 1699, various reports and messages, Schommer (Elmhurst, New York) to Bech, September 7, 1940.

118　Norbert Le Gallais worked in Brussels and lived with his family in Luxembourg for some time before retiring and settling in Venice with his wife Rita Eckstein and their two children, Catherine and Hugues.

119　Cordell Hull (1871-1950), Secretary of State from 1933 to 1944.

120　Benjamin Sumner Welles (1892-1961), Under-Secretary of State from 1937 to 1943.

121　AMgdL 1697, official correspondence Le Gallais to H.R.H., notes on official interviews in Washington, 1st category.

122　Carrier, Thomas J., *Washington, D.C.: A Historic Walking Tour (Images of America)*. Charleston, Arcadia 1999.

123　*The New York Times*, "Welles' Collection of Screens on Sale", February 15, 1925.

124　*The New York Times*, Harold B. Hinton, "Welles: Our Man of the Hour in Cuba", August 20, 1933, *The New York Times*, Celestine Bohlenjan, "Benjamin Welles, Biographer And Journalist, Is Dead at 85", January 4, 2002.

125　*Evening Star* (Washington, D.C.) 1854-1972, April 3, 1940.

126　*Evening Star*, April 7, 1940.

127　Marjorie Merriweather Post (1887-1973), owner of General Foods, Inc. used a large part of her fortune to collect art, in particular pre-revolutionary Russian art, and her third husband, Joseph Edward Davies (1876-1958), Democrat, Ambassador to Russia and then to Belgium from 1938 until 1939, from where he was accredited as a Minister in Luxembourg.

128　*Evening Star*, April 18, 1940.

129　*Evening Star*, May 2, 1940.

130　Bernard Zimmer, who died in September 1970 in New York, aged 81, arrived in the United States in 1905. He was President of the organising committee of the Luxembourg pavilion, President and CEO of the American Zinc Company and Vice-President of the American Metal Company, and Honorary Consul General since December 1946. Heisbourg 1940, p. 77.

131　The Luxembourg Relief Fund, to which we shall return later.

132　Heisbourg 1940, p. 77.

133　AE-AW, letter from Dupong to Le Gallais of November 24, 1941.

134　ANLux, Heisbourg Fund, letter from Le Gallais to Bech of September 11, 1943.

135　Jacques Lennon (1913-2015), businessman and Honorary Consul in New York.

136　Jacques Lennon joined the US Army in 1943 and was seconded to North Africa and Italy.

137　*Evening Star*, October 5, 1941.

138　Information provided by the Grand Ducal Court in September 2004. The building was sold in 1962 by the Administration des Biens to the Luxembourg State.

139　*110 Years of diplomatic relations between the Grand Duchy of Luxembourg and the United States of America*, published by the Government of Luxembourg.

140　Eleanor Maloney (1903-2000) worked from 1940 to 1973, when she retired at the age of 70.

141　Eleanor Maloney died on January 11, 2000 in a retirement home in Duluth, St. Louis County, Minnesota, and was buried in her hometown.

142　The transmission time from Venice to Washington was five days, as stated in Eleanor Maloney's June 23 letter to Le Gallais based on Le Gallais' letter of June 18, AE-AW.

143　Dean G. Acheson (1893-1971), member of the Democratic Party, Undersecretary of State from 1945 to 1947 and Secretary of State from 1949 to 1953 under President Truman.

144　AE-AW, letter from Eleanor Maloney to Le Gallais of September 12, 1955.

145 Pierre Elvinger (1903-1967), Secretary General at the Ministry of Justice in Montreal. After the war, he became Government adviser at the Ministry of Foreign Affairs.

146 Name of an American actress.

147 Meeting in 2002 with Mrs. McKenna married Elvinger.

148 Marguerite of Lynar, Countess (1871-1959), lady-in-waiting of the Grand Duchess.

149 Von Bayern, Irmingard, *Jugend-Erinnerungen: 1923-1950*. EOS Verlag 2010, p. 113.

150 Countess Theresa Kerssenbrock (Mrs. Maloney writes the surname Kerssenbruck) (1888-1973), accompanied the imperial family since the First World War. Until the end of her life she remained with former Empress Zita, born Princess of Bourbon-Parma and sister of Prince Félix of Luxembourg.

151 Princess Antonia of Luxembourg (1899-1954), then Royal Princess of Bavaria (Crown Princess of Bayern).

152 Corneille Staudt (1895-1957), Vice-Consul of Luxembourg in New York.

153 Princess Hilda of Luxembourg (1896-1979) was the widow of Prince Adolf of Schwarzenberg.

154 Prince Adolphe de Schwarzenberg (1890-1950) was married to Princess Hilda of Luxembourg.

155 AE-AW, correspondence of Eleanor Maloney with Le Gallais of August 1, 1952.

156 Letter sent by the Countess to Eleanor Maloney in 1953/5, private archives.

157 AE-AW, letter from Grand Marshal of the Court Loesch to Ambassador Le Gallais of December 19, 1951.

158 Haag and Krier, letter from Le Gallais to Prince Félix in early July 1940, p. 190.

159 Georges Theunis (1873-1966), Prime Minister of Belgium from 1921 to 1925 and from 1934 to 1935. Governor of the National Bank of Belgium from 1941 to 1944.

160 Carlos Martins Pereira e Souza (1884-1965), Brazilian diplomat, embassy counselor in Tokyo in 1934 and 1935 and Ambassador in Washington from 1939 to 1948.

161 Heisbourg 1940, p. 152.

162 Haag and Krier, p. 198, letter from Le Gallais to Bech of July 19, 1940.

163 Telegram (Naval Communication Service of Trenton) of July 23, 1940 and letter from the Assistant Secretary of the Treasury to the Secretary of State of July 26, 1940. According to a letter from the Department of the Navy to the Secretary of State of October 16, 1940, the Grand Ducal family's transport costs on the Trenton were estimated at $360.73. National Archives at College Park.

164 Heisbourg 1940, p. 156.

165 *Idem.*

166 Heisbourg 1940, p. 184.

167 Rubin, Nancy, *American Empress: The Life and Times of Marjorie Merriweather Post*. iUniverse, Indiana, United States 1995, pp. 264 *et seq*. Large camp in the Adirondacks in New York State where many of the country homes of the most influential American families were located.

168 Even, Pierre, *Die Silberkammer der Luxemburger Dynastie*, exhibition catalogue, 2012, p. 37.

169 *Documents on Canadian External Relations 1939-1941*, Volume II / Part II, Volume 8.

170 Camille Gutt (1884-1971), Belgian politician and financier, Minister of Finance from 1940 to 1945, first Managing Director of the International Monetary Fund from 1946 to 1951.

171 Haag, Emile, *Une réussite originale. Le Luxembourg au fil des siècles*, Editions Guy Binsfeld, p. 367.

172 Pimentel, Irène and Ramalho, Margarida, *O Comboio de Luxemburgo*, Esfera dos livros, p. 99.

173 Message from Prince Félix delivered to the American Legation in Lisbon on August 19, 1940, cable from the Prince to Sumner Welles dated September 18, 1940 and acknowledgement dated September 23, National Archives at College Park.

174 Linden, André, "Léif Lëtzebuerger ... dir dohém a mir hei baussen...". The radio speeches of Grand Duchess Charlotte in exile, "ët wor alles net esou einfach". *Questions sur le Luxembourg et la Deuxième Guerre mondiale*. Luxembourg 2002.

175 AMgdL 1697, official correspondence Le Gallais to H.R.H., notes on official interviews in Washington, 1st category. Le Gallais note from his conversation with Welles of March 27, 1941.

176 Heisbourg, 100 Joer Lëtzebuerger Dynasty, p. 66.

177 AMgdL 1699, various reports and messages, Schommer (Elmhurst, New York) to Bech, September 7, 1940.

178 AMgdL 1699, various reports and messages, Dupong to Bech, September 5, 1940.

179 Letter from Information Commissioner Georges Schommer to Minister Victor Bodson.

180 https://industrie.lu/deMuyserTabouraing.html

181 Léon Schaus (1905-1982), Councillor of the Legation, Secretary General of the Government in exile; was after the war director of the tax administration and member (Vice-President since December 1953) of the Council of State until his resignation in 1977.

182 Haag and Krier, p. 115.

183 AMgdL 1699, various reports and messages, Schommer (Elmhurst, New York) to Bech, September 12, 1940.

184 Haag and Krier, p.124

185 Dave Hennen Morris (1872-1944), ambassador to Belgium from 1933 to 1937 and, therefore, co-accredited to the Grand Duchy, one of Joseph Davies' predecessors.

186 Alex Bonn (1908-2008), Luxembourg lawyer exiled in the United States during the war and future President of the Council of State.

187 Heisbourg 1940, p. 219.

188 Princess Alice, Countess of Athlone (1883-1981), granddaughter of Queen Victoria, wife of Prince Alexander of Teck (1874-1957) who became Earl of Athlone in 1917. This brother of Queen Mary became Governor General of Canada in June 1940.

189 Stanley Woodward (1899-1992), acting Chief of Protocol in 1940, then Chief of Protocol at the White House under President Roosevelt, and ambassador to Canada under President Truman.

190 This letter does not appear in the archives of the Embassy in Washington. AMgdL, exchange of letters between the President and the Envoy Extraordinary and Minister Plenipotentiary.

191 ANLux, Heisbourg Fund, AE-AW, Dupong file 1940-1941 (WD1-WD189), letter from Le Gallais to Bech of November 12, 1940.

192 Heisbourg 1940, p. 216 (no reference to archives).

193 ANLux, Heisbourg Fund, AE-AW, Dupong file 1940-1941 (WD1-WD189), letter from Le Gallais to Bech of November 12, 1940 on his accreditation to the President, 8 November.

194 Coutu, Jean-Claude, *La millionnaire de Mascouche: le manoir seigneurial de 1930 à 1954*. Société de développement et d'animation de Mascouche, 2006

195 Trausch, Gilbert, *Joseph Bech*; p. 97.

196 Heisbourg 1941, p. 78.

197 Telegram of December 30, 1940 (received State Department - January 22, 1941), National Archives at College Park following a telegram of end-of-year greetings of December 27, 1940 signed "Charlotte".

198 The Consulate of the Czech Republic is located there at present.

199 Hazel Kemp Colville (1889-1961), alias "La millionnaire de Mascouche", the seigneurial estate purchased in 1930.

200 Isabel Leighton and Bertram Bloch are the authors of *Marie-Adelaide: A Play*. New York, Rialto Service Bureau. See also Theodore Marburg, *The Story of a Soul, Based, in Outline on Edith O'Shaughnessy's 'The*

Life of Marie Adelaide, Grand Duchess of Luxemburg', and on the Official proceedings of the Luxemburg parliament, Philadelphia, Dorrance and Company, 1938.

201   Heisbourg 1941, p. 33, from NA850A. 00/95.

202   Walter Franklin George (1878-1957), politician of the State of Georgia. Democratic Senator and President pro tempore of the Senate from 1955 to 1957.

203   Lewis Dominic Thill (1903-1975), Republican Congressman from Wisconsin from 1939 to 1943.

204   Heisbourg 1941, p. 17.

205   Lord Halifax, Edward Frederick Lindley Wood (1881-1959), British politician, ambassador to the United States from 1940 to 1946.

206   Heisbourg 1941, pp. 43-44.

207   AMgdL 1697, Le Gallais letter to Bech of February 7, 1941, official correspondence Le Gallais to H.R.H., notes on official talks in Washington, 1st category.

208   Trausch, Gilbert, *Joseph Bech*; p. 105.

209   Heisbourg 1941; p. 45.

210   ANLux, AE-0015, Bodson Fund.

211   AMgdL 1697, letter from Le Gallais to Bech of February 18, 1941, official correspondence Le Gallais to H.R.H., notes on official interviews in Washington, 1st category.

212   John Marsch (died July 29, 1954 at the age of 85), born in Saeul, had left Luxembourg at the age of 18 for the United States. He was President of the Luxembourg Chamber of Commerce in Chicago and Honorary Consul General from 1935.

213   Heisbourg 1941, p. 59, letter from Bodson to Krier of February 4, AEL-GT EX 527,0023.

214   Heisbourg 1941, p. 60; AE-ALW, Bech file.

215   ANLux, Heisbourg Fund, draft letter from Grand Duchess to Minister Bech with the words "draft" and "not dispatched".

216   Victor Bodson left for London in August 1941.

217   Heisbourg 1940, pp. 222-223.

218   Heisbourg 1941, p. 47.

219   Letter from Dupong to Le Gallais of February 3, 1941, WD 61, AmgdL.

220   AMgdL 1699, various reports and messages, Bech to Dupong, January 5, 1941. Haag and Krier, Emile, p. 299, letter from Bech to Dupong of January 5-8, 1941.

221   Heisbourg 1941, p. 50.

222   Heisbourg 1941, letter from Bodson to Krier of February 4, 1941, AE-Gt EX 527,0023, p. 53.

223   AMgdL 1697, official correspondence from Le Gallais to H.R.H., notes on official interviews in Washington, 1st category, Le Gallais speech at the Waldorf Astoria in New York, February 27, 1941.

224   Weitz, Paul, *Charlotte von Luxemburg*, Editions Saint-Paul, 1988.

225   Linden, André, "Léif Lëtzebuerger ... dir dohém a mir hei baussen... ", the radio speeches of Grand Duchess Charlotte in exile, "ët wor alles net esou einfach". Questions sur le Luxembourg et la Deuxième Guerre mondiale. Luxembourg 2002.

226   AMgdL 1697, official correspondence Le Gallais to H.R.H., notes on official interviews in Washington, 1st category, excerpt of a letter from Le Gallais to Dupong of June 15, 1942 "about a Gallup Poll".

227   Robert Serebrenik (1902-1965), Chief Rabbi of Luxembourg since 1929.

228   American Jewish Joint Distribution Committee was an American Jewish humanitarian organisation based in New York. There is an entire file containing information not only on the arrival of refugees in Luxembourg during the 1930s, but also on the emigration, under trying conditions, of hundreds of Jews between August 1940 and October 1941.

229 Albert Nussbaum (1898-1978) was Commissioner for Emigration of the Jewish population since November 30, 1940 and Director of Transmigration for the American Joint Distribution Committee.

230 Heisbourg 1941, p. 270, Nussbaum arrived in New York in 1942.

231 The tragic story of this third train that failed to bring the passengers from Luxembourg to their destination was described by Irène Pimentel and Margarida Ramalho in *O Comboio de Luxemburgo*, Esfera dos Livros 2016, p. 181.

232 Heisbourg 1941, p. 252.

233 Artuso Report, p. 217 referring to Grosbois, Thierry, *Le gouvernement luxembourgeois en exil*, Hémecht 2005, p. 28.

234 Heisbourg 1941, p. 246.

235 Koch-Kent, Henri, *Vu et entendu, vol. 2, Years of Exile 1940-1946*, Luxembourg, Imprimerie centrale 1986, p. 308. Gordian Troeller (1917-2003) was a Luxembourg journalist, photographer and documentarian who fought in the Spanish Civil War on the Republican side.

236 Heisbourg 1942-1943, p. 182.

237 René Blum (1889-1967), lawyer, diplomat and politician (LSAP) and one of the most active leaders in the 1937 referendum against banning the Communist Party ("Maulkuerfgesetz"). Following this defeat of the Minister of State Joseph Bech, René Blum became Minister of Justice until his resignation on April 6, 1940. After the war he became ambassador to the Soviet Union.

238 Heisbourg 1941, p. 23, excerpt from AE-ALW, Dupong file.

239 ANLux, Heisbourg Fund, AE-AW/64, letter from Albert Nussbaum in New York to Le Gallais of May 28, 1942.

240 Heisbourg 1941, p. 285.

241 Bodson later received the honour of "Righteous Among the Nations" for helping German Jews escape persecution under the Nazi regime.

242 ANLux, AE-AW-2119, fate of Luxembourg nationals and Jews during World War II.

243 ANLux, Heisbourg Fund, mention AE-AW/7 gov, letter from Alex Bonn to Le Gallais of June 6, 1941.

244 Heisbourg 1941, p. 274, and ANLux-AW, Heisbourg Fund, Bech file, letter no. 17, letter from Le Gallais to Bech of July 15, 1941.

245 Artuso Report, pp. 218-219 referring to Grosbois, Thierry, *Le gouvernement luxembourgeois en exil*, Hémecht 2005, pp. 28-29.

246 ANLux, Bodson Fund, box 35 anc 27 CDRR 00235.

247 Heisbourg 1941, p. 280.

248 Koch-Kent, Henri, *Vu et entendu*, p. 179.

249 Pimentel, Irene and Ramalho, Margarida, *O Comboio de Luxemburgo*, p. 171.

250 ANLux, Heisbourg Fund.

251 Heisbourg 1940, p. 195.

252 Heisbourg 1941, p. 282.

253 Heisbourg 1941, p. 93.

254 Heisbourg 1941, p. 93.

255 AMgdL 1699, various reports and messages, Dupong (Montreal) to Bech (London), November 18, 1940.

256 ANLux, Heisbourg Fund, letter from Le Gallais to Dupong of November 30, 1942 - WD 404.

257 ANLux, Heisbourg Fund, letter from Dupong to Le Gallais of November 18, 1942 - WD 10.

258 Wolff, André, *Memories: A Mission in the United States*, Luxembourg, Imprimerie Saint-Paul 1950, p. 15. Wolff was Information Commissioner of the Grand Duchy in the United States.

259 The Belgian ambassadors to the United States of the time of Le Gallais were count Robert van der Straten-Ponthoz (1935-1945), Baron Robert Silvercruys (to Canada until December 1944) 1945-1959.

260 Also in a letter to Victor Bodson.

261 Regarding the accredited ministers, see also AE-AW, letter from Dupong to Guill Konsbruck of August 23, 1943 also concerning the accreditation to the Grand Duchess of the new representative Mr. Ray Atherton, Ambassador from 1943 to 1948 and successor of Mr. Jay Pierrepont Moffat, American Ambassador to Canada from 1940 in 1943, who died in January at the age of 47.

262 A property had been considered half an hour from New York near Hyde Park.

263 AMgdL 1699, various reports and messages, Dupong from London to the Grand Duchess, June 18, 1941.

264 Weitz, Paul, *Charlotte von Luxemburg*, Editions Saint-Paul, 1988.

265 Letter from Member of the House of Representatives George Holden Tinkham of July 31, 1940 and response from the acting Secretary of State of August 7, 1940, National Archives at College Park.

266 Heisbourg 1941, p. 114; AE-ALW, Bech dossier, letter from Le Gallais to Bech of July 17, 1941.

267 AMgdL 1689 and AMgdL 5365.

268 AE-AW, July 16 letter from Guill Konsbruck to Le Gallais on the July 1941 purchase of the farm.

269 AE-AW, letter of May 21, 1943 from Guill Konsbruck to the owner of the last leased property at Glen Cove, Long Island.

270 Waller, George Platt, *Defiant Diplomat George Platt Waller: American Consul in Nazi-occupied Luxembourg 1931-1941*; Lanham, Rowman & Littlefield 2014, p. 166. George Platt Waller (1889-1962), was American chargé d'affaires in Luxembourg from 1931 until May 10, 1940. He departed for the United States on August 1, 1941 and returned to Luxembourg at the end of 1944. John Clarence Cudahy (1887-1943) was American ambassador to Poland from 1933 to 1937, Minister to Ireland from 1937 to 1940, ambassador to Belgium in 1940, and minister accredited in Luxembourg from February 12, 1940 (Bulletin of the Grand Duchy of 1940).

271 Letter from Le Gallais to Dupong of March 14, 1942, ANLux, AE-AW.

272 Heisburg, *100 Joer Lëtzebuerger Dynastie*, p. 67.

273 AE-AW, letter from Konsbruck to Schaus of October 16.

274 Koch-Kent, Henri, *Vu et entendu*, p. 199.

275 AE-AW, letters from Guill Konsbruck of August 30 and September 2, 1941.

276 Fred Gilson was, during World War II, chairman of the American Committee for Luxembourg Relief Incorporated and Vice-Consul / chancellor of the Grand Duchy of Luxembourg in Chicago.

277 AE-AW, letter from Le Gallais of September 20, 1941.

278 AE-AW; Le Gallais letter to Mr. Schommer of September 30 and *Evening Star*, October 5, 1941.

279 *Evening Star*, October 27, 1941. Princess Marie-Gabrielle, after Heisburg 1941, p. 176.

280 Letter from Schaus to Guill Konsbruck of October 9, 1941, also addressed to André Wolff.

281 Letters of October 18 and 20, 1941.

282 Heisbourg 1941, p. 177. Krier-Becker, Lily, *Pierre Krier* (manuscript); p. 174.

283 Heisbourg 1941, p. 215.

284 The United States entered the war following the attack on Pearl Harbor on December 7, 1941.

285 This is the rail overpass called "Biisserbréck" at the northern exit of Luxembourg railway station.

286 Citation of briefs by Justice Minister Bodson, private archives.

287 Heisbourg 1940, p. 230, extracted from AE-GT EX 385, pp. 2-3.

288 Heisbourg 1941, p. 198, AEL-ALW, Bech file.

289   Heisbourg 1941, p. 201, AEL-ALW, Government R file (reports), or ANLux, AE-AW-0724.

290   Heisbourg 1942-1943, p. 15, AEL-ALW, Government file R (reports).

291   Heisbourg 1942-1943, p. 314.

292   Heisbourg 1942-1943, p. 17.

293   http://www.fdrlibrary.marist.edu/daybyday/daylog/january-14th-1942/ (accessed June 1, 2019).

294   Heisbourg 1941, p. 203.

295   Heisbourg; 1941, p. 204, letter from Le Gallais to Bech of May 28, 1941; and AMgdL 1697, official correspondence from Le Gallais to H.R.H., notes on official interviews in Washington, 1st category.

296   These documents are partly reproduced in Heisbourg's book.

297   Matthew Woll (1880-1956), was Vice-President of the American Federation of Labor during World War II and a Luxembourg-born American who played an important role in labor union relations.

298   Heisbourg 1942-1943, p. 40.

299   Major-General William Joseph Donovan (1883-1959), was a soldier, lawyer, and the head of the OSS (Office of Strategic Services) during World War II. After the war he initiated the creation of the CIA.

300   http://www.fdrlibrary.marist.edu/daybyday/daylog/june-5th-1942/

301   Heisbourg 1942-1943, p. 52.

302   Léon Pasvolsky, Special Assistant to the Secretary of State.

303   Herbert Feis, State Department Economic Advisor.

304   AMgdL 1697, official correspondence Le Gallais to H.R.H., notes on official interviews in Washington, 1st category, undated note written by Le Gallais following a conversation between Bech and Pasvolsky, Special Assistant to the Secretary of State, found with a Le Gallais post-war note dated July 15, 1942.

305   Address of His Excellency, Joseph Bech, Minister of Foreign Affairs of Luxembourg before the Committee on Foreign Affairs, House of Representatives, Wednesday, June 3, 1942, United States Government Printing Office, Washington, 1942, p. 6-7, and Trausch, Gilbert, *Joseph Bech*; p. 131.

306   Heisbourg 1942-1943, p. 47.

307   Bernard J. Cigrand (1866-1932) was a dentist and university professor.

308   AMgdL 1697, official correspondence from Le Gallais to H.R.H ., notes on official talks in Washington, 1st category, letter from Le Gallais to Dupong of June 20, 1942.

309   Louis Ensch (1895-1953) was a Luxembourg engineer, and the general manager of Belgo-Mineira in 1936.

310   AE-AW, June 19, 1942 according to Guill Konsbruck report.

311   *Evening Star*, July 26, 1942.

312   Heisbourg 1942, p. 72.

313   AMgdL 1697, official correspondence from Le Gallais to H.R.H., notes on official talks in Washington, 1st category, letter from Le Gallais of February 12, 1943.

314   This is an allusion to the qualification of Bech as a master sorcerer by the elder of the aide-de-camp's two sons, when Bech had impressed him. The latter reported to everyone that the *Gréssten Hexeméschter aus Portugalien* had written to him. Private archives.

315   *New York Times*, August 1, 1942.

316   Heisbourg, *100 Joer Lëtzebuerger Dynasty*, p. 67.

317   Heisbourg 1942-1943, p. 56. *Evening Star*, July 26, 1942.

318   Heisbourg 1942, p. 74.

319   Letter from Guill Konsbruck to Léon Schaus of August 21, 1942.

320   Heisbourg, *100 Joer Lëtzebuerger Dynasty*, p. 67.

321   Heisbourg 1942-1943, p. 90.

322   Heisbourg 1942-1943, p. 57.

323   ANLux-AE 13182, letter from Le Gallais to the US Secretary of State on September 8, 1942.

324   Kayser, Steve, "The Neutrality of Luxembourg from 1918 to 1945", *Forum*, June 2006, pp. 36-39; and Stronck, Gaston, *Le Luxembourg et le Pacte Atlantique. De la neutralité à l'alliance*, doctoral thesis in history defended in 1991 at Montpellier 3.

325   Heisbourg 1942-1943, p. 90-95.

326   ANLux-AE 13182, letter from Le Gallais to Secretary of State of September 8, 1942.

327   October 8, 1942.

328   Heisbourg 1942, p. 109.

329   AMgdL 1697, official correspondence from Le Gallais to H.R.H., notes on official talks in Washington, 1st category; letter from Le Gallais to Bech of October 16, 1942.

330   AMgdL 1697, official correspondence from Le Gallais to H.R.H., notes on official talks in Washington, 1st category, letter from Bech to Le Gallais of October 9, 1942.

331   AE-AW, letter from Guill Konsbruck to Léon Schaus of October 26, 1942.

332   Carl Brugmann (1899-1967) was Swiss Ambassador to the United States from 1939 to late 1954. He was married to Mary Wallace, daughter of Secretary of State Henry C. Wallace and sister of Vice President Henry A. Wallace.

333   Henry A. Wallace (1888-1965) was American Vice-President from 1941 to 1944.

334   Thomas Terry "Tom" Connally (1877-1963) was a Democratic representative from Texas in both the House of Representatives (1917-1929) and the Senate (1929-1953).

335   Martha, Princess of Sweden (1901-1954) became Crown Princess of Norway in 1929 by marrying Prince Olav.

336   Margarethe, Princess of Denmark (1895-1992) was the wife of Prince René of Bourbon-Parma, the sister-in-law and a great friend of the Grand Duchess. She lived with her family in New York City during the exile.

337   Report in the Heisbourg collection, ANLux, probably from Le Gallais.

338   Weitz, Paul, *Charlotte von Luxemburg*, 1988.

339   Wolff, André, *Information Commissioner of the Grand Duchy...*, p. 23.

340   AE-AW, letter from Eleanor Maloney to Guill Konsbruck of November 4, 1942.

341   AMgdL 1697, official correspondence from Le Gallais to H.R.H., notes on official talks in Washington, 1st category, cable from Le Gallais to Bech no. 25/42.

342   AMgdL 1697, official correspondence from Le Gallais to H.R.H., notes on official talks in Washington; 1st category; letter from Le Gallais to the Grand Duchess of December 12, 1942.

343   AMgdL 1697, official correspondence from Le Gallais to H.R.H., notes on official talks in Washington; 1st category; letter from Le Gallais to the Grand Duchess of November 28, 1942.

344   Heisbourg, *100 Joer Lëtzebuerger Dynastie*, p. 70.

345   James Bryant Conant (1893-1978) was president of Harvard University from 1933 to 1953 and a diplomat.

346   Letter from Le Gallais to Cordell Hull of September 15, 1942, National Archives at College Park.

347   AE-AW, letter from Le Gallais to Bech of November 28, 1942.

348   Eugene Meyer (1875-1959) was President of the World Bank and the Federal Reserve and owner of the *Washington Post*.

349   AE-AW, letters from Guill Konsbruck of January 7 and 11, 1943, letters from Konsbruck to Le Gallais of January 1 and 12, 1943.

350   AE-AW, letter from Le Gallais to Guill Konsbruck of January 6, 1943.

351   AE-AW, letter from Konsbruck to Le Gallais of January 12, 1943, and Heisbourg 1942-1943, p. 214.

352   Heisbourg 1942-1943, p. 217. Report from Dupong's interview with Sumner Welles and AMgdL 1697, official correspondence from Le Gallais to H.R.H., notes on official talks in Washington, 1st category, letter from Le Gallais to the Grand Duchess of February 12, 1943.

353   Heisbourg 1942-1943, p. 223 and ANLux, AE-AW-2139.

354   AMgdL 1697, official correspondence from Le Gallais to H.R.H., notes on official talks in Washington; 1st category.

355   Serge Rips was member of the Board of Economic Warfare, whose scope included the Grand Duchy of Luxembourg.

356   AE-AW, letter from Guill Konsbruck to Léon Schaus of March 3, 1943.

357   Edward Steichen (1879-1973) was a world famous photographer born in Luxembourg.

358   Herbert Clark Hoover (1874-1964), 31st President of the United States (1929-1933) or his son Herbert Hoover Jr. (1903-1969), Under-Secretary of State from 1954 to 1957 under President Eisenhower.

359   Heisbourg 1942-1943, p. 303.

360   AE-AW, letter from Konsbruck to Le Gallais of March 10, 1943.

361   Heisbourg, *100 Joer Lëtzebuerger Dynasty*; p. 70.

362   Earl Warren (1891-1974) was Governor of California from January 4, 1943 for ten years, and later became Chief Justice on the US Supreme Court.

363   AE-AW, letter from Guill Konsbruck to Prince Félix of April 29, 1943.

364   ANLux, AE-AW, Heisbourg Fund, Dupong folder, letter from Dupong to Le Gallais of April 13, 1943, the date 20 being added in pencil.

365   ANLux, AE-AW-Bech, letter from Bech to Le Gallais London of May 12, 1943.

366   René Harf was a doctor of law, formerly a lawyer in Luxembourg and a close friend of Alfred Loesch, management advisor to the Tax Administration.

367   AE-AW, letter from Eleanor Maloney to Guill Konsbruck.

368   Letters from the American embassies in Paris (January 3, 1945) and Luxembourg (May 8, 1947), National Archives at College Park.

369   AE-AW, letter from Léon Schaus to Guill Konsbruck of September 24, 1943.

370   AMgdL 1697, official correspondence from Le Gallais to H.R.H., notes on official talks in Washington; 1st category, excerpt of a note summarizing a conversation between President Roosevelt, M. Bech and the Luxembourg Minister in Washington, September 28, 1943.

371   Heisbourg, *100 Joer Lëtzebuerger Dynastie*, p. 70.

372   AE-AW, letter from Bech to Le Gallais of May 23, 1944.

373   Heisbourg 1942-1943, p. 307.

374   Norbert Le Gallais had also sent his Christmas greetings via the National Broadcast Company on December 20, 1940 after a letter from his father Hugues Le Gallais to Georges Schommer of December 9, 1940. ANLux, Heisbourg Fund.

375   AE-AW, letters from Léon Schaus to Guill Konsbruck of December 16, 1943 and January 4, 1944.

376   Heisbourg 1942-1943, p. 374.

377   Henri Hoppenot (1891-1977) was the delegate of the provisional Government of the French Republic to the United States in 1944.

378   Heisbourg 1943-1944, p. 33.

379   AE-AW, letter from Le Gallais to Konsbruck of April 19, 1944.

380 Heisbourg 1943-1944, p. 46, AE-ALW, Dupong file, letter from Dupong written in Montreal to Le Gallais of May 2, 1944.

381 Heisbourg 1943-1944, p. 31.

382 Heisbourg 1943-1944, p. 260.

383 On May 19, 1944, Dupong informed General Eisenhower of the composition of the Military Mission to the Supreme Headquarters Allied Expeditionary Force (SHAEF).

384 Heisbourg 1943-1944, p. 311, AE-ALW, Konsbruck dossier.

385 AE-AW, letter from Le Gallais to Konsbruck of August 3, 1944.

386 Heisbourg, *100 Joer Lëtzebuerger Dynasty*, p. 69.

387 Union of Luxembourg Resistance Movements (*Unio'n*).

388 *Volksdeutsche Bewegung* (VdB) can literally be translated as "German ethnic movement". It was a Nazi movement that existed in Luxembourg during the World War II occupation.

389 ANLux, AE-AW-0724.

390 AE-AW, letter from Joseph Bech to André Wolff of September 7, 1944.

391 Heisbourg 1943-1944, p. 73, and AE-AW, letter from Le Gallais to Bech of September 13, 1944.

392 Letter from Le Gallais to Dupong of December 11, 1944, AE-AW.

393 Publication of the City of Luxembourg.

394 Le 17 (see Heisbourg, *100 Years of the Luxembourg Dynasty*, p. 73) or 19 (see *Luxembourg Bulletin* April 1945).

395 AE-AW, letter from Konsbruck to Le Gallais of February 16, 1948 and subsequent correspondence.

396 https://sip.gouvernement.lu/dam-assets/publications/bulletin/1947/BID_1947_10/BID_1947_10.pdf.

397 CDF 45-49 RG 59, Box 3317, two documents on Luxembourg, letter from chargé d'affaires Waller, Octave 1946, ceremony dedicated by the bishop to the Americans, May 14, 1946. Memorandum of Conversation, State Department, about the conversation between Le Gallais and the Secretary of State prior to a trip by Le Gallais to Luxembourg (June 4, 1946).

398 *Evening Star*, October 27, 1941 and Krier-Becker, Lily, *Pierre Krier* (manuscript), p. 174.

399 Heisbourg 1942, p. 66.

400 Hubert Pierlot (1883-1963), Prime Minister of Belgium from September 27, 1944 to February 7, 1945.

401 Giscard d'Estaing, Antoine, *Leopold III: Un Roi dans la tourmente*, Brussels, Racine 1995, p. 257.

402 AD 1/178 (April 19, 1943), Delegate to represent Lux at Food Conference, Central Files of the State Department.

403 Heisbourg 1942-1943, p. 239-246.

404 Heisbourg 1943-1944, p. 12.

405 William Clayton (1880-1966) was a businessman and Assistant Secretary of State for Economic Affairs. Truman appointed him Under-Secretary of State for Economic Affairs (1946-47), ANLux, Heisbourg Fund, letter from Le Gallais to Dupong of May 27, 1943.

406 Heisbourg 1943-1944, p. 12 and *Evening Star*, September 18, 1944.

407 Heisbourg 1943-1944, p. 10.

408 ANLux, Heisbourg Fund, Le Gallais speech.

409 ANLux, Heisbourg Fund, letter from Le Gallais to Bech of March 7, 1941.

410 Heisbourg 1943-1944, p. 49.

411 800.515/1201 (June 9, 1944), Minister of Luxembourg will be the only representative to the Financial and Monetary Conference, and 800.515/1239 (June 14, 1944) Lux delegate to the Monetary Conference.

412 Central Files of the State Department Archivist / Textual Reference Branch (RDT2), National Archives at College Park.

413 AE-AW, letter from Dupong to Le Gallais from June 1944.

414 Charles Heuertz was a management advisor at the Social Insurance Office.

415 This was to be recalled during an interview at the State Department in 1952 in connection with the air deal that the United States was really not interested in concluding with the Grand Duchy.

416 Trausch, Gilbert, *Joseph Bech*, p. 115.

417 Kayser, Steve, *The Neutrality of Luxembourg from 1918 to 1945*, *Forum*, of June 2006.

418 Stronck, Gaston, *Le Luxembourg et le Pacte Atlantique. De la neutralité à l'alliance*, p. 150.

419 Peter Fraser (1884-1950) was a trade unionist, a member of the Labor Party, and Prime Minister of New Zealand from 1940 to 1949.

420 Albert Calmes (1881-1967) was an economist, banker and historian.

421 *London News Chronicle*, July 11, 1945, National Archives at College Park.

422 *The Key West Citizen* (Key West, Fla.), 1879 – current, March 18, 1949.

423 Hector Dieudonné, a Belgian, Managing Director of Columeta.

424 Paul Georges Marie Kronacker, Baron (1897-1994) was a Liberal, a Member of the Belgian Parliament from 1939 to 1968, and Minister of Provisions in the Van Acker Governments (1945-46).

425 AE-AW, letter confirming cable from Konsbruck to Le Gallais of September 21, 1945.

426 Firm from Marion, OH manufacturing and selling various types of excavators.

427 AE-AW, André Wolff to Konsbruck, March 5, 1946.

428 AE-AW, Konsbruck to Le Gallais, March 14, 1946.

429 AE-AW, Konsbruck to Le Gallais, September 16, 1946.

430 Burks Summers (1898-1977), businessman and diplomat.

431 AE-AW, letter from Le Gallais to Konsbruck, January 18, 1946.

432 Regener, Gilles, "Welcome to Luxembourg!", *Forum*, June 2012, pp. 33-36.

433 *Idem*. "Promotion économique du Luxembourg – investissements américains au Luxembourg et en Europe, 1958-1970", ANLux, AE-AW-1403.

434 Embassy archives, AE-AW (see also under Arbed, as the message concerns the situation in relation to the steel industry and the lack of oil as well as the need to diversify the Luxembourg economy).

435 Stronck, Gaston, *Le Luxembourg et le Pacte Atlantique. De la neutralité à l'alliance*, p. 224.

436 Aloyse Meyer (1883-1952) was director of Arbed, also during the period of the German occupation during the Second World War. Shortly before the liberation in September 1944 he was arrested by the Gestapo and deported as a *Schutzhäftling* to Germany. He was freed in April 1945. After the war, he again managed the company before becoming Arbed's chairman of the board in April 1947. Schoentgen, Marc, "'Heim ins Reich'? Die Arbed-Konzernleitung während der deutschen Besatzung 1940-1944: zwischen Kollaboration und Widerstand" *Forum*, February 2011.

437 D'Ansembourg, Gaston, comte d', *Au bon vieux temps*, p. 81.

438 ANLux, Bodson Fund, box 21 anc 17 CDRR-00169, Victor Bodson correspondence.

439 Heisbourg 1941, p. 158.

440 Koch-Kent, Henri, *Vu et entendu - vol. 2. Years of Exile 1940-1946*, p. 351.

441 ANLux, Heisbourg Fund, with mention AE-AW/7 gouv, letter from Le Gallais to Barbanson of March 28, 1942.

442 ANLux, Heisbourg Fund, AW-Bech, letter from Bech to Le Gallais of May 12, 1943.

443 AMgdL 1697, official correspondence between Le Gallais to H.R.H., notes on official interviews in Washington; 1st category.

444   Translation: Meyer is a good friend, but we must be careful.

445   Translation: Unlocking Luxembourg assets in the United States.

446   Alan Goodrich Kirk (1888-1983) was US Ambassador to Luxembourg from 1946 to 1949.

447   *Ennis Daily News*, September 17, 1946, reprinted by the *Washington Post* on September 17, 1947.

448   AE-AW, letter from Le Gallais to Konsbruck of November 24, 1946.

449   Andrew Russell Pearson (1897-1969) was one of American's best-known columnists, notably for his column in the unionized newspaper *Washington Merry-Go-Round*.

450   Translation: It was not his function to mask enemy interests.

451   AE-AW, letter from Konsbruck to Le Gallais of December 5, 1946.

452   AE-AW, according to a document of April 17, 1947 from the Luxembourg Government to the American Government.

453   AE-AW, letter from Guill Konsbruck of January 11, 1947.

454   "Le Gallais bei Clayton", *Escher Tageblatt*, February 2, 1947.

455   René Schmit (1907-1975) was head of department at the Central Administration from 1945.

456   Victor Bück (1889-1957) was ARBED Commissioner, a Luxembourg industrialist and Honorary Consul of Portugal in Luxembourg.

457   AE-AW, letter from Konsbruck to Le Gallais of June 7, 1948.

458   James Martin was a lawyer with the US Department of Justice and was head of the Decartelisation Service of the military Government in Germany after the Second World War. , Luxembourg is often mentioned in his book, *All Honorable Men*, published in 1950.

459   AE-AW, letter from Konsbruck to Le Gallais, November 8, 1946.

460   AE-AW, letter from Le Gallais to Konsbruck, November 21, 1946.

461   This led to the US Information and Educational Act of 1948.

462   Christian Herter, was a member of the House of Representatives from Massachusetts (1943-1953). AE-AW, letter from Konsbruck to Le Gallais of November 7, 1947.

463   AE-AW, letter from Hugues Le Gallais of November 19, 1947.

464   AE-AW, letter from Konsbruck to Le Gallais of February 2, 1949.

465   Dr. Joseph Horatz, was Chairman of the Board of Directors and Managing Director of Fellen & Guilleaume Carlswerk AG, Köln-Mülheim (1952).

466   AE-AW, letter from Konsbruck to Le Gallais of August 27, 1951.

467   AE-AW, letter from Le Gallais to Konsbruck of September 14, 1951.

468   AE-AW, letter from Guill Konsbruck of October 27, 1951.

469   AE-AW, various files.

470   Letter Otto Bartning to Aline Mayrisch of December 23, 1946, CNL, Mayrisch Fund. Otto Bartning (1883-1959), the Berlin architect who designed the Maternité Grande-Duchesse Charlotte, inaugurated on March 10, 1936.

471   AE -AW 2028, correspondence from July 1942 to January 1945.

472   March 12, 1948 according to the letter of March 8, but March 11 according to his own CV, the handing over of the copies having perhaps preceded the handing over itself.

473   Johannes Coenraad Kielstra (1878-1951) was Minister of the Netherlands in Mexico and Guatemala (1944-1948).

474   Etienne Ruzette, Baron (1894-1960) was Minister of Belgium in Mexico and had been posted in Luxembourg in the 1920s.

475   Lester Bowles Pearson (sometimes called "Mike", 1897-1972) was a Canadian diplomat and statesman, Member of Parliament since 1948.

476   Alain du Parc Locmaria (1892-1973) was Belgian Ambassador to Canada.

477   Dr. J. H. van Royen was Ambassador of the Netherlands to Canada from 1947 and to the United States from 1950.

478   Brooke Claxton (1898-1960) was a lawyer, professor of commercial law and federal politician from Quebec. Appointed Secretary of State for External Affairs in the Liberal Government of Prime Minister Louis St. Laurent in 1948, he was elected as a member of the Liberal Party and shortly afterwards appointed Minister of Defence from 1946 to 1954 in the cabinets of Mackenzie King and Louis St. Laurent.

479   William Lyon Mackenzie King (1874-1950) was Prime Minister of Canada from 1921 to 1926, from 1926 to 1930 and from October 23, 1935 to November 15, 1948.

480   Louis Stephen St-Laurent (1882-1973) was Prime Minister of Canada (1948-1957).

481   *Evening Star*, April 15, 1951.

482   *Evening Star*, March 31, 1951.

483   Heisbourg 1943-1944, p. 264.

484   From October 10, 1940 to October 10, 1944 – Fulgencio Batista Zaldívar; from October 10, 1944 to October 10, 1948 – Ramón Grau San Martín; from October 10, 1948 to March 10, 1952 – Carlos Prío Socarrás; from March 13, 1952 to January 1, 1959 – Fulgencio Batista Zaldívar.

485   ANLux-AE-09915.

486   *Evening Star*, October 8, 1948.

487   Rubén Fulgencio Batista y Zaldívar (1901-1973) was President of Cuban from 1952 to 1959.

488   Carlos Saladrigas Zayas (1900-1956) was a Cuban conservative politician and diplomat, Minister of Foreign Affairs (1933 and 1955-1956), and Prime Minister (1940-1942).

489   Miguel Ángel de la Campa y Caraveda (1882-1965) was a Cuban diplomat, lawyer and author. He served from 1906 to 1958 as a diplomat in Spain, Italy, Mexico, Japan and the United Nations. He was Minister of Foreign Affairs from 1937 to 1940 and from 1952 to 1955. His last post was as Ambassador to the United States from 1955 to 1958.

490   Henry de Torrenté (1893-1962) was an envoy (from 1955) and Ambassador (from 1957 to 1960) of Switzerland to the United States.

491   Pierre Majerus (1908-1998) remained as head of mission in Rome until 1974.

492   *Evening Star*, January 24, 1952

493   *Evening Star*, January 26, 1951

494   *Revue*, no. 34, August 22, 1953

495   Heisebourg Fund, ANLux, letter from HLG to Dupong, to Montreal, May 17, 1943

496   *Evening Star*, April 9, 1950

497   Oral testimony, November 27, 2018

498   *Evening Star*, March 31, 1951

499   Pearl Reid Mesta, born Pearl Skirvin (1889-1975), was an American socialite and diplomat. A member of the Republican Party, the Democratic Party, and then again the Republican Party, she was the American chief of post in Luxembourg between 1949 and 1953.

500   https://www2.gwu.edu/~erpapers/myday/displaydoc.cfm?_y=1950&_f=md001631JUNE 26, 1950

501   John Foster Dulles (1888-1959), a Republican, was Secretary of State from 1953 to 1959 under President Eisenhower.

502   *Evening Star*, November 18, 1947.

503   Hans Roger Madol (real name Gerhard Salomon; 1903-1956), was President of the Luxembourg Society, a bibliographer, journalist, and diplomat.

504   Sacheverell Sitwell (1897-1988), 6th Baronet, was an English poet and essayist.

505   Heisbourg 1941, p. 139.

506   It was not until 1963, during her state visit to the United States, that the Grand Duchess met Edward Steichen at the Embassy in Washington.

507   The "Family of Man" exhibition at the Château de Clervaux with a sign showing the locations of the exhibition.

508   AE-AW, letter of June 24, 1952 from Eleanor Maloney.

509   AMgdL 1697, official correspondence Le Gallais to H.R.H., notes on official interviews in Washington; 1st category; excerpt of a letter from Le Gallais to Dupong of April 7, 1941.

510   Dostert, Paul, *Les finances du gouvernement luxembourgeois en exil (1940-1945)*, publication on the occasion of Gilbert Trausch's 80th birthday.

511   AE-AW, Le Gallais letter to Bech of June 9, 1952

512   Walter Lippmann (1889-1974) was an American intellectual, writer, journalist and polemicist. He wrote for the *New Republic*, the *World* and the *New York Herald Tribune*.

513   Lambert Dupong (1917-2000) was a lawyer and the son of Minister of State Pierre Dupong. Oral testimony of a family member in 2018.

514   *Evening Star*, February 12, *Evening Star*, March 28, 1941.

515   *Evening Star*, October 17, 1941.

516   *Evening Star*, August 2, 1942.

517   *Evening Star*, April 30, 1944.

518   *Evening Star*, November 1, 1942.

519   *Evening Star*, May 16, 1943.

520   *Evening Star*, May 19, 1943, *Evening Star*, June 6, 1943.

521   *Evening Star*, March 30, 1941, *Evening Star*, October 28, 1943, *Evening Star*, October 22, 1945, *Evening Star*, April 15, 1948.

522   *Evening Star*, October 24, 1943.

523   *Evening Star*, May 7, 1944.

524   *Evening Star*, October 12, 1945.

525   *Evening Star*, December 10, 1944, *Evening Star*, December 10, 1944, *Evening Star*, December 17, 1944.

526   *Evening Star*, March 2, 1945.

527   *Evening Star*, September 23, 1945.

528   *Evening Star*, December 2, 1945.

529   *Evening Star*, February 3, 1946.

530   *Evening Star*, November 18, 1947.

531   *Evening Star*, February 6, 1948.

532   *Evening Star*, April 1, 1951.

533   *Evening Star*, October 7, 1951.

534   *Evening Star*, October 24, 1951.

535   Vijaya Lakshmi Nehru Pandit (1900-1990) was an Indian politician and diplomat, the first woman President of the United Nations General Assembly. She was the sister of Indian Prime Minister Jawaharlal Nehru and the Indian Ambassador to the United States and Mexico from 1949 to 1951.

536   Wiley T. Buchanan (1913-1986) was appointed Minister in Luxembourg in 1953. When both countries decided to raise their respective missions to Embassy level two years later, he was promoted

to Ambassador. He held this position until he became Head of Protocol in 1957 (until 1961) and then Ambassador to Austria.

537 Sir Percey Claude Spender (1897-1985) was a former Australian Foreign Minister, Australian Ambassador to the United States from 1951 to 1958 and Member of the International Court of Justice (1958-1967).

538 Charles de Beistegui (1895-1970) was a decorator and collector.

539 AE-AW, letter of August 9, 1952 Eleanor Maloney to Le Gallais.

540 Heisbourg 1943-1944, p. 4.

541 Edwin Martin "Pa" Watson (1883-1945) was a Major General, secretary and intimate of Franklin Delano Roosevelt.

542 Patricia Mountbatten (1924-2017) was the eldest daughter of Lord Louis Mountbatten. In 1946 she married John Knatchbull, 7th Baron Brabourne, CBE (1924-2005).

543 Lady Annabel Vane-Tempest-Stewart (b. 1934) was the wife of businessman Mark Birley.

544 Legal adviser / State Department to the Under-Secretary June 17, 1954, National Archives at College Park.

545 Information from the Treaty Service of the Luxembourg Ministry of Foreign and European Affairs.

546 CDF 45-49 RG 59, Box 3318, National Archives at College Park.

547 Does not seem to have been completed until 1962.

548 Note verbale from Le Gallais. Memorandum of conversation with Le Gallais on the subject. Memorandum of conversation with officials on the same subject. CDF 45-49 RG 59, Box 3318, National Archives at College Park.

549 *Evening Star*, September 22, 1951.

550 Air Agreement File, National Archives at College Park.

551 Note from the American Legation to the State Department, May 14, 1952, National Archives at College Park.

552 Extract from presentations by Corinne Schroeder, "Le Gallais a Korea", AE-AW-0291, AE-07799.

553 Pierre Pescatore (1919-2010) was a Luxembourg professor and judge at the European Court of Justice. He worked at the Ministry of Foreign Affairs from 1946 to 1967. He was one of the Luxembourg Government's representatives during the negotiations leading to the Treaty of Rome.

554 Pierre Wurth (1926-2008) was a Luxembourg diplomat.

555 Henry Ford II (1917-1987) was an American industrialist. The grandson of the founder of the American automobile industry, he served as an alternative delegate to the United Nations in 1953 under President Eisenhower.

556 Excerpt from presentations by Corinne Schroeder, "Le Gallais a Korea", AE-AW-0291, AE-07799.

557 ANLux, AE-AW-0726, speech by Le Gallais given on August 24, 1953.

558 Deputy to Dean Rusk (1909-1994), future Secretary of State from 1961 to 1969 under Presidents Kennedy and Johnson.

559 Beus, J.G. de (1909-1991) was Minister of the Netherlands in the United States until September 1954.

560 AMgdL 1699, various reports and messages, Bech to Dupong, January 5, 1941, Trausch, Gilbert, *Joseph Bech*, p. 99, letter from Joseph Bech to Pierre Dupong of January 8, 1941.

561 ANLux, AE-AW 0727, in the presence of his wife and son, expressly mentioned.

562 The *Luxembourg Bulletin* is an information brochure in English published by the Luxembourg Government. Depending on the changing places of residence of the sovereign, the President of the Government Pierre Dupong, the Minister for Foreign Affairs Joseph Bech, the Minister for Labour Pierre Krier, the Minister for Justice Victor Bodson, residing mainly in the United Kingdom, Canada and the United States, the *Luxembourg Bulletin* appeared from July 1942 to September 1945 in two

non-identical issues, one in London, the other in Montreal and New York (until issue No. 12, February-April). From number 13, October-November, the brochure was finally published only in New York.

563 Linden, André, "Léif Lëtzebuerger ... dir dohém a mir hei baussen... ". The radio speeches of Grand Duchess Charlotte in exile; "ët wor alles net esou einfach", Questions sur le Luxembourg et la Deuxième Guerre mondiale, Luxembourg 2002.

564 Wolff, André, Information Commissioner of the Grand Duchy in the United States, *Memories: A Mission in the United States*, Imprimerie Saint-Paul, Luxembourg 1950, p. 30. In it, he mentions a broadcast by the National Broadcast Company, called "Victory rally" and sponsored by the Metropolitan Opera Guild under the auspices of the *New York Times* by Minister of State Dupong on February 20, 1943. The Speaker of the Belgian House of Representatives Van Cauwelaert was also one of the speakers. The Grand Duchess, Belgian Ambassador Theunis and Minister Le Gallais attended the event.

565 ANLux, AE-AW-0725, interviews given and speeches delivered by Pierre Dupong, Joseph Bech, Perle Mesta, André Wolff, Hugues Le Gallais, Pierre Krier and the Grand Duchess, draft speech by Le Gallais for Dupong.

566 Trausch, Gilbert, *Joseph Bech*, pp. 132-133.

567 Heisbourg 1942-1943, p. 36.

568 *Evening Star*, September 18, 1944, and Wolff, André, Information Commissioner of the Grand Duchy in the United States, Memories: A Mission in the United States; Imprimerie Saint-Paul, Luxembourg 1950, p. 79.

569 Ceremony of Luxembourg Freedom Charter held on September 17, 1944 in the Council Chamber City Hall. "Luxembourg hailed on ancient freedom", *New York Times*, September 18, 1944.

570 *Luxembourg Bulletin*, No. 9, August 1945, pp. 2-4 (Linden André, "«Un beau petit pays?» Bilder und Diskurse um das Luxemburg der fünfziger Jahre", in *Le Luxembourg des années 50: une société de petite dimension entre tradition et modernité*, Publications scientifiques du musée d'Histoire de la Ville de Luxembourg, Luxembourg 1999.

571 Stronck, Gaston, *Le Luxembourg et le Pacte Atlantique. De la neutralité à l'alliance*, p. 147.

572 *New York Herald Tribune* of August 19, 1947.

573 James Byrnes (1882-1972) was Secretary of State from 1945 to 1947 under President Truman.

574 André Visson (Akivisson, Isidore) was an American journalist of Russian origin.

575 Georges Bidault (1899-1983) was a French Resistance fighter and statesman. He was a Companion of the Liberation.

576 ANLux, Heisbourg Fund, letter from Le Gallais to Bech of April 22, 1946.

577 George Marshall (1880-1959) was Secretary of State from 1947 to 1949 and US Secretary of Defence from 1950 to 1951 under President Truman.

578 Source: Marshall Foundation.

579 The treaty establishing the European Defence Community was signed in Paris exactly one year earlier, on May 27, 1952.

580 Hellé, wife of Henri Bonnet (1888-1978), was a French politician and diplomat, French Ambassador to the United States from 1944 to 1954.

581 William Armistead Moale Burden II (1906-1984) was a banker, collector, philanthropist and Ambassador to Belgium under President Eisenhower.

582 Alberto Tarchiani (1885-1964) was an Italian journalist, politician, diplomat and Ambassador to the United States from 1945 to 1955.

583 Hubert Miles Gladwyn Jebb (1900-1996), 1st Baron Gladwyn, was a British diplomat and politician, notably Secretary General of the United Nations (inaugural/acting) from October 1945 to February 1946. He was Permanent Representative to the United Nations from 1950 to 1954.

584 Maurice Frère (1890-1970) was a Belgian engineer and financier.

585 Dirk Spierenburg (1909-2001) was a Dutch diplomat and politician. He was a member of the ECSC from 1952 to 1962.

586   AE-AW, letter from Le Gallais to Eleanor Maloney of September 11, 1958.

587   Lesch, Paul, *Playing Her Part. Perle Mesta in Luxembourg*, American Chamber of Commerce in Luxembourg 2001.

588   John Davison Rockefeller 3rd (1906-1978) was an entrepreneur and philanthropist, member of the third generation of the Rockefeller family, son of John Davison Rockefeller Junior and Abby Aldrich Rockefeller. From 1932 to 1978, he was married to Blanchette Ferry Rockefeller (1909-1992).

589   *Evening Star*, May 18, 1946.

590   Meyer Robert Guggenheim (1885-1959) was a colonel in the US Army.

591   Unger, Irwin, Unger, Debi, *The Guggenheims – a family history*, p. 188.

592   AE-AW, letters from Eleanor Maloney to Le Gallais in Seal Harbor of June 7, 8, 10, and 20, 1956, and in Venice, June 25, 1956.

593   AE-AW, letter of July 5, 1956.

594   Oliver Shewell Franks, Baron, then Lord Franks (1905-1992) and his wife Barbara, née Tanner. Franks was British Ambassador to the United States from 1948 to 1952.

595   AE-AW, letter of July 18, 1956.

596   Joseph Luns (1911-2002), Dutch Minister of Foreign Affairs from 1952-1971 and Secretary General of NATO.

597   ANLux, AE-AW copy notes from Bech to Le Gallais of February 24, 1958.

598   Clarence Douglas Dillon (1909-2003) was an American diplomat and politician, Ambassador to France from 1953 to 1957 and Secretary of State for the Treasury (1961-1965). He was the future father-in-law of Prince Charles of Luxembourg.

599   Hubert Ansiaux (1908-1987), baron, was a Belgian banker, governor of the National Bank of Belgium from 1957 to 1971 and chairman of the board of the Université libre de Bruxelles. He was appointed Director of the National Bank of Belgium in 1941.

600   The Rapacki Plan was presented by the Polish Foreign Minister, Adam Rapacki, on October 2, 1957 to the UN General Assembly. This limited plan, called "demilitarisation in Central Europe", proposed a nuclear-free zone.

601   Bech had obviously made a joke of it by talking about "deterrorising".

602   Manilo Giovanni Brosio (1897-1980) was an Italian lawyer, diplomat and politician.

603   Charles Burke Elbrick (1908-1983) was an American diplomat. From 1953 to 1957 he was Assistant Under-Secretary of State for European Affairs. He was promoted to Assistant Secretary of State for European and Eurasian Affairs in 1957.

604   AE-AW, letter from Eleanor Maloney to Le Gallais of May 20, 1958.

605   Paul Schulté was a Luxembourg diplomat.

606   AE-AW, letter from Le Gallais to Cortina d'Ampezzo of August 13, 1958.

607   Many crossed-out words follow, that Le Gallais scribbled down with a state of nervousness, only to strike them out later.

608   NLux, Heisbourg Fund.

609   The *MS Vulcania* was an Italian ocean liner in service from 1929 to 1974.

610   Felix Frankfurter (1882-1965) was a American lawyer, professor and jurist who served as Associate Justice of the United States Supreme Court.

611   Theodore Francis Green (1867-1966) was a Rhode Island politician. A Democrat, he served as the 57th Governor of Rhode Island (1933-1937) and as Senator (1937-1961).

612   Probably Mary C. Pratt Herter, wife of Christian Herter, Governor of Massachusetts (1953-1957) and then Secretary of State (1959-1961).

613   Lambert Schaus (1908-1976) was a lawyer, Member of Parliament, Minister of Economy and Trade (1946-1947), Member of the City Council (1948-1952), Envoy Extraordinary and Minister

Plenipotentiary (1953-1955), and Ambassador to Belgium (1955-1958). On June 18, 1958, Schaus was appointed representative of Luxembourg at the inaugural edition of the European Commission.

614   Georges Heisbourg (1918-2008) was first Ambassador in Washington from 1958 to 1964, then in The Hague, Paris, at the West European Union in London, in Moscow, at the Council of Europe and in Bonn. He was married to Hélène Pinet.

615   Source: Marshall Foundation.

616   Wilhelm von Munthe af Morgenstierne (1887-1963) was Norwegian Ambassador to the United States from 1942 to 1958.

617   AE-AW, letter from Eleanor Maloney to Le Gallais of August 18, 158. Heisbourg was in Washington between thie letter of August 18 and a letter from Eleanor Maloney to Le Gallais of August 21.

618   AE-AW, letter from Eleanor Maloney to Le Gallais of September 11, 1958.

619   AE-AW, letter from Eleanor Maloney to Le Gallais of September 9, 1958.

620   ANLux, AE-AW 257.

621   AE-AW, letter from Eleanor Maloney to Le Gallais of September 22, 1958.

622   AE-AW; letter from Eleanor Maloney to Le Gallais of September 24, 1958.

623   AE-AW, letter from Le Gallais of October 1, 1958. On October 10, 1958 Le Gallais wrote from Hotel Raphael in Paris, saying that he will be back in Venice on October 15.

624   AE-AW, letter from Eleanor Maloney to Le Gallais of May 26, 1958.

625   It is the Museum of the Settecento veneziano that would house, much later (circa 2014) the collection of porcelain by Marino Nani Mocenigo.

626   Henri, Prince of Bourbon-Parma, Count of Bardi (1851-1905) was the second husband to Princess Aldegonde of Bragança, who was the sister, among others, of Grand Duchess Marie-Anne of Luxembourg and the Duchess of Parma.

627   Giacinto Auriti (1883-1969) was an Italian diplomat and art collector. He was Ambassador to Japan from 1933 to 1940.

628   Guido Perocco (1916-1997) was an art historian, and the Director of the Museum of Modern Art at Ca' Pesaro in Venice.

629   Harry S. Truman (1884-1972), President of the United States from 1945 to 1953, and his wife Elisabeth Wallace Truman (1885-1982).

630   Aspasía (or Aspasie) Mános (1896-1972) was a Princess of Greece and Denmark, the wife of King Alexander I of Greece, and the mother of Queen Alexandra of Yugoslavia.

631   Virginia Caroline Bacon, née Hall (1920-2016) was married in 1946 to Harold H. Bacon of Washington.

632   George Frost Kennan (1904-2005) was an American diplomat, political scientist and historian whose ideas had a strong influence on American policy towards the Soviet Union after the Second World War.

633   John Alexander Pope (d. 1982), Director of the Freer Gallery of Art, married in 1947 to Annemarie Henle Pope, who died in 2001 at the age of 94. He was Deputy Director of Exhibitions of the American Federation of Arts in Washington, D.C., and later Head of the Travelling Exhibitions Department of the Smithsonian Institution.

634   Ninette de Valois (née Edris Stannus; 1898-2001) was a dancer and choreographer.

635   Valentina Dutko was a Russian dancer who founded the National Ballet School and Company in 1953.

636   Lord Harcourt was Economic Counsellor in the 1950s at the British Embassy in Washington.

637   Olga Nicolis dei Conti de Robilant (1900-1996) was the wife of Antonio Alvares Pereira de Melo, Marquis of Cadaval.

638   Princese Urraca of Bourbon-Sicily (1913-1999).

639   Vittorio Winspeare (1912-1995).

640   Christiane Rodenbourg-Loesch (b, 1932) was the daughter of Marshal of the Court Alfred Loesch, who had been deported to Silesia.

641   Emmanuel, called Manu, Tesch (1920-2011), member of the Arbed College of Commissioners from 1958, and his wife, Thérèse, née Laval (1921-2008).

642   Juan de Liedekerke de Pailhe (b. 1927), married in 1951 to Gisèle de Maleingreau d'Hembise (b. 1928), daughter of Adrien de Maleingreau d'Hembise and Marie-Jeanne Pescatore.

643   Giovan Battista Nani (1616-1678) was born and died in Venice. He was a historian and became, at the age of 25, Ambassador of Venice in France.

644   Daniele Varè (1880-1956) was an Italian diplomat posted in Beijing, Geneva, Copenhagen and Luxembourg.

645   According to a letter of late October 1962, private archives.

646   AMgdL 4517-1, letter from Ambassador Pierre Majerus to the Grand Marshal of the Court of December 28, 1964.

647   *Idem.*

INDEX

Note: This index does not include the names mentioned most often in the book: Hugues Le Gallais, Grand Duchess Charlotte and Prince Felix of Luxembourg, Pierre Dupong, Joseph Bech, Guill Konsbruck. Persons mentioned solely in the notes have not been included either. Pages referring to the notes are in italics.